Deleuze and Guattari and Fascism

Deleuze Connections

'It is not the elements or the sets which define the multiplicity. What defines it is the AND, as something which has its place between the elements or between the sets. AND, AND, AND – stammering.'

Gilles Deleuze and Claire Parnet, *Dialogues*

General Editor
Ian Buchanan

Editorial Advisory Board

Keith Ansell-Pearson

Rosi Braidotti

Claire Colebrook

Tom Conley

Gregg Lambert

Adrian Parr

Paul Patton

Patricia Pisters

Deleuze and Guattari and Fascism

Edited by Rick Dolphijn and Rosi Braidotti

EDINBURGH
University Press

Edinburgh University Press is one of the leading university presses in the UK. We publish academic books and journals in our selected subject areas across the humanities and social sciences, combining cutting-edge scholarship with high editorial and production values to produce academic works of lasting importance. For more information visit our website: edinburghuniversitypress.com

Grateful acknowledgement is made to the sources listed in the List of Illustrations for permission to reproduce material previously published elsewhere. Every effort has been made to trace the copyright holders, but if any have been inadvertently overlooked, the publisher will be pleased to make the necessary arrangements at the first opportunity.

Edinburgh University Press Ltd
The Tun – Holyrood Road
12(2f) Jackson's Entry
Edinburgh EH8 8PJ

First published in hardback by Edinburgh University Press 2022

Typeset in 10.5/13 Adobe Sabon by
Cheshire Typesetting Ltd, Cuddington, Cheshire, and
printed and bound by CPI Group (UK) Ltd,
Croydon, CR0 4YY

A CIP record for this book is available from the British Library

ISBN 978 1 3995 0522 2 (hardback)
ISBN 978 1 3995 0523 9 (paperback)
ISBN 978 1 3995 0524 6 (webready PDF)
ISBN 978 1 3995 0525 3 (epub)

Contents

Part II Situated Fascisms

Part III Patriarchal Fascism

Illustrations

Abbreviations

AO Gilles Deleuze and Félix Guattari, *Anti-Oedipus*, trans. R. Hurley, M. Seem and H. R. Lane, with a preface by M. Foucault and an introduction by M. Seem, Minneapolis: University of Minnesota Press, 1977. Translation of *L'Anti-Oedipe: Capitalisme et schizophrénie I*, Paris: Minuit, 1972.

B Gilles Deleuze, *Bergsonism*, trans. H. Tomlinson and B. Habberjam, New York: Zone Books, 1991. Translation of *Le Bergsonisme*, Paris: Presses Universitaires de France, 1966.

C1 Gilles Deleuze, *Cinema 1: The Movement Image*, trans. H. Tomlinson and B. Habberjam, London: Athlone, 1986. Translation of *Cinéma 1, L'Image Mouvement*, Paris: Minuit, 1983.

C2 Gilles Deleuze, *Cinema 2: The Time Image*, trans. H. Tomlinson and R. Galeta, London: Athlone, 1989. Translation of *Cinéma 2, L'Image-Temps*, Paris: Minuit, 1985.

CC Gilles Deleuze, *Essays Critical and Clinical*, trans. D. W. Smith and M. A. Greco, Minneapolis: University of Minnesota Press, 1997. Translation of *Critique et Clinique*, Paris: Minuit, 1993.

CM Félix Guattari, *Chaosmosis, an Ethico-aesthetic Paradigm*, trans. P. Bains and J. Pefanis, Bloomington: Indiana University Press, 1995. Translation of *Chaosmose*, Paris: Galilée, 1992.

CS Félix Guattari, *Chaosophy: Texts and Interviews 1972–1977*, trans. D. L. Sweet, ed. S. Lotringer, introduction by F. Dosse, Los Angeles: Semiotext(e), 2009.

D Gilles Deleuze and Claire Parnet, *Dialogues*, trans. H. Tomlinson and B. Habberjam, New York: Columbia University Press, 1987. Translation of *Dialogues*, Paris: Flammarion, 1977.

DI Gilles Deleuze, *Desert Islands and Other Texts 1953–1974*, trans. M. Taormina, ed. D. Lapoujade, New York: Semiotext(e), 2004.

DR Gilles Deleuze, *Difference and Repetition*, trans. P. Patton, New York: Columbia University Press, 1990. Translation of *Différance et répétition*, Paris: Presses Universitaires de France, 1968.

EP Gilles Deleuze, *Expressionism in Philosophy: Spinoza*, trans. M. Joughin, New York: Zone Books, 1992. Translation of *Spinoza et le problème de l'expression*, Paris: Minuit, 1968.

ES Gilles Deleuze, *Empiricism and Subjectivity: An Essay on Hume's Theory of Human Nature*, trans. C. V. Boundas, New York: Columbia University Press, 1991. Translation of *Empiricisme et Subjectivité. Essai sur la Nature Humaine selon Hume*, Paris: Presses Universitaires de France, 1953.

F Gilles Deleuze, *Foucault*, trans. S. Hand, Minneapolis: University of Minnesota Press, 1988. Translation of *Foucault*, Paris: Minuit, 1986.

FB Gilles Deleuze, *Francis Bacon: The Logic of Sensation*, trans. D. W. Smith, New York: Columbia University Press, 2003. Translation of *Francis Bacon: Logique de la sensation*, Paris: Editions du Seuil, 1981.

K Gilles Deleuze and Félix Guattari, *Kafka: Toward a Minor Literature*, trans. D. Polan, Minneapolis: University of Minnesota Press, 1986. Translation of *Kafka: pour un literature mineure*, Paris: Minuit, 1975.

LF Félix Guattari, *Lines of Flight: For Another World of Possibilities*, London: Bloomsbury, 2011.

LO Gilles Deleuze, *Letters and Other Texts*, trans. A. Hodges, ed. D. Lapoujade, South Pasadena, CA: Semiotext(e). Translation of *Lettres et autres textes*, Paris: Minuit, 2015.

LS Gilles Deleuze, *The Logic of Sense*, trans. M. Lester, with C. Stivale, ed. C. V. Boundas, New York: Columbia University Press, 1990. Translation of *Logique du sens*, Paris: Minuit, 1969.

MR Félix Guattari, *Molecular Revolution. Psychiatry and Politics*, London: Puffin, 1984.

NP Gilles Deleuze, *Nietzsche and Philosophy*, trans. H. Tomlinson, Minneapolis: University of Minnesota Press, 1983. Translation of *Nietzsche et la philosophie*, Paris: Presses Universitaires de France, 1962.

OL Gilles Deleuze and Félix Guattari, *On the Line*, New York: Semiotext(e), 1983.

PI Gilles Deleuze, *Pure Immanence, Essays on A Life*, trans. A. Boyman, New York: Zone Books, 2001.

PP   Gilles Deleuze, *Negotiations*, trans. M. Joughin, New York: Columbia University Press, 1995. Translation of *Pourparlers*, Paris: Minuit, 1990.

PS   Gilles Deleuze, *Proust and Signs*, trans. R. Howard, Minneapolis: University of Minnesota Press, 2000. Translation of *Proust et les signes*, 3rd edn, Paris: Presses Universitaires de France, 1976.

S   Gilles Deleuze, *Spinoza: Practical Philosophy*, trans. R. Hurley, San Francisco: City Lights, 1988. Translation of *Spinoza: philosophy pratique*, 2nd edn, Paris: Minuit, 1981.

SC   Félix Guattari, *Schizoanalytic Cartographies*, trans. A. Goffey, London: Bloomsbury, 2013. Translation of *Cartographiques Schizoanalytiques*, Paris: Galilée, 1989.

SM   Gilles Deleuze, *Masochism: An Interpretation of Coldness and Cruelty*, trans. J. McNeil, New York: G. Braziller, 1971. Translation of *Preséntation de Sacher-Masoch*, Paris: Minuit, 1967.

SS   Félix Guattari, *Soft Subversions: Texts and Interviews 1977–1985*, trans. C. Wiener and E. Wittman, Los Angeles: Semiotext(e) Foreign Agent Series, 2009.

TE   Félix Guattari, *The Three Ecologies*, trans. I. Pindar and P. Sutton, New York: Continuum, 2008. Translation of *Les trois ecologies*, Paris: Galilée, 1989.

TF   Gilles Deleuze, *The Fold. Leibniz and the Baroque*, trans. T. Conley, Minneapolis: University of Minnesota Press, 1993. Translation of *Le pli. Leibniz et le Baroque*, Paris: Minuit, 1988.

TP   Gilles Deleuze and Félix Guattari, *A Thousand Plateaus: Capitalism and Schizophrenia*, trans. B. Massumi, Minneapolis: University of Minnesota Press, 1987. Translation of *Mille plateau: capitalisme et schizophrénie, II*, Paris: Minuit, 1980.

TR   Gilles Deleuze, *Two Regimes of Madness: Texts and Interviews 1975–1995*, trans. A. Hodges and M. Taormina, ed. D. Lapoujade. New York: Semiotext(e), 2006.

WP   Gilles Deleuze and Félix Guattari, *What is Philosophy?*, trans. H. Tomlinson and G. Burchell, New York: Columbia University Press, 1994. Translation of *Qu'est-ce que la philosophy?*, Paris: Minuit, 1991.

Introduction: How to Live the Anti-fascist Life and Endure the Pain

Rick Dolphijn and Rosi Braidotti

We have been led to believe that fascism was just a bad moment we had to go through, a sort of historical error, but also a beautiful page in history for the good heroes. We are further led to believe that there were real antagonistic contradictions between the fascist Axis and the Allies.

Félix Guattari, CM, 239–40

How can one keep from destroying oneself through guilt and others through resentment, spreading one's own powerlessness and enslavement everywhere, one's own sickness, indigestion and poison? In the end, one is unable to even encounter oneself.

Gilles Deleuze, S, 23

Against Historical Fascism, or, a Practical Philosophy of Everyday Immunisation against the Negative or Restrictive Effects of Power

Historical fascism as a macro phenomenon is by now a well-studied chapter of Western and world history. Based on the holistic organicism of early twentieth-century philosophies of life, and their sexualised and racialised hierarchies that divide and conquer different sections of humanity, European fascism is a necropolitical system of power which celebrates its own partial vision of life. Fascism is, then, a philosophical system that advocates a transcendental entity embodied in the European Man as the epitome of evolution and European culture as the motor of human civilisation. It is also an undifferentiated vitalist system that subjects all humans and non-humans under one universal law – that of the allegedly superior master race. This translates into the discourse and practice of the 'white man's burden' as a gendered and racialised project of ontological disqualification of multiple 'others'. The fascist worldview favoured a corrupt notion of human transcendence, a demented masculinism and a flair for esoteric and often obscurantist theories of racial and antisemitic domination and white supremacy. This is a mix which *has always* defied scientific rationality while claiming to operate on its behalf. This transcendence came with a celebration of life, of youthfulness and of human *potestas*, associated with a pseudo-spiritualist celebration of a 'cosmic soul' or Eurocentric mystical spirit, which was used as a tool of discrimination. The fascist versions of a deterministic notion of 'vitalism', however, were both opposed to and seduced by technological mechanisms, the rule of technology,[1] and a modernist dehumanising narrative of progress.

Throughout their work, Gilles Deleuze and Félix Guattari always resisted the historicist reading of issues of contemporary culture at large. Or, at least, they practise what can be called an 'immanent historicism', a synchronic rather than diachronic reading of events, as Buchanan put it (2001). Yet a much more rigorous analysis is needed, particularly when it comes to fascism, which should be regarded – alongside slavery and colonialism – as the deepest ethical failure inflicted by and upon Europe. Fascism is the wound that runs through the heart of Europe and all its people, and it is a wound that will not heal. In fact, today, the legacy of fascism, its nepotist economics and technologies, is fully integrated in the state structure, its hierarchical political system, and everlasting patriarchal bias, while it is also operative on a global level. Therefore this book set itself the ambitious goal of mapping the presence of fascism in *all* its global appearances. Of course, we didn't come close to covering the global span, but we made a start.

It is to Deleuze and Guattari's credit that they take seriously the task of exposing the essentialist fallacies of self-replicating fascism, and then proceed to de-Nazify European philosophy from within, as Michel Foucault famously stated in his foreword to the English-language edition of *Anti-Oedipus*. Foucault stressed this aspect of their philosophical project and argued that Deleuze and Guattari do not simply offer a 'new philosophy' or theory by being a 'flashy Hegel' or something of that kind. What they propose is rather a shift of perspective away from dialectics, into a Spinozist political ontology. Resting on the parallelism of mind–body and a critical renaturalisation of all living entities within a shared desire to persevere and grow in their existence and relational abilities, critical Spinozism proposes an ethical indexation system for political actions and values. The nature–culture continuum of Deleuze's life philosophy is not given as a holistic block, but as a materially embedded differential system. At the origin is heterogenesis. Foucault refers to this project as a practical philosophy of everyday immunisation against unifying master theories and the negative or restrictive effects of power.

This heterogeneous approach can also be described as a 'lifestyle', in the new materialist sense of an embodied and embedded praxis of affirmative becoming. Based on the collectively driven task of overturning negative affects and forging a social horizon of hope, this is also a neo-stoical 'anti-oedipal lifestyle', as the title of their book suggests, that rejects authoritarianism in the fundamental sense. Grounded and relatively humble, its rigorous ethics of affirmation also exposes the despotic undercurrents and micro-instances of power formations. These include nasty patriarchal violations, systemic neo-colonial appropriations, racist and antisemitic exclusions, ecocide, and the capitalist devastations of a world in love with its own fantasised power. Taking on the everyday violence of gestures of humiliation, violation, murder and exploitation, that nasty streak which cannot help but hurt others, driven by a sick sense of entitlement, Deleuze and Guattari set themselves to identify the social pathology of fascism and target it. All of which can best be described as a *critical and creative form of thinking and living 'the anti-fascist life'*.

The new materialist philosophy of immanence put forward by Deleuze and Guattari advances a serious critique of the philosophical roots of European fascism. In our reading, Deleuze and Guattari are indeed committed to detoxifying the practice of philosophy from the appeal of racism, nativist nationalism, and patriarchal, neo-colonial authoritarianism in two significant ways. The first is prominent in this volume – the critique of the collective desire for power, defined as the worship of the strong leader and, next to him, the naturalisation of inequalities through violently enforced sexualised and racialised hierarchies.[2]

The second way, enfolded in the first, comes with a more foundational philosophical concept of life. Deleuze and Guattari reject the undifferentiated holism that lies at the core of death-bound fascist philosophies of life. What they introduce instead is heterogeneity and heterogenesis at the conceptual core of what we used to refer to as 'nature'. Matter, the living and generative matter that we call nature, as manifested in forms of individuated organisms, species and peoples, can be seen as bounded, yet fluid. Any specified individuated organism is in fact an instantiation of possible life flows, and consequently also a temporary reduction of the force of virtual inhuman and non-human flows of becoming. Rather than glorifying or even sacralising a transcendent notion of 'Life', Deleuze and Guattari forcefully argue that there is no life as one system, just ongoing flows and transformations of entities, relations and forces. Life is a complex interrelation of multiple *zoē/*

geo/techno-systems (Braidotti 2019). It is a general ecology of complex relations that is constituted by the circulation of transversal modes of assemblage, in a dynamic exchange that defines reciprocal forms of specification or determination. For us people of the Third Millennium, it also supports the recomposition of the human/non-human nexus by inscribing the technological apparatus as second nature.

In short, shaping the anti-fascist life is not just a matter of political activism – though that remains paramount: it is *a quintessentially philosophical project* of recognising the fascist wounds as they traverse our thinking and our being, which needs to be fought within the discipline and with the methods and concepts of the discipline. The anti-fascist life begins by replacing any appeal to naturalised hierarchical orders, rejecting the social constructivist approach that reduces nature to culture. But what we also need is an alternative understanding of how philosophies of life engender mechanisms of death; how biopower breeds necropolitics. And even more importantly, to define ethics as the endeavour to compose and cultivate just a life – one ethical life led by the principle of joy of affirmation. We shall return to this.

The Continuing Presence of Fascism

One always thinks against one's times, in spite of the times and out of concern for one's times, if one wants to think in an anti-fascist manner. In the frantic and soul-searching months following the May 1968 insurrection, when Gilles Deleuze and Félix Guattari had just met, had found their common 'non-carnal birth' and become 'friends of thought', they drew some drastic conclusions about the ethics and politics they had inherited from the generation of the historical anti-fascists who preceded them, not the least Sartre, Malraux and Fanon. The Marxist analyses of capital and power had not produced the promised results in May 68, nor were they yielding the promised paradise in the Soviet Union.

The problem ran deep and posed a conceptual dilemma: for one thing, at that time, several fascist dictatorships were still operational in Europe, let alone in other parts of the word. In Spain Franco had ruled undisturbed since the 1930s, Portugal and Greece were ruled by military dictators and the entire Soviet Empire was one big dictatorship run by genocidal rulers who claimed to act on behalf of the world proletariat. So, the narrative of historical fascism was far from over in the 1970s and the phenomenon of fascism could not be reduced to a past event confined to the early twentieth century as a (deviant) form of the totalitarian state. Nor is it the case that the nefarious phenomenon that was this 'historical error' was resolved by the Allied forces once and for all in 1945 on the beaches of Normandy and in the ruins of Hiroshima and Nagasaki. Primo Levi's latter years and writings argue powerfully that this is far from the truth. In his last work, *The Drowned and the Saved*, written a year before his death, he refers to this as 'the Gray Zone'. Remembering life in the concentration camp and how its survivors (of which he was one) understood their experiences afterwards, he stresses: 'The enemy was outside but also inside. There was no clearly defined "us". There were more than two contenders, and, rather than one border, there were many blurred borders, perhaps countless, one between every person and every other' (Levi 2015: 2431).

Félix Guattari and Gilles Deleuze did not *believe* that this 'historical' take on fascism was actually working as an antidote. The historical narrative of fascism that has shaped the anti-fascist social imaginary of the post-war generations has undergone some radical revisions with the rise of information and media society, from the 1960s onwards. Whereas classical fascists loved their radio broadcasts and pioneered filmed propaganda, liberal democracies in the post-war years favoured television and film as their media, as Guattari noted. Especially television, which, during the 1970s and 1980s gave form to the living room, and much more than the radio ever did, found itself at the centre of everyday family life. Spellbinding TV, much more so than the riot police, now played a crucial role in the spread of what Guattari analysed at a conference in 1979 as a new movement he referred to as the 'worldwide development of a new form of fascism' (SS, 236). In his efforts to set up a 'plan for the planet' (as the original paper was called), Guattari considered it of the greatest importance to monitor the ways in which everyday fascism would reveal itself through an all-pervasive deployment of communication technology, on a scale likely to impact the social imaginary:

> This new regime will not act only through the instrumentality of governments, but through all the elements that contribute to the education of the work force, to the moulding of every individual and the imposing of a particular lifestyle – in other words through a multitude of systems of semiotic subjugation operating in schools, commercial sport, the media, advertising and all the various techniques used to 'help people . . .' (SS, 238)

Talking about how fascism caused cinema to meet its 'first death', Deleuze also noted that in his time, fascism found the means to express itself in television broadcasts: 'Because television is the form in which new powers of "control" become immediate and direct' (PP, 75). Nowadays, the social media applications and digital platforms that control the news (Twitter and Facebook primarily, but more than ever the alternative sites and platforms of the alt-right) have taken over the task of exercising social control. Deleuze and Guattari always warned us that fascism does not 'start in the past', nor does it stay there. Fascism happens in the present, according to the present, and is situated and real (and disturbing) *in the name of the present*. The reason for this problematic longevity is that fascism is vitally installed in our systems and lives and in our psychic and imaginary landscapes. This occurs through what Deleuze and Guattari in *Anti-Oedipus* call *microfascisms*; very site-specific practices that somehow proliferate around the desire for strong power. This can range from the appeal to coercive consumption, strong nationalist and patriarchal values, and incitement to racism and xenophobia. Promoting detention, expulsion, exclusions and imposing poverty and deprivation are just some of the popular tools used to achieve this.

Contemporary microfascism takes place within the social sphere but thrives first on the psychic areas of our collective social pathology: an imaginary enamoured with power. Again, we turn to Guattari who nicely summarised this:

> I repeat: what fascism set in motion yesterday continues to proliferate in other forms, within the complex of contemporary social space. A whole totalitarian chemistry manipulates the structures of state, political and union structures, institutional and family structures, and even individual structures, inasmuch as one can speak of a sort of fascism of the superego in situations of guilt and neurosis. (CS, 236)

Therefore, fascism is not just part of our day and age, but also of ourselves, of our conscious and unconscious structures, and of the technologies attached to them, as they root in our very desires. This is what Guattari was referring to in the text quoted above entitled 'Everybody wants to be a fascist'. This is also the take on fascism that is key to their joint philosophical oeuvre (notably *Anti-Oedipus* and *A Thousand Plateaus*) as it aims to explore the anti-fascist life. As they put it in the latter book (TP, 251): 'It is too easy to be antifascist on the molar level, and not even see the fascist inside you, the fascist you yourself sustain and nourish and cherish with molecules both personal and collective.'

The conviction that sustains this volume is that it is important to *name and resist* all the new forms of microfascism that are emerging all around and within us. Microfascism brings about the paradox of a desire that desires its own repression and its un-freedom. It is a prerogative of the democratic system that is in the hands of its electoral majority, and in times of rising populism it cannot be easily immunised against its own reactionary elements. This is unfortunately the recipe of contemporary illiberal and populist movements. Defined as the love for a strongman, fascism promises to solve all your problems: to make the trains run on time, to restore the British Empire, to solve the world's problems by tweeting abuse at imagined enemies late at night, and – inevitably – to chase away all foreigners, all transgressive others, all gender-non-conforming people, *all the non-aligned subjects*.

Contemplating the state of the present, one is struck by the delusional, infantile but also homicidal quality of a desire that desires its own extinction and marries into the cult of destruction. This is a systemic blockage of the affirmative force of desire. It produces an endless implosion of what could have been a mode of becoming. This is precisely the kind of negativity that anti-fascist subjects need to be on guard against. And let us emphasise this once more; the fascist must be traced not only in the 'other', but also within yourself. 'The fascist inside you' is this totalitarian entity that dispels relational connections and instils suspicion and hatred. It leads to scapegoating instead of pursuing adequate understandings of one's condition. One can only undo the fascist inside by acknowledging one's attachment to dominant identity formations and power structures. The acknowledgement is the precondition for the practical task of changing the negative habit into affirmative relations. This praxis requires opening up to others and co-constructing alternative social structures and alternative desires that sustain the task of transforming the negative. Returning desire to its affirmative structure is a way of learning to live the anti-fascist life, that is to say, a life affected by others, a life equally wounded. Yet always a life that is aware of its relational competence and responsibility, and in search of ways to endure the pain by transforming it into a source of information, for action-oriented knowledge.

In *A Thousand Plateaus*, Deleuze and Guattari discuss the more conceptual dimension of their anti-fascism. Opposing the view that confines this to a discrete event in a past historical time, they make a sharp distinction between what Protevi (2000) calls 'molecular fascism' and 'molar totalitarianism'. The difference between the two is qualitative: they use the terms molar and molecular to describe (respectively) the macropolitics of power (as we see this, for instance, in the state) versus the micropolitics of power (as, for instance, in the commons). The differences are of speed and scale, of ethical forces and modes of relation. Deleuze and Guattari prioritise the molecular becoming, and stress that the micropolitical fits much more the nature of contemporary fascism.

Fascism, according to Deleuze and Guattari, is today more algorithmic or procedural as it does not find its origin in the totalitarian state, but rather in 'a thousand tiny fascisms' that traverse and discipline the practices of everyday life in so many ways.

The manipulations currently practised by populist movements and their reckless leaders aimed at spreading hatred, divisiveness and racism come to mind, of course. Furthermore, populist, nationalistic anti-intellectualism is on the rise again, with the internet facilitating not only instant communication, but also daily outpourings of vitriol. But these extreme examples are not where fascism stops. Michel Foucault rightfully recognised microfascisms everywhere: 'How do we rid our speech and our acts, our hearts and our pleasures, of fascism? How do we ferret out the fascism that is ingrained in our behaviour?' (AO, xiii). Guattari goes even further than that, by stating that fascism shares in a micropolitical economy of desire, 'inseparable from the evolution of productive forces' (CM, 245) of Integrated World Capitalism. This is in line with Todd May's 'critique' (2013) that the masses not only desired fascism, as Deleuze and Guattari seem to suggest, but also anticipated it, so that their individual desires proved deeply fascist in a myriad of ways.

In sum, instead of *tracing a history of totalitarian macropolitics* that finds its origin in the state, Deleuze and Guattari *map a geography of fascist micropolitics* as it traverses the mental, social and environmental fabric, eventually finding a prolific resonance with the centralised or molar state. Fascism proliferates in many different forms: 'rural fascism and city or neighbourhood fascism, youth fascism and war veteran's fascism, fascism of the Left and of the Right, fascism of the couple, family, school, and office' (TP, 214). The fascist revolution never works like a totalitarian organism, but spreads all over, like a disease. Fascism is always a cancerous multiplicity of contaminating bodies that is able to expand in all directions.

The Anti-fascist Method as a Clinical and Critical Praxis

That cancerous multiplicity of bodies doesn't just travel via the realm of words. It is rather the case that microfascism always proliferates within material – embodied and embedded – beings and all living matters. The psychic dimension of microfascism displays therefore a viral aspect, which opens up a pathological but also parasitological narrative within the anti-fascist life argument. This is of relevance at the time of writing, when the planet is in the grip of the Covid-19 pandemic, and autocratic leaders stand out for their denial of the existence of the virus altogether, or their opportunistic attempt to suspend completely of the rule of law by imposing a perpetual state of emergency in society. They – notably Trump, Putin, Bolsonaro, Johnson and Orban – have also displayed total incompetence in the management of public health and disease control. What is the alternative?

Michel Serres reminds us that the best narrative depiction of contemporary parasitology is not Camus' much-acclaimed *The Plague* (as many suggest these days) but rather Molière's *Tartuffe ou l'Impositeur*, the classic comedy of the pious fraud who cleverly works his way into Orgon's family. For whereas *The Plague* is still a moralising narrative on survival, *Tartuffe* is about the politics of exclusion, about the long negotiations through which, slowly but steadily, the treachery becomes apparent and is taken care of. Confronted with an unknown evil – a virus or a disease – that has entered the household and lurks around for opportunities to further harm and even destroy its unity, the story of *Tartuffe* raises important questions about hospitality and hostility. What does it mean to be a good host, when the actions of the evil intruder (the virus) are potentially harmful and hard to detect? How does one process the negative and potentially lethal charge of a relation? By extension: to what extent does biopower coexist with necropolitics?

Contemporary critical culture is in the thrall of the biopolitical. Notions of biopower, biopolitics, and their negative counerparts: Thanatospolitics, necropolitics, positive and negative forms of power, etc. have become something of a 'buzzword' (Lemke 2011). As many philosophers stress the necropolitical aspects of the biopolitical (Agamben 1998; Esposito 2008; Mbembe 2003) as the biopolitics of life itself (Rose 2007; Rabinow 2003; Hardt and Negri 2009). Serres, like Deleuze and Guattari, approaches biopower beyond the limitations of social constructivist methods, which impose a nature–culture distinction that subjects living matter to the dictates of an all-powerful social code. The materialist politics of immanence, on the other hand, stress differential located positions and their strong relational power. Biopower, in this approach, is clearly not only the power to let live, but also that of letting die, 'because power is situated and exercised at the level of life, the species, the race, and the large-scale phenomena of population' (Foucault 1978: 137). The ancestral threats to human survival represented by famine and epidemics have been reshaped by more calculated management of the interaction of human life and death. The impressive knowledge of and power over life developed by modern science and biopolitics, finds its counterpart in a formidable death-machine, which includes wars and weapons of all kinds, including nuclear, chemical and bacterial means. All technology is war technology. If the point of Thanatos-politics is not just the exercise of sovereign will, but rather the biopolitical management of populations, then 'massacres have become vital' (Foucault 1978: 137).

The genocidal aspects of biopower are brought to the foreground by Agamben (1998), who defines *bios* as the result of the intervention of sovereign power upon living matter. Biopower is that which can reduce the subject to 'bare life', that is to say *zoē* as mortality. The being-alive-ness of the subject (*zoē*) is identified with its perishability, vulnerability to death and extinction. The equation of biopower with Thanatos-politics is a further argument in the case Agamben builds against the political project of modernity, with a distinct anti-feminist twist (Cooper 2009).

This aggressive – even militaristic – and dualistic approach to immunology is constitutive of biopolitical theories, where it is currently taken as an analogy for contemporary politics and governance. For instance, Esposito's work on biopolitics (2008) explores the immunological political economy of hospitality and hostility. It is slightly disappointing that what was originally a politics of life – biopolitics – which also included a reappraisal of the politics of dying and letting die, has become almost exclusively focused on the thanato-political pole. But considering the scale of the contemporary devastation, this reduction is understandable. Nonetheless, there is something missing from the dominant immunological paradigm proposed by Esposito, Agamben, Nancy, and others today. What is missing is a philosophy of life that is not dualistically opposed to, and hence intrinsically bound up with, non-life. That is to say: an affirmative philosophy of life.

The immunological paradox is not only about death and destruction, but also the virtual potential for regeneration and endurance. It refers to the process by which the same element – for instance a virus – doubles up as a potential vaccine. This 'intruder' (Nancy 2008) triggers the infection or the disease, but also creates a first line of defence against it. The first line of autoimmunological defence gestures towards a cure or secures immunity from the very disease that is triggering the composition of the encounter. This is also, incidentally, Derrida's definition of the *pharmakon*. The autoimmunological principle states that the pathogen that is injected in controlled doses into the body does not destroy the entirety of the organism but helps the immune system to learn how to defend itself. *The ethics of immunity proposes not the exclusion, but the incorporation and vicarious substitution of the vital/lethal other.*

Serres emphasises this generative interconnection of living matter, the generative continuum between life and death, and degrees of non-living and quasi-dying. Like Deleuze and Guattari, he calls for a much more fundamental and more intimate relational connection between constituted bodies and intruding agents, whether viruses or microbes of any biota. They propose a powerful figuration of a co-creative and collaborative model between separate yet related organisms, agents and living matter. This is the original form of transcorporeality (Alaimo 2010), which generates a web of multiple relations, including the work needed to produce collaborative autoimmunity. It points to the heterogeneous co-creation of hospitable and sustainable environments – the convergence of hospitality and hostility, to the point of transformation of both. By extension it allows us to rethink political and ethical interactions based on a materially grounded understanding of transversal subject-formation. This is anti-fascism at the molecular level.

How do we recognise the evil inside us, how do we avert its threat and search for ways to live a good life, acknowledging (unlike the historians) that the expulsion of Tartuffe is not how the story ends (nor how it should be remembered: it is the process of recognising that should be remembered, the sensitivity, the alertness, the negotiation). This is what we are aiming at when we pose the question: how do we live the anti-fascist life and endure the pain? Crucial is the parasitology proposed by *Tartuffe*, as Serres reads it: a parasitology that does not demand that society (the host) close itself off from its outside, nor that it open itself up completely: 'The parasite gives the host the means to be safe from the parasite. The organism reinforces its resistance and increases its adaptability. It is moved a bit away from its equilibrium and it is then even more strongly at equilibrium' (Serres 2007: 193). Serres notes that this is exactly what happens in Molière's play: by first welcoming Tartuffe into the family, with great scepticism from some of its members and enthusiasm from others, the Orgon family (through fierce debates, negotiations and an occasional laugh) searches to identify precisely in what way this unknown guest is harmful to them. Crucial here is that in the process, the family *finds itself anew*. Serres thus praises the generous hosts, willing to face the virus, willing to drink a small sip of the poison (*virus* refers to poison in Latin), not afraid to be confronted with its own possible death. And as it puts itself at stake, it finds 'a new equilibrium', the family reinvents itself, undergoes a metamorphosis. How? *By turning the virus into the vaccine.* This is what Serres concludes: 'With the expulsion of Tartuffe, Orgon's family is vaccinated against the next devout man' (2007: 193).

In the preface to the French edition of *Essays Critical and Clinical*, Deleuze calls for a similar search for health when he says that the authors who have been dear to him throughout his life are the ones able to cure language from its diseases, by '"drilling holes" in language in order to see or hear "what was lurking behind"' (CC, lv), as Samuel Beckett would say; by finding a language in language that has so much more to say to us, and immediately introduces us to a better life. Of course, all the authors dear to Deleuze, from Antonin Artaud to Virginia Woolf, are in search of this health in different ways. What they share is this clinical approach, that is to say a gradual immunisation process, by making friends with the disease. Ethically, this requires a sharp eye for the innumerable microfascisms, the acknowledgement of serious disagreements that, through fierce debates, negotiations and maybe even an occasional laugh, can be recognised, debated and drilled out. In his book on literature, Deleuze called this a critical and clinical approach. Spinoza, taking up the generalist perspective, simply called it ethics, stressing that the primary task of ethics is to detoxify you. It is important to stress the pathological aspects of this fascist micropolitics, its sickness, its poisonous dimensions, which Spinoza is also quick to emphasise in his ethics.

The microfascist practices that are of our concern are not to be 'recognised', they have to be discovered, over and over again. Learning from Foucault, Deleuze and Guattari saw that more and more, macro-powers are accompanied by a series of micro-powers:

> What we have is no longer the Schoolmaster but the monitor, the best student, the class dunce, the janitor, etc. No longer the general but the junior officers, the non-commissioned officers, the soldier inside me, and also the malcontent: all have their own tendencies, poles, conflicts, and relations of force. (TP, 224–5)

This is how the oppressed do not just vote for their oppressor, the strong leader, but are all also offered the tools and the promise of being him.

The politics of resentment and negativity has a long history as a tool of fascist domination, which repeats itself periodically with astounding force. Its components are always the same: sexism, misogyny, homo- and transphobia, racism, antisemitism, white supremacy, contempt for science and human intelligence in general; a cult of violence. A very manifest death drive expressed in an apocalyptic imaginary of decline, destruction and a frantic state of emergency. Fear, resentment and xenophobia are the poison, the sickness of the self-hatred that is being projected outward as a generalised disenchantment with just about everything, starting with democracy. Masses of disaffected individuals readily turn to strongmen who promise to hear their pain and offer solace. Politicians are quick to manipulate this mass of negativity into violent and usually unfounded but efficient exercises in scapegoating. This is the core of microfascism: a cult of negativity, a sick love of unchecked power, the cult of narcissistic egotistical personality, hatred for the rest of the world. It is about turning the negative into hyper-negativity: turning expressions of pain into cries of revenge, a quest for justice into a mockery of it, the willingness to speak truth to power into the ability to lie shamelessly. Turning fear into hatred, vulnerability into rage, cynicism and opportunism.

As the contributions to this volume show, microfascism proliferates on the left as well as the right of the political spectrum. The right recycles well-tested appeals to sacralised notions of authentic cultural identity, pursuing the refrain of blood and soil. Nativist ethno-nationalism is the key to today's right-wing populism. On the left, working classes exhausted by decades of economic injustice and neoliberal austerity, coupled with fear and rejection of immigrants and especially of Islam, turn to xenophobic and neo-nationalist populism. In both cases, socio-economic deprivation is a compelling motive, but the driving force is a wave of negative affects. And the unifying elements are misogyny, racism and indifference to the environmental crisis.

Affirmative Ethics as Key to the Anti-fascist Life

Deleuze's rereading of Spinoza's ethics of joy is the remedy against the microfascist cult of negativity and the social poison it spreads, coupled with Guattari's incisive analysis of the power of the media to infantilise us and make us desire our own demise – the media as a massive contemporary microfascist machinery. Affirmative ethics is the antidote, the immunity shot against the social pathology of polarised hateful rejection of the interdependence that makes us all function as humans. Reaching an adequate understanding of the conditions that led us to this predicament is the necessary starting point. And such an understanding can only be elaborated collectively by comparing notes – cartographies, analyses, probes and insights of where we are at. Achieving an adequate understanding of our real-life conditions is an essential prerequisite. Accordingly, we devote an entire section of this volume to accounts of the vulnerability of representative democracy as a system.

But the function of epistemological clarity is to lead to ethical action, to activate the desire for affirmation, starting from the composition of a plane of immanence. This project includes a critical reappraisal of community-building as the basis for collective action, aimed at affirming forms of social and ethical interaction and respect for freedom. Relational webs need to be set up on the basis of affirmative values and shared insights. We need to move beyond dialectical oppositions, beyond the logic of violent antagonism, beyond military dualisms to reach a pacifism of matters. This task is aided by accurate political cartographies of the power relations that we inhabit and by which we are structured. This requires a proper understanding of how to live together in a more-than-human world. That alone is hard work.

Knowing that affirmation is the empowering ethical force that increases our ability to relate and take in others, to take on more of the world, and that negativity is the opposite – a decrease of our relational capacity and empathy for others – choosing joy means choosing action, rather then reaction. Negativity and resentment, on the other hand, are conducive to paralysis and stagnation. More than ever therefore we need forms of political opposition that are rich in alternatives, concrete in propositions and attached to everyday projects. This is not a simple or pain-free process, but anger alone is not a project; it needs to become a constitutive force directed not only 'against', but also in favour of something.

Confronted by the pit of negativity of political leaders who wish us ill while pretending to care, faced by their dishonesty and violence, we will echo Deleuze and Guattari and say: No thank you, we would prefer not to follow you. The crucial question however is: who and how many are 'we', those who desire an anti-fascist life? 'We' may well agree and be against the alliance of neoliberalism with microfascisms and multiple fundamentalisms, but we need to compose together a plane of agreement about what our shared hopes and aspirations are. We need to agree on what we want to build together as an alternative. We need fierce discussion, negotiation and an occasional laugh in order to discover these new forms of fascism, but also to reinvent ourselves (to unite more strongly at a new equilibrium, as Serres would say). Critique and creation work hand-in-hand, as do the critical and the clinical aspects of ethical praxis (see Braidotti 2016).

Thus, our volume is ambitious: while denouncing the proliferation of microfascisms, we want to repeat the same question: who and how many are 'we'? To what extent can 'we' say that 'we' are in this together? We want to express solidarity, while avoiding hasty recompositions of one 'humanity' bonded in fear and vulnerability. We prefer to defend complexity, heterogeneity and multiple ways of being anti-fascist, that is to say, an affirmative definition of what binds us together.

The way to activate a contemporary version of the anti-fascist life is to cultivate the ethics of affirmation and start from the project of composing a 'we' that is grounded, accountable and active. This is the collective praxis of affirmative politics, which Deleuze and Guattari encourage us to embrace against the toxic negativity of the social context. In the midst of our technologically mediated social relations and in response to the paranoid rhetoric of our post-truth democratic leaders, how can we labour together to construct affirmative ethical and political practices? How can we work towards socially sustainable horizons of hope through resistance? What tools can we use to resist nihilism, escape consumerist individualism and get immunised against xenophobia? The answer is in the doing, in the praxis of composing alliances, transversal connections and in engaging in difficult conversations about what troubles us. *'We' need to re-radicalise ourselves together.*

This volume demonstrates to what an extent 'we critical philosophers' have at hand powerful theoretical models: from Spinoza to Donna Haraway, from Foucault to Deleuze and Guattari. And 'we feminists' have rich practical precedents as well: from Olympe de Gouges to Sojourner Truth, from the Riot Grrls to Pussy Riot, via the cyborg-ecofeminists, the xeno-feminists, anti-racist mobilisations and post-anthropocentric environmental, transnational justice activists. They constitute a multitude of alternative ways of processing the pain of exclusion while aspiring to self-determination. They are capable of triggering new social imaginaries and igniting unexpected political passions. These sources of inspiration for alternative forms of anti-fascist subjectivity are built on affirmative praxis. They teach us that resistance to the microfascism and violence of the present requires the creation of modes of affirmative relation and of ethical interaction – of alternative communities – based on the pursuit of shared desires for a collaborative ethics of affirmation and freedom.

And this is why Deleuze and Guattari are *always already* doing philosophy in a very different way: thinking is not a consequence, it is a cause, and thus it does not originate in rational knowledge (as Descartes made us believe), as it is not dependent upon a being, it is a collective productive process, a practice, a force. The aim of Deleuze and Guattari scholarship is not to follow or repeat these ideas on an issue such as fascism, but rather to deterritorialise and reterritorialise these precious thoughts in twenty-first-century practices (Evans and Reid 2013).

We, the generous hosts, as Serres would say; we, the responsible elders – as Indigenous philosophies would say (Viveiros de Castro 2015), need to open all our doors of perception and windows of interception to

the state of fascism today. Delving into these twenty-first-century practices, we start this book (the first part) by focusing on the global threats
that have manifested themselves in our everyday lives. John Protevi
rereads *Anti-Oedipus* (including the preface to the English translation
by Foucault and the introduction by Mark Seem), showing us how
radical Deleuze and Guattari's theory of human nature actually is, and
how the economy of violence central to it matters for us today. Zeynep
Gambetti then shows us why this emphasis on immanence, in Deleuze
and Guattari's take on fascism, is so important, and why rereading
Arendt allows us to map microfascisms in the light of contemporary
action and resistance. Christian Alonso starts from the environmental
degradation of today, using especially Guattari's critique of fascism and
the reactionary order it produced, to look at biohacking and the way art
is able to open our eyes to the more-than-human catastrophes of today.
Goda Klumbytė and Lila Athanasiadou take another major theme in
twenty-first-century life as they analyse 'smart cities', and the way the
algorithms facilitating this new form of control reveal a long history of
managerial fascism (from Pinochet to Alphabet), and strategies of subjectification (smart cities are the social machines Deleuze and Guattari
talk of in *Anti-Oedipus*). Siddique Motala turns our attention to the
universities we teach at, showing how the narratives of darker times (in
this case the fascism of apartheid) give form to our education industries
in many ways today. Shiva Zarabadi asks us to look at another very
cruel contemporary machine that might seem new but finds its origins
in racist and colonialist machineries, which she refers to as 'the terrorist
machine'; the ontological force, installed by cognitive capitalism, that
labels terrorism, counterterrorism and being Muslim as debt. Finally,
Patricia MacCormack makes us look at ourselves, at our human exceptionalism and asks us to rethink the concept of life and question the
possibility of a life that is not anthropocentric, as she harshly concludes
that the Anthropocene is the human Reich.

The second part of this book, entitled 'Situated Fascisms', offers
analyses of fascisms at work in different parts of the contemporary
world. Simone Bignall takes us to Australia to give us insight into the
complex political manoeuvres of the Australian government when it
comes to asking for forgiveness of Indigenous Australians regarding
the colonial violence that has been exercised over these communities
until today. Angela Balzano studies the neo-conservative, xenophobic
and misogynist fascism at work in contemporary Italy, giving insight
into how the pro-life movement, together with the Church, shows how
neo-fascism entails a strong need to discipline women 'for the sake of

the state'. Woosung Kang delves into how *Anti-Oedipus* was a book not so much pro-revolution but more anti-counterrevolution; stressing its ethics and its search for a different life, he marks how these claims were taken up in the intellectual circles of Korea, with their reading of nomadism, of cultural differences, and keeping in mind the imperialism that has long haunted the Korean people. Contemporary Spain, under the rule of fascism until the mid-1970s, is studied by Mónica Cano Abadía; the silence, the trauma and the knowledge that the beast is somehow still there give rise to very troubling practices of remembering and forgetting, in the light of the rise of populism. Rick Dolphijn reads the life of Joë Bousquet, the French poet who was wounded in the First World War, became an icon of Surrealism during the rise of fascism, and showed us how fascism has wounded Europe (until today), while living his own life, in pain but beautifully, through the arts. Arash Ghajarjazi takes us to nineteenth-century Iran, where cholera came with the rise of Shiism, the strong monomaniac semiotics that gave rise to fascistophilic thinking, a curse that has ruled the country for two centuries. We close this part by looking at Athens, as Stavros Kousoulas studies its urban ecology in post-Olympic (2004) times, noting that its common urban unit (the *polykatoikia*), which used to regulate urban involution, has started to matter differently (it was decoded, deterritorialised), eroded on every level due to reactive politics, fear of immigrants and 'idiocy'.

The third and final part of this book deals with patriarchal fascism and offers concrete case studies of the sexualised and gendered modes of oppression that happen to us all. Christine Daigle kicks off by noting that the virtual regimes we all inhabit confront us with a variety of toxic fascist regimes that in different ways inflict pain upon us 'transjective beings'. As Daigle coins this term; entangled with others in a variety of (virtual) geographies, she asks us to bear witness to these virtual fascisms and fight their toxicity. Delphi Carstens and Evelien Geerts, in search of the fascism inside, look at the fascist strands of *Lebensphilosophie* that privilege *bios* over *zoē*, and pave the way for the neoliberal desires that go after their own oppression; building a Body without Organs that refuses to subject itself to *bios* but affirms all forms of life and matter/ energy is what they aim at instead. Ruth Clemens and Becket Flannery, departing from a Guattarian ecosophy, study the alt-right and the way in which their neo-archaic notions of white masculinity are not just strategies of subjecting gender and the body, but also aim at agriculture, diet and culture at large. Finally Natalie Dyer, Hollie Mackenzie, Diana Teggi and Patricia de Vries make us look at Deleuze and Guattari's first form of resistance, what they refer to as *becoming woman*, to analyse how the protest pop and punk band Pussy Riot resist Trumpism by searching for the anti-fascist life: through women's fluidity and labiality they practise resistance affirmatively, in harmony with all forces of life and of the earth.

All the contributions in the three parts of this volume, while offering us a rigorous analysis of how fascism matters in our times, aim at searching for ways to endure the pain, to live our lives in harmony with the more-than-human world and with ourselves. Deleuze stressed just that when he talked of his admiration for Primo Levi and how he is able to convince us that the Nazi camps gave *all of us* 'a shame at being human' (PP, 172). The shame Levi is talking about concerns not only our responsibility for Nazism or fascism. It is the shame of being unable, not seeing how to stop our comrades, our fellow human beings, our co-citizens and of course also ourselves from becoming fascists. *It is the shame of somehow having become comprised within it.* Of not having been able – or willing – to contribute enough to immunising the body politic from this sickness. Of having let it happen again, on our watch.

It is for this reason that this book *had* to be written, and that the conferences, the seminars and the readings groups that preceded it, *had* to take place. It had to be written by all of us, for us all, together.

Notes

1. The Futurist movement, and its inevitable suicide, is emblematic of this double pull.
2. In this respect Deleuze's analysis is compatible with Erich Fromm's definition of fascism (2001 [1941]) as the abdication of personal responsibility and Wilhelm Reich's (1970 [1933]) idea of a popular, eroticised desire for a strongman to relieve us from the freedom to make our own choices.

References

Agamben, G. (1998), *Homo Sacer: Sovereign Power and Bare Life*, Stanford, CA: Stanford University Press.

Alaimo, S. (2010), *Bodily Natures: Science, Environment, and the Material Self*, Bloomington: Indiana University Press.

Braidotti, R. (2016), 'Don't Agonize; Organize!', *e-flux Conversations*, 14 November, <http://conversations.e-flux.com/t/rosi-braidotti-don-t-agonize-organize/5294> (last accessed 13 May 2022).

Braidotti, R. (2019), *Posthuman Knowledge*, Cambridge: Polity.

Buchanan, I. (2001), 'Deleuze's "Immanent Historicism"', *Parallax*, 7 (4): 29–39.

Cooper, M. (2008), *Life as Surplus: Biotechnology and Capitalism in the Neoliberal Era*, Seattle: University of Washington Press.

Cooper, M. (2009), 'The Silent Scream – Agamben, Deleuze and the Politics of the Unborn', in R. Braidotti et al. (eds), *Deleuze and Law*, Basingstoke: Palgrave Macmillan.

Esposito, R. (2008), *Bios. Biopolitics and Philosophy*, Minneapolis: University of Minnesota Press.

Evans, B., and J. Read (2013), 'Introduction: Fascism in all its Forms', in B. Evans and J. Read (eds), *Deleuze and Fascism; Security, War, Aesthetics*, Abingdon: Routledge, pp. 1–12.

Foucault, M. (1978), *The History of Sexuality Vol. 1*, New York: Pantheon Books.

Fromm, E. (2001 [1941]), *Escape from Freedom*, Mountain View, CA: Ishi Press.

Hardt, M., and A. Negri (2009), *Commonwealth*, Cambridge, MA: Harvard University Press.

Lemke, T. (2011), 'Critique and Experience in Foucault', *Theory, Culture & Society*, 28 (4): 26–48.

Levi, P. (2015), *The Complete Works of Primo Levi Part III*, New York: Liveright.

May, T. (2013), 'Desire and Ideology in Fascism', in B. Evans and J. Read (eds), *Deleuze and Fascism; Security, War, Aesthetics*, Abingdon: Routledge, pp. 13–26.

Mbembe, A. (2003), 'Necropolitics', *Public Culture*, 15 (1): 11–40.

Nancy, J.-L. (2008), 'The Intruder', in *Corpus*, New York: Fordham University Press, pp. 161–70.

Protevi, J. (2000), '"A Problem of Pure Matter": Deleuze and Guattari's Treatment of Fascist Nihilism in *A Thousand Plateaus*', in K. Ansell-Pearson and D. Morgan (eds), *Nihilism Now! 'Monsters of Energy'*, Basingstoke: Palgrave Macmillan, pp. 167–88.

Rabinow, P. (2003), *Anthropos Today: Reflections on Modern Equipment*, Princeton, NJ: Princeton University Press.

Reich, W. (1970 [1933]), *The Mass Psychology of Fascism*, New York: Farrar, Straus and Giroux.

Rose, N. (2007), *The Politics of Life Itself: Biomedicine, Power and Subjectivity in the Twenty-first Century*, Princeton, NJ: Princeton University Press.

Serres, M. (2007 [1982]), *The Parasite*, Minneapolis: University of Minnesota Press.

Viveiros de Castro, E. (2015), 'Who is Afraid of the Ontological Wolf?', *The Cambridge Journal of Anthropology*, 33 (1): 2–17.

PART I

TWENTY-FIRST-CENTURY FASCISMS

PART F

TWENTY-FIRST CENTURY
FASCISMS

Chapter 1

Human Nature and Anti-fascist Living

John Protevi

Nietzsche's 'Herd' Myth

Foucault's preface to the English translation of *Anti-Oedipus* gives it the alternate title of *Introduction to the Non-Fascist Life* – an 'art of living counter to all forms of fascism' – and offers a frightening invocation of the 'fascism in us all'. This will be our entry into the main thrust of this chapter: how we can construct a notion of human nature such that we are not condemned to be forever fighting a deep drive to microfascism as the desire to have all human relations be those of command.

Writing in 1982, Foucault explains how, for a certain time in France (he specifies 1945–65) critical social thought had Marx and Freud as its obligatory reference points, along with 'the greatest respect' for sign-systems. This conceptual field was also the underlying border of the usual readings of late 1960s social movements: 'A war fought on two fronts: against social exploitation and psychic repression ... had returned and set fire to reality itself: Marx and Freud in the same incandescent light' (AO, xi–xii). While these two thinkers are certainly present, *Anti-Oedipus* is not a new Marx–Freud synthesis, Foucault continues; it's not a new system of thought, a 'flashy Hegel'. Rather, *Anti-Oedipus* is an 'art', a guidebook helping us address the following: 'how does one introduce desire into thought, into discourse, into action?' (AO, xii).

But 'desire' has two valences in *Anti-Oedipus*, fascist and revolutionary, paranoid and schizophrenic, molar and molecular. To achieve the latter, we must defeat the former, which lives as 'the fascism in us all, in our heads and our everyday behavior, the fascism that causes us to love power, to desire the very thing that dominates and exploits us' (AO, xiii). We must insist, however, that this 'fascism in us all', if we are to be faithful to Foucault and to Deleuze and Guattari, must not be an ineradicable part of human nature, but must instead be a historical artefact, an 'assemblage'.

Hence some of Foucault's suggestions: be multiple, not totalising; never 'terrorise' your readers, never claim to have found 'the pure order'; be joyous, 'do not think one has to be sad to be militant'; above all, 'do not become enamored of power' (AO, xiii). These last two are connected: never be sad in that specifically Spinozist sense of bringing yourself and other people down, of sapping their horizontal power of friendship and cooperation in favour of a vertical power of command.

So, memorable suggestions, well worth revisiting, pondering and implementing.

At this point, however, I'd like to shift attention to the other prefatory piece to the English translation of *Anti-Oedipus*, the introduction by Mark Seem. There he adds a third great thinker, Nietzsche, to the mix, highlighting two aspects of desire diagnosed in the *Genealogy of Morals* (Nietzsche 1997) upon which *Anti-Oedipus* will focus: first, the direct libidinal investment of economic flows, and second, the desire for security. Regarding economic flows, Seem directs our attention to 'the Nietzschean theory of affects and intensity . . . a theory of desire and will, of the conscious and the unconscious forces, that relates desire directly to the social field and to a monetary system based on profit' (AO, xviii). And regarding security, Seem directs us to Nietzsche's critique of security-seeking churches: 'Such a set of beliefs, Deleuze and Guattari demonstrate, such a herd instinct, is based on the desire to be led, the desire to have someone else legislate life' (AO, xvi). Here again we find microfascism; something like 'even when I cannot command, at least someone will be in command, telling me what to do'.

Whatever the merits of Nietzsche's critique of the early Christians and their *ressentiment*-mongering in their appeal to the downtrodden of the Roman empire, to the extent that Nietzsche in the *Genealogy* meant the 'herd' to refer to pre-state or non-state nomadic foragers, he is spectacularly wrong from the perspective of contemporary anthropology, both in terms of putative economic practices (which Nietzsche sees in terms of 'debt') and their putative political desires (which are seen as the desire to be 'led').

The critique of 'debt' is subtle and perhaps ultimately only terminological. The use of 'debt' by Nietzsche (and by extension Deleuze and Guattari) is criticised by David Graeber (2012) as projecting individualism and a money economy onto pre-state society. Obligations in pre-state society were not oriented to the restoration of pre-contract individuality as are 'debts'. The initiation rites or 'theater of cruelty' described by Clastres and by Deleuze and Guattari are crucial parts of the anti-state mechanisms preserving the political positivity of 'primitive' egalitarianism (Clastres 1989: 177–88; AO, 188–91). In being initiated, you are being obliged to distribute production in a way that prevents the hoarding of personal property that might enable ascent to a commanding position because it requires '*dépense*' or extravagant expenditure and consumption by others. Initiation rites have an ambiguous position in an economy of violence. Even though they can be torturous, they are voluntary or, better, key elements in social desiring-production. You are constituted by your desire to distribute to others and consume what they give you. So, for Clastres, initiation rites inscribe the 'Anti-One' group law; they are hence anti-state mechanisms (Clastres 1994: 93–104). In *Anti-Oedipus*, Deleuze and Guattari see initiation rites as anti-exchange rites: they are not oriented to the restoration of previous equality, but are designed to produce a web of obligations. They produce 'mobile blocs of debt', and hence are anti-state: they are not centred on any transcendent point, but circulate endlessly. Initiation thus ensures the saturation of the social field with always-unequal relations and provokes the 'anti-production' that prevents stockpiling of property, thus weakening any pretension to a transcendent command position (AO, 184–92).

While the debt vs obligation issue is certainly interesting, the real bite in bringing anthropology to bear on the connection between Nietzsche and Deleuze and Guattari's analysis of fascism comes from the economy of violence of non-state peoples, which, with the help of Boehm (2012a; 2012b) and Scott (2009; 2017), we find in the margins of the 'apparatus of capture' chapter of *A Thousand Plateaus* (TP, 424–73; Sibertin-Blanc 2016; Smith 2018). According to Boehm (2012b), the nomadic forager economy of violence has an anti-state effect by preventing the centralised power of the would-be alpha or dominating 'head'. By killing the would-be dominators among them, such non-state peoples – thought by Nietzsche to be a herd seeking a commander – aim at preserving autonomous egalitarianism, or, precisely, a form of non-state life that would be equally be anti-fascist life. That is to say, the non-state 'herd' so little wants to be led, to have someone else legislate for them, that their entire way of life is dedicated to preventing being incorporated into states where they would be dominated. Thus, the analysis of the genesis of fascism must include the analysis of the genesis of the state, and the various forms of resistance to the state. A bit further on in this essay, I will thus distinguish the anti-state economies of violence of two types of non-state peoples: nomadic egalitarian foragers and the sedentary horticultural 'societies without the state' of Clastres. While Clastres sees war as the main way in which his non-state peoples avoid the state, forager violence, by being restricted to individuals, is anti-war as well as anti-state.

Implications for a Theory of Human Nature

Before we pursue some of the specifics of non-state peoples, we should pause and address a classic issue. As I don't think we can get away from an implied notion of human nature in our philosophy I will be as upfront as I can. My notion of human nature is 'a multiplicity of pro-social politically inflected affective cognition'. I will explain those terms in a moment, but before that we should discuss the risks and rewards of even broaching a concept of human nature.

For much too long, exclusion from political participation or even personhood was justified by a thick conception of human nature, one we can define as copying, explicitly or implicitly, the characteristics of 'White Man'. (I'm operationally defining personhood, using terms from the Greeks, as those whose mistreatment would warrant a charge of *hubris*: paradigmatically, treating a free adult man like a woman, child or slave.) These thick conceptions converged on an idea of culturally induced rational control of brutal, recalcitrant and at best tamable emotions. And the accounts of an essentially violent emotional constitution held in check by culturally induced top-down cognitive structures leave us with a pessimism that forecloses many political reforms based on positive and bottom-up care and cooperation capacities, labelling them as idealistic fantasies.

Despite that history, I think a philosophical intervention to reclaim human nature is worth the risk. For one thing, past efforts to destroy the above-sketched concept because of its abusive consequences and replace it with social constructivism have left those sympathetic to the constructivist position open to charges of adopting a naïve and politically motivated reliance on cultural anthropology at the expense of evolutionary biology. (Hence the real struggle is between an ultra-Darwinist evolutionary psychology and a combination of cultural anthropology and empiricist cultural psychology. For a strong presentation of social constructivism based on the latter perspectives, see Prinz 2012.) But we don't have to give up on the life sciences to distance ourselves from the old notion of human nature, and to rescue quite a bit of what made social constructivism appealing, namely deep cultural variability. As I will detail below, there are live debates at the intersection of biological, evolutionary *and* cultural anthropology that put the above long-standing assumptions about human nature in question.

To return to my notion of human nature as 'a multiplicity of prosocial politically inflected affective cognition', if 'prosociality' is the default setting, then the following is an anti-fascist ethical standard that finds support in an evolutionary account of human nature: *act such that you nurture the capacity to enact repeatable active joyous encounters of positive sympathetic care and fair cooperation for self and others without qualification.*

This is an exhortation to a way of life rather than full-fledged moral imperative. It is also just a first-order account; I won't enter into meta-ethical territory, and I'm leaving the principle's relation to law-making to one side. I can say that whatever your principle of moral judgement, a grasp of evolved human nature is important for your moral pedagogy, how to get to where we should be from where we are. I avoid the naturalistic fallacy in that I don't claim that my standard is *correct because* it is grounded in evolved human nature. But I do think showing that evolved human nature is congruent with that standard is a needed intervention in contemporary debates in philosophy, anthropology and psychology.

Human nature is a multiplicity. A multiplicity is composed of the virtual patterns, triggers and thresholds of a set of interacting intensive processes. 'Virtual' is a term of ontological modality – a pattern of walking does not exist in the same way that any one actual series of steps exists. Rather, we should say that the virtual pattern 'insists' in those actual series. An assemblage is a set of actual interacting processes in which thresholds in the patterns of those processes – in the relations among the processes – trigger qualitative changes in the behaviour of the system. An assemblage is informed by the multiplicity that it actualises or, if you like, 'incarnates'.

The multiplicity of human nature is a virtual differential field of bio-neuro-cultural processes insisting in different existing actual assemblages of politically inflected affective cognition. Although this is a thin conception of human nature, it's not purely formal: it has some content, that is, a prosocial orientation: a primary orientation to sympathetic care and fair cooperation, which is nonetheless admitting of rational egoist-driven violence and competition under duress. Our 'norm of reaction' includes rational egoism, even if bio-cultural evolution has – to date – converged on sympathetic care and fair cooperation (Barker 2015; Ostrom 2005). Furthermore, with certain territorialisation processes – accelerating with states and agriculture – prosociality comes with a gradient favouring the in-group.

We could think here of the resonance of this notion of human nature as a multiplicity of bio-cultural processes with Sylvia Wynter's 'sociogenic principle' (Wynter 2001). Wynter invokes a deep plasticity whereby social patterns of experience use biological capacities for the targeted release of neurotransmitters to produce feeling structures. Wynter takes her cue from Fanon's analysis of how 'black skins' are overlain by 'white masks' and how the pathologies of colonialism can become deeply embodied in both coloniser and colonised.

Rather than being essentialist (necessary and sufficient conditions) or teleological (a completed state), the human nature concept here can only be nomological (Machery 2008; Barker 2015), describing general outcomes for most people under loosely defined environmental situations, and without pejorative boundary-setting for those whose performance is atypical. Mine is a thin conception, but it has enough content that its ramifications are of philosophical interest.

To repeat, then, human nature is a multiplicity of 'prosocial politically inflected affective cognition'. When our early hominin ancestors moved on to the plains, they encountered a highly variable environment necessitating collaboration. Counter-intuitively – but why do we have *this* intuition? – the world was too dangerous to afford competition, let alone war (Kelly 2005; Sterelny 2014). We therefore evolved towards great plasticity of intelligent behaviour to the extent that we engaged in 'niche-construction': we changed our environment so that it could be inherited in predictable ways but never so rigidly as to disallow cultural change (Barker 2015).

Together, then, plasticity and niche-construction mean that humans have evolved so that most are open to prosocialisation processes. 'Prosocialisation' entails being evolutionarily prepared to be intellectually and emotionally invested in, though never determined by, the social and somatic patterns we inhabit and that guide our caring and cooperative relations – and even our stressed violent and competitive relations – with those around us.

Cultural accrual is not naively progressivist; many cultures produce vastly unequal distributions of costs and benefits, very often intertwined with gender and race distinctions. Some even reach the point where we emotionally invest in being dominated. As Spinoza put it, sometimes we fight for our domination as if it were our salvation. This is the problem of fascist desire, the desire to have command and obedience be the sole form of human relation. I also hasten to say that when those social patterns conflict, rational moral reflection and collaborative discussion can and should intervene – and they conflict quite often, even in forager band societies that earlier generations would have characterised as 'simple'. Humans have been arguing about what is the right thing to do for a very long time; we are 'political animals' even before or outside the restricted sense of 'polis' as city; in fact, I'd say there's more political/moral reflection and discussion in 'simple' egalitarian forager bands than in the households and imperial courts of 'complex' hierarchical situations, where commands are issued and obeyed or resisted. We could say that prosocialisation is always fracturing and being repaired with both affective and cognitive remediation qua sympathetic care and moral argument – as Deleuze and Guattari say in *Anti-Oedipus*, 'desiring machines only work by breaking down'.

Live Debates over Human Nature in Contemporary Anthropology

Two such debates are 1) challenges to the long-dominant 'Chimpanzee Referential Doctrine' (CRD) for the Last Common Ancestor (LCA) for the *Pan* (chimpanzees and bonobos)/*Homo* lineages; and 2) whether, in the *Homo* lineages, inter-group 'coalitionary violence' was widespread and intense enough to form the primary selection pressure for human altruism.

The CRD. The CRD posits extant chimpanzees as the best model for the *Pan/Homo* LCA (Vaesen 2014; Gonzalez-Cabrera 2020). If you reject the CRD, you can remain agnostic as to the LCA, and begin your analysis of modern humans within the hominin line, maintaining that chimpanzee, bonobo and human traits had independent evolutionary origins; or you can adopt a 'mosaic' conception of the LCA, such that it should be modelled with both bonobo-like and chimp-like traits. If you accept the CRD, you're pushed in the direction of a deep roots theory of violence and war, which means that establishing intra- and inter-group peace entails an uphill battle against the grain of human nature (Wrangham and Peterson 1996; Kitcher 2011).

This brings us to some high stakes issues in moral psychology. If you accept the CRD, conscience is a top-down cognitive control of emotions driving one to dominate others. In a way that echoes Nietzsche's analysis of the herd versus the aristocrats, conscience is rooted in fear of group punishment, that is, conscience is an adaptation to 'social selection' against would-be dominators by an egalitarian group, up to and including capital punishment (Boehm 2012b). The difference from Nietzsche is that such 'herd' production of conscience is not a late, post-state, cultural psychological struggle, but a straightforward and early, pre-state one. But in this picture, joy in collaboration vanishes and in its place would be mere relief at behaviour that doesn't attract punishment, or at best satisfaction at having obeyed ethical precepts.

If you accept conscience as derived from fear of punishment directed at dominators, that doesn't mean you have to throw up your hands, but your main path to social improvement is to reinforce and/or supplement the teaching of explicit moral principles by child-rearing practices and social institutions for the detection and punishment of dominance bids resulting from failures of conscience (Kitcher 2011). If you reject the CRD, conscience is still top-down, but has two origins: physical punishment for dominance bids but also social punishment (rebukes) for failed care and cooperation such as quitting or non-sharing (Tomasello 2016). Here, emotion doesn't have to be *only* a primitive source of trouble to be controlled so that later evolved and rationally based care and cooperation can have room to operate; it can *also* include a positive impulse to care and cooperation that can be nurtured. So, if you reject the CRD it's easier for you to root the normative standard of active joyous encounters of care and cooperation in human nature.

War and prosocial human nature. Since Darwin's suggestion in *The Descent of Man*, it has been widely thought that war was a primary selection pressure for altruism and prosociality in human evolution. According to this narrative, we are the descendants of victors in warfare.

> When two tribes of primeval man, living in the same country, came into competition, if (other things being equal) the one tribe included a great number of courageous, sympathetic and faithful members, who were always ready to warn each other of danger, to aid and defend each other, this tribe would succeed better and conquer the other. (Darwin 2004 [1871]: 113)

The thesis that widespread pre-state warfare provided the selection pressure for prosociality is, however, bitterly disputed. Here the basic question is whether war is a universal human experience, or whether it only occurs in certain social circumstances, namely, the state (Fry 2013). While critics of the universal war thesis admit that nomadic forager groups have individual-level murder and revenge killing and even group 'executions' of murderous individuals, they deny that they have warfare as anonymous group-level conflict in which any member of the opposing group is fair game (Kelly 2000). The critics of universal war also look askance at using current violence rates among contemporary foragers as transparent access to our evolutionary past (thus treating them as 'living fossils'), by reminding us of the need to look at them in the context of state contact and subsequent territorial constriction and/or rivalry over trading rights (Ferguson 2008). For these thinkers, then, we are not the descendants of victors; we are the descendants of cooperators whose sharing in times of crisis avoided war – to repeat what I said above, war really doesn't pay for nomadic foragers: there's too much to lose and too little to gain (Kelly 2005; Sterelny 2014).

If we were essentially or even simply strongly predisposed to killing due to a warfare selection pressure – whether or not that is continuous with chimpanzee lethal raiding (Wrangham 1999) – military and police training efforts would be towards control, when in fact the effort is towards enabling. Now such enabling has, to be sure, made great strides, with training using live-fire realistic targets aimed at reflex and quick decision or 'shoot/no-shoot' engagements (Protevi 2008). We can of course extend this analysis of training to the living conditions, initiation rites and other training procedures of gangs, guerrilla groups and so on. Not only do we 'have to be taught, carefully taught' to hate, as *South Pacific* tells us, we have to be trained to kill effectively.

The Economy of Violence of Nomadic Forager Bands

Nomadic egalitarian foragers are not angelic and pacific creatures. But their economy of violence is both anti-war and anti-state. There is no teleology here in discussing processes that ward off or instantiate statification; states are not the 'mature' form of social life and non-state societies possess their own positivity in mechanisms for warding off state formation. Even as they have for the most part abandoned unilinear 'evolutionary' theories of social 'stages' (Widerquist and McCall [2017] provide a brief overview), anthropologists would still acknowledge that the nomadic forager band is the social form for the vast majority of human life, prior to the institution of the state. (Scott [2017] synthesises new research that calls into question any notion of a 'Neolithic Revolution' which simultaneously – or even quickly and necessarily – brought together states, urbanism and agriculture as a clean break from foraging.) Despite current research showing more variability than previously acknowledged among currently living foragers (Kelly 2013), we can cautiously speculate that pre-state nomadic forager bands were most likely egalitarian or 'acephalic'; that they practised 'fission–fusion' and frequent inter-band visiting, rendering group identity fluid; that they often had a gendered division of labour, though with little specialisation within genders; and that while there was most likely a prestige gradient relative to prowess, group discussion was the decision-making process; hence, while there was rhetoric and persuasion, there was no top-down command (Kelly 2000; Boehm 2012b; Sterelny 2014).

According to Boehm (2012b), the nomadic forager economy of violence has an anti-state effect by preventing the centralised power of the would-be alpha or dominating 'head'. Boehm is an expert in the ethnography of contemporary nomadic foragers. He cautions against the 'living fossil' view, though he attempts cautious extrapolation to pre-state social existence. The forager economy of violence focuses on intra-group personal violence. Here we find individual acts of fighting and murder, and group response of ostracism, exile or killing, that is, 'capital punishment'. Intra-group anonymous violence is a void category for nomadic foragers; everyone knows everyone else in the group.

We turn now to inter-group violence. The term 'inter-group' is tricky as fission–fusion practices mean that forager group membership is fluid, so strict boundaries are difficult to establish. Nonetheless, there is evidence of inter-group personal violence or vengeance. Individual, personalised acts of fighting or murder call for a group response of permitting individualised vengeance targeting only the murderer. Boehm (2012b) cites cases where a murderer is killed by his own kin and the corpse is then presented to the victim's family; this is quite clearly an anti-war gesture. According to Boehm, then, vengeance is an anti-war process; it prevents escalation to anonymous inter-group violence. So, for Boehm, forager economies of violence are (intra-group) anti-state and (inter-group) anti-war.

We could say that Boehm is upping the ante in glossing Nietzsche's *Genealogy* (Nietzsche 1997): 'Of course the herd of weaklings ganged up and killed the solitary strong ones! You say that like it's a bad thing, when in fact, it's the secret of human evolution!' Of course, Nietzsche is not *complaining* about social selection or about the development of conscience (that which interferes with free-riding or domination by warning about group retribution); he is not resentful that this has occurred; he is not saying what he says as a moral argument about what *should* have happened – 'See what you lot have done? Wouldn't it have been better if the herd had stayed in its place way back when?' So, Boehm is not really defeating Nietzsche, since Nietzsche himself would certainly expect the descendants of herd manoeuvres to think this way – 'of course lambs do not like lions! Why should they?'

The ethnography of contemporary foragers shows multiple anti-war mechanisms, including toleration of inter-group vengeance to head off feud. Feud – as opposed to vengeance – would allow targeting any member of the other group, but this requires a 'calculus of social substitution' that not all forager societies have, per Kelly (2000: 10). Feud would be on the way to anonymous inter-group violence or war. In feud, there is collective duty to avenge wrongs that is directed at a group which holds collective responsibility for the wrongs committed by its members. According to Kelly (2000), this pattern holds only in 'segmented' societies (those in which marriages and other social ties are regulated across sub-group formations such as lineages); many nomadic forager bands are 'unsegmented' and hence practise only personal vengeance rather than collective feud.

Sterelny (2014) notes that foragers have no territorial motivation to attack, as they do not invest much labour in the land and have no interest in permanent occupation (though this point is nuanced by Scott [2017], who notes that permanent settlement is compatible with foraging when a multi-food site can be found in resource-rich wetlands, whereby foragers can access multiple food webs by remaining in place and allowing the resources to come to them, rather than them chasing the resources). Sterelny also notes the psychological implausibility that war provided a selection pressure for our evolved traits of intra-group cooperation, which does not seem compatible with also selecting for people who are able to easily access the berserker rage useful in inter-group war. It would be, Sterelny claims, too difficult to partition such aggression solely into war; it would be too difficult to suppress its in-group expression. But such in-group expression is what triggers anti-alpha capital punishment.

Kelly (2005: 15298) sketches a geo-eco-techno-social multiplicity that results in a period of 'intrinsic defensive advantage'. The geographical aspect is that defenders know their territory and can hold ambush positions. The ecological aspect is that low population density meant defenders could flee if needed. The technological aspect is that single-kill thrown weapons allow the infliction of damage from afar on invaders with low risk to defenders. The social aspect is that invading parties would be non-specialists while defenders would have throwing skills developed in hunting. Kelly concludes that, faced with such a period of defensive advantage, foragers developed positive peace-seeking inter-group mechanisms (diplomacy, feasts, contests).

With a universal war anthropological perspective, you assume hostility to be the default setting for inter-group relations, and war, prior to being territorially motivated, aims at women-capture qua acquisition of reproductive resources. But this is not the only possible materialist position, as peace-seeking mechanisms are just as materialist as war. In fact, per Kelly (2005), they allow more efficient resource exploitation: the two sides are not afraid to exploit to the border of their territories, as they would be if border raids were frequent. For Kelly, then, it's a shift to state military specialisation that allows strikes at the home camp that shifts the balance and allows state territorial acquisition and enslavement warfare.

A Non-war-based Hypothesis for Evolved Prosociality

So, if there was a time before war, then what was our selection pressure for prosociality? It was *obligate collaborative foraging*, which, evolving by mutualism and reciprocity, is not group-level selection. This, and not warfare, was the selection pressure for anger control or 'self-domestication' and for cognitive and affective capacities for joint attention allowing for the development of prosocial capacities of care and cooperation beyond kin, even to the point of psychological altruism, in which the ends and needs of others motivate our action. This line of thought (Tomasello 2016; Sterelny 2014) allows for evolved egalitarian sentiments to positively contribute to mutualistic cooperation. The selection pressure here would be collective self-defence against non-human animal predators and so-called 'power scavenging' in which hominins cooperatively chased predators from their kills.

Our ancestors did indeed develop ways to detect and punish bullies and shirkers and so to suppress our dominance-enabling hair-trigger temper and violent reactive aggression, as in the so-called Human Self-Domestication hypothesis. But they also genuinely and positively developed an emotional structure that can motivate us, their descendants, to search for the joy we directly find in cooperation, sharing and helping. This means that foragers don't settle for cooperation simply out of the fear that not cooperating would unleash the bullies and shirkers that lurk within all of us (Gaus 2015).

For most people, most of the time, it's a little bit of both. It's not impossible to find pure examples of bullies and cooperators, devils and saints, but either pure state seems relatively rare. What we have to watch out for is having our social structures tilt towards rewarding bullies and shirkers. (Barker [2015] thinks bullies might be expressing a developmental switch in a norm of reaction model which produces a behaviour set adapted to circumstances of violent uncertainty.) But that also means we can work with human nature, and not against it, to work towards institutions that would support our hortatory ideal. It's a matter of nurturing a deep capacity for care and cooperation, and expanding it so it is without qualification, not a matter of desperately fighting a single deep drive to dominance.

An Anti-fascist Politics of Joy

You get joy in joining an assemblage that increases your power. To live anti-fascistically, however, we must distinguish active and passive joy in Spinoza's sense: active joy comes when you have an adequate idea and are an adequate cause of the increase in power in an encounter; that is, when your singular essence is positively contributing to the increased power, as opposed to simply being passively uplifted by external forces. Our capacity for mutually active joyous encounters gives us the potential to resolve the conflict of egoism and altruism, as in those cases increasing my power increases yours.

Here we need the distinction between *pouvoir* and *puissance*. *Pouvoir* is transcendent power: it comes from above. It is hylomorphic, imposing form on the chaotic or passive material of the emotions or the mob. In its most extreme manifestation, it is fascistic: it is expressed not simply as the desire to rule, but more insidiously as the longing for the strong leader to rescue us from the chaos into which our bodies politic have descended. *Puissance*, on the other hand, is immanent self-organisation. It is the power of people working together to generate the structures of their social life. The difference between *pouvoir* and *puissance* allows us to nuance the notion of joyous and sad affect with the notions of active and passive power.

Consider the paradigm case of fascist joy. The Nazis at the Nuremberg rallies were filled with joyous affect, but this joy of being swept up into an emergent body politic was passive. The Nazis' joy was triggered by the presence of a transcendent figure manipulating symbols – flags and faces – and by the imposition of a rhythm or a forced entrainment – marches and salutes and songs. Upon leaving the rally, they had no autonomous power (*puissance*) to make repeatable mutually empowering connections. In fact, they could only feel sad at being isolated, removed from the thrilling presence of the leader.

We then come back to our ethical standard: does the encounter produce repeatable, mutually active joyous affect in enacting positive care and cooperation? Does it increase the *puissance* of the bodies, that is, does it enable them to form new and mutually empowering encounters of care and cooperation outside the original encounter?

A final remark. I've tried to keep this essay neutral with regard to classic questions in political philosophy. But I don't think I can make it all the way to the end, for, to develop capacities for active joyous encounters for self and others without qualification, we need positive or substantive liberties that enable claims on material support and appropriate care. One must be protected, cared for and nurtured to reach one's potentials. I think there is a possible connection with the Sen/Nussbaum capabilities approach, but it must be 'without qualification', to ward off the implicit economic productivity and political performance orientation of Sen and Nussbaum that Eva Feder Kittay detects. That's why I go with the capacity for joy that Kittay finds expressed in her daughter's life: 'But I have since learned – from her, from the disability community and from my own observations – that she is capable of having a very good life, one full of joy, of love, of laughter' (Kittay 2005: 110).

It's only then, relieved of the anxiety produced by artificial scarcity and its attendant egoism, that we have institutionalised the means to develop our prosocial potentials, whatever the register – art, science, politics, philosophy, love – for singular differentiations of the multiplicity of human nature. It's only then that we can continue to explore what we – self and others, without qualification – can become. It's then that we can truly live non-fascistically.

References

Barker, G. (2015), *Beyond Biofatalism: Human Nature for an Evolving World*, New York: Columbia University Press.

Boehm, C. (2012a), 'Ancestral Hierarchy and Conflict', *Science*, 336 (6083): 844–7.

Boehm, C. (2012b), *Moral Origins: The Evolution of Virtue, Altruism, and Shame*, New York: Basic Books.

Clastres, P. (1989 [1974]), *Society against the State*, trans. R. Hurley and A. Stein, New York: Zone Books. Translation of *La Société contra l'état*, Paris: Minuit.

Clastres, P. (1994 [1980]), *Archaeology of Violence*, trans. J. Herman, New York: Semiotext(e). Translation of *Recherches d'anthropologie politique*, Paris: Seuil.

Darwin, C. (2004 [1871]), *The Descent of Man*, New York: Penguin.

Ferguson, B. (2008), 'Ten Points on War', *Social Analysis*, 52 (2): 32–49.

Fry, D. (2007), *Beyond War: The Human Potential for Peace*, New York: Oxford University Press.

Fry, D. (2013), 'War, Peace and Human Nature: The Challenge of Achieving Scientific Objectivity', in D. Fry (ed.), *War, Peace, and Human Nature*, Oxford: Oxford University Press, pp. 1–21.

Gaus, G. (2015), 'The Egalitarian Species', *Social Philosophy and Policy*, 31 (2): 1–27.

Gonzalez-Cabrera, I. (2020), 'On Social Tolerance and the Evolution of Human Normative Guidance', *The British Journal for the Philosophy of Science*, 70 (2): 523–49.

Graeber, D. (2012), *Debt: The First 5,000 Years*, New York: Melville House.

Kelly, R. (2000), *Warless Societies and the Origin of War*, Ann Arbor: University of Michigan Press.

Kelly, R. (2005), 'The Evolution of Lethal Intergroup Violence', *Proceedings of the National Academy of Science*, 102 (43): 15294–8.

Kelly, R. L. (2013), *The Lifeways of Hunter-Gatherers: The Foraging Spectrum*, Cambridge: Cambridge University Press.

Kitcher, P. (2011), *The Ethical Project*, Cambridge, MA: Harvard University Press.

Kittay, E. F. (2005), 'Equality, Dignity, and Disability', in M. A. Lyons and F. Waldron (eds), *Perspectives on Equality: The Second Seamus Heaney Lectures*, Dublin: The Liffey Press, pp. 93–119.

Machery, E. (2008), 'A Plea for Human Nature', *Philosophical Psychology*, 21 (3): 321–9.

Nietzsche, F. (1997 [1887]), *On the Genealogy of Morality*, trans. Carol Diethe, Cambridge: Cambridge University Press. Translation of *Zur Geneologie der Moral*, Leipzig: Neumann.

Ostrom, E. (2005), 'Policies that Crowd Out Reciprocity and Collective Action', in H. Gintis, S. Bowles, R. Boyd and E. Fehr (eds), *Moral Sentiments and Material Interests: The Foundations of Cooperation in Economic Life*, Cambridge, MA: MIT Press, pp. 253–75.

Prinz, J. (2012), *Beyond Human Nature: How Culture and Experience Shape the Human Mind*, New York: W. W. Norton.

Protevi, J. (2008), 'Affect, Agency, and Responsibility: The Act of Killing in the Age of Cyborgs', *Phenomenology and the Cognitive Sciences*, 7 (2): 405–13.

Protevi, J. (2019), *Edges of the State*, Minneapolis: University of Minnesota Press.

Scott, J. C. (2009), *The Art of Not Being Governed: An Anarchist History of Upland Southeast Asia*, New Haven: Yale University Press.

Scott, J. C. (2017), *Against the Grain: A Deep History of the Earliest States*, New Haven: Yale University Press.

Sibertin-Blanc, G. (2016 [2013]), *State and Politics*, trans. Ames Hodges, New York: Semiotext(e). Translation of *Politique et État chez Deleuze et Guattari*, Paris: Actuel Marx.

Smith, D. (2018), '7000BC: Apparatus of Capture', in H. Somers-Hall, J. Bell and J. Williams (eds), *A Thousand Plateaus and Philosophy*, Edinburgh: Edinburgh University Press, pp. 223–41.

Sterelny, K. (2014), 'Cooperation, Culture, and Conflict', *British Journal for the Philosophy of Science*, 67 (1): 1–28.

Tomasello, M. (2016), *A Natural History of Human Morality*, Cambridge, MA: Harvard University Press.

Vaesen, K. (2014), 'Chimpocentrism and Reconstructions of Human Evolution (a Timely Reminder)', *Studies in History and Philosophy of Biological and Biomedical Sciences*, 45: 12–21.

Widerquist, K., and G. McCall (2017), *Prehistoric Myths in Modern Political Philosophy*, Edinburgh: Edinburgh University Press.

Wrangham, R. (1999), 'Evolution of Coalitionary Killing', *American Journal of Physical Anthropology* 110 (Supplement 29): 1–30.

Wrangham, R. and D. Peterson (1996), *Demonic Males: Apes and the Origins of Human Violence*, New York: Houghton Mifflin.

Wynter, S. (2001), 'Towards the Sociogenic Principle: Fanon, Identity, the Puzzle of Conscious Experience, and What it is Like to be "Black"', in M. F. Durán-Cogan and A. Gómez-Moriana (eds), *National Identities and Sociopolitical Changes in Latin America*, New York: Routledge, pp. 30–66.

Chapter 2

Immanence, Neoliberalism, Microfascism: Will We Die in Silence?

Zeynep Gambetti

It is no longer the age of cruelty or the age of terror, but the age of cynicism, accompanied by a strange piety.

Deleuze and Guattari, AO, 225

On ne crèvera pas en silence!

Gilets jaunes

Gilles Deleuze famously wrote that '[a] snake's coils are even more intricate than a mole's burrow' (PP, 182). The serpent represents the mode of functioning of 'control societies' in which institutions have lost both their relevance and their capacity to stratify, enclose and enshrine. If Deleuze's premonitions are to be taken seriously (as they should be), we would need to consider the possibility of molecular formations or pseudo-planes of immanence replacing the rigid stratifications that were once the mark of twentieth-century fascisms. Given that new forms of domination breed – and will breed – from within control societies, we would need to ask what it would mean to cease thinking of fascism as a molehill, as a closed system with identifiable spaces and practices of command, internment and murder. What would it mean instead to think of it as a serpent that does not hold captive, but kills through immanent undulations and modulations, rapid and flexible variations, and the extended execution of the Final Solution?

The question necessarily emerges from the present-day context that is marked, on the one hand, by growing indifference to the plight of others, and on the other, by the alarming resonance that far right discourses find in societies across the globe. Our indifference to those who incur social death is manifest at the molecular level, at the level of the streets we walk, as we step over the extended limbs of those stranded on the pavement, turning our heads not to notice. But we have also become apathetic to the fate of migrants, drowning in hundreds in the Mediterranean, or to black bodies being shot, or neighbours being evicted, or colleagues losing their contracts for failing to comply with the grant-hunting requirements of the neoliberal university. The eruption of Covid-19 on the global scene might have temporarily equalised our exposure to the forces of nature or of life in the barest sense, but new categories of 'disposable bodies' are now being constituted at great speed. We have come to internalise the idea that the exposure of certain portions of the population to the virus is a necessary evil. The Covid-19 pandemic is exacerbating fascistic tendencies and has revealed that 'letting die' can take on new forms. Instead of collectively inventing a politics of care, of giving and protecting life, we react with *ressentiment*, protesting against the vaccine while consuming more and more luxury goods. The pandemic also brings to the forefront how incapable and unwilling political elites across the ideological spectrum are in 'making live'.

As for the rising popularity of the far right, scholars of fascism would surely reserve the F-word to such episodes only. It would seem that quotidian indifference to precariousness, as demonstrated by undisturbed practices of living and falling back upon our habits, even when caught up in a pandemic, is not comparable with the far right's disregard for the fate of outliers. They warn us not to dilute the term 'fascist', lest it is so hollowed out that it fails to perform its critical function. So be it. But still, what if the idea of a clean break between us and them served to exonerate us, by providing us with a comfortable position of externality from which to critique far right ideologies without asking the question of whether we, too, might be involved in reproducing some of the practices that we explain away as being exceptions or abominations? What if Michel Foucault was right in stating that, in addition to historical fascism, the strategic adversary in our day and age is 'the fascism in us all, in our heads and in our everyday behavior' (AO, xiii)?

The urge to dissociate our micro-practices from fascist dispositions stems in part from the fact that far right movements represent themselves as *alternatives* to the existing political system. They contest the purported dissolution of identities within a globalising world, point a finger at immigrants, and denounce what they see as the 'liberal hegemony' and 'gender ideology'. But if we take such discourses at face value, we would not only end up reinforcing this representation. We would be dispensing with asking ourselves whether today's fascistic tendencies actually constitute a break with existing practices and discourses. For what exactly are the existing practices and discourses that we think the far right has set out to destroy? If we have an idealised version of liberal democracy in mind (rule of law, universal rights, free and fair elections, independent judiciary, and legitimacy based on rational debate and scrutiny), we might first like to reflect upon whether that ideal hasn't already been hollowed out, long before the far right reappeared on the political scene as a major force.

This chapter is an exercise in engaging with the concepts and functions populating Gilles Deleuze and Felix Guattari's (schizo)analysis of fascism. Immanence will constitute the conceptual pivot of the chapter. I contend that one must think through and expose the unresolved tensions in the philosophy of immanence in order to take the measure of the perils in store for contemporary anti-fascist struggles. Without such an exercise, we would fail to comprehend how new forms of fascism are insidiously emerging from within our everyday practices, contaminating our chances of standing against them. By inquiring into the triple aspect of immanence as 1) the self-perpetuating movement of capitalist accumulation processes, 2) the most treacherous feature of microfascisms, and 3) paradoxically, one of the conditions of resistance and revolution, I ask how a notion can be made to carry so much contradictory weight. The aim is not so much to trace the itinerary of the concept, but rather to put it into an echo chamber where it would resonate with other figures of immanence, borrowed notably from Michel Foucault and Hannah Arendt, so as to bring out its real import. Although sketchy, the last part of the chapter aims to formulate the conditions under which an immanent notion of power might serve as a basis for rethinking the struggle against fascism in contemporary societies.

From Capitalist Immanence to Microfascism

Immanence is a heavy-duty notion in Deleuze and Guattari's individually and jointly produced work. From the philosophical point of view, immanence implies a univocal ontology according to which there is no essence that precedes existence and no existential principle of hierarchy that organises beings on a scale running from lack to perfection. Espousing this purely positive ontology, Deleuze and Guattari denounce the Platonic superimposition of the realm of Ideas over the phenomenal realm and the Cartesian separation of mind and matter as just as illusory as the transcendent God of theology (WP, 44–51). Univocity entails rejecting transcendental guarantees of identity, on the one hand, and the value of negation in accounting for individuation, on the other. Instead of a dialectical confrontation between identities that negate each other in a pre-determined or logically pre-determinable sequence, the philosophy of immanence endorses the notion of self-differentiation. All individuating instances are construed as generating through potentially infinite and immanent differentiations within a multiplicity of relations. As such, immanence implies the fully positive coexistence of potentials, the latter conceived as so many virtual powers or energies that are not and cannot be indefinitely channelled into distinct forms. Constructing a transcendental empiricist philosophy enables Deleuze and Guattari to associate identity thinking, binary logic, representative thought and hierarchical models with coding and overcoding practices that must be dismantled. In other words, immanence constitutes the very basis of Deleuze and Guattari's *critical* ontology, their very premise of critique.

In accordance with such an ontology, liberation calls for the dissolution of strata, codes, or modalities of subjectivisation that impose order, uniformity and regularity on to the real. The ethics of becoming, as developed by Deleuze and Guattari, demands the severing of affective attachments to identities and to overcoding machines such as the state and capital, just as much as it espouses a vision of the world as impersonal, interconnected and populated by potentially infinite singularities. Instead of the 'IS', this is a world of the 'AND' in which both the subject/object dichotomy and the self/other dichotomy are cast off. Unlike Kantian morality, which requires transcending the real in order to attain autonomy or moral excellence, an ethics of becoming calls for a truly immanent actualisation of pure potentials.

I do not have to state the numerous merits of such a philosophical position – not in this volume in any case. But I do want to start introducing the difficulties associated with immanence in Deleuze and Guattari's own analyses, since the looming threat of fascism is a serious one and it will not do to celebrate immanence without a critical examination. To start immediately with the first difficulty: in Deleuze and Guattari's thought, immanence is not the exclusive trait of an ethics of becoming, but also of capitalism. This presents us with a complex problem associated with immanence at the level of concrete social formations, at the level of *real* immanence as opposed to a virtual one that can only be *actualised*.[1] Deleuze and Guattari distinguish capitalism from former modes of production through its capacity to break down existing codes, that is, hierarchies or privileges that reproduce and legitimise inequality in pre-capitalist societies. In the latter, codes territorialise wealth and labour by attaching them to specific places, forms of life and specific persons (for instance, landed aristocracy vs. serfs in Europe), thereby circumscribing production processes within more or less fixed arrangements and limits. Following Marx, Deleuze and Guattari portray capitalism as partially liberating. Capitalism decodes, that is, it sets production free of some of its former fetters. It replaces codes with an axiomatic that functions by generating, quantifying and conjoining two flows: flows of labour and flows of money. Axiomatic operations are considered self-evident. In Jason Read's words, 'they lay down a particular formula, a particular system of equivalences, and this cannot be argued with [. . .] one only needs to act in accordance with the quantitative flows' (2008: 146). Instead of compromising or allying with instances exterior to production (the state, the landed aristocracy, geographically delimited markets, bankers), capitalism develops its own reproductive articulation. It is both axiomatically and practically immanent to the socius it creates. It is self-reflexive, reproducing itself from within: 'Capitalism becomes filiative when money begets money, or value a surplus value' (AO, 227). From this point onwards, capital accumulation abjures all exterior limits, but has only an interior one which it reproduces by constantly displacing it. This is rendered possible through the deterritorialising tendency in capitalism.

> At the same time as capitalist deterritorialisation is developing from the center to the periphery, the decoding of flows on the periphery develops by means of a 'disarticulation' that ensures the ruin of traditional sectors, the development of extraverted economic circuits, a specific hypertrophy of the tertiary sector, and an extreme inequality in the different areas of productivity and in incomes. Each passage of a flux is a deterritorialization, and each displaced limit, a decoding. Capitalism schizophrenizes more and more on the periphery. (AO, 231–2)

Note that decoding and deterritorialisation are integral to the workings of capital. This presents us with a conundrum since, even though Deleuze and Guattari qualify capitalist deterritorialisation as *relative* and instead call for *absolute* deterritorialisation along lines of flight as the means through which the internal limits of capital must be dismantled (WP, 88), they nevertheless leave us in a grey zone, a zone of indiscernibility between relative and absolute, capitalist and revolutionary immanence. We know, of course, that capitalism's filiative production of surplus value is conditioned and thus relatively bound to a machine of anti-production (the state, its police, army and apparatuses of science and technology). But Deleuze and Guattari also contend that the 'apparatus of antiproduction is no longer a transcendent instance that opposes production, limits it, or checks it' (AO, 235). As a self-reflexive process of generating and conjoining flows of abstract labour and exchange value, capitalism succeeds in capturing and immersing all that it encounters into its axiomatic. The state, too, is put to the service of capital to regulate productivity and assure its reproduction. In regard to this capacity, it must be conceded that capitalism constructs an 'entire field of immanence' (AO, 228). It leaves no 'outside', as it were. So much so that the spectre of the *Communist Manifesto* lurks between the lines in Deleuze and Guattari's world-historical narrative of the globalisation of capital:

> So what is the solution? Which is the revolutionary path? [. . .] To withdraw from the world market, as Samir Amin advises Third World countries to do, in a curious revival of the fascist 'economic solution'? Or might it be to go in the opposite direction? To go still further, that is, in the movement of the market, of decoding and deterritorialization? (AO, 239)

One is tempted to ask whether in 1972, when *Anti-Oedipus* was completed, the socio-historic world seemed more hopeful, if not 'ripe' for revolution. Did it appear to draw closer to liberating itself from transcendental fetters (the state, autonomous institutions, external limits) such that the modes of immanence characterising capitalism could be depicted as potentially facilitating an emancipatory transition towards non-axiomatic experiments in becoming? Even so, one significant difficulty that cannot be readily resolved is how to distinguish between immanence as a principle of revolutionary becoming and the immanence characterising capitalism. Another concerns the question of how to overcome the cynicism which necessarily emanates from the physical field of immanence constructed by capitalism: 'there is not a single economic or financial operation that, assuming it is translated in terms of a code, would not lay bare its own unavowable nature, that is, its intrinsic perversion or essential cynicism' (AO, 247). As we shall see below, cynicism will prove to be a formidable obstacle in the way of reassembling desires. Yet another difficulty arises when Deleuze and Guattari portray not only capitalism, but also fascism as immanent in *A Thousand Plateaus*. There is, as it were, a sea-change between the two volumes of *Capitalism and Schizophrenia* on the question of fascism. This merits a closer look, not only because it is one of the points of controversy in Deleuze scholarship, but also because it stands in the way of conceiving of molecular assemblages capable of actualising virtual connections rather than pulling us into the abyss.

To begin with, *Anti-Oedipus* locates the conditions of the emergence of fascism within capitalism. Capitalism's schizophrenic drive, the setting loose of flows of desire operated by capital's destitution of codes and modes of life, paradoxically results in the reappearance of 'artificial, residual, archaic' forms of territorialisation, some of which nourish fascistic tendencies (AO, 257–8). The fascist 'solution' to the radically axiomatic thrust of capitalism is to restratify by investing in codes of racial or national superiority. The production of fascistic bodies must be analysed within this setting, Deleuze and Guattari suggest. They note how Wilhelm Reich exclaimed: 'no, the masses were not deceived, they desired fascism, and that is what has to be explained' (AO, 257). The desire for fixity, a backlash to the disarticulations operated by capitalism, is at the same time a desire for power. The massifying dynamics of capitalist modernity detach individuals from traditional communities and personified rule, but submit them to an impersonal propulsion over which they have little or no control. As Eugene Holland notes: 'Mid-century European masses weren't ideologically tricked into fascism: they actively desired it because it augmented their feelings of power' (2008: 76).

A Thousand Plateaus rectifies the somewhat sketchy argument in Anti-Oedipus. The question is the same: 'Why does desire desire its own repression?' (TP, 215) But this time the answer is significantly different. Fascism is not a reaction; on the contrary, it is bred as an interiority in capitalist societies. The term that must be retained is 'microfascism', which is one of the most significant contributions of Deleuze and Guattari to understanding what I consider to be a form of 'fascism from below' (Gambetti 2020). Instead of locating fascism in a regime or party, 'microfascism' conceives it as a destructive desire, a surge that is as diffuse as it is dangerous. The admonition that 'every politics is simultaneously a *macropolitics* and a *micropolitics*' (TP, 213) should in fact advise us against the dangers of looking for signs of fascism exclusively in the macropolitics of signification, subject-formation, party organisation, and in historical signs of domination (the swastika, the KKK, the Nazi salute, the skinhead, etc.). Fascism is 'a cancerous body rather than a totalitarian organism' (TP, 215), according to Deleuze and Guattari, a movement that captures the masses from within rather than a state or army apparatus that represses them. Because it continually generates a micropolitics of insecurity by fluidifying or shattering codes and erecting mechanisms of paranoid libidinal investment, capitalism tends to foster cancerous outgrowths at the micro level that are either suicidal or are caught up in a desire for destruction. In every de-institutionalised medium and in every social niche, a cancerous tissue is ready to gnaw and create a black hole:

We would even say that fascism implies a molecular regime that is distinct both from molar segments and their centralization. Doubtless, fascism invented the concept of the totalitarian State, but *there is no reason to define fascism by a concept of its own devising*: there are totalitarian States, of the Stalinist or military dictatorship type, that are not fascist. The concept of the totalitarian State applies only at the macropolitical level, to a rigid segmentarity and a particular mode of totalization and centralization. But fascism is inseparable from a proliferation of molecular focuses in interaction, which skip from point to point, before beginning to resonate together in the National Socialist State. (TP, 214, emphasis added)

One of the fundamental claims advanced here is that we should avoid looking for fascism in molar structures only. This flies in the face of the vast majority of historical or political studies of fascism that take Mussolini's programmatic declarations at face value and claim that the F-word cannot be used to describe sociopolitical processes unless there is a state takeover. Deleuze and Guattari propose an unconventional take on fascism, construing it as a particular assemblage of desire. It is crucial to note, with Holland, that they also evade psychologism by articulating desire to machinic production: desire 'is what a variety of social assemblages (capitalism, nuclear families, the State, institutional state apparatus and other institutions) determine it to be' (2008: 86). Microfascist desire is produced when social assemblages are too violently pitched into a void, when molar processes of overcoding, themselves never ideological but material, are destratified in such a way as to leave behind only the debris of former strata (TP, 163). Each assemblage then closes up on to itself, in its own black hole, converting its petty insecurities into clarities and certitudes, and escaping the forces that bind it into a greater organism generating signification. These instances of runaway conformity, as John Protevi (2000: 172) depicts them, are not creative but destructive of the stratum on which they are attached: they gnaw at it, blocking desire and endlessly reproducing 'assembly-line personalities'. Another point that deserves attention in Deleuze and Guattari's concept of microfascism is that there is nothing in the molecular (or that which escapes capture by larger assemblages of power) that is intrinsically liberating. The molecular is not up for celebration as opposed to the molar, not unconditionally. Completed twelve years after 1968, *A Thousand Plateaus* is more cautious about the potential benefits of exasperating capitalism's lines of flight. Even the cherished notion of the Body without Organs (BwO) does not escape being tainted by fascism. In its full state, the BwO is a pure non-stratified matrix of intensity, 'the field of immanence of desire' (TP, 154). But Deleuze and Guattari also speak of fascism as a BwO, albeit an empty one that desires its own annihilation. They concede that distinguishing the fascist BwO from a full one is not at all evident:

> the material problem confronting schizoanalysis is knowing whether we have it within our means to make the selection, to distinguish the BwO from its doubles: empty vitreous bodies, cancerous bodies, totalitarian and fascist. The test of desire: not denouncing false desires, but distinguishing within desire between that which pertains to stratic proliferation, or else too-violent destratification, and that which pertains to the construction of the plane of consistency. (TP, 165)

Obviously, there is much unresolved tension in this (newer) account of fascism. Much to our despair, Deleuze and Guattari's position oscillates between vindicating schizophrenic tendencies, on the one hand, and dreading cancerous outgrowth, on the other. Not only is desubjectification, deterritorialisation or constituting war machines not enough to eschew fascism (or even to short-circuit the apparatuses of capture), but one should also avoid a 'too-violent destratification' at all costs, they tell us, since 'the worst that can happen is if you throw the strata into demented or suicidal collapse, which brings them back down on us heavier than ever' (TP, 161).

Why this shift from defining fascism as a rigid, paranoid and molar state of catatonia to portraying it as a rapid, manic, molecular concentration of suicidal lines of flight? Although Holland (2008: 79) faults Deleuze and Guattari for wrongly following Paul Virilio's path in construing fascism as suicidal, Protevi goes to great pains to show that the shift is indeed consistent, both with the conceptual schemes of the second volume and with historical fascism. He remarks that the state's relation to fascism is construed in a different manner in *A Thousand Plateaus*. Fascism is no longer a solution to capitalism, but 'a war machine stronger than the State', a realisation of 'pure flow' (Protevi 2000: 179, 183). But how can pure flow be brought to resonate with a state apparatus? Microfascism, the proliferation of a thousand monomanias and self-evident truths bestowing each individual with the mission of becoming a self-appointed judge or SS officer, turns out to be impossible to capture by the overcoding apparatuses of the modern state if the latter were to retain its structures, its bureaucratic administrative system, its standing army and clearly demarcated institutions. Implied is the idea that the fascist state is no longer a state, but a war machine – or rather, a state taken over by a war machine. In the Nazi state, Protevi (2000: 178) writes, what thwarts the possibility of reterritorialisation is the 'manic ascension into a war frenzy'. That is, the cancerous cells of microfascism gone berserk are not 'tamed' within a stable and segmented state. On the contrary, the state itself goes berserk. As an empty BwO whose only object is war, the fascist state realises the impossible: it manages to remain submerged within the field of immanence to the bitter end.

Curiously, Protevi's manifest confirmation of the historical import of the concept of microfascism gets lost on Holland (2008: 74), who enlists him as an ally to reject the analysis in A Thousand Plateaus. The usefulness of grasping fascism as a war machine that takes over the state is problematic, Holland maintains, since even Deleuze and Guattari concede that the state continues to command the fascist war machine. In Holland's view, the inversion of the roles of state and war machine happens only in the 'postfascist' era after the Second World War 'as the global-capitalist war machine subordinates all political and social considerations to the aim of capital accumulation' (2008: 82). Yet Holland's dismissal of the relevance of microfascism to account for historical fascisms would be unsustainable if the nature of the Nazi state were problematised along with that of the war machine. For what allows us to assert that the state remains intact when it fuses with a war machine? To reiterate Franz Neumann's provocative thesis, it is unclear whether Nazi Germany was a state in the modern sense of the term:

> it is doubtful whether National Socialism possesses a unified coercive machinery, unless we accept the leadership theory as a true doctrine ... There is no need for a state standing above all groups; the state may even be a hindrance to the compromises and to domination over the ruled classes. (Neumann 2009: 468–9)

Following Neumann's analysis but attributing much more unity to the totalitarian machine, Hannah Arendt also claims that Nazi Germany (and Stalin's USSR, both totalitarian in her view) are not total states but non-states. Both Hitler and Stalin, she writes, 'held out promises of stability in order to hide their intention of creating a state of permanent instability' (Arendt 1973: 391). Destabilisation entailed preventing 'normalization from reaching the point where a new way of life could develop' (1973: 391). The paradoxical conjunction between movement and state could not be achieved solely on the basis of ideology and propaganda; it called for a structural transformation of state and society. Instead of being monolithic and architectonic, as most scholars of totalitarianism take it to be, totalitarianism necessarily implies shapelessness according to Arendt. Every function of the administration was duplicated by some organ in the party, laws and regulations proliferated without abrogating previous ones, authority was endlessly divided and delegated while at the same time being concentrated within a central core. Arendt writes:

> One should not forget that only a building can have a structure, but that a movement [. . .] can only have a direction, and that any form of legal or governmental structure can only be a handicap to a movement which is being propelled with increasing speed in a certain direction. (1973: 398)

The gist of this argument is that fascist totalitarianism should be conceptualised through its tendency to eradicate clearly segmented structures that might 'territorialise' the movement and serve to condition or command it. The laws of motion replace positive laws in such a way that law coincides with the actual direction of the movement. This constructs a peculiar form of immanence that detaches itself from conditioned existence. The state of perpetual movement and instability, which are the distinctive traits of fascist totalitarianism, according to Arendt and Neumann, imply a self-referential and self-perpetuating system that deprives whoever is caught up in it of any means of transcending the given or the present: 'All that matters is embodied in the moving movement itself; every idea, every value has vanished into a welter of superstitious pseudoscientific *immanence*' (Arendt 1973: 249, emphasis added).

Unwittingly, Deleuze and Guattari restate this insight into fascism as a peculiar form of molarity that sets all strata into perpetual motion:

> The most we can say is that the State apparatus tends increasingly to identify with the abstract machine it effectuates. This is where the notion of the totalitarian State becomes meaningful: a State becomes totalitarian when, instead of effectuating, within its own limits, the worldwide overcoding machine, it identifies with it, creating the conditions for 'autarky', producing a reterritorialisation by 'closed vessel', in the artifice of the void. (TP, 223)

The void, it must be conceded, is not a territory, neither in the conventional sense nor in the sense Deleuze and Guattari attribute to it, that is, a vector of motion and spatio-temporal attachment. The black hole, another image that Deleuze and Guattari offer to illustrate the void, puts the suicidal character of the fascist state in stark relief: a black hole is an all-powerful nothingness, pure matter that destroys all matter. No wonder Protevi qualifies the Nazi state as an 'ascending, burning, manic, "schizo"' type of nihilism being projected towards 'zero intensity' (2000: 185). The totalitarian state 'couples "resonance" with a "forced movement"' (TP, 224), itself becoming a black hole even as it keeps a thousand black holes in a relation of resonance with each other.

Figures 2.1– 2.3 These three figures illustrate the distinction between a constitutional state, a repressive authoritarian state and a fascist totalitarian state. Figure 2.1 depicts a constitutional state, a Body with Organs (an organism) that is stratified on the inside and has boundaries that separate it from other organisms on the outside. But it leaks in several places: lines of flight leak out of both the inner compartments and the exterior ones. In repressive authoritarianism (Figure 2.2), however, all stratifications and boundaries are rigid, extremely molar and so constricted that only a few leaks, if any, are possible. Fascism, on the other hand, sets desire into chaotic motion rather than curbing it (Figure 2.3). It is the setting loose of a thousand demons of all shapes and sizes that eventually begin to resonate with each other in such a way that they begin to move in the same direction, gnawing at everything they encounter as well as at each other. The thick shell represents the totality – achieved either by total war in historical fascisms or by total monetisation in today's neoliberal empire.

To cut a longer story short, if my reading of Deleuze and Guattari's emphasis on microfascism is correct, it must be conceded that there is a *qualitative* difference between repressive authoritarianism and fascism, even when the latter is construed as a state takeover. Authoritarian and fascist sociopolitical formations differ in *nature*, not in degree. Fascism is a squeezing and jostling about rather than a repressing; its incoherent 'totality' is achieved by imminent conjugation rather than through an external junta.

Leaving this analysis as it is without being able to further develop it within the scope of this chapter, I would like now to turn now to another problem, that of 'post-fascism'. For the complexities and pitfalls associated with immanence as a philosophical notion and a heuristic device do not seem to be exhausted once we leave historical fascisms behind and enter into a world in which 'closed vessel' conditions cannot be reproduced owing to the global nature of capitalist interdependency.

The Thousand Little Black Holes of Neoliberalism

Are we really beyond fascism in the so-called post-fascist era? If so, why is it that Deleuze and Guattari feel the need to warn us against microfascisms? I suggest that in order to understand the societal dynamics that warrant sounding the alarm against the resurgence of fascism, we must take leave of *Capitalism and Schizophrenia* and engage with Deleuze's short piece 'Postscript on Societies of Control' (originally published in French in 1990) and the Foucauldian analyses that underlie it.

In what Deleuze calls 'control societies' and what Foucault alternately names 'regulatory power', 'security' or 'biopolitics', it becomes apparent, *ex post facto*, that the institutional mainstay of capitalist formations at the beginning of the twentieth century was not entirely immanent. That is to say that, with the exception of the nihilist thrust of the fascist war machine resonating in a state, the possibilities for coding and overcoding had not totally disappeared despite capitalist globalisation. Molecular social assemblages regulating desire remained concentrationary and closed systems in which disciplinary apparatuses functioned to instill norms (or codes) in discontinuous, segmentary and hierarchised ways. But between 1968 and 1990 it would seem that one layer of strata constituting societies in the global North was removed or hypostatised in such a way that flows of money, credit, information, pleasure, fear, desire, sickness and violence could no longer be subjected to disciplinary moulding. Replacing institutional apparatuses, Deleuze tells us, is 'control', a continuous system that allows for short-term variations but simultaneously tends towards a state of perpetual metastability. Capitalism also transformed itself: the corporation replaced the factory, enclosed spaces of production and circulation were replaced by the liquidity of stock markets and credit money. In short, it is only at the end of the twentieth century that we encounter a crisis of the institutions, a 'general breakdown of all sites of confinement – prisons, hospitals, factories, schools, the family' (PP, 178).

Deleuze builds upon Foucault's insight into how disciplinary power was supplemented and to a certain extent made redundant by a new type of regulatory power whose full measure Foucault took in the late 1970s and early 1980s. On Foucault's account, disciplinary power stands in a position of exteriority to what it disciplines. The norm that serves to control, supervise, train and admonish bodies comes from an instance that is socially and phenomenologically distinct from these bodies. The school teacher imposes an educational standard developed within the scientific and pedagogical apparatuses on students who are but bodies precisely because of the exteriority of the norm. In certain respects, the disciplinary relay is on a par with the juridico-political sovereign whose law is dictated from a standpoint above and beyond the law. This 'relative autonomy' of the institutions, as it were, is dismantled by a biopolitics of governmentality. Control, writes Deleuze, 'is the name proposed by Burroughs to characterize the new monster, and Foucault sees it fast approaching. Paul Virilio too is constantly analyzing the ultrarapid forms of apparently free-floating control that are taking over from the old disciplines at work within the time scales of closed system' (PP, 178).

This was, of course, foreseen in *A Thousand Plateaus* by Deleuze and Guattari. Citing Foucault, Deleuze and Guattari had already portrayed a society in which a micropolitics of insecurity contaminated every nook and cranny. There is 'no longer the Schoolmaster but the monitor, the best student, the class dunce, the janitor, etc.', they wrote. 'No longer the general, but the junior officers, the noncommissioned officers, the soldier inside me, and also the malcontent' (TP, 224–5). These constitute a 'multitude of black holes' that act 'as viruses adapting to the most varied situations, sinking voids in molecular perceptions and semiotics. Interactions without resonance' (TP, 228). The exact societal dynamics, however, were never as clearly spelled out as in Deleuze's 'Postscript'. To illustrate with one striking sentence that resonates all too clearly with what we are going through today: 'Family, school, army, and factory are no longer so many analogous but different sites converging in an owner, whether the state or some private power, but transmutable or transformable coded configurations of a single business where the only people left are administrators' (PP, 181). Accounting for this change is no small feat and cannot be done satisfactorily in a short chapter. Suffice it to note that if a violent destratification of the socius is taking place at the turn of the twenty-first century (as Deleuze suggests) and we can no longer blame industrial capitalism for deterritorialising feudal modes of production and ways of life, we must confront neoliberalism head on to distinguish the peculiar form of immanence that characterises it from that of industrialisation.

The era of neoliberal immanence has in fact been the cause of much anxiety (particularly among liberals for whom there is no way out other than hanging on to the *idea* of the rule of law despite its grandiose implosion in practice) and much exaltation (particularly among scholars from the left for whom the direct confrontation of productive forces and empire was the harbinger of revolutionary struggle). But in my view, neither camp could foresee that the millennial neoliberal task was to achieve sameness without recourse to the Leviathan and to capture from within. Tocqueville's suspicion of democratic government as a soft power that takes care of everything, leaving citizens passive and uncritical, seems to have been replaced by the impersonal power of marketisation, demanding active but equally uncritical adjustments. The particular type of freedom promoted by neoliberalism is doubly treacherous: on the one hand, it turns the individual into a 'dividual', as Deleuze puts it, that is, into data to be prompted, modulated and controlled through networks of communication and capitalisation (PP, 180). On the other hand, citizenship now entails the willingness to accept austerity measures, personal and collective sacrifices, wage and budget cuts, and the unequal distribution of the burdens of the debt economy, as Wendy Brown perceptively tells us (2015: 210–16). The tyranny of the majority is exercised by the statistical curve whose lower end spells social death. Those that end up there are not only left to die, but are also moralised: they are leeches, losers, the unfit. They are no longer considered as equally rights-bearing individuals as all others. Despite the fact that liberal rights remain universal in theory, they have long become conditional in practice.

It was indeed Foucault who foresaw in *Security, Territory, Population* how, as a technology of power, biopolitical security worked by making use of the risks inherent in aleatory trajectories in such a way as to 'secure' the well-being of the population taken as a whole. As opposed to disciplinary techniques, security is concerned with inducing aggregate behaviour by regulating flows without blocking them. Despite the tricky name Foucault gives it, 'security' does not enclose, but pretends to follow the movements of the population. It does not devise norms or codes of conduct that transcend the segments of the population on which they are to be applied. In other words, instead of codifying, it produces generalised desires. It fabricates standard deviations and derives normality curves from what it presents as the 'natural' vital activity of the population. It renounces the aim of monitoring each and every body; it undulates like a serpent rather than casting moulds.

By opting for the term 'population', Foucault avoids employing the more conservative word 'masses', laden as it is with pejorative connotations and assumptions. He nevertheless theorises massification and atomisation. As a mass phenomenon, constructing a population requires identifying (or rather, inventing) biological risks that need to be controlled. The art of government that corresponds to population derives from political economy. Instead of prescribing or decreeing, techniques of intervention take on the form of 'letting do' (*laissez faire*), that is, of inciting and stimulating, but also of 'letting die', since it is only when some are threatened with losing their lives that desire and aversion can be manufactured. Allowing 'free play' to forces that cancel each other out or produce shifts in normality curves generates a form of freedom that is radically different from the freedom to say 'No' to the sovereign. Foucault's redefinition of liberal freedom as an ultimately utilitarian rationality, whereby both innovation and self-constraint inhere in the individual in its capacity as utility maximiser, cannot be isolated from the embeddedness of this freedom into the engineered movements of larger biopolitical wholes. In other words, apparatuses of security are assemblages that simultaneously induce risk-taking and conformity, individualisation and massification. I suggest that it is Deleuze, rather than Foucault, who saw how it was neoliberalism that ushered this new order in and realised this new state of immanence:

> Marketing is now the instrument of social control and produces the arrogant breed who are our masters. Control is short-term and rapidly shifting, but at the same time continuous and unbounded, whereas discipline was long-term, infinite, and discontinuous. A man is no longer a man confined, but a man in debt. (PP, 181)

Underscoring how Deleuze and Guattari urge us to seek the monotheism behind every despotism, Matthew Thiessen adds: 'In the case of today's despotic capitalism, the monotheistic component is the capacity for endless credit and debt *creation* which, in time, literally becomes a monolithic all-consuming force' (2012: 116).

What I want to retain from Foucault's conceptualisation of population is the idea that as soon as power takes over life – that is, becomes biopolitical/securitarian – it becomes indistinguishable from the *immanent* movement of its object. Security reconstructs the space of the social in such a way that positive law becomes redundant, or rather, is taken over by a series of other laws – the laws of supply and demand, of capital flows, demographic laws, the laws of optimal societal development, and so forth. And we might ask in the place of Foucault: what happens when normality curves and indirect interventions induce aggregate behaviour? 'Truth' becomes embedded in the movements of the population – it too becomes immanent. The flip-side of this 'immanent regime of truth' (that of the life of the population and its statistically generated knowledge) is that it is necessarily fluctuating. This decoding or deterritorialisation of truth digs the black hole of cynicism.[2]

The proliferation of risks and sources of insecurity at the molecular level, whether they take the form of debt, precariousness, social deprivation or simply losing out in the game of competitiveness, 'are not just unwanted consequences or negative side effects but essential conditions and positive elements of liberal freedom' (Lemke 2014: 65). What Foucault was describing as 'liberal' has been called 'neoliberal' ever since. To be sure, Foucault went overboard with his fascination with neoliberal thought in *The Birth of Biopolitics*. But he was aware that the practices of neoliberalism were characterised by 'a relative devaluation of legal forms of regulation and the creeping development of an *authoritarian security regime* that operated against and beyond legal prescriptions and codes' (Lemke 2014: 66, emphasis added). Securitarian biopolitics breeds insecurity and existential dangers, but removes the legal and institutional forms of protection against these. Indeed, generating new forms of disposability is *absolutely necessary* for the functioning of neoliberal governmentality. Unless everyone is potentially put at risk, it would be impossible to 'secure' aggregate desire. It is only when social safety nets and constitutional guarantees against reducing individuals to manageable inert matter are systematically dismantled that risk becomes 'productive'. Only then is each and every 'man in debt' faced with the prospect of being disposed of by the system. And (here's the catch): it is only then that 'a thousand black holes' are created in every niche, including our very own. To put it bluntly: no matter how deeply we might feel attached to the liberal norms of a now bygone era, we act in ways that uphold the idea that rights are conditional and precarity is a fate. We fail to repoliticise our condition or transcend the parameters of life as a population. Cynicism abounds: 'exploitation comes to be a seen as a fact of life, part of the general human condition, rather than as the impetus for revolutionary awakening [since] money is that object that has the potential to stand in for all possible objects – it becomes the universal object of desire' (Read 2008: 152). Living an 'as if' life turns us at best into cynics, but at worst into fascists, racists, sexists or xenophobes. As Deleuze and Guattari exclaim: 'It's too easy to be antifascist on the molar level, and not even see the fascist inside you, the fascist you yourself sustain and nourish and cherish with molecules both personal and collective' (TP, 215).

But what would it take to resist this new condition? How are we to avoid becoming cancerous BwOs and instead turn ourselves into creative BwOs or liberating war machines? And with whom are we to form rhizomatic relations if our neighbours are busy constituting themselves into human capital? Deleuze and Guattari, it must be remembered, turn to the artist to bring into life the missing 'people':

As Virilio says in his very rigorous analysis of the depopulation of the people and the deterritorialization of the earth, the question has become: 'To dwell as a poet or as an assassin?' The assassin is one who bombards the existing people with molecular populations that are forever closing all of the assemblages, hurling them into an ever wider and deeper black hole. The poet, on the other hand, is one who lets loose molecular populations in hopes that this will sow the seeds of, or even engender, the people to come, that these populations will pass into a people to come, open a cosmos. (TP, 345)

Foucault is less poetic. Once the securitarian-neoliberal apparatus starts to construct molecular populations, the name of the force capable of standing against it is 'the people':

[t]he people comprise those who conduct themselves in relation to the management of the population, at the level of the population, as if they were not part of the population as a collective subject-object, as if they put themselves outside of it, and consequently the people are those who, refusing to be the population, disrupt the system. (Foucault 2007: 43–4)

The insight expressed here must be given its due, for it expresses the danger lying ahead: what if the solution consisted not in becoming impersonal and 'dividual', as in population, but in (re-)becoming 'people' by reconstructing a form of externality? A more terrifying question follows. What if the far right is ahead of us, doing what we failed to do: refusing to be a 'population' so as to become a 'people'?

If we allowed ourselves to remain at the level of ideology, we would surely consider the fascist remedy to fluidity as proof of the far right's will to break with the system. It is striking to realise how much the far right appropriates tropes from the left and the new left, criticising the egotism and consumerism that market society disseminates as well as the hyper-individualism that underlies it (Friberg 2015: 28). But at a closer look, it is possible to notice continuities between the neoliberal biopolitics of immanence and the 'cure' that the far right proposes. The far right does not advocate a return to the intrinsic value of each and every life, but wants to authoritatively pre-arrange disposability. Instead of spreading out the risks associated with the predatory version of neoliberal capitalism to the whole population, it designates an out-group that would need to be disposed of so as to reduce the precarity of the in-group. This in-group is defined through demographics and the lifestyle choices of a majority as much as it is through purportedly biological traits (Shaw 2018: xi). As such, the far right remains within the neoliberal biopolitical paradigm instead of departing from it, but wants to authoritatively reproduce the ways in which it functions. Its aim is to secure the very curves that derive 'normality' from the demographics of the majority and to dispossess minority populations instead of leaving things to chance or to the market. On the one hand, the far right craves for difference as opposed to the uniformity imposed by the market, but cannot construe of any other difference than that related to identity. On the other hand, it craves for identity as opposed to constant fluctuation and differentiation through the impersonal laws of the market, but cannot construe of any identity other than that which is axiomatically produced by statistics. The risks associated with neoliberal discourses of freedom are projected on to an alien or enemy that then comes to epitomise risk. Put differently, the far right wants to retain the conditionality of rights but designates ethnic or racial identity as the condition for enjoying them. We must admit, nevertheless, that it *politicises* the distribution of aggregate levels of precarity: the selection is to be made by will power instead of by impersonal forces.

As to whether the far right succeeds in calling into being a people to come, the answer is negative. The whole meaning of the cancerous cell analogy is brought to light when the far right aim of fostering a race or ethnicity-based identitarianism is taken into consideration. Geared towards propagating racial superiority and exclusivity, the fascist cell produces nothing new, but rather gnaws on existing social tissues, contaminating and disfiguring them, and sucking out their life. This is also why fascism is empty, despite its ideological haughtiness – it shifts things about, consuming and discarding them along the way.

It must be obvious by now that *A Thousand Plateaus* was not mistaken as to the affinity between the diffusion of power into the capillaries of society (into various disciplinary apparatuses) and the proliferation of cancerous BwOs. I would take one step further and suggest that biopolitical dispositifs in the neoliberal age are even more productive of fascist black holes at the molar and global levels than Deleuze and Guattari (and Foucault, for that matter) could ever foresee. And yet, the Final Solution might never become an option in the twenty-first century, not only because the global market is too integrated to allow for 'closed-vessel conditions', but perhaps also because it is largely redundant: the biopolitical rationale of 'letting die' comes in very handy and suffices. The molehill is no longer required if one succeeds in undulating like the serpent, not only within national boundaries, but also globally. Blown out of proportion, Foucault's securitarian paradigm functions to induce global aggregate desires by creating worldwide risks and threats. The latter are not what political parties across the spectrum aim to reduce – politics today consists of *generating* the existential dangers that are indispensable for the reproduction of neoliberal capitalist accumulation. But the suicide of the democratic alternative does not need the state as vector: the mafia, hedge funds, aficionados of conspiracy theory, multinational corporations, evangelists, anti-gender theorists now operate internationally and are all suitable replacements for the state. Any instance that brings the thousand black holes to resonate together (not only nationally, but also globally) will suffice to resurrect fascism in novel and unforeseen forms.

This brief exposé might be enough to drive in the message that neither the liberal trope of calling back the constitutional state nor the post-structuralist mantra of dismantling all forms of power are likely to provide a bulwark against the pseudo-plane of consistency in which neoliberal capitalism, biopolitical security and microfascism enter into an echo chamber. Without devaluing the theoretical and practical spaces of freedom opened up by deconstruction and disarticulation in the past, it looks as if societies of control in our day and age can only be undone through a renewed ability to construct and rearticulate. Immanence, not rigid segmentarity, seems to be the problem today.

We Lack Creation – and Power

We now have a true conundrum on our hands, one that is imposed upon us by conditions that Deleuze and Guattari predicted but did not live to witness. The three different realisations of immanence, the capitalist, the microfascist and the neoliberal, are entering into perverse connections with each other, but the people to come would have to be interpellated from within this complex and sinister set of assemblages.[3] How is one to reckon with this, think from within it on how to confront, resist and change it?

Revolution, Deleuze and Guattari write, 'is absolute deterritorialization even to the point where this calls for a new earth, a new people' (WP, 101) and '[p]hilosophy takes the relative deterritorialization of capital to the absolute; it makes it pass over the plane of immanence as movement of the infinite and suppresses it as internal limit, *turns it back against itself so as to summon forth a new earth, a new people*' (WP, 99, emphasis in the original). Granted, but what is a 'new earth', if it is not going to remain artistic or philosophical? And what figure of power corresponds to that capacity to summon forth a new people, since such a capacity would need to be acquired under present conditions and despite them? Such questions seem to preoccupy Antonio Negri who, in a conversation with Deleuze, asks: 'How can minority becoming be powerful? How can resistance become an insurrection? Reading you, I'm never sure how to answer such questions, even though I always find in your works an impetus that forces me to reformulate the questions theoretically and practically' (PP, 173). Deleuze himself admits that there is a 'tragic or melancholic tone' in the way he and Guattari conceive of the war machine. The war machine is not only a force capable of deterritorialising capitalism, but also of generating fascistic black holes. 'We lack creation', Deleuze and Guattari write. '*We lack resistance to the present*' (WP, 108, emphasis in the original).

The difficulty, to my mind, springs from the tension in Deleuze and Guattari's thought between revolution as deterritorialisation and revolution as creation. Deterritorialisation implies relinquishing molar identities, universals, transcendent structures and notions. It is a negative moment. Creation, on the other hand, is affirmative: it implies the inventing of new spaces, relations, modes of becoming. It necessarily involves spatial and temporal form-giving. To Deleuze and Guattari, I am tempted to respond: we do not only lack resistance to the present, we lack the *power* to create.

The notion of power has an ambivalent status in both Deleuze's own work and in the texts he wrote in collaboration with Guattari. The power to be affected that Deleuze praises in Spinoza is approvingly redubbed 'force' in his book on Nietzsche, but *A Thousand Plateaus* lists power among the four potentially fascist dangers that lines of flight get caught up in (TP, 228–9; Protevi 2000: 178). Power is construed as a 'center' that always procures its power from impotence: 'the only purpose these centers have is to translate as best they can flow quanta into line segments (only segments are totalizable, in one way or another). But this is both the principle of their power and the basis of their impotence' (TP, 225).

But why should power not be salvaged through the Spinozist idea of capacity, as the ability to form connections and thereby transform each degree of power into a combined force? Why conceptualise power as consisting solely of the state or disciplinary apparatuses or blocks on desire? Paraphrasing Arendt (and drawing her into dialogue with both Spinoza and Deleuze–Guattari as an unexpected ally), I suggest we reappraise power, a notion that derives from the Latin *potentia*, the equivalent of the Greek *dynamis*. Arendt claims that power is always a power potential that is actualised only 'where men [*sic*] live so close together that the potentialities of action are always present' (1958: 201). In one of his most explicit comments on revolution, Deleuze seems to come close to thinking of power as generated collectively from below, as the acting-together of a plurality, rather than as an abstract machine:

> [w]hen a minority creates models for itself, it's because it wants to become a majority, and probably has to, to survive or prosper (to have a state, be recognized, establish its rights, for example). But its *power* comes from what it's managed to create, which to some extent goes into the model, but doesn't depend on it. A people is always a creative minority, and remains one even when it acquires a majority. (PP, 173, emphasis added)

The stakes involved in engaging in such a reconceptualisation are as follows: 1) Capitalism, especially in its neoliberal phase, generates black holes of impotence that are then filled with microfascist forms of sedimentation. 2) Black holes are themselves a function of social assemblages of securitisation gnawing upon the debris of former strata (that of the institutions), violently torn apart by practices of 'letting do' and 'letting die'. 3) The generalised cynicism emanating from social formations themselves is an obstacle in the way of reharnessing any progressive ideology, liberal or socialist, in the service of overcoming neoliberal and microfascist pragmatics. The only bulwark to cynical pragmatics is a creative pragmatics. To sum up, because of the above, there is a need to 1) reinvent power as a cure to impotence; 2) forge horizontal connections as a cure to microfascist attachments; 3) pragmatically rekindle the *belief* in the power of acting together. But the most crucial point is this: we urgently need to devise ways of actualising collective power, since without power, the global capitalist machine cannot be outdone. No anti-fascist struggle can ever dispense with leaving that formidable machine untouched.

To continue reflecting along this path, we need to concede that unlike authority, power cannot be the property of an institution or of a person. Power is always a degree of power, a capacity to be affected as well as the capacity to affect. And yet, contra Deleuze, power cannot be a totally impersonal or imperceptible force, either, since it creates the collective actor, the 'people' as it were, albeit only retrospectively, as a function of its own horizontal assemblages and connections. Collective action must be conceived as an activity that prefigures the people, rather than a mode of disruption or deterritorialisation. It must also be conceded that neither the actors nor their connections can be given in advance, but must be forged along the way. Most importantly, the double nature of power as both immanent and transcendent must be reckoned with. To be sure, the power to be generated by horizontal minorities will be immanent to the moving and acting multiplicity. But that same power will also be transcendent because it will be the common basis upon which to constitute a shared world ('a new earth') and forms of self-organisation (preferably without organs that reintroduce rigid segmentarity). Power, conceived in this way, would precede law and institutionalisation.[4] Furthermore, we would need to admit, with Arendt, that any living power could 'only be actualized but never fully materialized' (1958: 200). From this we must derive the idea that power, like freedom, can only be expressed in the act, in act-uality. All other forms of power are derivatives of this basic premise. This formulation of collective action allows us to conceive of power as a negative force, transcending the present and constituting a break with its temporalities and modalities, while at the same time founding new communities without hypostatising into a *potestas* or an axiomatic. The creation of a 'people' requires thinking immanence together with transcendence, differentiation together with connection.

To illustrate what I am proposing without really being conclusive, let me very briefly consider two contemporary social movements, the *gilets jaunes* and *Ni Una Menos*, to see if we can distinguish between cancerous, empty BwOs and fuller ones. Despite their being infiltrated by the far right, the *gilets jaunes* have succeeded in creating cohesion without any visible structure or leader since November 2018. Their demands raise eyebrows on the left, since they do not conform to leftist checklists. And yet the *gilets jaunes* wielded so much power that President Macron had to send security forces, not only to protect the Champs-Elysées, but also to break up the agoras at the roundabouts. I would advance the tentative hypothesis that the *gilets jaunes* are the mirror image of the far right. Both the *gilets jaunes* and the far right are war machines; the latter is rigid and has no other object than war, and the former constitutes a form of militancy that is so open and structureless that it cannot found a new 'people'. Runaway conformism and runaway rebelliousness. Many dismiss the *gilets jaunes* as being irremediably ambiguous in their message and future orientation. But as opposed to the far right, the *gilets jaunes* do not try to unite under an axiomatic. They, too, voice biopolitical concerns in an age of biopolitics, but they also stand up against disposability and politicise precarity in order to eliminate it, not to control and redirect it against out-groups. They decry the so-called 'exigencies' of neoliberal market rationality and demand that the logic of extraction from the poor towards the rich be reversed. They resurrect the *cahiers de doléance*, inventing a form of transcending the present by reclaiming past forms of popular expression, without, however, seeking to restore the past, the *Ancien Régime* or a mythical origin. They offer to turn streets and roundabouts into agoras, devising new territories for the unlikely coming together of alternative visions of society. They are not involved in an absolute deterritorialisation, but do constitute a fleeting form of power from below. But their micro-certainties and disgust with the 'system' may, at any time, turn cancerous since they remain at the mercy of sad passions, reactive instead of proactive. They are the 'malcontent', the empty BwOs.

As distinct from the *gilets jaunes*, *Ni Una Menos* is a creative minoritarian movement. The name ('not one less') evokes negativity, but the women involved in this movement are connecting struggles being waged by those who are projected to the outer limits of neoliberal schizophrenia. Starting out as a movement against male violence, *Ni Una Menos* evolved into a struggle against patriarchal, colonial and capitalist forms of violence. This was made possible by mapping out the dynamics of 'neoliberalism from below' (Gago 2017: 2) and diagnosing how each and every body is trapped in distinct but similar ways. This turned them into a movement-event in which one 'wound would be the living trace and the scar of all wounds' (LS, 149). Violence against the female (trans or non-trans) body, when perceived as a body-territory, could be interlinked with other territorial logics of aggression, exploitation and extraction. Overflowing the borders of Argentina, the movement went from hashtag to global strike, altering both the labour strike as a political repertoire and feminism as a depository of signs. The 'feminist strike' actualised a line of flight, it was 'strengthened because of its *impossibility* (women cannot strike but desire to do so)' (Gago 2019: n.p.). From #NiUnaMenos to #WeStrike, the movement also altered the notion of the working class by building connections between reproductive and productive labour, domestic and migrant labour, neo-colonisation and precaritisation. Their power can be considered a *potentia* that, according to Deleuze and Guattari, establishes 'transversal communications between heterogeneous populations' (TP, 239). Such transversal encounters (or rather, the organisation of such encounters) created dynamics and subjectivities that could not have been deduced from predefined identities or interests, thus transcending the present. But more importantly, *Ni Una Menos* eschews becoming a tragic or melancholic instantiation of a war machine, a mere saying 'no', by remaining connective and affirmative. The movement simultaneously affirms the value of all forms of labour, of body-territories, and invents alternative modes of caring for each other to overcome powerlessness and atomisation.

To be fair, the slogan 'We will not die in silence' of the *gilets jaunes* and the 'Not one less' of the feminist movement in Argentina both express the desire to disrupt neoliberal processes and cease being a population. These slogans do not seem explicitly anti-fascist, but as Deleuze and Guattari argue, 'this is never an ideological operation but rather an economic and political one' (TP, 223). Both movements are riding on lines of flight out of capitalism, but *Ni Una Menos* also prefigures innovative ways of transcending black holes. And to recall the following words by Max Horkheimer: 'whoever is not willing to talk about capitalism should also keep quiet about fascism' (1989: 78). This is especially true today under neoliberal-biopolitical conditions.

Notes

1. The difference between the real and the actual, the possible and the virtual is elaborated at some length by Deleuze in *Bergsonism*. The process of realization of the possible, he writes, is subject to rules of resemblance and limitation: 'realization involves a limitation by which some possibles are supposed to be repulsed or thwarted, while others 'pass' into the real. The virtual, on the other hand, does not have to be realized, but rather actualized; and the rules of actualization are not those of resemblance and limitation, but those of difference or divergence and of creation' (B, 97). Actualization is a creation, not a sterile doubling in the plane of reality of what is posited as possible.
2. Interestingly, there is another figure of cynicism that lurks behind Foucault's scheme of biopolitical governmentality, as different from the cynicism of abstractions in Deleuze-Guattari. For the latter, see Read 2008.
3. I would be tempted to use the term 'perverse connection', owing to the inherently molecular and deterritorialized nature of capitalism, microfascism and neoliberalism, instead of 'conjugation.' For the distinction, see TP, 220.
4. This idea that power precedes institutions would also resonate with Antonio Negri's notion of constituent power.

References

Arendt, H. (1958), *The Human Condition*, Chicago: University of Chicago Press.
Arendt, H. (1973), *The Origins of Totalitarianism*, New York: Meridian Books.
Brown, W. (2015), *Undoing the Demos: Neoliberalism's Stealth Revolution*, New York: Zone Books.
Foucault, M. (2007), *Security, Territory, Population. Lectures at the Collège de France 1977–1978*, Basingstoke: Palgrave Macmillan.
Friberg, D. (2015), *The Real Right Returns*, London, Arktos
Gago, V. (2017), *Neoliberalism from Below. Popular Pragmatics and Baroque Economies*, Durham, NC: Duke University Press.
Gago, V. (2019), 'Eight Theses on the Feminist Revolution', *Toward Freedom*, 10 September, <https://towardfreedom.org/story/eight-theses-on-the-feminist-revolution/> (last accessed 13 May 2022).
Gambetti, Z. (2016), 'Risking Oneself and One's Identity: Agonism Revisited', in J. Butler, Z. Gambetti and L. Sabsay (eds), *Vulnerability in Resistance*, Durham, NC: Duke University Press, pp. 28–51.

Gambetti, Z. (2020), 'Exploratory Notes on the Origins of New Fascisms', *Critical Times*, 3 (1): 1–32.

Holland, E. (2008), 'Schizoanalysis, Nomadology, Fascism', in I. Buchanan and N. Thoburn (eds), *Deleuze and Politics*, Edinburgh: Edinburgh University Press, pp. 74–97.

Horkheimer, M. (1989), 'The Jews and Europe', in S. E. Bronner and D. M. Kellner (eds), *Critical Theory and Society*, London: Routledge, pp. 77–94.

Lemke, T. (2014), 'The Risks of Security: Liberalism, Biopolitics, and Fear', in V. Lemm and M. Vatter (eds), *Government of Life: Foucault, Biopolitics and Neoliberalism*, New York: Fordham University Press, pp. 59–74.

Neumann, F. (2009), *Behemoth. The Structure and Practice of National Socialism 1933–44*, Chicago: Ivan R. Dee.

Protevi, J. (2000), '"A Problem of Pure Matter": Fascist Nihilism in *A Thousand Plateaus*', in K. Ansell-Pearson and D. Morgan (eds), *Nihilism Now! 'Monsters of Energy'*, Basingstoke: Palgrave Macmillan, pp. 167–88.

Read, J. (2008), 'The Age of Cynicism: Deleuze and Guattari on the Production of Subjectivity in Capitalism', in I. Buchanan and N. Thoburn (eds), *Deleuze and Politics*, Edinburgh: Edinburgh University Press, pp. 139–59.

Shaw, G. (2018), 'Introduction: An Alternative to Failure', in G. Shaw (ed.), *A Fair Hearing. The Alt-Right in the Words of its Members and Leaders*, [Budapest]: Arktos Media, pp. ix–xv.

Thiessen, M. (2012), 'Infinite Debt and the Mechanics of Dispossession', in R. Braidotti and P. Pisters (eds), *Revisiting Normativity with Deleuze*, London: Bloomsbury, pp. 115–30.

Chapter 3

Generative Contaminations: Biohacking as a Method for Instituting an Affirmative Politics of Life

Christian Alonso

Introduction

Today, we are witnessing a burgeoning of reactionary forces that are taking over institutions and using their electoral majorities to privatise the public sector, dismantle the welfare state and move backwards in terms of equality, sustainability, and labour and financial regulation. In addressing the conditions of the emergence of these authoritarian populisms, cultural theorists have maintained that their success lies in the way that real problems, lived experiences and unattended contradictions are represented within a logic that pulls them towards the interests of the right wing. While this view goes beyond an overly simplistic position of moral and political purity, it still does not explain the existence of tyranny and servitude. In the years before Margaret Thatcher was elected as UK prime minister in 1979, the psychoanalyst, philosopher and activist Félix Guattari developed a theory of fascism that managed to explain how the energy of the masses was placed at the service of a reactionary social order. According to Guattari, the intensification of the dynamics of hierarchisation, exploitation and segregation that proliferated with the advent of neoliberal capitalism converges on the spreading of a new type of fascism on a planetary scale. Unlike previous forms of authoritarian fascism, this new regime operates in the interiority of subjects and its main goal is to ensure that 'each individual assumes mechanisms of control, repression, and modelization of the dominant order' (SS, 258). His thesis is that fascism has abandoned the order of molarities – collective equipment, political parties and ideologies – and nowadays exists molecularised, dusty and imperceptible in the social body. The reason why today 'everybody wants to be a fascist' (CS, 154) can be explained only on the basis of a constitutive relationship between desire and fascism. A desire that, as conceived by Deleuze and Guattari, has neither an object nor belongs to any expert; on the contrary, it produces the real and lies within everyone's reach.

The Guattarian account of molecular fascism operates within the coordinates of integrated world capitalism, that is, it offers a perspective that helps us grasp how libidinal production is currently being captured and remote-controlled by an economy that stands on the axiom of profit. The hypothesis is that capitalism produces and distributes a 'subjectivity of generalized equivalence' (CM, 22) by which modes of being remain absorbed by semiotic operators in accordance with a logic in which values of use, exchange and desire are situated on the same plane. This equation impoverishes subjectivity by imposing on it certain axiological territories and operations that diminish its ethical, aesthetic and political dimension, and by reducing its intrinsic qualities of alterity, singularity and difference to binary and lineal relations (CM, 104). Capitalistic subjectivity homogenises every mode of existence through an encoding of activities, thoughts and behaviours. Machinic capitalism, grounded in techno-scientific improvements, has miniaturised its logistics and thereby manages to seep into our psychic territories, intervening in the 'basic functioning of the perceptive, sensorial, affective, cognitive, linguistic behaviours' (SS, 262). How exactly does this colonisation of the social unconscious occur? What does it mean that capitalism has molecularised its means of action? What are the precise procedures it activates to codify existential modalities? Under which conditions do these new forms of subjugation emerge? Finally, how can mechanisms of resistance be conceived and put into practice?

Responding to these questions, I will discuss a transdisciplinary, research-based bio-art project in conjunction with a Guattarian eco-machinics of semiotic rupture and subjective recomposition. In so doing, various issues will be addressed: how can we apprehend the inherent creativity of modes of existence? To what extent does this understanding facilitate an enrichment of our relationship with a 'more-than-human' alterity and, at the same time, challenge ongoing capitalistic subjections? How does art get involved in the transformation of modes of being, feeling, thinking and acting, and allow the cultivation of an art of attentiveness to the trans-species interconnection that brings about the transversal phenomenon of climate change? How can artistic imagination be combined with social machines and political action in trying to offer a critical and creative response to environmental devastation, social inequality and the homogenisation of habits of thought? In short, how can we think about the intersection between an ecological conception of art and an understanding of existence as an ecological creation, as two strategies actively engaged in the construction of a sustainable future? My goal is to evaluate the possibilities for defining art as an aesthetic technology for the production of heterogeneous subjectivations and multispecies material ecologies that move beyond the axiomatics of capitalisation and signification and are governed by new modes of care, affect and accountability. Deleuze and Guattari's micropolitics of desire will operate as our framework, because by facilitating a direct contact with the referent this methodology contributes to the formation and transformation of subjectivity, which prevents any distinction between social goals and social practices. In other words, any post-representational analysis always entails an existential pragmatics.

The Repressive/Emancipatory Conditions of the New Machinic Regime

When trying to understand the functioning of molecular fascism, one should turn one's attention to the distinction made by Guattari – both singly and together with Gilles Deleuze – between signifying and asignifying semiotics, which provides the basis for the description of different functions of signs operating within the economy, power relations and subjective production. Advanced capitalism stands on a dual semiotic register when mobilising the mechanisms of 'social subjection' and 'machinic subservience' by which they effectively homogenise subjectivity (SS, 261–4). Social subjection produces us as subjects through the assignment of subjective codes, inducing individuals to adapt themselves to prefabricated representations in relation to sex, race, identity, nationality, professional sector, job position and so on. It exerts control by means of personological delimitation, in a similar way to Foucauldian disciplinary techniques based on 'individualizing governmentality' (Foucault 2006; 2008). Relying on the molar logic of representation and meaning, and evolving through the paradigm of communication, subjection based on signifying semiotics takes material form by means of adapting to well-defined roles and functions so as to meet the needs of power. Machinic subservience, on the one hand, operates by asignifying semiotics, that is to say by signs that do not engender any effect of signification – such as mathematical and musical writing, data syntax and stock market codes – which open up the possibility of direct contact with their referent, thus participating in countless experimentations that unfold within the paradigm of enunciation. As argued by philosopher Maurizio Lazzarato (2014: 37), machinic subservience transforms the individual (I) into a relay (it) made of inputs and outputs, capable of either facilitating or blocking the transmission of operational and informational flows running across the productive, consumerist and regulatory cybernetic capitalist network.

Whereas signifying semiotics refers to the molar level of well-defined representations that operate upon individuals, asignifying semiotics works at the molecular level of existence – pre-individual, infra-social and post-representational – in which subjects are recognised by their capacity to be traversed by signs that swirl in flows of information, capital, data, consumption and desire. In this change of register, there is a shift from the transcendental identity and its consideration as a compound of form and matter to an immanence of relations that conceives subjectivity as an intensive and differential force, that is to say, a modulation of expression and content. The coercive coordinates of advanced capitalism are defined by both the functions of the induced acquisition of standardised subjective avatars and by the coupling of each individual's nervous system to the productive machinery. The combined operations of the two types of semiotics lead to what Guattari called the 'society of integration' (SS, 77), that is, a new order that would coexist with the Foucauldian disciplinary society and the Deleuzian society of control. The microfascism of machinic capitalism materialises when desire remains subjected to redundancies of signification and of interaction. When this happens, subjectivity becomes emptied of its inherent polivocity – or, as Guattari would put it, it gets dragged it into a 'black hole' inhabited exclusively by semiotics of power. Nevertheless, this black hole not only has disempowering effects, but also injects subjectivity with an unprecedented creative energy, in the sense that the emptiness left can be filled up with new matters of expression capable of avoiding dominant redundancies and significations of power; thereby, this withdrawal might well constitute the operational condition for forging a new resistance.

The value of Guattari's post-representational thought consists in its being able to explain the production of a subjectivity that is not only logocentric but also 'machinocentric' (Lazzarato 2006). In other words, the effects of signifying and asignifying semiotics provide evidence that the ontological character of subjective formations is neither homogenetic nor something that belongs to the realm of the individual; on the contrary, it is heterogenetic and made up of 'collective assemblages of enunciation' inhabited by a myriad of economic, technological and ethological components that cannot simply be considered as human (MR, 221). Even though Guattari admits that subjectivity is not bound to any single dominant agency in absolute terms – God, Capital, the Signifier – in the context of a society of integration, the possibility of a politics of resistance must be constructed. Guattari believed that the programmed flow of capitalist semiotisation could be effectively interrupted by an ethico-aesthetic practice of existential self-production and by a politics of self-management capable of engendering heterogenetic subjective territories. He developed his analytical-pragmatic ecosophical perspective with the aim of regenerating damaged existential territories, making them habitable again by enhancing the singularisation, the alterification and the complexification of subjectivity. He endeavoured to develop a method to analyse unconscious formations that was not limited either to the notion of the human individual or to its embodiments in groups or institutions, and that was capable of breaking with the familiarist frameworks that confine subjectivity to interpersonal relationships. One of these methods is the 'ecosophic object', composed of four components: energetic-signaletic flows, processual machinic phyla, universes of value and existential territories (SC, 56–7). This perspective manages to transversalise the molar with the molecular, the actual with the virtual, the possible with the real, the affects with the effects.

The transformative potentialities of the Guattarian ethical-aesthetic navigational tool lies in the complex connections across the registers of subjectivity, the socius and the environment, and the articulations that these four components allow. Inasmuch as a post-representational analysis always entails a pragmatics, this methodology is useful not only to study unconscious formations but also to map out and produce singularised existential socio-biotechnical formations. Here the role of maps is not representation, communication or signification, but rather the engendering of references and the production of collective assemblages of enunciation. It is about the creation of heterogeneous existential modalities that aim to activate processes of social production and, eventually, planetary transformations. This kind of constructivism implies both a rupture with significations that are dominant in the social field and a singularised composition of experience on a subjective level. Nevertheless, Guattari insists that subjectivity can work 'for the better and for the worse' (Guattari 2008: 57, my translation) – that is, it can either be repressive or liberating. In other words, subjectivity can deteriorate into a 'capitalist homogenesis' characterised by a 'brutalizing mass-mediatization', or it can be enriched through a 'machinic heterogenesis' in which an 'invention of new universes of reference' could take place (Guattari 2008: 59, my translation). The same happens with technology: it may constitute a catalyst of affirmative developments – namely, a decentralised connectivity provided by the internet or the renewed sense of alterity enabled by bionic prosthesis – as well as of negative ones – such as environmental degradation and surveillance systems. Everything depends on the articulation between material flows, machinic phyla, universes of value and existential territories occurring in each specific situation.

In Guattari's view, the ecosophic logic is currently manifested in realms such as the sciences, industry and works of art – these are domains in which 'the systems of signs that they put into play already form an intrinsic part of the material of their production' (LF, 96). This is why Guattari emphasises these kinds of practices – and art practice in particular – in his ethical-aesthetic paradigm. The artwork is similarly comprised of signifying and asignifying semiotics. The encounter with art, described by Guattari as the zero degree of creativity, enables the reappropriation of the conditions of the production of subjectivity. Appropriation amounts to a singularised, not transcendentally subjected existence, which can be intensified by means of the creation of an affective order, resulting in a subjective production of an aesthetic order. The combined operations of art's mixed semiotics molecularise the unitary subject and bring about a collective, polyphonic and transindividual subjectivity. The aesthetic dimension of ecosophy refers neither to a conception of the artist as a personological representation nor to an idea of art as an institutionalised or disciplined practice. Although borrowed from art, this dimension's creationist nature proliferates well beyond the field of artistic production, and it refers to a generalisation of subjective creativity that extends to all practices and all areas of knowledge. Nevertheless, this generalisation of aesthetics does not diminish the specificity of art; on the contrary, its involvement in the ecosophical analysis helps accentuate a rupture with established models, without sacrificing its internal coordinates. Art thereby becomes the main source of inspiration for the ecosophic metamodelisation, given its endless task of inventing coordinates, which defines it as the production of productions. Art thus constitutes an existential operator, an engine for the creation of complex, heterogeneous and transversalised subjective formations that describes its ecosophical quality.

Mary Maggic – also known as Mary Tsang – is an artist and biologist who defines herself as a 'non-binary fluidic multiplicity' and who works at the intersection of biotechnology, cultural discourse and civil disobedience. *Open Source Estrogen* (henceforth, OSE) is a collaborative, experimental and speculative research project initiated in 2015 that brings together do-it-yourself science, body and gender politics, and the ethics of hormonal manipulation. The project seeks to develop an open-source protocol that anyone could use to produce oestrogen in the kitchen. As stated in Mary Maggic's video presentation entitled *Housewives Making Drugs*, the cookery matters here because 'the kitchen is a politically charged space prescribed to women as their proper dwelling, making it the appropriate place to prepare an estrogen synthesis recipe'. As the artist hopes, the appropriation of hormonal production and administration 'would allow women and transgender females to exercise greater control over their bodies by circumventing governments and institutions' by providing them with the means to create their own birth-control pills, to self-manage gender transition, to alleviate menopausal symptoms, and so on.[1] Acknowledging both a conceptual and methodological bond with works such as *Open Source Gendercodes*, led by artist and biologist Ryan Hammond (2015, ongoing), or *Transplant* by the art collective Quimera Rosa (2016, ongoing), OSE fosters public amateurism in the development of tools, protocols and wetware for low-cost, accessible and participatory oestrogen-biohacking workshops. These are the coordinates of a project that first and foremost strives to raise awareness of the cultural representations and molecular biopolitics that govern our bodies and to act out new modes of existence that do not involve oppressive relationships.

Determinism as a Biopolitical Tool and a Monetary Surplus

OSE's point of departure is a concern with the xenoestrogenic pollution that is causing morphological mutations, neurological disorders and physiological damage to both human and non-human species. Also known as endocrine-disrupting molecules (EDCs), xenoestrogens such as atrazine, bisphenol A (BPA), dichlorodiphenyltrichloroethane (DDT) and polychlorinated biphenyls (PCBs) are types of non-biodegradable synthetic hormones that compromise the hormonal balance of bodies and alter the regular functioning of oestrogens. The latter have a fundamental role for the proper functioning of the endocrine, neurological and immunological system, and determine mood, metabolism and reproductive development. Xenoestrogenic molecules were first isolated, sourced and marketed by pharmaceutical, chemical and petrochemical companies in the 1930s, which had a great interest in commercialising hormones that were said to rectify so-called 'gender deviations'. The association between sexual/gender identity and hormonal chemical composition can be traced back to the 'discovery' of hormones as biological agents. In 1905 the British physiologist Ernest Starling first defined hormones as 'chemical messengers' that are 'carried from the organ where they are produced to the organ which they affect by means of the blood stream' (quoted in Henderson 2005: 9). At that time, the Anglo-French-American physician Charles Brown-Séquard claimed that testicles contained the essence of masculinity – testosterone – while ovaries contained the essence of femininity – oestrogens.

As the father of organotherapy, Brown-Séquard believed that every bodily organ produced an agent with a possible therapeutic use. Therefore, he theorised that testicular extracts would have rejuvenating effects in men and that the retention of semen should lead to increased strength, vigour and sexual desire (Borell 1976; Brown-Séquard 1889). Another pioneer of endocrinology, the Austrian physiologist Eugen Steinach, asserted that homosexuals were not 'real men' because they lacked 'male' sex hormones, and that homosexuality could be 'cured' by means of testosterone injections. After carrying out multiple experiments on mice, he claimed that ovaries grafted on to a neutered male produced feminisation, while testes grafted on to a female produced masculinisation. The female masculinised specimen was said to display features of virility – such as intolerance, aggressiveness and jealousy towards rivals – whereas the male effeminate exemplar displayed a predisposition towards nurturing, caring, devotion and patience (Steinach 1920). French surgeon Serge Voronoff, in turn, performed more than fifty operations by which testes from monkeys were transplanted into men. In most cases, castration was unilateral (it involved the grafting of one testicle), as doctors wanted their patients (whom they believed to be heterosexual) to be able to marry and procreate.

In all four examples – Starling, Brown-Séquard, Steinach and Voronoff – the belief that the cells of an organism might be inscribed with traits of masculinity or femininity provided a biological explanation of same-sex sexual orientation based on a connection between the somatic and the behavioural, and this belief legitimised hormonal therapy to treat homosexuality. The notion of the hormonal body signalled a new physiological understanding that could explain sexual desire in terms of gender identity.

These practices provide evidence of a decisive critical question: pre-existing notions of gender are inscribed into scientific research and medical practice, and operate as a standard of how bodies should look anatomically and behave psychologically. According to Maggic, although both ovaries and testes produce testosterone and oestrogens, 'scientists deliberately sourced hormones from their codified gender assignments'. According to this view, 'the hormones are literally sexed, given sexes of their own' (Tsang 2017: 6). This constitutes a 'somatic fiction' in which gender representations are codified by hormonal composition, which leads to the belief that oestrogenic hormones produce a female body, while testosterone produces a male body. Binary conceptualisations and classifications have thoroughly informed not only psycho-medical discussions of sex and gender, but also legal and cultural considerations. Today, hormones are still largely seen as biological determinants of sexual identities, and social institutions validated by fields such as biology, embryology and endocrinology reinforce a strict dualistic-antagonistic model that systematically excludes transgender, genderqueer, pangender, genderfluid, among others. Beyond their particularities, all these trans experiences have one thing in common: in many countries being trans is still considered a pathology, under the diagnosis of 'gender identity disorder' or 'gender dysphoria'. As argued by Castro-Peraza et al., pathologising in this way promotes the denial of access to healthcare for trans people, compromises the right to corporal integrity, and limits the right to a legal personality, to found a family and to be free from degrading treatment. These discriminatory and stigmatising dynamics constitute human rights violations that infringe the Universal Declaration of Human Rights and the Yogyakarta Principles (Castro-Peraza et al. 2019: 4).

Capitalism has always benefited from the heteronormative, deterministic and constraining representations of sex and gender through the production, accumulation and distribution of sexed hormones. In the 1920s and 1930s European and North American biochemists Adolf Butenandt, Tadeus Reichstein and Edward Adelbert Doisy characterised various steroid hormones, including oestrogen, testosterone and progesterone. Their 'discovery' inaugurated a race by pharmaceutical companies to conquer sex hormones for clinical use. The first to be isolated was pregnanediol, in 1928, from pregnant mare urine. The second was oestrone, in 1929, from the urine of pregnant women. The third was androsterone, in 1931, extracted from the urine provided by workers and prisoners at the Prussian Police Academy in Berlin. The fourth was progesterone, in 1934, extracted from ovaries. Lastly, testosterone, in 1935, was obtained from bull testes (Nieschlag and Nieschlag 2019: 205). In what would eventually be considered as the golden age of steroid biochemistry, scientists endeavoured to uncover a synthetic oestrogenic molecule that would produce enough physiological effects to be able to be commodified as a product. The first of these was Bisphenol-A (BPA), which was first synthesised in 1891, although the exploration of its commercial possibilities did not occur until the

1930s, when British biochemist Edward Charles Dodds identified its oestrogenic properties. Dodds also developed diethylstilbesterol (DES), a powerful oestrogenic substance commercialised in the 1940s together with conjugated equine oestrogens (CEE), as the basis of Premarin, an oestrogen medication popularised in the 1950s. Both DES and Premarin were aimed at treating 'female problems' such as menstruation, menopause, nausea during pregnancy, miscarriages and women who were 'too masculine'.

The prescription of synthetic oestrogens such as BPA, DES and CEE to women of all ages persisted until 1960, when the combined oral contraceptive pill became the cornerstone of modern hormonal therapy. As pointed out by Maggic, the history of oestrogen therapy reveals to what extent the chemical-gender somatic fiction serves the interests of an exclusive heteronormativity that perpetuates a social order in which the question of what and who is constructed as normal and natural is taken for granted:

> the arena of reproduction is another politicized space of hormonal management and lucrative pharma-capitalism. Depending on the body, class, and country one is born into, the oral contraceptive pill on one hand is marketed as liberating a woman from reproductive burden, and on the other hand operates as a tool for mass population control. (Tsang 2017: 7)

Here Maggic addresses the complex question of how a critique of hormonal production-distribution as a coercive tool may coexist with a recognition of how the sexual revolutions of the twentieth century were unleashed precisely for access to these hormones. The biopolitical side-effects of both molar and molecular normalising mechanisms become evident in the bodily and social experience of people whose gender identity differs from the one allocated to them at birth. Transgender or intersex people are born with physical, hormonal or genetic traits that are neither wholly female nor wholly male, a combination of female and male, or neither female nor male. Children born with intersex bodies are often subjected to medical interventions to 'normalise' sex characteristics that are not based on evidence of an unhealthy body but rather on beliefs and narrow social norms.

This is how these 'unruly bodies', as Maggic names them, are also

> treated as a disobedient object that must be disciplined through hormonal control. From the medicalisation of bodies born [with] ambiguous genitalia, to the discrimination of trans-bodies by the pharmaceutical industry, to the disqualification of female intersex athletes from competitions based on above average testosterone levels. (Tsang 2017: 7–8)

However, synthetic hormones are not only a mechanism for subjecting dissident corporalities and subjectivities, but also one that pollutes environments and compromises the health of human and non-human bodies. Today, wherever we are, we are continually exposed to a myriad of xenoestrogenic endocrine disruptors, carcinogens, neurotoxins, asthmagens and mutagens, from our regular contact with plastic water bottles, birth-control pills, parabens, food preservatives, personal care products, kitchen cleaners, insect repellents, pesticides, factory-farmed meats, solvents, and so on. The worldwide bioaccumulation of these hazardous chemicals – known as persistent organic pollutants (POPs) – poses serious problems to our health: cancers (breast, ovarian, prostate and testicular), neurological and neurobehavioural problems, immune system breakdown, heart disease, diabetes and obesity (Colborn and Clement 1992). Rachel Carson's *Silent Spring* (1962) was among the first studies to alert a worldwide audience to the health risks associated with exposure to chlorinated hydrocarbons such as DDT, which jeopardises the liver's capacity to maintain hormonal balance, which could potentially lead to cancers of the reproductive organs.

Soon after the United States Environmental Protection Agency banned the use of persistent xenoestrogens such as DDT (1972) and PCB (1979), the scientific literature on the continuing and long-term health effects of chemical pollutants, such as the synthetic versions of oestradiol and progesterone present in birth-control pills, proliferated. In 2020 the European Union acknowledged endocrine disruptors as a global challenge and has passed specific legislative obligations aimed at phasing out xenoestrogens that contaminate the water, air, soil and food supply. However, as environmentalist Giovanna Di Chiro has established (2010: 208), despite extensive evidence proving the carcinogenic effects and the immunological, metabolic, mutagenic and neurological problems brought by xenoestrogens, the narrative that has reached mainstream media and even scientific discourses focuses mainly on the challenge these pollutants pose to the stability and reliability of the human male's reproductive system and sexual orientation. As pointed out by Di Chiro (2010: 201), headlines describing the effects of endocrine-disruptor pollutants in terms of 'chemical castration', 'feminisation of nature', 'de-masculinisation' and 'ova-pollution' leading to 'sexuality and sexual disorders' such as those of hermaphrodite frogs (male frogs with ovaries growing in their testes as a result of exposure to the pesticide Atrazine) show that 'the dominant anti-toxics discourse deployed in mainstream environmentalism adopts the potent rhetoric that toxic chemical pollution is responsible for the undermining or perversion of the "natural": natural biologies/ecologies, natural bodies, natural reproductive processes'.

The reaction to the threat to virility and masculinity is twofold: on the one hand are the endocrine-disruptor deniers who reject the idea that a 'real man' could be negatively affected; on the other hand are those who support the thesis, believing that xenoestrogens are blurring the 'natural' divide between men and women and producing abnormal bodies (feminised males, intersex people and hermaphrodites). Either way, Di Chiro concludes with a key point: the debates about chemical contamination were not simply about an impending human health problem, but also concerned a newly troubled masculinity that threatens the social order. As noted by Maggic, the truly disrupting power of xenoestrogens is that they bear witness to the fact that 'sex is not produced deterministically through chromosomes, genetics, or gonad-produced hormones, but modulated through industrial by-products of our anthropogenic activities' (Tsang 2017: 10). Importantly, xenoestrogenic compounds compel us to acknowledge that bodies are inherently queer, in the sense that 'these chemicals problematize our fixed notions of gender sex, and prompt us to view our bodies as changeable substrates – a malleability inherent to our biological makeup but alien to our prescribed constructs of (eco)heteronormativity' (Tsang 2017: 10). Seen in this light, the biopolitical agency embedded in xenoestrogens is immersed in a fundamental paradox: the heteronormative-capitalistic power relations that are releasing the endocrine disruptors into the environment, and which are thereby queering bodies, will later pathologise all those dissident subjectivities that do not fit heteronormative and dualistic subjective representations.

Becoming Molecular as a Tool to Undermine Molar Stratifications

While there is sustained reason for concern, the focus on the gender-bending, feminising and demasculinising as anti-normal and anti-natural effects of xenoestrogens ends up strengthening the forces behind environmental and social unsustainability and naturalises homophobia, queer-phobia and even carcinogenic diseases. In trying to respond to the necropolitics at work in the production and distribution of xenoestrogens and in the reinforcement of a transcendental system of representation, Mary Maggic wonders if there might be another way of thinking, feeling, relating, caring and acting. Can we recycle the residues of eco-normativity that are distilled from a dominant anti-toxicity discourse that appeals to pre-existing cultural norms of gender balance, normal sexual reproduction and the homeostatic balance of nature? Today we inhabit ecosystems polluted by agricultural, pharmaceutical and petrochemical industries. The plastics-derived molecules present in our urine, blood and faeces can be seen as making us alien and posthuman. Significantly, not only are our bodies are being chemically and physiologically altered, but so too are our notions of fixed gender and of a unitary subject of transcendental reason and rational consciousness. That is, our bodies are physically disrupted just as the social norms outlining strict distinctions between male and female and what counts as human and what does not are also challenged. OSE is asking how we, as affected bodies, might reframe toxicity without reinforcing a standard of purity. How can we face a shared vulnerability in order to produce new alliances based not on anxiety and catastrophic end-of-the-world narratives but on trans-species alliances? Can we shift from 'toxic shame' to 'toxic embrace' as a strategy to disrupt hormonal technologies of capitalistic detritus and heteronormative social-subjection mechanisms?

Maggic and their collaborators are acting out methodologies aimed at developing protocols and raising public awareness as a mechanism for bioresistance, providing insights into how to shift from environmental toxicity (hormone disruption) to body and gender sovereignty (hormone dissonance). The project comprises three parts. The first, *Estrofem! Lab*, begins with the question: 'can we harness civic action to create DIY/DIWO protocols and recipes for hacking hormones that are founded in both equity and accessibility?' (Tsang 2017: 23). Within this section, three main protocols are developed: YES-HER yeast oestrogen biosensors, urine-hormone extraction and DIY solid phase extraction. All these protocols are performed collaboratively with non-expert citizens, through what Maggic calls 'workshopology', defined as a 'collaborative hands-on experimentation as an iterative process and design strategy that takes feedback from its own mishaps, accidents, and participant experiences in order to develop new methodologies in the future' (Tsang 2017: 24). This becomes a means of becoming familiarised with these biohacking and speculative design methods, fostering a public amateurism and learning together in a horizontal, non-hierarchical way. The first protocol aims at developing an affordable technique for detecting xenoestrogens in the environment through a species of yeast that has been genetically modified to contain Human Estrogen Receptor (HER), a biosensor that becomes an extension of our bodies. The second protocol strives to create a less-than-10-dollar method for separating hormones present in urine and processing them through a glass column made from a recycled glass bottle containing cigarette filters, silica gel and methanol. The third involves the extraction of hormonal pollutants in water samples from river and urban fountains, the removal of microbes and other particles, and the dissolution of xenoestrogens with an organosulphur compound.

The project defines itself as open source in the sense that the generated protocols are shareable, hackable and constantly improved. Another sense comes from the recognition that, insofar as xenoestrogens are ubiquitous, they are available for us to hack and to collaborate with. A third sense comes from the principle of equity and accessibility with which the open recipes for oestrogen synthesisation are generated. For the second part of the project, Maggic came up with a Martha Stewart-style cooking show titled *Housewives Making Drugs*, in which two transgender woman put into practice the *urine-hormone extraction* protocol, now redefined as a culinary recipe, in a kitchen setting. The show opens with the speculative question: what if it were possible to make oestrogen in the kitchen? Trans-femme stars Jade and Jade teach the audience at home how to prepare their own hormones. The first step involves the extraction of oestrogens from their urine. These are then refined and recycled back into their bodies. This protocol therefore becomes an open-source recipe for producing and managing a DIY hormonal therapy, one that manages to domesticate xenoestrogens through hormone-hacking procedures. It also operates as a decolonising practice of 'gender hacking' that unravels how bodies are socially managed, disciplined and pathologised, providing ways for taking over our own gender transformation. The intensification of the mutagenic effects of xenoestrogens helps the realisation of a 'queer futurity'[2] that results from 'hacking dualistic violence in order to become(ing) together', as noted by philosopher Laura Benítez (2019: 79). This is how the project considers the micro-performativity of hormones as an agential power of not only molecular colonisation but also molecular collaboration: 'from these xeno-forces arise xeno-solidarities'.[3]

The third and final part of the project, *Hormone Micro Performance*, includes diverse implementations of the protocols developed at the *Estrofem! Lab*, collaborative performances with other artists and distinct user interactions. It is divided in two subparts. The first, *Micro Performativity of Sex Hormones*, was performed when the show *Interacting Art* was hosted at the Raumschiff Gallery in Linz (2016). Maggic asked the other participant artist for a urine sample so that their hormones could be extracted and displayed as a shrine-like installation. These samples were connected to oxygen masks, allowing the audience to smell and amplify the micro-colonisation of chemically signalling pheromones that live outside the body. Next to the installation, Maggic's suitcases containing all the materials used to test the protocols were displayed. The disclosure of the biohacking process was aimed at demystifying the black-box scientific method and questioning the sterility and purity of the laboratory and the white box: 'the open lab installation shows biology and biochemistry for what it is: messy, uncontrollable, and open for mutations and subjectivities outside of institutional access and normalization' (Tsang 2017: 47). The second subpart, *Molecular Queering Agency* (2016), consists of a fictional computer animation that invites participants not to react with sex panic to the ongoing hormonal colonisation but to acknowledge our bodies as permeable interfaces that constantly experience mutations as we inhabit queering environments. It therefore attempts to show the decisive implications of molecular trespassing for the field of molar representations, by focusing on its potential for heterogenesis and transversality (SC). The three-step-process script invites participants to shift from phobia in relation to gender ambiguity, intersexuality and threats to human reproducibility towards an ecosophical articulation that strives to implement a life-centred egalitarianism in our intoxicated world.[4]

More-than-human Communisation

OSE speaks more broadly to the question of how we can manifest an entangled, material-semiotic notion of community that would do justice to the more-than-human nature of our world. In a globally interconnected and technologically mediated world determined by the regimes brought about by necropolitics (Mbembe 2003), biopiracy (Shiva 1999) and dispossession (Sassen 2014), humans are exposed in a similar way to animals, rivers and oil to those extractivist, exploitative and commodifying practices through which capitalism accumulates value. This perspective undermines the modern belief that we can live in isolation from the environment and shows that we maintain a constitutive relationship and consequential implication with the larger world. Furthermore, it brings the issue of collective coexistence to the foreground and impels us to imagine a notion of community beyond social presence, negotiation and consent. OSE brings forth a transversalised, process-oriented, open-ended and contingent notion of community that extends beyond the human – ranging from climatic phenomena and geological formations to molecular life, bacteria and viruses – and inscribes alien bodies in dense networks of material interaction. It develops a more inclusive politics that stands for the integrity, health and diversity of bodies without reproducing the eugenics discourse of the-normal-as-the-natural. As we have seen, reactionary, technocratic environmentalism might argue for ecological justice while reinforcing a heteronormative system of representation that constrains the possibilities of life. In this sense, OSE enacts Roberto Esposito's account of communisation as a model of affirmative politics that in turn needs to be seen in conjunction with that of immunisation.

The meaning of the term 'community' is today entangled with notions of belonging, identity and property – this is, with one's self and with what one owns. Its earliest sense, conversely, is defined by what is contrary to one's own possession, by what is non-appropriable, and by what belongs to everyone. The Latin roots of community are a combination of *cum* and *munus*, designating both 'gift' and 'task', a reciprocal duty to give. Far from protecting a subject within a shared property, the former meaning of community conveys rather a loss: what one considers as one's own vanishes as the communal arises. This entails expropriating the self in favour of the other and full exposure among members of a community. It is precisely this aspect against which modernity activated a process of immunisation, describing *comunitas* and *immunitas*. In the twentieth century, social relations were fully biopoliticised in a double process that, on the one hand, aims at protecting life and, on the other, induces its own destruction. This becomes clear with Nazism, where conservation of life is based upon the absolute value of one race, and other populations are seen as dispensable. Here a politics that includes not only management but also the transformation of *bios* raises the question of what counts as a human life to be preserved, and what does not, not only in relation to what was believed to be 'outside' the human (animals, plants) but also within humans (Jews, Roma people, gays, lesbians and Afro-descendants). The immunitarian apparatus is fully committed to the strengthening of *a* life at the expense of inducing the death of *another* life within society, as happens in autoimmune diseases. After 9/11 we have shifted to a diffuse, abstract fear in which preventive war seems not an exception but the 'sole form of global coexistence' (Esposito 2013: 76). The paradox is that war waged in the name of security ultimately multiplies the risks the proponents want to avoid.

Given this situation, Esposito wonders whether there is another way of thinking and practising biopolitics today, one that would replace a transcendent politics 'about' life (*biopotere*) with an affirmative politics 'of' life (*biopotenza*) based on an immanent norm to bodies and a collective and differential subjectivation. While Esposito's emphasis on the performative nature of community remains crucial when configuring a multi-agential assemblage defined by the continuous production of difference and engagement in becomings, feminist new materialisms and posthuman onto-epistemologies are putting forward modes of inquiry that help us grasp community's nomadic and immanent substratum in a more post-anthropocentric key. One is Rosi Braidotti's notion of a posthuman subjectivity, defined as a 'relational subject constituted in and by multiplicity', that is, 'a subject that works across differences and is also internally differentiated, but still grounded and accountable', which signals 'an embodied and embedded and hence partial form of accountability, based on a strong sense of collectivity, relationality and hence community building' (Braidotti 2013: 49). These communities or assemblages are defined by Anna Tsing (2015: 23) as 'open-ended gatherings' that 'allow us to ask about communal effects without assuming them', and that 'show us potential histories in the making'. As Silvia Federici has argued, this transversal account of community action implies ceasing to consider the notion of community as a 'gated reality, a grouping of people joined by exclusive interests separating them from others, as with communities formed on the basis of religion or ethnicity', meaning instead 'a quality of relations, a principle of cooperation and of responsibility to each other and to the earth, the forests, the seas, the animals' (Federici 2012: n.p.).

Conclusion

OSE can be perceived as fuelling a pragmatics of existence across environmental, social and mental ecologies, which counteracts repressive power relations currently impacting bodies on both a micropolitical and a macropolitical level. Maggic's 'becoming-molecular' constitutes a decisive strategy when grasping the pollution our bodies are exposed to at the level of particles, raising awareness about the biopolitical dimension of taken-for-granted gender/sex determinisms and harmful, naturalised, heteronormative representations, and about gaining access to open-source oestrogens and DIY hormonal therapies. The implementation of the Estrofem hacklab recipes mobilises an elemental shift from molecular colonisation (biopower) to molecular emancipation (bioresistance) in which social subjection/machinic subservience operations are put on hold in favour of a procedural self-production of subjectivity in the direction of singularisation, alterification and complexification. This ecosophical articulation occurs by means of an affirmative biopolitics that disrupts immunitarian dynamics and recomposes a more-than-human assemblage not ruled by identity and property but by a nomadic subjectivity invested in a reciprocal gift-giving, a politics of 'being-with'. The self is expropriated in favour of a mutual becoming in which each component of the multispecies assemblage is exposed to generative contagion with one another, restoring community bonds. In sum, Maggic's nomadic laboratories are hacking microfascist colonisations of the body, gender and environment by means of non-profit practices of communisation driven by the desire to live in a world based on trans-species solidarity. The simultaneous redefinition of a post-anthropocentric, more-than-human assemblage and the constant emergence of a processual machinic subjectivity pave the way for a non-immunised, radical communitised existence from which new modes of care, affect and accountability could be experienced.

Notes

1. See Mary Maggic, *Housewives Making Drugs*, 2015, 00:20-00:30, available at <https://vimeo.com/143059738> (last accessed 20 September 2020).
2. See Heather Davis, 'The Queer Futurity of Plastics, conference at Sonic Acts Festival', 2016, available at <https://player.vimeo.com/video/158044006> (last accessed 26 May 2019).
3. Available at <https://maggic.ooo/Estrofem-Lab> (last accessed 26 May 2019).
4. See Mary Maggic, *Molecular Queering Agency*, available at <https://vimeo.com/372133054> (last accessed 5 October 2020).

References

Alonso, C. (2018), 'Placing Life at the Centre: Towards a More-than-human Cosmopolitics', in M. Di Paola (ed.), *Cosmopolitics and Biopolitics*, Barcelona: Edicions de la Universitat de Barcelona, pp. 111–30.
Alonso, C. (ed.) (2019), *Mutating Ecologies in Contemporary Art*, Barcelona: Edicions de la Universitat de Barcelona.
Benítez, L. (2019), 'Monism, Immanence and Biohacking. Hacking Dualistic Violence', in C. Alonso (ed.), *Mutating Ecologies in Contemporary Art*, Barcelona: Edicions de la Universitat de Barcelona, pp. 69–80.
Borell, M. (1976), 'Organotherapy, British Physiology, and the Discovery of the Internal Secretions', *Journal of the History of Biology*, 9 (2): 235–68.
Braidotti, R. (2013), *The Posthuman*, Cambridge: Polity.
Brown-Séquard, C. (1889), 'Notes on the Effects Produced on Man by Subcutaneous Injections of a Liquid Obtained from the Testicles of Animals', *The Lancet*, 134 (3438): 105–7.
Castro-Peraza, M. E., et al. (2019), 'Gender Identity: The Human Right of Depathologization', *International Journal of Environmental Research and Public Health*, 16 (6): 1–11.
Colborn, T., and C. Clement (eds) (1992), *Chemically Induced Alterations in Sexual Development: The Wildlife/Human Connection*, Princeton, NJ: Princeton Scientific Publishing.

Di Chiro, G. (2010), 'Polluted Politics? Confronting Toxic Discourse, Sex Panic, and Eco-Normativity', in C. Mortimer-Sandilands and B. Erickson (eds), *Queer Ecologies: Sex, Nature, Politics, Desire*, Bloomington: Indiana University Press, pp. 199–230.

Esposito, R. (2008), *Bíos: Biopolitics and Philosophy*, Minneapolis: University of Minnesota Press.

Esposito, R. (2013), *Terms of the Political. Community, Immunity, Biopolitics*, trans. R. N. Welch, New York: Fordham University Press.

Federici, S. (2012), 'Feminism and the Politics of the Commons', in D. Bollier and S. Helfrich (eds), *The Wealth of the Commons: A World beyond Market & State*, Amherst, MA: Levellers Press, 2012, <http://wealthofthecommons.org/essay/feminism-and-politics-commons> (last accessed 26 May 2019).

Foucault, M. (2006), *The History of Sexuality I. The Will to Knowledge*, trans. R. Hurley, London: Penguin.

Foucault, M. (2008), *The Birth of Biopolitics. Lectures at the Collège de France 1978–79*, trans. Graham Burchell, New York: Palgrave Macmillan.

Guattari, F. (2008), *La Ciudad Subjetiva y Post-mediática. La Polis Reinventada*, Cali: Fundación Comunidad.

Haraway, D. (2008), *When Species Meet*, Minneapolis: University of Minnesota Press.

Henderson, J. (2005), 'Ernest Starling and Hormones: An Historical Commentary', *Journal of Endocrinology*, 184 (1): 5–10.

Lazzarato, M. (2006), 'Semiotic Pluralism and the New Government of Signs. Homage to Félix Guattari', trans. Mary O'Neill, in *Transversal. European Institute for Progressive Cultural Policies*, 1–7, <https://transversal.at/transversal/0107/lazzarato/en> (last accessed 26 May 2019).

Lazzarato, M. (2011), *The Making of the Indebted Man. An Essay on the Neoliberal Condition*, Los Angeles: Semiotext(e).

Lazzarato, M. (2014), *Signs and Machines. Capitalism and the Production of Subjectivity*, Los Angeles: Semiotext(e).

Mbembe, A. (2003), 'Necropolitics', *Public Culture*, 15 (1): 11–40.

Nieschlag, E., and S. Nieschlag (2019), 'Endocrine History. The History of the Discovery, Synthesis and Development of Testosterone for Clinical Use', *European Journal of Endocrinology*, 180 (6): 201–12.

Sassen, S. (2014), *Expulsions: Brutality and Complexity in the Global Economy*, Cambridge, MA: Harvard University Press.

Shiva, V. (1999), *Biopiracy*, Cambridge, MA: South End Press.

Steinach, E. (1920), *Verjüngung durch experimentelle Neubelebung der alternden Pubertätsdrüse*, Berlin: Julius Springer.

Tsang, M. (2017), *Open Source Estrogen: From Biomolecules to Biopolitics. Hormones with Institutional Biopower*, Cambridge. MA: Massachusetts Institute of Technology.

Tsing, A. L. (2015), *The Mushroom at the End of the World: On the Possibility of Life in Capitalist Ruins*, Princeton: Princeton University Press.

Chapter 4

Algorithmic Governmentality and Managerial Fascism: The Case of Smart Cities

Goda Klumbytė and Lila Athanasiadou

Introduction

The historical beginnings of smart cities can be traced back to early computational models such as Jay W. Forrester's *Urban Dynamics* research with MIT's Urban Systems Laboratory (1969), large-scale data gathering and analysis initiatives such as the Community Analysis Bureau in Los Angeles (1974), or projects that expanded network infrastructures such as *De Digitale Stad* in Amsterdam (1994). Contemporary smart cities combine predictive computational modelling, decentralised data gathering, a sophisticated technical infrastructure and algorithmic management by big tech. One of the earliest large-scale experiments in smart governance was Salvador Allende's project Cybersyn. In the early 1970s, after nationalising 150 industries, the democratic socialist government of Chile decided to reorient their production towards social needs. To accomplish this, Allende's team replaced the 'invisible hand of the market' with a transparent central system that fostered intra-scalar decision making through direct worker participation and autonomy for each factory's management, while holding a fast-track for the government to take control in the case of an emergency.

Cybersyn sought to replace managerial elites by responding to the question of management with the help of communication technology and cybernetics facilitated by a low-tech infrastructure. An amalgam of CYBER-netics and SYN-ergy, the project emerged from the need to consolidate production of goods with consumer demand in order to construct simulations of the market. The Chilean chief engineer Fernardo Flores, with the help of British cybernetics engineer Stafford Beer, designed a 'nervous system' that used real-time data from 400 telex machines placed on sites of production and logistical points connected to a single IBM mainframe computer positioned in the government's control room (Medina 2014). Allende's goal was to build a decentralised economic system as a way to re-engineer socialism into a smoother, less bureaucratic governmental system than the Soviet Union's. The system was designed to create a balance: a fit between labour power, consumer satisfaction, energy use and productivity, with goals reoriented towards efficiency of production and distribution of goods but not maximum profits. It created a centralised government operating on a decentralised infrastructure and an economic system that was simultaneously governed by the workers, the factory managers and the group of engineers and politicians operating within the control room.

Cybersyn did not only act as a real-time market simulation and decision-making tool but also as a mechanism to forecast the impact of economic policies. Besides Cybersyn, Flores and Beer tested Cyberfolk, a direct democracy tool that calculated 'happiness levels' throughout the entire Chilean population through an 'algedonic gradient' – from the Greek *algos*, pain, and *hedoni*, pleasure – accessed through the public TV network, which allowed citizens to give feedback to the government on every top-down decision taken through a device hooked up to their televisions (Morozov 2014).

Only a few years after its launch and after surviving a series of US-orchestrated nationwide strikes in 1973, project Cybersyn was brought to a halt by Pinochet's fascist authoritarian regime.[1] The military coup, rebranded as a 'protected democracy', was supported not only by foreign powers but also by private interests that, while rejecting Allende's socialist vision, devised new ways to utilise the technological infrastructure that his engineers built (Durán-Palma et al. 2005: 65–89). After a modernisation sponsored by the US government, the Chilean military and intelligence agencies expanded their databanks and accumulated personal records on citizens, classifying them as potential dangers. The way Pinochet's coup appropriated and used the cybernetic utopia marked 'a related historical turning point, when cyber-utopia transmuted into cyber-terror, and technology was used not to increase "real-time happiness" – unto "complete bliss" – but to instil raw pain' (Grandin 2014).

The fate of Cybersyn demonstrates how neoliberalism and fascism can intersect in both the discourse and the technical logic of a contemporary equivalent – smart cities – and how the technical and algorithmic infrastructure can sustain and channel the proto-fascist desire shaped by neoliberal fantasies. Particularly today, with smart technologies being utilised in cities both to track Covid-19 infections and to manage social distancing, as well as tracking subjects deemed 'unruly' (such as those who gather to protest) or 'suspicious' (such as those marked by racialised and sexualised difference), it is important to ask what kind of desire informs and is invested in contemporary forms of sociality and the operation of smart cities. We argue that in asking this question it is also crucial to take into account the technical infrastructures that can transmit, aid and amplify affective investments.

In this chapter we look at the smart city's technical structure, its modes of power and the way they produce the desiring subject. We argue that through a conjunction between a specific technical infrastructure, algorithmic governmentality as a modus operandi and neoliberal imperatives, which inform the desire for a 'good life' through consumption, smart cities can produce what could be described as managerial fascism. Encompassing both fixity (of categories and people that are locked into them) and acceleration (of profit, modulations, modes of control), managerial fascism has the capacity to scale beyond the concrete instances of urban life and towards a cancerous Body without Organs of fascist desire expressed in an image of society as a normalised statistical distribution. We conclude the chapter with some avenues for lines of flight and the generative potential of smart cities.

Smart Cities and Algorithmic Governmentality: Technology Meets Cybernetics Meets Algorithmics

The term smart cities appeared around 2008 in the midst of a recession in the global West, when technology firms such as Cisco and IBM shifted their business models from providing hardware and software to the private sector, to providing products and consultancy for a variety of 'problems' to cities and governmental bodies (Paroutis et al. 2014). Since then, smart cities have become an umbrella-term to refer to any technological urban prosthesis, from DIY environmental sensors, to the Internet of Things, 'smart' urban furniture, efficient energy grids, to video surveillance analytics. In this chapter we do not engage with any local, small-scale technological solutions but rather tackle the dominant logic and understanding of 'smartness' itself as the integration of physical, technological and algorithmic infrastructures employed in the planning and governing of cities that serve private interests. Smart cities have been criticised by urbanists, privacy specialists, technology journalists and political theorists as a chimera of technofascism and neoliberal managerialism disguised behind an image of sustainable economic growth and technological efficiency (see, for instance, Greenfield 2013; Morozov and Bria 2018; Krivý 2018). Generally, smart cities operate as private–public initiatives, through which technology firms minimise the power of governing bodies while still benefiting from the legal and institutional support a government body can offer. Their promise is that through an overlay of the physical urban space with digital technological capacities, a better, faster, more efficient and more sustainable city can be built.

The merging of the physical and the digital and the idea of feedback between them points to cybernetics as a system model for smart city management. From its inception, cybernetics has been concerned not only with self-organisation but also with prediction (Wiener 1985). It posits the possibility of engineering order out of disorder by regulating the flows of communication through command and control, arising from information about patterns of action and interventions in those patterns through feedback loops. An early encounter of cybernetics and technology with urbanism can be traced back to the late 1960s with experiments such as the installation *SEEK* in New York's Jewish Museum by Nicholas Negroponte of the Architecture Machine Group, which demonstrated both the potential and the problems of a responsive environment.[2] The management and stability of such a system is engineered based on pattern discovery and prediction. To speak of the sustainability of the system would mean to speak of its self-regulation and possible carefully engineered 'nudges' to trigger desired patterns.

With second-order cybernetics, a system self-regulates based on positive feedback that enacts non-linear systemic changes that allow for emergent properties. The system is conceived as open, with the operator not enacting control but being an observing node in a system that is organised as a network. Within urbanist discourse, second-order cybernetics was immediately embraced as celebrating uncertainty, unpredictability and non-linear systemic changes, as the observer became part of the system with the ability to affect the observed, and thus 'obliterate the observer's hope of impartial, objective prediction' (von Foerster 1984: 258). However, the contemporary smart city proliferates on a legitimisation of prediction models and speculation scenarios over explanatory descriptive models, not as an attempt to prevent undesired results by re-establishing a desired state but as an attempt to preclude possibilities by defining patterns of action. This is particularly noticeable in urban governance technologies such as integrated data management systems and predictive policing tools, aimed at predicting the geographical locations where crime is likely to occur, and potential offenders or victims,[3] which in recent years have been criticised for reproducing racial and other biases (Angwin et al. 2016; Kaufmann et al. 2019). In other words, with second-order cybernetics, the goal is no longer simple prediction but active pre-emption.

If cybernetics gave smart cities a systemic concept of governance, contemporary algorithmics – the science of algorithm design and operation – adds a powerful technological tool for prediction and pre-emption, which enables algorithmic governmentality.[4] Algorithmics of smart cities create grounds for specific forms of governmentality by drawing on two functions of contemporary algorithmic systems: the capacity to derive categorisations (identifying discrete values and addressing questions about the likelihood of a particular data point belonging to a certain category) and estimations (estimating continuous values and addressing questions about the expected value of a particular data point in time).[5] In order for algorithms to be able to perform these functions, they are 'trained' by running iteratively through datasets to 'discover' patterns: statistical correlations, which can be described by a function, generalised enough to act as a prediction scheme for new datasets previously 'unseen'. This predictive capacity is at the basis of contemporary smart applications and resonates with the anticipatory logic that is proposed by the global imaginary of the smart city as a space that responds to uncertainty and risk based on pre-emption, precaution and preparedness (White 2016).

In this process of data-based production of prediction, significant de- and reterritorialisations are performed through a series of abstractions. Apart from technological abstractions and formalisations, the data that the algorithm trains on and processes is abstracted from its context, being detached from the specific individuals and locations that produced the data – in other words, deterritorialisation through decontextualisation and disembodiment. This process is followed by a reterritorialisation of data as information, structured and categorised, rendering it usable for algorithmic processing. The crucial moment of deterritorialisation is enacted through detaching the specific instances of correlation found among data points from specific datasets and generalising these correlations into patterns that in turn form the bases for the so-called predictions. These de-/reterritorialisations through abstraction render the algorithmic system highly modular and endow it with high combinatorial potential, making algorithmic governmentality both attractive and effective for neoliberal smart city projects.

The last two moves of abstraction and de-/reterritorialisation are loci for a great deal of algorithmic bias – such as racial, gender or class bias. Datasets have been shown to be non-representative and prejudiced towards certain populations: for example, a facial recognition algorithm might be trained on a dataset that mostly contains white faces, and thus fail to identify or misidentify persons of colour. Further, because algorithmic predictions act on the future based on historical data, they are often found to reproduce structural biases and inequalities, such as racial bias in the correlation with crime in predictive policing and recidivism prediction systems. The results of the application of such algorithmic prediction systems could therefore be seen as striating, creating sediments upon sediments of historical and material patterns of interaction that solidify into normative structures and insert algorithmic forms of governmentality into the structures of sociality. Algorithmic governmentality is thus a specific mode of proliferation of forms of governance that surpass the governing bodies and instead insert themselves in the socio-technical fabric as modulations of control (PP): rapid, continuous, self-organising and self-perpetuating nodes embedded at all levels of the overall system.

In smart cities, such governmentality perfectly merges cybernetics and algorithmics: modulations are automated and deliver just-in-time control based on pre-described rules and goals of the system. Algorithmic governmentality aims at tweaking or nudging towards desired behaviour, and it operates within the algorithmic logic of pre-emptive prediction and real-time intervention. This 'real-time' governmentality operates on a system that is legitimised based on how efficiently it fits/negotiates between its parameters. The efficiency of the system lies in its flexibility and its capacity to adapt and change, therefore capitalising on difference instead of merely attempting to suppress it. With algorithmic governmentality the system does not have desired states as in earlier cybernetic experiments, but instead attempts to replace discrete goals by creating a fit between a variety of parameters resulting in modulated fitness landscapes. As Deleuze notes, modulation of control is about curating the field of actions rather than imposing explicit prohibitions (PP). Simultaneously, however, all these modular landscapes are overcoded by financial profit imperatives that ultimately facilitate the alignment of all the contested vectors of desire with capital.

One example of how cybernetics and algorithmics give rise to the specific mode of algorithmic governmentality is Google Sidewalks' flexible algorithmic 'outcome-based code' (Sidewalk Labs 2017: 120) that replaces traditional zoning laws. In October 2017 Sidewalk Labs, a subsidiary of Alphabet, the parent company of Google, launched the Quayside project, a partnership with Waterfront Toronto that aspired to build a series of neighbourhoods from the internet up . . . merging the physical and the digital into a living laboratory for urban innovation . . . designed for radical flexibility, enabling the best ideas to be refined in real time and creating a cycle of ongoing improvement driven by the feedback of residents and the energy of entrepreneurs. (Sidewalk Labs 2017: 12)

One of its innovative pillars was its vision of replacing static urban regulations and zoning by planners and designers with a new system that rewards good performance while 'enabling buildings to adapt to market demand for mixed-use environments' (Sidewalk Labs 2017: 120). While Sidewalk Labs criticises strict top-down zoning for stifling innovation and creating segregation, its performance-based code does not replace top-down zoning but cedes the decision-making power to an algorithm, bypassing discretionary elements of local decision making that characterise hybrid approaches to planning (Schulze and Webb 2020). Local government here is substituted by a proliferation of technocratic governmentality (modes of governing) enabled by the algorithmic infrastructure. Deregulation, when coupled with goals that align with profit making, remains in favour of a 'survival of the fittest' type of logic that actively hinders the participation of minor voices in the decision-making process. Sidewalk Labs was finally scrapped in July 2020 after a series of controversies regarding data privacy, real estate price spikes and strong opposition from housing activists and locals, but it does serve as an interesting case study of the forms of governmentality that big, tech-driven smart cities espouse and encourage.

The Emergence of the Multi-level Infrastructure of Dividuality

In effect, algorithmic governmentality both creates and relies on what we would call 'the infrastructure of dividuality'. Following Deleuze, 'dividual' here is opposed to the 'individual' subject (PP, 180), and algorithmic governmentality provides the material technical infrastructure for such subject formation. The properties of a dividual are captured by the technological apparatus of algorithms as aggregate 'cloud identities' that are constructed during the process of abstraction – and extraction – of patterns from data based on actions (and not words or inherent attributes). Wendy Chun suggests that algorithms employed in network science that operate in the same abstraction logic manage to 'target key intersectional identities' instead of tracking explicitly racial, sexual or other differences (2018: 65). Differences are instrumentalised to create tighter and more precise categories, forcing singular patterns to fit into existing general categories, turning the 'imitation game' into an 'identification game'.[6]

The recognition of the pattern does not happen at the level of the individual but that of the demographic: individual actions indicate collective behavioural patterns on the 'supra-dividual' level.[7] Since singular actions are used to build the pattern on the level of the demographic, 'correlations ... are not made based solely on an individual's actions and history, but rather the history and actions of others "like" him or her' (Chun 2018: 75). On the level of the infra-dividual, data (environmental, social, economic, material) coalesce into patterns – abstracted, deterritorialised flows – and are employed to build a statistical numerical representation – a reterritorialisation – that acts as the ground for the model/simulation of the city and constructs the supra-dividual categories. However, the patterns extracted on the supra-dividual layer both create epistemological models used for analysis but also operate as pre-emptive mechanisms, extracting patterns of behaviour and monetising them as intention by re-engineering and directing desires via new services that are being introduced in the city.[8]

Flows of re- and deterritorialisation in the smart city are supported and facilitated by a specific type of numerical space that the algorithmic infrastructure of the city creates. This space is characterised by articulations of what Deleuze and Guattari call a 'Numbering Number' and a 'Numbered Number' (TP, 118). The numbering number is the autonomous arithmetical organisation that appears when something gets distributed in space, as opposed to when space is divided or distributed itself, which is what occurs in the space ruled by the numbered number. On the level of technical infrastructure – the computational space of binary code, formal language, erasure of boundaries between different domains or different forms of entities – a smooth space is created upon which algorithms work as diagrammatic procedures, as vectors.

Technical objects – such as algorithms – move through such space iteratively (and rhythmically), working ordinally (ascribing positions) without cardinality (counting). In that sense they form what Sandra Robinson calls a 'vital network' – a dynamic, relational and generative assemblage that is self-organising in response to the heterogeneity of contemporary network processes, connections and communication (Robinson 2016). Such a network of interactions between technical elements and procedures is vital because it is still self-organising, but unlike a cybernetic system, it is molecular and not self-contained. That is to say, it is more akin to swarms and meshwork and is not entirely concerned with subjects and networks where entities or nodes are clearly identifiable. This vital network of infrastructure that roots in the smooth space of the numbering number is concerned only with procedures, not with outputs. However, the state – and also the company – extracts value from this rhythmic, smooth procedure by subjecting algorithmic organisation, vectoral movement to counting and statistical management, creating thus a metered, striated space of the numbered number.

The striated space gets further reproduced and solidified into graspable forms: patterns and categories, which are then reorganised in real time to build more models and services. Crucially, this process of modelling and operationalisation of models has a diagrammatic relation to reality: a double operation of analysis and action renders the models self-fulfilling prophecies that simultaneously produce the realities they are trying to represent. This contributes to a naturalisation of historical and social phenomena such as segregation, due to the fact that already existing conditions are assumed to be 'random' and therefore neutral, while at the same time the nature of the algorithms used amplifies and normalises these existing conditions.[9] The modulating power of control is injected at the level of infrastructure itself, thus inscribing modes of control into daily techno-social routines, normalising forms of control and power at the same time as they are providing support for them (Datta and Odendaal 2019).

The subject here is further dividualised, becoming a modular assemblage that gets assembled and disassembled computationally, exhibiting different patterns and attributes depending on the query. Its diagram becomes operational, shifting from a social concept to a social-technical one and working as a self-actualising mechanism, producing what it is monitoring. Jennifer Gabrys argues that 'the very responsiveness that enables citizens to gather data does not extend to enabling them to meaningfully act upon the data gathered, since this would require changing the urban "system" in which they have become effective operators' (Gabrys 2014: 22). The citizen is not the liberal subject with the agency to act and intervene in her environment: while citizens might act as sensors, they do not have to actively register in the system. In the meantime, algorithmic logic remains a black box, making decisions appear objective and natural and foreclosing the virtual through its preemptive logic of control.

Management of Difference and Inscription of Neoliberal Desire

Both Deleuze and Guattari highlight that regulatory, economic and other structures of production produce and are sustained by specific lines of subjectification and investment of desire (TP, TE). Our central argument is that within a smart city the lines of subjectification as well as forms of affective investment are co-constructed through technical infrastructures and modes of algorithmic governmentality. As Deleuze and Guattari proclaim, 'desire belongs to the infrastructure' (AO, 348). This is not to say that infrastructure forms the base for desire's superstructure, but rather, as Guattari points out in *The Three Ecologies*, that the techno-scientific processes and the processes of subjectification, as well as economic and juridical processes, are all simultaneously operating mechanisms marked by rhizomatic, non-linear relations with each other. Capitalism, contrary to previous modes of production, however, does not aim at reproducing one specific code or model of organisation, but rather through deterritorialising previous forms of investment of desire capitalism frees desire and turns it into a force of production (Read 2008). Simultaneously, an immediate reterritorialisation is happening: new loci of investing desire are created, and the trajectories for becoming subject get rerouted through the act of consumption.

Large-scale smart city initiatives that foster partnerships between private tech conglomerates and supranational organisations operate on a scale that facilitates a reinvestment of desire through a smooth infrastructure and an algorithmic logic that is profoundly intra-scalar, totalising and operation-oriented. Cardullo and Kitchin have argued that EU initiatives such as the European Innovation Partnership for Smart Cities and Communities (EIP-SCC) have been successful in extending 'entrepreneurial urbanism' by encouraging the privatisation of public assets, the marketisation of public services (including housing and public space previously provided by the state) and the scaling up of market-driven technological solutions to urban problems through 'mimetic adaptation' (Cardullo and Kitchin 2018). It is important to stress that the urban problems described by the EIP-SCC are only framed within calculable frameworks of energy and time efficiency, sustainability (longevity versus cost) and freedom of choice within market constraints. As we have argued above, by removing local regulatory frameworks such as local committees and community decision making, these initiatives allow public work to be 'marketised, deregulated and privatised', consequently transforming the rights of citizens into choices, 'with citizens framed increasingly as consumers' (Cardullo and Kitchin 2018: 5).

The commodification of civic life in its totalising extent turns the political state into a corporate one – a modular, just-in-time provider of services and enough social control to produce new codes that can be injected as fuel for capitalist de-/reterritorialisations. The shift is not only systemic but also ideological as it adopts neoliberalism as the underlying urban logic, promoting the new highly skilled labour class and all its adjacent lifestyle 'qualities' such as competitiveness, dematerialisation of work, focus on well-being. The combination of top-down neoliberal policies and their enactment through algorithmic governmentality only accelerates the striation of the social fabric of the city. Such striation relies on existing racial, class and gender segregations, as well as sedimenting them further both by creating new 'knowledge' from data patterns as well as by discursively positioning cities as 'smart', and thus as correspondingly 'young', 'tech savvy', 'connected'. From the way individual actions are instrumentalised to both create categories and affirm them (by making them statistically probable) we can conclude that difference is not only a property to be managed but is rendered fully operational between the processes of data analysis and the enactment of the models built.

The link between abstraction and representation, data analysis and pattern recognition, is big data analytics. Data analytics through network science is able to read data as meaningful information and gather it into comprehensible sets using clustering algorithms predominantly based on the logic of homophily. Clustering algorithms have diverse applications as they are employed for any classification of data. Alex Singleton discusses their use in the context of geodemographics, a field whose focus is to 'effectively code people and the places in which they live into aggregate groupings based on shared attribute similarities' (Singleton 2016: 231). Homophily as a logic follows the theory that similarity breeds connection (McPherson et al. 2001). Wendy Chun problematises its uncritical use in the discipline of network science, tracing its origin to a 1954 text by sociologists Lazarsfeld and Merton that looked into 'the dynamic processes through which the similarity or opposition of values shape the formation, maintenance, and disruption of close friendships' (Lazarsfeld and Merton 1954: 28). Being only one of the ways social groups were formed, homophily – far from being a naturally occurring phenomenon – is a tool, and like any tool it anticipates and produces its results. As Chun argues, homophily 'assumes and creates segregation; it presumes consensus and similarity within local clusters, making segregation a default characteristic of network neighbourhoods' (2018: 76). By recognising connections only as acts of free will, it 'erases historical contingencies, institutional discrimination, and economic realities' (Sinan et al. 2013). Homophily logic operates by amplifying identity, relying on the 'discovered' patterns, and by creating connections between them through highlighting the similarities while ignoring the differences.

By becoming axiomatic within network analysis, homophily transforms the inductive logic to a deductive one, naturalising similarities between groups. This, in turn, breeds a certain kind of 'political monoculture', in which rights are redefined through consumption patterns and the dividual cells are tasked with correspondingly savvy 'self-management'. From 'technical machines', through the algorithmic infrastructure and the homophily principle that permeates it, smart cities turn into 'social machines' (AO, 30–1). But as Deleuze and Guattari warn in *Anti-Oedipus*, 'there are no desiring-machines that exist outside the social machines that they form on a large scale; and no social machines without the desiring-machines that inhabit them on a small scale' (AO, 340). Urban services released to the public as trial runs in the urban context ground the connection between the social machines and the desiring ones. With the logic of trial runs and constant demos (Halpern and Günel 2017), smart cities use the dependency of citizens on corporations to introduce services that will gradually allow people to relinquish their privacy in return for increased comfort. Comfort is the underlying cause that network scientists attribute to the success of the principle of homophily (Chun 2018: 79), since it translates into familiarity, certainty and consensus, making what deviates from the norm uncomfortable and therefore unpleasant. Thus on the micropolitical level, comfort informs the desire for smart cities, which, on the macropolitical level, resonates with and amplifies the assimilation to the statistical average, obsessive risk and uncertainty management, and the logic of repetition of the same that dictates their operations.

Guattari suggested that capitalism is 'a power operation before it becomes a profit operation' as its function is diagrammatic and therefore more operative than merely representational (SS, 252). It is not hard to observe that the diagram of the global imaginaries of smart cities easily aligns with the three core processes of neoliberalism – privatisation (with privatised technical infrastructure and data), deregulation (through real-time decentralised decision making) and commodification of every part of citizens' lives. Nevertheless, simultaneously one can trace its desire-producing tactics within the operational logic of fascism: namely totalising control, desire of sameness, and repetition resonating with the diagram of capital. The algorithmic infrastructure links the micro and macro levels of desiring production while operating as a social-technical machine, a diagram. However, coupled with homophily as the main logic, the content of the operation alludes to the logic of a structure, rather than a diagram that performs through feedback loops towards eternal return (CS, 154–75). Smart cities, when driven by their global profit-oriented imaginaries of neoliberalism and pre-emptive hope (Halpern and Günel 2017), are thus marshalling the management of difference by constantly producing techniques for reterritorialisation to follow the deterritorialising effects of capitalism.

Managerial Fascism and the Cancerous BwO

The concept of managerial fascism in smart cities arises through a conjunction between a specific technical infrastructure, algorithmic governmentality as a modus operandi and neoliberal imperatives, which inform a desire for 'fitness' and the 'good life' through consumption. Eugene Holland notes that in *Anti-Oedipus* and *A Thousand Plateaus* fascism is conceptualised rather differently (Holland 2008). If in the former fascism is characterised by a certain stagnation and fixity of desire, in the latter it is rather described as an intensification of speed, a cancerous Body without Organs (BwO) and suicidal line of flight. Holland tries to resolve this contradiction by arguing that since desire is always already socially engineered, specific historical circumstances need to be accounted for in order to identify specific instances of fascistic tendencies. Following this line, we argue that the managerial fascism that emerges through the neoliberal model of the smart city encompasses both fixity and acceleration.

On the level of infrastructure, as mentioned earlier, algorithmic processing of information forms a smooth space for the circulation of productive forces. It is productive and smooth because it allows for multiple connections between human and non-human elements, forming a hybrid ecosystem. Neoliberal rendering of the smart city deploys a capitalist machine upon this smooth space for value extraction, and this extraction is facilitated by managerial algorithmic governmentality. Subsuming productive connections, such governmentality creates resonance between the neoliberal imperative for 'fitness', stifling the flows, striating them into statistical averages and data aggregates – and the fascist suicidal line of flight, which moves at increasingly accelerating speeds, threatening and effectively crossing the very limits of cybernetic equilibrium of the system. This specific resonance between neoliberal capitalism and fascism has also been pointed out by Chaudhary and Chappe (2016) in their analysis of the emergence of the figure of the 'supermanager' in the bureaucratic structure of the Third Reich, far before it became the key figure in neoliberalism. Relying on Franz Neumann's analysis of the managerial aspects of the Nazi regime, they argue that the role of the 'supermanager' was to smooth over the power differences in society.

The genealogy of the function of corporate smart cities and their algorithmic government can thus be traced back to the emergence of this 'managerial elite' during the Nazi period and connected to the emergence of 'supermanagers' who operate in the smooth infrastructure of neoliberalism. The supermanager's role in the smart city is replaced by an algorithmic infrastructure that can automate and optimise this process. The bureaucratic apparatus in a smart city to an extent is replaced by the algorithmic apparatus of management through prediction and pre-emption that similarly smooths over the power differences. Processing decontextualised data as 'neutral' and 'objective' information, this algorithmic apparatus suspends uncertainty and actualises the virtual while bypassing subjectivity and selectivity (Rouvroy and Stiegler 2016).

Furthermore, managerial fascism requires the production of a certain kind of body politic. As Protevi argues, this entails the production of bodies whose 'affective-cognitive patterns and triggers fit the functional needs of the system' (Protevi 2018: 72). It has a compositional (personal and group or civic) and a temporal scale (punctual events, mid-term habit/training/development and long-term history). Managerial fascism, aided by algorithmic governmentality, produces constructed collectivities and a body politic that is geared further towards 'fitting': it is not that there are no possibilities of choice, but rather that the possibility of choice is always already structured by the query categories and patterns of action that are offered as the only options, while optimisation 'for the best' imposes a teleological goal of fitness.

The desire for the 'good life' here becomes a desire for absolute objectivity and certainty – ever on the horizon, as an unattainable yet desirable goal – overcoded with the imperative for limitless, cancerous consumption. In other words, managerial fascism postulates ever-increasing productivity, while at the same time designating those subjects and processes that are not 'fit' as not only disposable but also threatening to further acceleration. Within managerial fascism, thus, everything that cannot be fitted into the pattern of harmonious rhythm needs to be expelled, disassembled or disintegrated through pre-emptive foreclosing of the very possibility of emergence. Aided by algorithmic governance and technological infrastructure with its corresponding smooth space, managerial fascism thus has the capacity to scale beyond the concrete instances of urban life and towards a cancerous BwO of fascist desire expressed in an image of society as a normalised statistical distribution.

Lines of Flight

What, then, are the possible lines of flight from managerial fascism? Where are the cracks in the smooth surface of algorithmic governmentality and how can those cracks be exploited to reinvest desire in the ecosophical (TE) multiplication of desires and differences? One possible line that forms within such cracks is the return to the smooth space of the numbering number that characterises the deeper level of algorithmic infrastructure. The space of the numbering number for Deleuze and Guattari is a space of potential, characterised, not unlike the machinic phylum, by high combinatorial potential (DeLanda 1997). Abstraction for them is not something to be shunned: on the contrary, for Deleuze the abstract is another way of talking about the intensive, which is not opposed to the concrete but rather to the discrete (Adkins 2016: 352–60). Computation, similarly, can be defined as a process of disentanglement from particulars, a science of 'concrete abstractions' (Colburn 2007). Abstractions are built from concrete entities, and through the processes of computing such abstractions are assembled into patterns of interaction that both describe and affect the electronic events that are to occur, as well as the singular-generic, concrete, material-discursive elements that comprise the abstractions. Perhaps then the operations of computing and algorithmic processes should be defined not as manipulations of discrete entities (which they of course also perform) but, at least to some extent, as diagrammatics that index relations and are productive rather than only descriptive (Klumbytė and Britton 2020).

Within such a framework another line of flight materialises: if abstractions are built from the concrete elements that are intensive and material-discursive, then, we argue, it matters where one abstracts from (Klumbytė and Britton 2020). The critique of the smart city does not rely solely on the datafication of everyday life. As Bernard Stiegler argues, 'the problem is not whether something can be digitised or not, rather the problem is: is it reducible to a calculus or not?' (Rouvroy and Stiegler 2016: 18). Everything is potentially digitisable and reducible to data, but data is not solely quantifiable itself, or rather it cannot be fully grasped in quantitative terms. In line with a feminist politics of location and situatedness, this points to a politics of 'thick data' (Wang 2016) and 'warm data' (Bateson 2017). Both of these concepts describe a data that is not rendered 'clean' and 'lean' for the obsessive generation of decontextualised patterns, but rather a data that bears connection to the subjects and environments that produced it, as well as, by extension, accountability to the historical and political conditions that it arises from and produces. Warm data is a way to place big data back into its context, conceptualised as a set of relations between systems that allow for quantitative data to be measured in the first place.

Despite the general tendency of smart city initiatives to be designed and presented as prototypes to be tested and reproduced elsewhere, the models they produce are also entangled in their social, political, cultural and economic specificities. As with data, models are also extracted from localities, deterritorialised and reterritorialised as alternative capital- and desire-generating models overcoding the same localities that they came from (Loukissas 2019). More attention thus needs to be paid to what kind of new territories are created. Furthermore, we propose that it is not the modelling or the prototyping that is the issue in itself, but rather the lack of creative diagrams and patterns of action. If models are rigid and abstract, diagrams are flexible, productive and active – perhaps diagrammatic thinking about urban spaces is an alternative route to smart city design.

Alternative diagrammatic approaches to smart and sustainable cities have been emerging also at the intersections of informatics and critical theory, particularly within urban informatics and sustainable (urban and otherwise) agriculture. For instance, Freeman et al. (2019) have explored 'fermentation' as a conceptual metaphor (or what we would call a diagram) for smart city design towards active placemaking that was employed in Taiwan by a community-based design collective City Yeast. The goal of reimagining the design of the smart city as a process of fermentation encouraged citizens to 'become yeast' and participate in the slow and engaging process of co-design. In a similar vein, Heitlinger et al. (2019) explored the concepts of commons, care and biocultural diversity as frameworks for co-designing sustainable smart urban agri-culture, disrupting the technology–nature divide and enacting a more ecosophical approach to city-making. Finally, Liu et al. (2019) propose symbiosis and companion species-based approaches to designing sus-tainable farming, which is attentive to multispecies encounters and livable worlds.[10]

As Guattari's ecosophical thought suggests (TE, CS), diagrammatic alternatives are often constructed aesthetically. Thus, not surprisingly, experimental and arts practices often become the loci for the emergence of new forms of being and thinking. In the domain of smart city design, one such locus was a project expressed by Humans of Simulated New York (Azizi 2018), a digital thought-experiment developed by writer/programmer Francis Tseng and artist Fei Liu. Based on a plethora of game-like city simulations that are historically based on predicting human behaviour and enacting policies accordingly, the researchers used real-life demographics from the New York City census to create a simulation game. Users are assigned characters and are asked to vote for policies that would benefit their avatar. By playing on Jameson's 'situational representation', the artists denaturalise the simulation, as the position of the player/user as individual subject is juxtaposed with the 'unrepresentable totality' of the socius. Simultaneously, by adding unpredictable factors in the simulation with a speculative character, they point to the limits of simulated models as predictive mechanisms while acknowledging their potential for creative imaginaries as instructive tools. Such use of data becomes a way to point out historical, social and political specificities as well as the economic imperatives that underline the smart city's function, and might contribute to challenging the contentious belief that planning equals self-organisation.

To conclude, we would like to point out that it is critical to realise that the space for political action lies in the gap between prediction and reality, especially since predictions can be self-cancelling as well as self-fulfilling (Silver 2012: 219). As Cybersyn's experiment shows, cybernetics and algorithmics can be used to decentralise structures and allow for greater control and involvement of citizens, especially when profit, market success, efficiency, technical elegance or smoothness of the infrastructure are not goals in themselves. Yet it can also create fertile ground for managerial fascism – a form of fascism that can emerge through smart cities as a result of the coalescence of algorithmic governmentality, the technical infrastructure of dividuality and the neoliberal imperative that produces and feeds on the desire for 'fitness' and sameness. We believe, however, that embracing diagrammatics not simply as a description of capitalism's operations but also as a conceptual tool for productive interventions can open up lines of flight away from the totalising resonances between neoliberalism and fascism.

Notes

1. It is important to stress that in referring to Pinochet's regime as 'fascist' we are borrowing from Jean Grugel's analysis, which distinguishes classic European fascism from its manifestation in Chile. Grugel describes the shared characteristics between Pinochet's regime and more traditional forms of fascism. These include 'anti- communism; anti-liberalism; anti-parliamentarianism; authoritarianism; anti-internationalism; populism; militarism; and corporatism' (Grugel 1985: 109–22).
2. The experiment featured a Plexiglas-covered environment inhabited by gerbils, and consisted of small movable blocks that were overseen and reorganised by a robotic arm. The computer extracted behavioural patterns from the gerbils

and through feedback loops prescribed the desired state for their environment in real time (Negroponte 1970: 23). Based on first-order cybernetics, the system was conceived as closed, with the operator enacting control as a homeostatic regulation that aimed for a state of order and equilibrium. Despite the utopian expectations the experiment finished unexpectedly when all the gerbils were found dead covered in their own excrement.

3. For an overview of predictive policing methods and tools, see Jansen 2018 (for European context) and Brayne et al. 2015 (for US-American context).

4. Governmentality is a term coined by Michel Foucault to demonstrate the connection between forms of power and subject formation, referring to the way the subject as an individual and the modern sovereign state co-constituted each other. Composed as an amalgam of *gouverner* and *mentalité*, governmentality highlights the modes of thought and rationality behind technologies of power (Foucault 2009: 144).

5. These functions are performed by machine-learning algorithms – that is, algorithms that are able learn patterns from data. For an overview of machine-learning algorithms and processes, see, for instance, Maini and Sabri 2017; and see Burrell 2016 for explorations of machine-learning-based image recognition.

6. Artist Hito Steyerl argues that modern computation is aiming at multiplying identities rather than obscuring them. She refers to the example of Facebook opening up its gender options beyond the binary as a way to refine the targeted advertising to its users. She argues: 'If you don't want to identify as man or as woman that's fine, but please check one of these fifty-plus boxes to state your precisely defined other type of gender, and we'll make sure to send you the appropriate ads. This is not an imitation game but an identification game' (Steyerl 2018: 12).

7. Here we borrow and rework Antoinette Rouvroy's terms 'infra-individual' and 'supra-individual' (Rouvroy and Stiegler 2016). Within the environmental, or what Rouvroy calls the 'infra-individual', level citizens are treated as sensors among other sensors and become part of human/non-human assemblages. Simultaneously, within the behavioural or 'supra-individual' layer, citizens are treated as aggregate data being abstracted as behavioural patterns to be enacted back upon the population.

8. Evgeny Morozov often argues that tech giants such as Google collect data and sell it to smaller startups that operate under its umbrella in order to create services to be reintroduced to the city, which in effect will generate more data to be sold (Morozov and Bria 2018).

9. Fuller and Hardwood reflect on the racism of Schelling's models of segregation as both operating 'by means of racial demarcation as an autocatalytic ideological given' and also providing 'a means of organizing racial division at a higher level of abstraction' (Fuller and Hardwood 2016: 62).

10. These are just three examples that were presented during the ACM's Human-Computer Interaction (CHI) conference in 2019. For more significant research in the area, see also proceedings of the recent editions of ACM's Designing Interactive Systems (DIS) conference, particularly the 2020 edition on More than Human Centered Design (https://dis.acm.org/2020/).

References

Adkins, B. (2016), 'Who Thinks Abstractly? Deleuze on Abstraction', *The Journal of Speculative Philosophy*, 30 (3): 352–60.

Angwin, J., J. Larson, S. Mattu and L. Kirchner (2016), 'Machine Bias', *ProPublica*, 23 May, <https://www.propublica.org/article/machine-bias-risk-assessments-in-criminal-sentencing> (last accessed 15 May 2022).

Azizi, A. (2018), 'Humans of Simulated New York', *Rhizome*, 3 April, <http://rhizome.org/editorial/2018/apr/03/humans-of-simulated-new-york> (last accessed 15 May 2022).

Bateson, N. (2017), 'Warm Data', 28 May, <https://norabateson.wordpress.com/2017/05/28/warm-data/> (last accessed 15 May 2022).

Brayne, S., A. Rosenblat and D. Boyd (2015), 'Predictive Policing', *Data & Civil Rights: A New Era of Policing and Justice*, 27 October, <http://www.datacivilrights.org/pubs/2015-1027/Predictive_Policing.pdf> (last accessed 15 May 2022).

Burrell, J. (2016), 'How the Machine "Thinks": Understanding Opacity in Machine Learning Algorithms', *Big Data & Society*, 3 (1): 1–12, <https://doi.org/10.1177/2053951715622512>.

Cardullo, P., and R. Kitchin (2018), 'Smart Urbanism and Smart Citizenship: The Neoliberal Logic of "Citizen-Focused" Smart Cities in Europe', *Environment and Planning C: Politics and Space*, 37 (5): 813–30, <https://doi.org/10.1177/0263774X18806508>.

Chaudhary, A. S., and R. Chappe (2016), 'The Supermanagerial Reich', *LA Review of Books*, 7 November, <https://lareviewofbooks.org/article/the-supermanagerial-reich> (last accessed 15 May 2022).

Chun, W. H. K. (2018), 'Queering Homophily', in C. Apprich, W. H. K. Chun, F. Cramer and H. Steyerl, *Pattern Discrimination*, Minneapolis: University of Minnesota Press, pp. 59–98.

Colburn, T. (2007), 'Abstraction in Computing', *Minds and Machines: Journal for Artificial Intelligence, Philosophy, and Cognitive Science*, 17 (2): 169–84.

Datta, A., and N. Odendaal (2019), 'Smart Cities and the Banality of Power', *Environment and Planning D: Society and Space*, 37 (3): 387–92, <https://doi.org/10.1177/0263775819841765>.

DeLanda, M. (1997), 'The Machinic Phylum', *TechnoMorphica*, http://v2.nl/archive/articles/the-machinic-phylum (last accessed 15 May 2022).

Durán-Palma, F., A. Wilkinson and M. Korczynski (2005), 'Labour Reform in a Neo-liberal "Protected" Democracy: Chile 1990–2001', *The International Journal of Human Resource Management*, 16 (1): 65–89.

Foucault, M. (2009), *Security, Territory, Population: Lectures at the College de France 1977–78*, Basingstoke: Palgrave Macmillan.

Freeman, G., J. Bardzell, S. Bardzell, S.-Y. Liu, X. Lu and D. Cao (2019), 'Smart and Fermented Cities', in S. Brewster, G. Fitzpatrick, A. Cox and V. Kostakos (eds), *Proceedings of the 2019 CHI Conference on Human Factors in Computing Systems – CHI '19*, New York: ACM Press, <https://doi.org/10.1145/3290605.3300274>.

Fuller, M., and G. Hardwood (2016), 'Abstract Urbanism', in R. Kitchin and S.-Y. Perng (eds), *Code and the City*, New York: Routledge, pp. 61–71.

Gabrys, J. (2014), 'Programming Environments: Environmentality and Citizen Sensing in the Smart City', *Environment and Planning D: Society and Space*, 32 (1): 30–48.

Grandin, G. (2014), 'The Anti-Socialist Origins of Big Data', *The Nation*, <https://www.thenation.com/article/archive/anti-socialist-origins-big-data/> (last accessed 15 May 2022).

Greenfield, A. (2013), *Against the Smart City*, New York: Do projects.

Grugel, J. (1985), 'Nationalist Movements and Fascist Ideology in Chile', *Bulletin of Latin American Research*, 4 (2): 109–22.

Halpern, O., and G. Günel (2017), 'FCJ-215 Demoing unto Death: Smart Cities, Environment, and Preemptive Hope', *The Fibreculture Journal*, <https://doi.org/10.15307/fcj.29.215.2017>.

Heitlinger, S., N. Bryan-Kinns and R. Comber (2019), 'The Right to the Sustainable Smart City', in S. Brewster, G. Fitzpatrick, A. Cox and V. Kostakos (eds), *Proceedings of the 2019 CHI Conference on Human Factors in Computing Systems – CHI '19*, New York: ACM Press, <https://doi.org/10.1145/3290605.3300517>.

Holland, E. W. (2008), 'Schizoanalysis, Nomadology, Fascism', in I. Buchanan and N. Thoburn, *Deleuze and Politics*, Edinburgh: Edinburgh University Press, pp. 74–96.

Jansen, F. (2018), 'Data Driven Policing in the Context of Europe', working paper in ERC-funded project *'Data Justice: Understanding datafication in relation to social justice' (DATAJUSTICE) starting grant (2018–2023)*, Data Justice Lab, Cardiff University, UK.

Kaufmann, M., S. Egbert and M. Leese (2019), 'Predictive Policing and the Politics of Patterns', *The British Journal of Criminology*, 59 (3): 674–92, <https://doi.org/10.1093/bjc/azy060>.

Klumbytė, G., and L. Britton (2018), 'Trans*re*lational Objects: In Search of a Common Strategy for Arts and Computation', lecture at the Institut für Kunst und Kunsttheorie, Intermedia programme, University of Cologne.

Klumbytė, G., and L. Britton (2020), 'Abstracting Otherwise: In Search for a Common Strategy of Arts and Computing', *ASAP/Journal*, 5 (1): 19–43, <https://doi.org/10.1353/asa.2020.0001>.

Krivý, M. (2018), 'Towards a Critique of Cybernetic Urbanism: The Smart City and the Society of Control', *Planning Theory*, 17 (1): 8–30.

Lazarsfeld, P. F., and R. K. Merton (1954), 'Friendship as a Social Process: A Substantive and Methodological Analysis', *Freedom and Control in Modern Society*, 18: 18–66.

Liu, S.-Y., S. Bardzell and J. Bardzell (2019), 'Symbiotic Encounters: HCI and Sustainable Agriculture'. in S. Brewster, G. Fitzpatrick, A. Cox and V. Kostakos (eds), *Proceedings of the 2019 CHI Conference on Human Factors in Computing Systems – CHI '19*, New York: ACM Press, <https://doi.org/10.1145/3290605.3300547>.

Loukissas, Y. A. (2019), *All Data Are Local: Thinking Critically in a Data-Driven Society*, Cambridge, MA: MIT Press.

Mackenzie, A. (2015), 'The Production of Prediction: What Does Machine Learning Want?', *European Journal of Cultural Studies*, 8 (4–5): 429–45.

Maini, V., and S. Sabri (2017), 'Machine Learning for Humans', *Medium*, 19 August, <https://medium.com/machine-learning-for-humans/why-machine-learning-matters-6164faf1df12> (last accessed 15 May 2022).

McPherson, M., L. Smith-Lovin and J. Cook (2001), 'Birds of a Feather: Homophily in Social Networks', *Annual Review of Sociology*, 27 (1): 415–44.

Medina, E. (2014), *Cybernetic Revolutionaries*, Cambridge, MA: MIT Press.

Morozov, E. (2014), 'The Planning Machine', *The New Yorker*, 6 October, <https://www.newyorker.com/magazine/2014/10/13/planning-machine> (last accessed 15 May 2022).

Morozov, E., and F. Bria (2018), *Rethinking the Smart City: Democratizing Urban Technology*, New York: Rosa Luxemburg Stiftung.

Negroponte, N. (1970), *The Architecture Machine Group*, Cambridge, MA: MIT Press.

Paroutis, S., M. Bennett and L. Heracleous (2014), 'A Strategic View on Smart City Technology: The Case of IBM Smarter Cities during a Recession', *Technological Forecasting and Social Change*, 89: 262–72.

Protevi, J. (2018), 'Bodies Politic', in R. Braidotti and M. Hlavajova (eds), *Posthuman Glossary*, London: Bloomsbury, pp. 72–4.

Read, J. (2008), 'The Age of Cynicism: Deleuze and Guattari on the Production of Subjectivity in Capitalism', in I. Buchanan and N. Thoburn (eds), *Deleuze and Politics*, Edinburgh: Edinburgh University Press, pp. 139–59.

Robinson, S. (2016), 'The Vital Network: An Algorithmic Milieu of Communication and Control', *communication +1*, 5 (1): Article 5, <https://doi.org/10.7275/R5416V0R>.

Rouvroy, A., and B. Stiegler (2016), 'The Digital Regime of Truth: From the Algorithmic Governmentality to a New Rule of Law', *La Deleuziana*, 3: 6–29.

Schulze Bäing, A., and B. Webb (2020), *Planning Through Zoning*, London: Royal Town Planning Institute.

Sidewalk Labs Toronto (2017), 'Vision Sections of RFP Submission', https://sidewalktoronto.ca/wp-content/uploads/2018/05/Sidewalk-Labs-Vision-Sections-of-RFP-Submission.pdf (last accessed 15 May 2022).

Silver, N. (2012), *The Signal and the Noise: Why So Many Predictions Fail – But Some Don't*, New York: The Penguin Press.

Sinan, A., L. Muchnik and A. Sundarajan (2013), 'Engineering Social Contagions: Optimal Network Seeding in the Presence of Homophily', *Network Science*, 1 (2): 125–53.

Singleton, A. (2016), 'Cities and Context: The Codification of Small Areas Through Geodemographic Classification', in R. Kitchin and S.-Y. Perng (eds), *Code and the City*, New York: Routledge, pp. 215–35.

Steyerl, H. (2018), 'A Sea of Data: Pattern Recognition and Corporate Animism (Forked Version)', in C. Apprich, W. H. K. Chun, F. Cramer and H. Steyerl, *Pattern Discrimination*, Minneapolis: University of Minnesota Press, pp. 1–22.

Von Foerster, H. (1984), 'Notes on an Epistemology for Living Things', in *Observing Systems*, Seaside, CA: Intersystems Publications, 2nd edn, pp. 257–72.

Tsang Wang, T. (2016), 'Why Big Data Needs Thick Data', *Medium*, 20 January, <https://medium.com/ethnography-matters/why-big-data-needs-thick-data-b4b3e75e3d7> (last accessed 15 May 2022).

White, J. M. (2016), 'Anticipatory Logics of the Smart City's Global Imaginary', *Urban Geography*, 37 (4): 572–89, <https://doi.org/10.1080/02723638.2016.1139879>.

Wiener, N. (1985), *Cybernetics: Or Control and Communication in the Animal and the Machine*, Cambridge, MA: MIT Press, 2nd edn.

Chapter 5

The Two Cartographies: A Posthumanist Approach to Geomatics Education

Siddique Motala

Introduction

This essay imagines how a pedagogy of resistance could be guided by a critical posthumanist orientation. Situated in a South African university of technology, I investigate the twin manifestations of power – *potestas* and *potentia* (restrictive and productive power respectively) – contained in a geomatics learning experience that affect the subjectification of students and educators alike. An immanent Deleuzian stance conceives of life as a process of creative power, and this helps me to explore the creative potential of storytelling as a micro-instance of pedagogical activism.

Geomatics is an umbrella term, and includes the disciplines of cartography, land surveying, geographic information systems (GIS), photogrammetry, geodesy and remote sensing. Current South African geomatics education is an extension of the old surveying education which was developed during the colonial and apartheid eras. The curriculum is overtly technicist and subtly politically loaded in a way that entrenches certain discourses and promotes specific subjectivities. Is apartheid fascism still haunting the geomatics curriculum? More than two decades after the official ending of apartheid, how would South African engineering curricula fare when asked if black lives matter?

Geomatics has been at the forefront of transdisciplinary and interdisciplinary research, so I am not arguing for transdisciplinarity in itself. Rather, I am promoting a type of transdisciplinary pedagogy that transcends the border between ethics and technology, between art and science. It seeks to find interconnections between the discursive communities of the 'hard' and 'soft' sciences. It is experimental, seeking out smooth pedagogical space among a sedimented and striated (TP) engineering curriculum that favours quantitative logic and promotes a normativity and worldview which is largely capitalist.

Cartography

For Braidotti, posthumanism is a navigational tool to map a set of material and discursive conditions, and this mapping is done by means of a cartography. This type of cartography accounts for subjects' location in space and time, and provides alternative representations in terms of *potestas* and *potentia* (Braidotti 2002). The cartography can be supplemented methodologically by reading together selected theorists (such as Deleuze, Braidotti, Barad, Haraway and Plumwood) with non-representational theory, and the critical cartographic insights of J. B. Harley. A cartographic analysis pays attention to 'micropolitical instances of activism, avoiding overarching generalizations' (Braidotti 2011: 269). The cartography is specific and is predicated on the embedded and embodied reality of the researcher.

In order to do justice to a reading of the present, there must be cognisance of the actual (what we are ceasing to be) while creatively imagining the actualisation of the virtual (what we are in the process of becoming) (Braidotti 2018a). Applying these considerations to a cartographic exploration of geomatics education in South Africa, a pertinent question is: does the current geomatics learning experience strive to offer a socially just education, or does it contribute to the perpetuation of a neo-colonial knowledge status quo? Furthermore, contexts are not only social. Surveyors are land professionals, and geomatics is intimately connected to issues of the land. The South African colonised land has resulted in the imposition of a system of land ownership, one that did not strictly exist in pre-colonial times. Advanced capitalism further exacerbates inequality by perpetuating a type of neo-apartheid spatiality. In this current Covid moment, it is clear that different students are differentially positioned with respect to the pandemic – their vulnerability to infection and chances of success are directly linked to place, history, capital and race. Additionally, the land has been altered by the effects of humankind on a planetary scale. Global warming affects South Africa in very specific ways – in Cape Town, we have recently experienced the worst drought in recorded history, and the scarcity of water is being touted as 'the new normal'.

Ethical accountability in the production of materialist cartographies can be supported methodologically by the 'politics of location' or 'situated and accountable knowledge practice' (Braidotti 2013: 51). A posthumanist analysis requires that I report on things from a standpoint, which is the space and time that I inhabit currently, that is, under the aegis of nomadic subjectivity, a difficult task, as the nomad is dynamic, multilayered, non-unitary, and situated within an ever-changing environment. At the present moment, the changing online environment should also be considered, with the evident proliferation of fake news and microfascisms. The cartography aims at unearthing the complexity, non-linearity, multilayered-ness and internally contradictory nature of the phenomenon under investigation, while situating it within an advanced capitalist society that multiplies difference for the purposes of maximising profit.

A pedagogy inspired by a posthumanist ethic is radically open to the future, situated, relational, affective and promotes active experimentation (Massey 2005; Braidotti 2018b). My pedagogy places emphasis on storytelling, counter-mapping and boundaries. The boundary is central to geomatics epistemology. Additionally, it is ubiquitous and pervasive in most aspects of culture. Geomatics, in general, creates hard boundaries, while a relational or Deleuzian ontology critiques the purpose and effect of these and other boundaries. A becoming is about the in-between spaces. Following a critical posthumanist path, I reterritorialise the boundary and insert it back into geomatics education via stories, focusing on how boundaries are transitory, permeable and topological. I also analyse actual boundaries that were created by geomatics practitioners – I trouble the notion of these boundaries being fixed, static or permanent.

A Posthumanist Pedagogy

Braidotti (2013) believes that critical posthumanism can help to facilitate responsible education in various ways. First, it can help in creating communities of learning that look like the society they reflect, serve and help to construct. There is an urgent need to transform the skewed demographic profile of success at South African universities. Additionally, there need to be concerted efforts to decolonise the curriculum to make it more accessible, interesting and relevant for local students (Badat 2015). Secondly, critical posthumanism can help to produce relevant knowledge 'that is attuned to basic principles of social justice, the respect for human decency and diversity, the rejection of false universalisms; the affirmation of the positivity of difference; the principles of academic freedom, anti-racism, openness to others and conviviality' (Braidotti 2013: 11).

Taking a monistic, Spinozist stance would require a focus on the powers of affirmation. Affirmative affects result in the relations between bodies being strengthened, sped up and enhanced. These are what Spinoza referred to as joyful passions, and serve as the counterpoint to sad passions that result in bodies being slowed down (S). Braidotti links these insights to the philosophy of Foucault, which sees power as being both restrictive (*potestas*) and productive (*potentia*). Power can be held in individuals or distributed across assemblages, and, being relational, can be used to produce positive or negative passions.

In the South African classroom, some students feel alienated since their knowledge is seen as less than, and a sense of shame is felt in sharing it in the same forum as privileged, Eurocentric knowledge. The shame provides an indication of the non-recognition of cultural and other knowledge of subordinate groups (Zembylas 2008). The hegemonic relations that exist in South African higher education are to the advantage of White, male and middle-class students and staff (Bozalek and Carolissen 2012). This dominant group defines the centre of the structure of the academy. Deviation from dominant norms results in large groups of students being described in terms of lack or deficit. However, movements such as #BlackLivesMatter and #RhodesMustFall can challenge these assumptions and inspire new pedagogies which activate joyful passions. A pedagogy of resistance must be attuned to silence – the silence on ethics in the geomatics curriculum, the silence of subjugated knowledge in South African society, and the silence of the environment in the time of the Anthropocene.

For centuries, oral storytelling has been the dominant method of transmitting cultural information for many Southern African indigenous groups. In South African higher education, storytelling has been reported as being an effective pedagogical tool, having both the ability to code discipline-specific knowledge (Motala and Musungu 2013) as well as being a space in which students engage in emotional and cognitive labour (Gachago et al. 2013). The combination of the ability of narrative to allow students to take on wider perspectives, its natural emphasis on geography and its power as a learning tool should make it particularly well suited to geomatics education. However, this is not a widespread practice and traditional engineering education is Western-centric and promotes a type of humanist interpellation. Over the years, several stories have found their way into my teaching through experimentation – in Deleuzian terms, through the search for a different image of thought (St Pierre et al. 2016). I tell stories, and then students are required to produce their own digital stories that combine maps and narrative. I mainly use stories from African history to grow a postcolonial consciousness.

Previously marginalised people are for the first time formulating 'their own narratives as subjects, producing a multiplication of discourses'

(Ferrando 2012: 12). A step towards understanding one's neighbours is listening to each other's stories, and 'story as methodology is decolonizing research' (Kovach 2009: 103). Stories are enactments, rather than just descriptions. Stories, like figurations, can assist us to imagine alternative subjectivities or realities. They can distil an otherwise complicated theory or ideology into a tangible, understandable product. 'We also live with each other in the flesh in ways not exhausted by our ideologies. Stories are much bigger than ideologies. In that is our hope' (Haraway 2003: 17). Haraway advocates for situated storytelling as a means of knowledge creation. She stresses the sympoietic nature of becoming-with as an important navigational tool. Rather than focusing on reconciliation or restoration, she focuses more modestly on getting on together, on partial recuperation. Stories help in this regard, but they can go even further, and fulfil the posthuman possibility of being both a navigational and analytical tool.

A Story from the South/A Cartography of Cartography

What follows is a shortened version of a story I tell in class. The story is shown in italics, and is iteratively co-produced by myself, students and GIS technology.

In 1657 Pieter Potter is asked by Jan van Riebeeck (the first Dutch commander of the Cape) to map the locations of the farms of the first free burghers. Although Potter is acknowledged to be the first Western surveyor who conducted work in South Africa, he actually had no technical training other than as an artist.

At the time, this artist/scientist boundary crossing was not unnatural, as it was prior to what would be called the 'cartographic reformation' by some historians of cartography, a period of approximately one hundred years (between 1670 and 1770) when cartography progressed from being recognised as an art to a science (Edney 2011). It is only over the last fifty years or so that a reconvergence between art and mapping has been seen. This destabilisation of the 'new' practice of cartography-as-science and the reinsertion of the 'old' art back into cartography runs counter to the supposed march of cartographic progress. This was not forward progress, as the excision of art helped to mask ethical aspects. The dropping of art corresponded with the acceleration of the impact and reach of technology and computerised cartography. The cartographic reformation saw the decline in decorative artistry on maps, usually produced by single skilled craftsmen. This was replaced by neutral white space, produced as a result of large-scale institutional surveys, using increasingly specialised instrumentation. Thus the cartographer went from being able to express themselves artistically to being part of a specialised production line. Today, national mapping agencies produce anonymous, standardised mapping. The scientific nature of maps helps to give them ideological legitimacy.

The land was allocated along the banks of the Liesbeeck River, so as to provide a water source. This part of the Cape Peninsula was visited by some of the indigenous Khoi tribes, as part of their annual migratory routes.

Maps of the early demography of Southern Africa at the time of the arrival of Europeans (mid-1600s) show the presence of the Khoi in different ways. The vast majority of the maps simply ignore their presence. Figure 5.1 is illustrative of this. It is a map that focuses on the land ownership of the Dutch. Containing no information about any indigenous people at all, such maps effectively erased their presence and normalised the idea of the land being empty and unconquered – *terra nullius*. Other maps show their dwellings in fixed positions, such as the 'Village de Hottentots' shown at the bottom right of an early map of Table Bay (Figure 5.2).

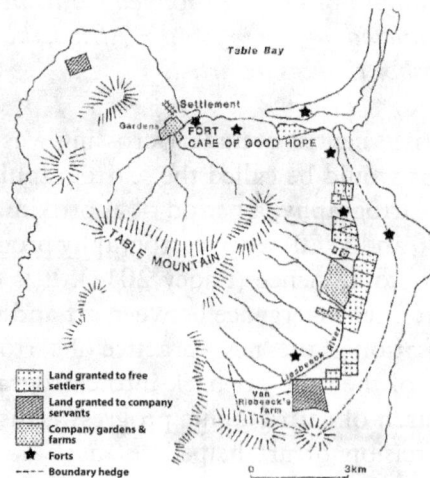

Figure 5.1 Locations of the first free burgher farms at the Cape.
Source: Christopher 1994: 14.

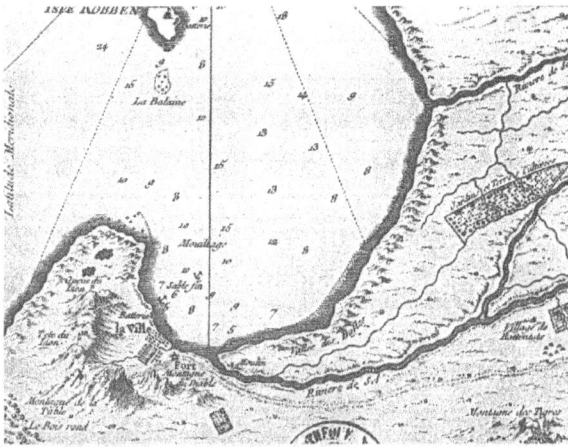

Figure 5.2 *Carte de la baye de la Table* (map of Table Bay).
Source: Glatigny, Estelle and Viljoen 2008: 309.

Figures 5.1 and 5.2 are single static maps and hence limited in their capacity to convey spatio-temporal information, such as the dynamic positions of Khoi tribes. The movement and interconnections of the Khoi cannot be inferred from a static map. Static maps or animated mapping (or indeed any other kind of mapping) have limitations as to what they can represent (Dawood and Motala 2015). The maps above are ostensibly intended to communicate spatial information on specific themes, such as Dutch land ownership or the topography of the Cape. While doing this, the mapping also participates in the creation of socio-material reality, which in this case was the creation of colonial South Africa. This link between the map as representation and the conception, articulation and structuring of the human world according to hegemonic social relations was one of J. B. Harley's major insights (Harley 1989; 1990; 2009).

The first Westerners who came into contact with the Khoi were astonished by their relationship with the land – it was linked to land use, rather than property, and boundaries would evolve according to the changing seasons. These fluid boundaries, communal living spaces, non-hierarchical inter-tribal relationships and nomadic wanderings were seen as savage and backward. A shift in this attitude is seen in the works of Deleuze and Guattari (TP) and Braidotti (2006).

Guided by the Christian morals of the time, Van Riebeeck felt responsible for helping to 'civilise' the Khoi and introduce them to the Christian way of life. This would be done effectively by conditioning Khoi children. Krotoa was about ten years old when she was taken into the Van Riebeeck household. She was renamed Eva, learned how to speak Dutch and adopted Christianity. She maintained contact with her people and was very useful to Van Riebeeck, who used her as an interpreter and negotiator. She helped him to develop a good relationship with the Khoi, who were able to provide cattle to the Dutch. Over time, Krotoa found herself in a difficult position. She was not fully accepted in Dutch society, and her own people distrusted her because she was viewed as a traitor when the Dutch–Khoi relations soured.

Following Plumwood (1993), various dualisms can be observed in the story and in the cartographic depictions of the Khoi. For example, civilised/uncivilised, Black/White and nature/culture are dualisms which are maintained by the characteristics of backgrounding (or denial), radical exclusion (hyperseparation), instrumentalism (objectification) and homogenisation (stereotyping). The Dutch masters depended on the land and the Khoi for their survival, yet focused attention away from the dependency through their mapping (backgrounding). The early settlers were particularly vulnerable and dependent on the Khoi for their supply of cattle. The Khoi were seen as a means to an end (instrumentalism) – their value was denied and subsumed under that of the colonisers. The Dutch went to great lengths to forge cordial relationships with the Khoi to secure their supply of cattle, such as the 'taming' of the 'savage' Krotoa. Their Christian morality also justified the objectification and homogenisation of the Khoi.

Although the representation of the locations of the Khoi on old colonial maps was varied, and the Khoi were allowed a degree of 'presence' on these maps, there is no doubt that the mapping assisted in the dispossession, removal or extermination of the indigenous people. The dominated Khoi are stereotyped in their depiction, and all internal differences (such as the difference between clans) are ignored – this is homogenisation. For example, the 'Village de Hottentots' (Figure 5.2) is iconic in that all Khoi settlements were depicted as simplified circular villages, ignoring any local variances. The nomadic Khoi's relationship to the land was viewed as primitive by the Dutch, and the discourse of the Dutch (including the mapping) normalised the hierarchy of human worth. By the logic of the Dutch, land ownership was superior to the agrarian and nomadic Khoi relationships. Most of the early maps, such as Pieter Potter's (similar to Figure 5.1), focus attention on the ownership of land by Whites, and omit the Khoi. This exhibits the dualistic mechanism of radical exclusion, in which the differences between cultures were magnified to create maximum separation, and naturalised the Dutch domination of the Khoi. Over time this culminated in the horrendous extermination of much of the Khoi and San population. Years later, Khoi and San were treated as sub-human by the European settlers, who were granted licences to kill the indigenous people who trespassed on their land. Associated with animals, Black bodies were given less worth than the land on which they were subjugated and killed.

Prior to Pieter Potter's surveying, the land of the Cape was considered to be the commonwealth of all the Khoi, regardless of tribal membership. Through his surveying, Potter marked the land and changed the way it would be seen and used. This would also lead to indelible changes in fauna and flora. The mapping played a part in the successful normalisation of colonisation. Every cartographic act was a performance intended to comply with, and propagate, specific social orders. These were Cartesian cuts that were enacted by surveyors or cartographers, separating objects of inquiry from subjects of empire. The ethics of the actions of surveyors are often dictated to them by the imperatives of their masters. For Pieter Potter, it was the VOC (Dutch East India Company) and Jan Van Riebeeck. For modern surveyors, it is the companies they work for, the allied professions that employ their services or others who have the economic power to influence land development. Modern-day surveyors are complicit in upholding dominant discourses, and as seen in South Africa, neo-apartheid spatiality. In large projects, surveyors work as part of large multi-disciplinary teams, as they might have during colonial times. Due to specialisation and a 'chain of command' of sorts, surveyors are made to feel that they do not have significant influence in ethical decision making. This distance between geomatics practitioners and ethics (as prescribed to them by the geomatics education assemblage) has an influence on their subjectification.

The settlement thus led to conflict, and Van Riebeeck decided to erect a line of defences, comprising forts, a strong wooden fence, and a line of wild almond trees comprising a boundary hedge. These were intended to keep out the Khoi, and thereafter transformed their nomadic wanderings. This boundary can still be observed physically – a small part of the hedge is alive in the Kirstenbosch Botanical Gardens. Figuratively, one can say that the whole hedge is still alive if one zooms out and looks at the map of the demography of Cape Town.

Figure 5.3 is a dot density map, showing the populations by race group. One purple dot = 100 White people, one yellow dot = 100 Coloured people, one green dot = 100 Black people and one red dot = 100 Indian people. The Liesbeeck River is shown as a light blue line, and the original location of the boundary hedge is shown as a red line. For a colour version of this map, see Motala (2020). One can see that the location of the original hedge is close to the apartheid boundary between White and Coloured areas, which is largely still in place in post-apartheid Cape Town.

The location of Van Riebeeck's hedge haunts the descendants of the first conflict. The boundary between settler and native, White and Black gets iteratively materialised. While public discourse shows a conscious effort towards post-apartheid land reform, most of the race-based spatial boundaries still exist and are propagated in South African cities and towns. 'Hauntology', a term coined by Derrida (1994) and used by Barad (2010; 2017), is about traces of the past that haunt the present and future. Barad advises us of the importance of being attuned to silence – she says that each worldly entanglement matters 'not just for what comes to matter but what is constitutively excluded from mattering in order for particular materializations to occur' (Juelskjær and Schwennesen 2012: 21). Harley

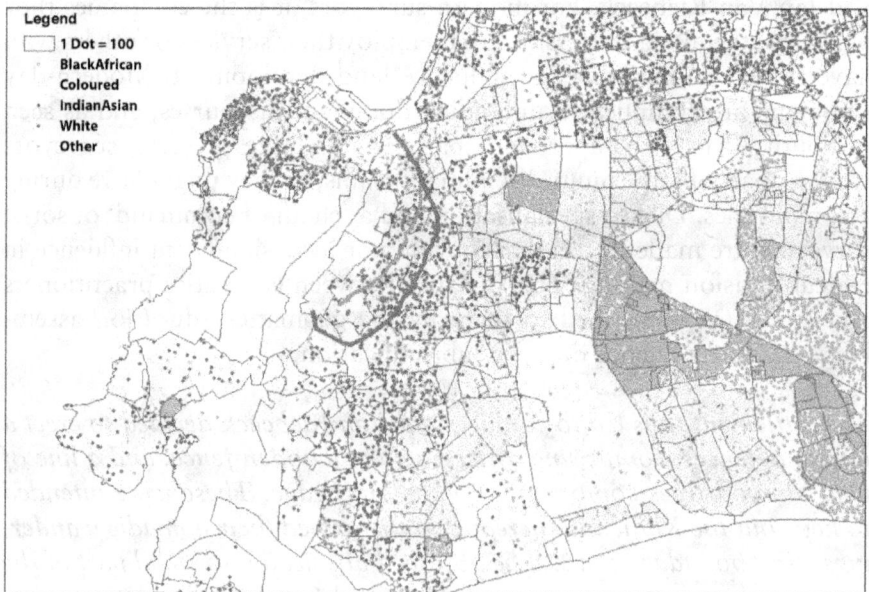

Figure 5.3 Location of Van Riebeeck's boundary overlaid on a dot density map.

notes that maps can speak volumes by their silence. Like Plumwood (1993), Spivak (1996), Braidotti (2006) and Barad (2017), he points out that silencing is an important aspect to note, so as to learn about the Other. Urban maps, for example, are not at the human scale and do not contain information about the quality of human life – the differential between the quality of White life and the life of others in South Africa is stark. Furthermore, mapping as we know it follows the Western paradigm of placing boundaries around 'resources'. These resources included native people, who were viewed as raw material to be exploited (Mbembe 2001). Non-representational theory investigates how bodies and subjects are actualised through their relationship with the world (Anderson and Harrison 2010). In this view, the world is not an inert backdrop of things, but is part of our fabric, as we are part of its fabric. Harley's point was about the qualitative shortcomings of maps in describing the human experience. A Deleuzian type of geography is one where geographers pay attention to 'a world of virtualities, singularities, and intensities, a world they are tempted to describe as haunted' (Buchanan and Lambert 2005: 9). Yet Buchanan and Lambert also acknowledge that a balance is needed between the Western mapping view and a Deleuzian geography, a balance between strata and lines of flight.

Critical cartography, like other critical practices, calls into question the claim by cartographers that cartography is a science (Crampton 2010). The development of cartography is closely linked to improvements in surveying and mapping instrumentation, and most importantly, accuracy. Accuracy became the primary metric by which progress in cartography was measured (Harley and Woodward 1987), and still carries much weight in geomatics educational practice. Accuracy is so important that it has become entwined with the geomatics conception of ethics (Crampton 1995). Critical cartography examines the relationship between knowledge and power, and in particular, how cartographers (often unwittingly) reinforce hegemonies by propagating powerful knowledge. Harley's insights show us that knowledge creation in mapping is far from objective. The fact that mapping is based on the scientific method makes map users believe that maps are value-free. Harley shows us the impossibility of an 'objective' map, as maps, by their very nature, are more than communicational and informational. This insight resonates with Deleuze and Guattari's argument in their chapter on the postulates of linguistics in *A Thousand Plateaus*. When cartographers internalise this supposed objectivity, the subjectivity that follows further entrenches humanism. There is an ontological insertion into geomatics of the Western subject via the rational scientific method.

Harley points out that the current climate of thought in cartography has not caught up with the complexities of modernity (which require, for example, an appreciation of ethics in cartography) and cartographers are prisoners of their own past (Harley 1989). This is because of the over-reliance on 'scientific' or 'objective' knowledge, and cartographers' unwillingness to attempt an epistemological shift in their interpretation of the nature of cartography. Read with Braidotti (2013), a troubling of the deference to the authority of the past is needed. Deleuze points out that the essence of beings should not be taken for granted, but must be appreciated in terms of the historical processes that helped to produce them (DeLanda 2006). Harley claims that cartographers' understanding of maps is not subtle enough for the realities of this increasingly complex world. I agree with this premise, and suggest that a posthumanist injection of *potentia* could benefit the inculcation of a different sensibility in engineering students. A different, Deleuzian map is required – one that is 'oriented toward an experimentation in contact with the real' (TP, 12).

For Harley, provoking self-criticism was the point of intellectual work in cartography. Other than shifting the sensibilities and practices of cartographers, such intellectual labour could 'contribute not only to a new richness in historical studies but also toward an enhanced social awareness that mapping must surely be "for people rather than for Man"' (Harley 1990: 2). Reading this quote with Braidotti, one can appreciate his anti-humanist stance, but one can also identify a deep anthropocentrism, as he cannot conceive of the value of mapping outside of humanity. Posthumanism can help to trouble his anthropocentric thought further. In order to accomplish this, a geo-centred sensibility is required. This sensibility envisages subjectivity at a global level, but also sees technology as an unbounded phenomenon and being as intimate to us as the nature we are part of. This is a difficult task, as it requires a decentring of the human subject. Braidotti's strategy of zoë-centred egalitarianism flattens the species hierarchy and takes seriously the health of the land. Geomatics practitioners thus need to ask: how can we relate differently to the land that we (and our technologies) are surveying with such accuracy? Is there a way to trouble our deeply ingrained humanism and anthropocentrism to listen to the land? With regard to the former (our humanism), Harley's anti-authoritarian insights can help. With regard to the latter, our ethics need a rethink in order to achieve this. The silence of geomatics towards the environment requires a more subtle understanding.

As a starting point, it should be noted that geomatics education is inherently non-anthropocentric. This is because much of geomatics theory is based on scientific principles that are grounded in the natural, mathematical and physical sciences. The dominant human (Anthropos) does not feature in many of the problems that geomatics practitioners and students are required to solve. Calculating coordinates of points, monitoring movements of the earth's surface, or producing a map of a piece of land do not seem to be human-centred activities. Furthermore, surveyors spend much time outdoors, involved in activities that bring them closer to the natural environment than many other professions. The issue is that the more insidious and linked problem, namely humanism, is masked by a profession that portrays itself, rather romantically, as being at one with nature.

The Subject of Geomatics

The figure of the surveyor arose out of a contingent array of historical processes. In the early colonial years, the need to mark, own and control access to land saw Pieter Potter produce the maps that he is famous for. The story of Van Riebeeck's hedge helps to trace some important entanglements related to colonialism, war, fascist apartheid planning, cartography and control. I cast a light on some important binaries so as to queer them at the same time. Consider the boundary hedge. The animate/inanimate and absent/present boundaries are not as clear cut as the boundary between settler and native. The hedge, although absent, was not erased in over 350 years of settlement at the Cape. It still keeps out the native in a hauntological entanglement with the land. The highlighting of the presence/absence of the hedge in my pedagogy is a cutting together/apart (Barad 2014) and a useful pedagogical/analytical device. A sensibility towards non-linear time is needed to be able to trace entanglements. Barad says: 'Travel-hopping is the embodied material labour of cutting through/undoing colonialist thinking in an attempt to come to terms with the unfathomable violences of colonialism in their specific material entanglements' (2017: 70). The spectre of the surveyor is always lurking in the shadows of boundaries that were created to keep the Others at bay (for a more complete treatment of hauntology as a pedagogy in my context, see Zembylas, Bozalek and Motala 2020).

Cartographers are more often than not passive about issues relating to ethics. Cartographic research shows practitioners to be largely pursuing excellence or innovation in technical areas (such as accuracy enhancement). Surveyors and cartographers often believe that they are 'observers', and that others (such as politicians) decide on the cartographic agenda. However, maps helped to create the myths of empire and nationalism. Harley notes that '[s]urveyors marched alongside soldiers, initially mapping for reconnaissance, then for general information, and eventually as a tool of pacification, civilization, and exploitation in the defined colonies' (Harley 2009: 132). It is into this non-innocent pedigree that student surveyors are being conditioned. Being able to come to terms with, and disidentify from, certain aspects of our shared past is important in the process of becoming. An experimental pedagogy, focusing on relationality and giving voice to the marginalised, is an exercise in becoming-minoritarian.

The 'model apartheid city' (Figure 5.4) was conceived by apartheid-era politicians with the assistance of town planners and surveyors. Surveyors helped to formalise the boundaries that have become so difficult, even in post-apartheid South Africa, to break down. Figure 5.4 is a tragic example of how the map, as a socially constructed image, went on to destroy lives and land. It was used as the reference for the ideal spatial arrangement of the apartheid city. Note how the primary factor

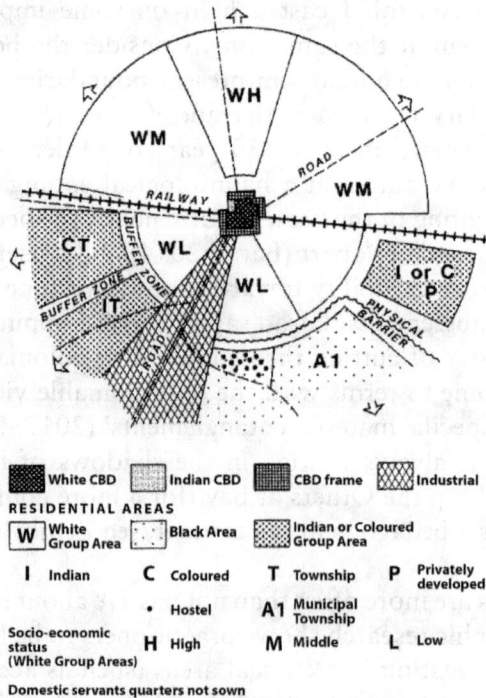

Figure 5.4 The model apartheid city. Source: Christopher 1994: 107.

that determined location was race. White group areas were separated from all other group areas by means of barriers such as railway lines or industrial areas. The map served as the blueprint for cities and towns in South Africa and was effectively and violently implemented. Note that there was maximum separation between Whites of 'high' socio-economic status and Blacks – the entanglement of race and economic status was formalised. Backgrounding was used to deny the reliance of the White population on Black labour. The map tellingly states 'Domestic servants' quarters not shown'. The spatial arrangement of the 'lower' groups in relation to the White groups is an example of instrumentalism, where the lower groups are incorporated into the fabric of the apartheid city as objects of production. Additionally, all lower groups are homogenised into their group areas, disregarding any internal differences.

Stories for *potentia*

The story that I have used in this chapter serves multiple purposes. It showcases my pedagogical approach, it is used to uncover and trouble dualisms, it is used as a device to forge connections across difference, and it critiques certain power structures while at the same time beginning to affirmatively transform the critique. The last point is achieved by, for example, critiquing the colonial power structures of the seventeenth century, while at the same time giving recognition to the subjugated voices of that period. It helps to reconstitute subjects (including myself, students and the characters in the stories) by tapping into *potentia*. Additionally, the story provides an exemplar of an affirmative combination of storytelling, counter-mapping and movement across boundaries. It is used to grow an awareness of alternative points of view and promotes dialogue. Following Braidotti (2006), my ethical practice involves an inquiry into relationships with alterity.

The story so far highlights one aspect of my pedagogical practice, namely my telling of stories. The other involves a more substantial shift of power relations. In response to the critique elicited by my stories, I seek out affirmative horizons of hope through boundary crossing of power relations. I convert the *potestas* contained in the geomatics curriculum into *potentia* by handing some of the power of pedagogy over to my students. This is done by allowing students to produce their own stories.[1]

Conclusion: What Was Produced?

The encounter between posthumanism, geomatics and storytelling is productive, and demonstrates a resistance to the interpellative power of *potestas*. It also puts the two cartographies of geomatics and posthumanism in conversation with each other.

Cartographers' over-reliance on 'scientific' or 'objective' knowledge blinds them to ethical issues. There is an overtly binary conception of cartography, which has over time come to be associated more with 'science' than 'art'. In geomatics and its related family of professions (for example, civil engineering, architecture and town planning), professional ethics is dominant and is associated with individuality, reliability, professional behaviour, legality and, most importantly for surveyors, accuracy. Each of these professionals might take care of their narrow ethical responsibilities (guided by professional ethics and focusing on legal and administrative compliance), but a more holistic view is lacking. It is not adequate to take the molecular view of looking at the details only. Even traditional oppositional strategies, such as feminism and socialism, have been criticised by Haraway for their rigidity and for their inability to reconcile contradictory standpoints: 'The political struggle is to see from both perspectives at once because each reveals both dominations and possibilities unimaginable from the other vantage point. Single vision produces worse illusions than double vision or many-headed monsters' (Haraway 1991: 154).

In cartography, the deep faith in representationalism emerges from the Cartesian worldview that separates subjects and objects, world and representation. This view is contested within the ambit of non-representational theory and critical cartography. Maps are not representations of the world 'out there'; rather, they help to construct the world.

It should be noted that Deleuze's ideas about cartography were always changing, and there are subtle differences between his writings, although maps and tracings primarily appear in his work on psychoanalysis or linguistics. In *A Thousand Plateaus*, the tracing is likened to arborescent, tree logic, while the map is akin to the rhizome. In *Essays Critical and Clinical*, he contrasts the cartographic with the archaeological. The archaeological approach, like the tracing, seeks out and confirms a dominant reality. In both, however, the map is experimental, non-hierarchical and in opposition to long-term sedimentation. Deleuze and Guattari do not fall into the trap of creating a dualism between maps and tracings: 'Have we not, however, reverted to a simple dualism by contrasting maps to tracings, as good and bad sides? Is it not of the essence of the map to be traceable?' (TP, 13). This conception of mapping is more aligned with Thrift's (2008) tenets of non-representational theory than traditional geomatics. Non-representational theory is about movement, it is anti-biographical, concerned with practice, and is experimental. Indeed, many non-representational theorists draw heavily on the work of Deleuze and Guattari (Vannini 2015).

My pedagogical activism, in the form of a storytelling intervention, is guided by my ethical stance and aligned with critical posthumanism. This alludes to the knowing-in-being ethico-onto-epistemology that is argued for by new materialists (van der Tuin 2014), which is similar to what post-qualitative researchers describe as a 'zig-zagging' between theory and practice (Jackson and Mazzei 2012; Lather 2016). The posthuman is, for Braidotti, 'both a genealogical and navigational tool' (2013: 5). This allows for zig-zagging not just between theory and practice as mentioned above, but also between critique and affirmation. This is a characteristic of new materialist theory that is allowed for in part by its dynamic conception of time. As Braidotti suggests, it is useful to be in an experimental mode and keep the 'process flowing and multifocused, refusing to both monumentalize the past and fetishize the future' (2014: 239). Seen as an apparatus, the storytelling intervention is 'constituted through particular practices that are perpetually open to rearrangements, rearticulations, and other reworkings' (Barad 2007: 170). Movement is important.

Boundaries are seen by surveyors as mostly static and permanent. However, boundaries are also inspiration for anti-dualist remedies, as they can be porous, fluid or move across space and time. Boundaries are markers of situatedness. My Cape Town stories are aimed at producing socially relevant knowledge while affirming the positivity of difference. Deterritorialising the boundaries of traditional maps, my pedagogy aims to expose the enclosure of old modes of thought (especially dualistic thought). For example, student stories that foreground subjugated knowledges resist incorporation by rediscovering a story for the underside. With a Deleuzian sensibility, new and fluid boundaries are actualised by collective experimentation. Boundaries, like the figurations of Haraway, have inherited non-innocent pasts that can be read diffractively (Sehgal 2014) for an affirmative transformation to take place. In these violent times, students are differentially marked by the learning experiences imposed on them, and this particular experience leaves a different type of mark on their bodies.

Acknowledgement

This work is based on research supported in part by the National Research Foundation of South Africa (Grant Number: 120845).

Note

1. I am unable to adequately report, due to space constraints, on the findings of the student storytelling intervention that I have been facilitating over the past few years. See Motala (2017) for more detail on the intervention and some analysis of student stories.

References

Anderson, B., and P. Harrison (eds) (2010), *Taking-Place: Non-Representational Theories and Geography*, Farnham: Ashgate.

Badat, S. (2015), 'Deciphering the Meanings and Explaining the South African Higher Education Student Protests of 2015–16', *Pax Academia: African Journal of Academic Freedom*, 1–2: 71–106.

Barad, K. (2007), *Meeting the Universe Halfway: Quantum Physics and the Entanglement of Matter and Meaning*, Durham, NC: Duke University Press.

Barad, K. (2010), 'Quantum Entanglements and Hauntological Relations of Inheritance: Dis/Continuities, SpaceTime Enfoldings, and Justice-to-Come', *Derrida Today*, 3 (2): 240–68.

Barad, K. (2014), 'Diffracting Diffraction: Cutting Together-Apart', *Parallax*, 20 (3): 168–87.

Barad, K. (2017), 'Troubling Time/s and Ecologies of Nothingness: Re-Turning, Re-Membering, and Facing the Incalculable', *New Formations*, 92: 56–86.

Bozalek, V., and R. Carolissen (2012), 'The Potential of Critical Feminist Citizenship Frameworks for Citizenship and Social Justice in Higher Education', *Perspectives in Education*, 30 (4): 9–18.

Braidotti, R. (2002), *Metamorphoses: Towards a Materialist Theory of Becoming*, Cambridge: Polity.

Braidotti, R. (2006), *Transpositions: On Nomadic Ethics*, Cambridge: Polity.

Braidotti, R. (2011), *Nomadic Theory: The Portable Rosi Braidotti*, New York: Columbia University Press.

Braidotti, R. (2013), *The Posthuman*, New York: Polity.

Braidotti, R. (2014), 'The Untimely', in B. Blaagard and I. van der Tuin (eds), *The Subject of Rosi Braidotti: Politics and Concepts*, London: Bloomsbury, pp. 227–50.

Braidotti, R. (2018a), 'A Theoretical Framework for the Critical Posthumanities', *Theory, Culture & Society*, 36 (6): 1–31, <https://doi.org/10.1177/0263276418771486>.

Braidotti, R. (2018b), 'Foreword', in V. Bozalek, R. Braidotti, M. Zembylas and T. Shefer (eds), *Socially Just Pedagogies in Higher Education: Critical Posthumanist and New Feminist Materialist Perspectives*, London: Bloomsbury, pp. xiii–xxvii.

Buchanan, I., and G. Lambert (2005), 'Introduction', in I. Buchanan and G. Lambert (eds), *Deleuze and Space*, Edinburgh: Edinburgh University Press, pp. 1–15.

Christopher, A. J. (1994), *The Atlas of Apartheid*, London: Routledge.

Crampton, J. W. (1995), 'The Ethics of GIS', *Cartography and Geographic Information Science*, 22 (1): 84–9.

Crampton, J. W. (2010), *Mapping: A Critical Introduction to Cartography and GIS*, Chichester: John Wiley.

Dawood, N., and S. Motala (2015), 'Evaluating an Animated and Static Time Series Map of District Six : A Visual and Cognitive Approach', *South African Journal of Geomatics*, 4 (3): 189–97.

DeLanda, M. (2006), *A New Philosophy of Society*, New York: Continuum.

Derrida, J. (1994), *Spectres of Marx: The State of the Debt, the Work of Mourning and the New International*, trans. Peggy Kamuf, New York: Routledge.

Edney, M. H. (2011), 'Cartography Without "Progress": Reinterpreting the Nature and Historical Development of Map Making', in M. Dodge (ed.), *Classics in Cartography: Reflections on Influential Articles from Cartographica*, Chichester: Wiley-Blackwell, pp. 305–29.

Ferrando, F. (2012), 'Towards A Posthumanist Methodology. A Statement', *Frame: Journal for Literary Studies*, 25 (1): 9–18.

Gachago, D., et al. (2013), 'Journeys across Difference: Pre-Service Teacher Education Students' Perceptions of a Pedagogy of Discomfort in a Digital Storytelling Project in South Africa', *Critical Studies in Teaching and Learning*, 1: 22–52.

Glatigny, P. D., et al. (2008), 'Inter Se Nulli Fines: Representations of the Presence of the Khoikhoi in Early Colonial Maps of the Cape of Good Hope', *South African Journal of Art History*, 23 (1): 301–17.

Haraway, D. (1991), *Simians, Cyborgs, and Women: The Reinvention of Nature*, New York: Routledge.

Haraway, D. (2003), *The Companion Species Manifesto: Dogs, People, and Significant Otherness*, Chicago: Prickly Paradigm Press.

Harley, J. B. (1989), 'Deconstructing the Map', *Cartographica*, 26 (2): 1–20.

Harley, J. B. (1990), 'Cartography, Ethics and Social Theory', *Cartographica*, 27 (2): 1–23.

Harley, J. B. (2009), 'Maps, Knowledge, and Power', in G. Henderson and M. Waterstone (eds), *Geographic Thought: A Praxis Perspective*, Abingdon: Routledge, pp. 129–48.

Harley, J. B., and D. Woodward (eds) (1987), *The History of Cartography*, Chicago: University of Chicago Press.

Jackson, A. Y., and L. A. Mazzei (2012), *Thinking with Theory in Qualitative Research*, Abingdon: Routledge.

Juelskjær, M., and N. Schwennesen (2012), 'Intra-Active Entanglements – An Interview with Karen Barad', *Kvinder, Køen Og Forskning*, 12: 10–23.

Kovach, M. (2009), *Indigenous Methodologies: Characteristics, Conversations and Contexts*, Toronto: University of Toronto Press.

Lather, P. (2016), 'Killing the Mother? Butler after Barad in Feminist (Post) Qualitative Research', in A. B. Reinertsen (ed.), *Becoming Earth: A Post Human Turn in Educational Discourse Collapsing Nature/Culture Divides*, Rotterdam: Sense Publishers, pp. 21–30.

Massey, D. (2005), *For Space*, London: Sage.

Mbembe, A. (2001), *On the Postcolony*, Berkeley: University of California Press.

Motala, S. (2017), 'In/between Science and Art: Posthumanist Ruminations on Geomatics Education', *Proceedings of the Fourth Biennial Conference of the South African Society for Engineering Education*, Cape Town, 14–15 June, South African Society for Engineering Education, pp. 194–204.

Motala, S. (2020), 'A Place-based response to Fikile Nxumalo', Critical Studies in Teaching and Learning (CriSTaL), 8(1): 50–59.

Motala, S., and K. Musungu (2013), 'Once upon a Place: Storytelling in GIS Education', in *13th SGEM GeoConference on Informatics, Geoinformatics and Remote Sensing*, vol. 1, International Multidisciplinary Scientific GeoConference SGEM2013, Albena, Bulgaria, 16–22 June, STEF92 Technology, pp. 821–8.

Plumwood, V. (1993), *Feminism and the Mastery of Nature*, Abingdon: Routledge.

Sehgal, M. (2014), 'Diffractive Propositions: Reading Alfred North Whitehead with Donna Haraway and Karen Barad', *Parallax*, 20 (3): 188–201.

Spivak, G. C. (1996), *The Spivak Reader: Selected Works of Gayatri Chakravorty Spivak*, ed. D. Landry and G. MacLean, New York: Routledge.

St Pierre, E. A., A. Y. Jackson and L. A. Mazzei (2016), 'New Empiricisms and New Materialisms: Conditions for New Inquiry', *Cultural Studies – Critical Methodologies*, 16 (2): 99–110.

Thrift, N. (2008), *Non-representational Theory: Space/Politics/Affect*, Abingdon: Routledge.

van der Tuin, I. (2014), 'Diffraction as a Methodology for Feminist Onto-Epistemology: On Encountering Chantal Chawaf and Posthuman Interpellation', *Parallax*, 20 (3): 231–44.

Vannini, P. (ed.) (2015), *Non-Representational Methodologies: Re-Envisioning Research*, New York: Routledge.

Zembylas, M. (2008), 'The Politics of Shame in Intercultural Education', *Education, Citizenship and Social Justice*, 3 (3): 263–80.

Zembylas, M., V. Bozalek and S. Motala (2020), 'A Pedagogy of Hauntology: Decolonizing the Curriculum with GIS', *Capacious*, 2 (1–2): 26–48.

Chapter 6

The Theatre of Everyday Debt-Cruelty: The Enfleshed Threat, Missing People and the Unbearable Strange Terrorist Machine

Shiva Zarabadi

A debt system or territorial representation: a voice that speaks or intones, a sign marked in bare flesh, an eye that extracts enjoyment from the pain . . . a savage triangle forming a territory of resonance and retention, a theatre of cruelty that implies the triple independence of the articulated voice, the graphic hand, and the appreciative eye. (AO, 185)

Introduction

In this chapter, I map the cynical flow of threat codes by considering the savage triangle of terrorism and counter-terrorism as a strange 'despotic machine' (AO, 198), threat as 'infinite debt' (AO, 217) and Muslim schoolgirls as 'missing people' (Braidotti 2018). Building on Seigworth, I ontologise the threat (of terrorism/counter-terrorism) as new 'lived socialities of debt' (Seigworth 2016: 16) to argue that the cynical over-coding (AO, 198) of threat in its 'new alliance and direct filiation' (AO, 223) with terrorism and counter-terrorism de-/reterritorialises Muslim schoolgirls into the affective and material racialising relations of indebtedness. I explore how threat can be worn as a 'debt-garment' (Seigworth 2016), how living-with-threat weaves through and between human and more-than-human bodies gradually and continuously altering the atmosphere of existence; as a garment it can be worn loosely or tightly, but cannot be easily got rid of (Seigworth 2016: 15–16). I follow threat as it is experienced by participants in my PhD research, in their everyday, ordinary, walking through London's Underground, then into university spaces, teaching halls and conferences. We walk and map our entanglements with threat and the terrorism capitalist-machine. Text boxes and images throughout the chapter show another layer of mapping the thinking, feeling, becoming with threat.

The Infinite Debt and the Terrorism Capitalist-machine

The Prevent policy as 'the appreciative eye' (AO, 185) of the terrorism capitalist-machine has extended its 'graphic hand' (AO, 185) into UK schools and students' lived, embodied and embedded experiences. As an anti-radicalisation duty and a security imperative enforced in UK schools (since 1 July 2015), it obliges teachers and school staff to be vigilant for signs of, or potentiality towards, extremism in students (HM Government 2021) and, if deemed necessary, to refer them to Channel.[1] The aim of the government's Prevent strategy is to disrupt what it believes to be a 'process of radicalisation' by strategically identifying and capturing 'would-be' terrorists at the beginning of this process, and rooting out extremism from its inception (HM Government 2021; Kundnani 2012).[2] According to this duty, it is Muslim students' views and ideas that are being monitored by schools, and not their actions. British-Bangladeshi Farah (Year 12), one of the Muslim participants in my PhD research, says, 'It's not only you have to be careful what you are saying, but you have to be careful with who you are now.' Since the biggest physical and ideological threat is posed by what are defined as radical 'Islamist' groups, Muslim students are considered prime suspects (Saeed 2017: 218); however, in a later review of the policy the government included right-wing extremism to ease complaints over the targeting of Muslim students.

The Muslim not-yet terrorists, the would-be terrorists and the risky racialised others, as 'missing people' (Braidotti 2018: 21), are one component of the virtual abstract terrorism capitalist-machine that has become affiliated to all dimensions of our ecologies of belonging: environmental, socio-economic, psychic (TE) and temporal. Counter-terrorism in general and the Prevent policy in particular, as a new assembled border-crossing, not only actualises new knowledge of Muslim 'missing people'[3] (Braidotti 2018: 19) but also attunes the public to a kind of 'thinking security' (Zarabadi and Ringrose 2018a) that is deeply entangled with our ordinary, everyday practices. In 'the affective atmosphere' (Anderson 2009) that counter-terrorism and the Prevent policy enable, threat becomes a living affective connection that endures, forms and intensifies bodies.

The obviousness, intertwined with the ordinariness, of thinking security silences some of the discursive, affective and material relations of threat. For instance, in the advertisement for the anti-terrorist hotline (Figure 6.1), the 'nothing, but' emphasises the 'thin air' (Tonstad 2016: 440) out of which threat and fear emerge, playing into the obviousness and ordinariness of thinking security, materialising the indebtedness of

Figure 6.1 Anti-terrorist hotline poster released by the National Counter Terrorism Security Office, 2017.

us all to fascist counter-terrorism, 'a forced, chosen, willed, hoped-for, feared indebtedness' (Tonstad 2016: 437).

As a new affiliated component to capitalist 'debt-mediated lives' (Deville and Seigworth 2015: 621), threat embraces, flows, lives and moves alongside human and more-than-human collective moments, movements and 'affectual materialities' (Deville and Seigworth 2015: 623). The relationship of the threat (of terrorism) to debt is that of 'the with and for' (Halberstam 2013: 11), which suggests how to be with and for in coalition, in embedded and embodied alliance with what I call threat-debt as the new more than exchange relations between affective capitalism, terrorism and missing people. This new 'savage triangle' (AO, 185) forms our territorial resonances and retentions. The mutual co-constitution of threat-debt does not emerge as a threat to economic relations of exchange and to future reimbursement, but more as a socio-political and cultural threat-debt relation that is allied with terrorism, racism, colonialism, Islamophobia and Muslim missing people. Threat weaves into debt relations, becoming another 'attachment device' enabling particular 'lures for feeling' (Deville 2015) in relation to the terrorism capitalist-machine. The threat (of terrorism) attunes the atmosphere of existence in the same way that living-with-debt gradually, affectively, materially and continuously folds and grows into and between new 'contact zones' (Ahmed 2014; Stewart 2007).

In line with the infinite demands of late capitalism, Muslim missing people incarnate the infinite debt to the terrorism capitalist-machine as an infinite responsibility of an indebted self to an ongoing reimburse-ment of other people's security. Tonstad suggests that 'the responsible self is the indebted self and the indebted self is the only responsible self', something that applies to Muslim missing people; the threatening body's potential to radicalisation is 'borrowed and already owed' (2016: 437) to the terrorism capitalist-machine. As with living with debt and the politics of ceaselessly repaying the borrowed, for instance student loans and Treasury bonds, threat enables the condition for missing people's 'debt of existence' (AO, 197), that is, the continuous borrowed being and becoming as a Muslim threatening body.

Ontologising threat as debt, inspired by Seigworth's 'ontology of debt', threat can be conceptualised as 'wearing a debt-garment' (Seigworth 2016: 15), an embodied, affective and material relation of indebtedness for Muslim missing people. To repay the borrowed is to redeem those moments of threat and fear that Muslim missing people owe to another (nation). Threat as a new affiliated debt of Muslim missing people cuts across every domain, going beyond exchange to an asymmetrical creditor–debtor power relation that allows an intimately embedded and embodied debt (Lazzarato 2012; Parikka 2011; Seigworth 2016; Deville and Seigworth 2015; Allon 2015). Unlike debt, which has to be borne personally and individually (Seigworth 2016: 20), threat as the Muslim missing people's debt to the nation's security has to be affective, mate-rial and social, where threat as capital becomes the predominant or great creditor of the terrorism capitalist-machine. Threat within the compulsory transparency culture is defined as an attempt by the security state 'to flatten the object of surveillance' (Hall 2015: 127) and 'to turn the world (and the body) inside out such that there would no longer be secrets or interiors, human or geographical in which terrorists or terror-ist threats might find refuge' (2015: 127), which becomes the archetype of social relations (Lazzarato 2012: 33) that modulates, attunes, breeds, subdues, adapts and shapes humans and more-than-human becomings. Since the enforcement of the Prevent policy in schools, Muslim missing children are constantly answering questions from their schoolmates about their hijab, religion and beliefs, such as 'Do you shower with that thing [hijab] on?' (asked of Maha and Hadil, two of my PhD research participants). The continuous de-/reterritorialising jokes, comments and mockery, the thinking security logic, the constant vigilance for any signs or risks of radicalisation that is enabled by the Prevent policy, all imply the same irredeemable debt and the impossibility of the debtors, the Muslim missing people, paying and terminating this relationship. However, the infinite desire of the terrorism capitalist-machine, or the 'great creditor' (Lazzarato 2012: 7), is not to be repaid, and not to end the racialised contract, but to stay within the confines of an infinite threat-debt relationship. This is what Puar (2017: 121) calls the 'debt trap', a 'simultaneous strategy of repression and liberation, enclosure and inclusion', the desire of the debtor missing people to repay the infinite demands of the creditor, and 'the infinite accountability and guilt before capital' (Lazzarato 2012: 7).

To materialise how threat moves and makes, I have walked with different groups of people in different spaces to rematerialise the everydayness and ordinariness of threat; the participants in my PhD research, my students on MA courses at UCL and diverse attendees at conferences. We walked and listened to the sounds of the London Underground and the new looping announcement: 'This is a security message. If you see something that doesn't look right, speak to staff or text British Transport Police on 61016. We'll sort it. See it, Say it, Sorted.'[4] On each walk, we extend the map-bodies-time-space into the already remattered thought-felts entanglements of other groups a few months/years earlier (Figures 6.2, 6.3). While we were walking, listening, feeling, thinking and making, we rematerialised what we walked with using colourful fabrics, safety pins, drawings, words, markers and glue. We entangled the past affected terror messages of others in another walking-with experience, my MA Sociology of Education students (the red jar in Figure 6.2), with our present experiences at the PhEmaterialisim Conference.[5] The

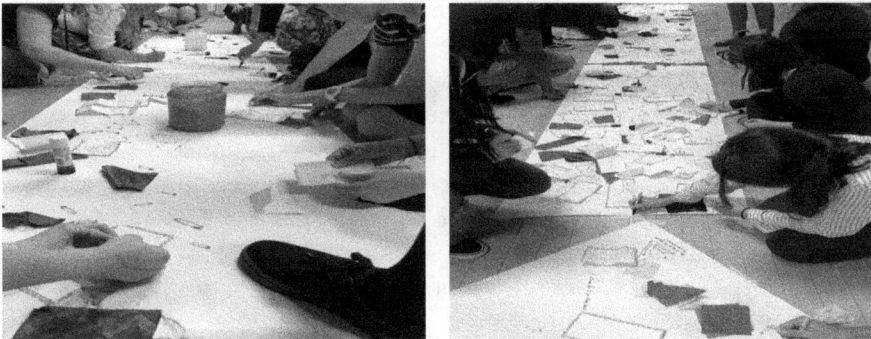

Figures 6.2–6.3 Left, first terror mapping (PhEmaterialisim Conference, UCL Institute of Education, June 2018; <https://www.ucl.ac.uk/ioe/events/2018/jun/phematerialism-2-matter-realising-pedagogical-and-methodological-interferences-terror-and-violence>); right, remapping the mapped terror walk (Sociology of Education master class, Institute of Education, October 2018).

delay of others in materialising their affective entanglements with the map, leaving empty spaces and open-ended points behind in the previous walking experiment, became the material and affective possibility for present feelings and thinkings to emerge on the map. Walking as 'an embodied way of knowing' (Vannini and Vannini 2017: 180) and always as a 'walking-with' (Springgay and Truman 2018) enabled a sensory entanglement with our bodies, more-than-human bodies, threat, everydayness, space and time.

Temporality and Threat

Threat as debt is a temporal, material and embodied event. Within contemporary capitalism, debt remobilises the individual and their social promise-making capacities for the future, to be determined by promises made in the past (Tonstad 2016: 434). The ability to make promises is a precondition of the debt and the project for the future (Parikka 2011). Lazzarato suggests that 'making a person capable of keeping a promise means constructing a memory for him, endowing him with interiority, a conscience which provides a bulwark against forgetting' (2012: 40). In a sense, memory, subjectivity and conscience begin to be produced within the domain of (debt) threat and the unforgivable surplus value of living as a threat to others. The same temporal logic and promise-making surrounding debt can be felt with threat, where you live through a prism of future risk, the threat of what might come next. Such 'affective futurity' (Massumi 2010: 66), in line with the pre-emptive logic of the Prevent policy, enables the double conditional logic of 'would have/could have' (Massumi 2010: 66). Within this logic, the Muslim child as an ontologised, racialised and threatening subject would have become either radicalised or a terrorist if s/he had had the chance; thus there is an overdetermined impossibility of this child not becoming a terrorist and being dislodged from the threat.

Hadil, a Muslim British-Bangladeshi girl and one of my PhD research participants (Year 12, private school, south-east London), depicts one unredeemable moment of her missing life:

> They make jokes, 'It's gonna be you next' [next Jihadi bride][6] and I just laugh, saying yeah, yeah, but NO [with strong and shaky voice, hand movement]. Even if they don't say anything, they think, 'Oh she is gonna be the one to go to Syria next'.

Halberstam, drawing on Harney and Moten in the opening of their book *The Undercommons: Fugitive & Black Study*, explains debt as 'living with brokenness', 'with being broke' and 'something that cannot be paid off' (2013: 5). I argue that the Prevent policy in UK schools is a component of the terrorism capitalist-machine, setting the scene for living with threat as brokenness. 'It's gonna be you next' materialises the future threat that has not yet happened in the here-and-now in this encounter at school, and reterritorialises Hadil, a would-be terrorist in the future, as a terrorist in the present. She carries and bears an 'always could-be identity' (Zarabadi and Ringrose 2018b: 67). With Harney and Moten (2013), the response to the call 'It's gonna be you next' is already there before the call happens, as 'You're already in something, you are already in it.' Hadil is already 'in the hold' (Harney and Moten 2013: 12), indebted into an unsettled feeling of never being on the right side of things (Harney and Moten 2013: 97); the debt that cannot be paid off to end the relation with debt, and the questions that cannot be answered to end the racialising questions of the terrorism capitalist-machine. The hold implies Puar's 'debt trap' (2017: 121) that Muslim missing people remain in. Being trapped in the hold is neither to stop nor to reach an end but to re-emerge as the temporal, spatial, affective charge of an emerging entanglement.

There is an intense relationship between these children and their futurity, as they are seen as 'a political field whose limit and horizon are reproductive futurism' (Edelman 2004: 27). For Muslim missing children this futurity manifests differently; their progress is not measured through educational development but through security logic. Inspired by Edelman's 'reproductive futurism' (2004: 27), I consider new futurity and security culture as 'pre- emptive futurism', to suggest how the futures of some children within this new terrorism capitalist-machine are entangled with the future security of the school, students, society and the nation. In the climate of threat and terrorism this pre-emptive futurism entangles the Muslim child in the future of the school, its students, the society and the nation. Future education and a future secure society depend on the Muslim child's paradoxical potential for threat. Following pre-emptive futurist logic, the threat of terrorism flows in viral replication rather than reproductive futurism (Puar 2017: 122). The 'present' Muslim child's potential for threat becomes the infinite debt to our future utopian society. I build on Coleman's (2017: 539) questions of 'who feels the future' to think of Muslim missing children as those who feel the future as more heavy, thick and sticky than others in the affective and material atmosphere that is enabled by capitalism and the terrorism capitalist-machine.

Such a climate of double conditional thinking, paradox and thinking security constitutes a different grammar of Muslim futurity, 'a grammar of anteriority' that in time comes before 'the tense of future real conditional' (Campt 2017: 114), creating the threat of would have had to happen. This affective grammar is situated in the embodied life of the Muslim child, embedding the conditional climate of paradox in that we do not know what will happen, but we imagine that it will/must happen. The challenge of Muslim futurity is the constant and perpetual necessity to endure commitment to the political imperative of what will have had to happen in the real conditional future, as it is tied to pre-emptive futurism thinking, feeling and becoming. The Muslim child's schooling experiences, situated between becoming and survival, are being affected by the climate of conditional paradox not only through policies such as Prevent but also through this 'grammatical practice of futurity' (Campt 2017: 116).

Debt time as straight time is the subjugated present to both the future and the past that comes at every moment already determined by the slow burden of debt (Tonstad 2016: 441). Overcoding present and future with threat from the terrorism capitalist-machine not only fulfils debt time's logic of 'nothing for free' (Tonstad 2016: 440) but also ensures that the indebted subject as a particularised (Muslim, black, Arab, Asian) subject stays with racialised differences and therefore with infinite debt.

In the threat-debt time, the memory has to be made not to conserve the past but to enable a memory of the future (Lazzarato 2012: 45). We have to feel Hadil as a present danger who, in the future, has to become the next Jihadi bride or be involved in terrorist attacks that haven't happened yet. Such memories of the future yet-to-come threat make risky Muslim missing people answerable to their future and the future of the nation. Munoz (2009: 22) maps another entry point to straight time, where in 'an autonaturalising temporality' the only possible future promised is that of reproductive majoritarian heterosexuality as, with the threat (of terrorism), the non-threatening future for some happens at the expense of others, the present risky missing people. For Munoz, the spectacle of the state is to restore its position through overt and subsidised acts of reproduction. Threat, marking the affective disjuncture and as one of the new affiliated by-products of the terrorism capitalist-machine, creates a sense of 'bad feeling', feeling fear and threat as a result of being queer, black, Muslim, non-white in straight time (Munoz 2009: 24). The experience of Muslim missing people under the terrorism capitalist-machine is a narrative of wish-fulfilment and a promise made 'which is not bound by its own time and the apparel of its content' (Munoz 2009: 24). For Munoz (2009: 165), this unboundedness interrupts straight time and the naturalised temporality attuned to making queer (missing people) unrealised and unthinkable. After Munoz, I argue that the unboundedness of the threat (of terrorism) is the vital component of the terrorist naturalised machine of straight time; it supplies present fears and threatening bodies that need to be vanished, a kind of investment in fairy tales that needs to be faced, in a certain way. This fabricated reality inculcates in us that the 'here and now' is not enough (Munoz 2009: 171) and needs to be acted upon. The promise of future redeemed debt is Munoz's 'desire for the good life' (2009: 182) and what we have been denied in 'straight time's choke hold', the condition of being left in waiting for another time that is not yet here, a 'call to a then-and-there' (2009: 187). A utopian call to a then-and-there secure society is entangled in how the terrorism capitalist-machine acts on Muslim missing bodies, keeping them in the hold, enabling the present feeling of fear from a threat that may or may not happen in the future.

Threat as a New Component of Capitalism

Threat-debt and terrorism as a new affiliated social relation become part of the reconfiguration of the institutional scaffolding of capitalist societies, moving beyond the terrorism narratives that justify control, surveillance and normalisation of security culture 'to governing from distance strategies through dividing practices and condemning large sections of the population to live bare life' (Joseph 2011: 34–5). Threat and the terrorism capitalist-machine not only create, divide and politicise our everyday mundane practices but also materialise forms of 'slow violence' (Nixon 2011) in the intimate everyday encounters of the Muslim missing people in my study. For Nixon, 'slow violence' extends, grows and unfolds the 'violent geographies of fast capitalism' (2011: 7). I argue that the extensions and contagions of threat (of terrorism) and the imperative to think about security propagated by pre-emptive logics as 'slow violence' does not refer to speed, but rather an affective viral vitality braided into all aspects of our everyday life.

Inas, a Muslim British-Bangladeshi girl (Year 12, state school, southeast London), and another of my PhD research participants, has been called ISIS by her friend at school:

In year nine I had a little fall-out with some girl, but she said she was joking but then it got a bit serious. But she was joking but she wrote a letter to me, an apology letter, said sorry a lot – she called me ISIS so, I got angry at her and my Jamaican classmate attacked her like physically, yeah it was quite a big thing, school and teachers got really angry and they were about to exclude her. She wrote a letter to me, she said sorry, but the school did treat this really as a big deal.

In a moment during an ordinary school day when Inas is called ISIS, she wears the threat 'debt-garment'. Being called ISIS as an 'intimate social and economic co-presencing' (Deville and Seigworth 2015: 618) pulls her into threat-debt, materialising the slow violence that grows from the terrorism capitalist-machine to Inas's body and other human and more-than-human bodies. Akin to debt, threat (of terrorism) as a lived variability of debt and credit fluctuates within and across all contexts:

> In the twitchy fibres and bumpy gooseflesh of your own sense of well-being, hanging half-suspended in the air of lecture halls and in the heavy atmospheres that emerge around dinner tables, in the muted gestures towards the supposed untouchability of finance capital in its well-tended opacities, in the tiny crack of a voice that replies when you ask innocently enough 'so, how are you doing?', in all of the architectures of attachment and alienation that can come to rigidify or dissolve without prior warning, and so much more. (Deville and Seigworth 2015: 618)

For Inas and Hadil, being called ISIS and the 'It's gonna be you next' joke as an 'intimate encounter' (Berlant and Edelman 2014: 119) 'isn't over when it ends, it goes on after it's all over'; and as an entry to the logic of (infinite) indebtedness (Graeber 2011: 15) it suffuses the most intimate ecologies of Inas's and Hadil's existence, saturating bodies, intimacies, materialities, habits and moods (Allon 2015: 698). For Inas and Hadil, the infinite threat-debt of Muslim missing people as 'intimate encounters' becomes impossible to repay and repair (Berlant in Berlant and Edelman 2014: 122–4), as they stay and animate their lived experiences as 'a debt of existence' (AO, 197). Missing people's infinite debt to the terrorism capitalist-machine stays and animates as 'the creditor has not yet lent while the debtor never quits repaying, for repaying is a duty but lending is an option' (AO, 197). Threat and the terrorism capitalist-machine 'overflow a new connective synthesis and inscription on the body of the old despotic territorial colonial and racialised machine' (AO, 198). This new inscription of threat and despotic state-proliferated security thinking allows the old colonial and racialised territorial inscriptions to live as new components of capitalism. Counter-terrorism and the Prevent policy in UK schools enable the operation of new alliances and overcodings; the old territorial unit of the obedient, passive, Muslim schoolgirl is now affiliated to threat and the terrorism capitalist-machine de-/reterritorialising them into the new visual category of 'terrorist look-alike'

(Puar 2007: 229), ISIS and Jihadi bride (Zarabadi and Ringrose 2018a: 85). Debt, as the unit of alliance for Deleuze and Guattari (AO, 185), and of threat for my research, codes the flows of desire and 'creates for man a memory of words (*paroles*)' (AO, 185).

The threat (of terrorism) territorialised by the counter-terrorist Prevent policy in UK schools makes up the bricks of the new despotic edifice, the terrorism capitalist-machine. Threat as debt functions as debility and embodied vulnerability (Puar 2017: 73) that constructs the microstates of differentiation and modulation of capacities (Puar 2017: 121). Building on Puar (2017: 74), I consider that threat-debt multiplies debilitated bodies and Muslim missing people through the terrorism capitalist-machine, security thinking and compulsory transparency culture. Puar (2017: 73) uses the concept of 'crippling debt' to map fiscal health as a form of capacitation and capacity. Similarly, the threat (of terrorism) as a form of crippling infinite debt affects bodily capacities through the construction of debility engendered by colonisation, securitisation, terrorism, war and racism.

The vital materiality of 'mind the gap', the ordinary known and lived Underground announcement mapped and remapped as a long red pinned fabric cutting across the surface. Red pinned fabric materialises the sonic embodied entanglement with the colonial affective geographies of everyday life, where sounds, bodies, materials, feelings and movements intra-act and continuously create different experiences of our relations to our own bodies and other human and more-than-human bodies. Red pinned fabric is how *Mind the Gap* is being felt-thought-experienced in the affective securitised atmosphere of London's Underground. Someone wrote: 'FEAR OF DIFFERENCE', the other extended it: 'I heard this first on the train from Gatwick. 20 stops. It played 10 times. I found

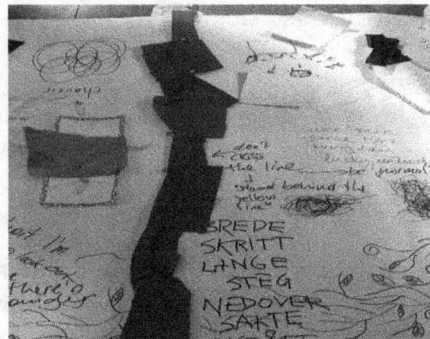

Figures 6.4–6.5 Left, red fabricated gap (June 2018); right, fabricated gap re-mattered with more affected data (October 2018).

myself saying the words to myself after leaving the train . . . again, again, again.' Someone else drew a line to this experience and wrote: 'THAT'S FEAR', and another: 'reminds me of nursery rhymes that remind children not to touch dangerous objects: PATRONIZING!!'

The Distribution of Threat: The Borrowed Sense

For risky Muslim missing people, living in intimate encounters with threat-debt, being in infinite debt relations and with a consistent bearing on unbearable racialisations within the terrorism capitalist-machine creates a 'felt-atmosphere' (Deville and Seigworth 2015: 622). For Glissant (2010: 17) this is a relation that is 'not lived absolutely (it would deny itself) but is felt in reality'. The threat (of terrorism) binds, constricts, releases, untenses and unfolds in the same way that debt and credit do (Deville and Seigworth 2015: 622). The new alliance of threat and the terrorism capitalist-machine compound a 'catastrophic multiplicity' of lived feelings, producing a 'complex storm of feeling, of aspects of world feeling each other in intense, unexpected and constantly mutating ways' that are not easily oriented to given habits of feeling, which remain unfelt and unthought (Murphie 2018: 19–23). The moments when Inas and Hadil encounter comments such as ISIS or 'It's gonna be you next' are when the call emerges, uniquely engaging them in a new and different collectivity of feeling, the catastrophic multiplicity that is made and remade within the negotiated avoidances or crossings into a new relational field. Within this potential lived field of feelings, Inas, Hadil and others are enabled to rejig and revalue everything in the school, their friendships, desires, memories, feelings and their next extended encounters. Massumi maps this moment:

> Deleuze and Guattari say that there is an intuitive collective understanding of where the limits are for a given field. Not going past the limits, avoiding tumbling over into a new field, is a marker of people's collective, affective investment, their differential attunement, towards staying in the relational field they're in, not because of how much they get per se, but because of the life-values, the quality of life, that this relational field affords them. (Massumi 2015b: 138)

The despotic terrorism capitalist-machine and the threat it proliferates in schools through the Prevent policy create a new temporal and spatial collectivity of feelings and a 'potential for feeling' (Whitehead 1978: 88). This new, crafted collectivity of threat becomes a site of community formation, not of those who speak or make a noise but of 'those whose feelings constitute the existing distribution of the sensible and those whose feelings are excluded' (Bargetz 2015: 589). Building on Bargetz's distribution of the sensible, the Muslim missing people are those whose feelings of being threatened with racial harassment are excluded. Muslims' feelings of being threatened as capital for the great creditor enable the terrorism capitalist-machine to move. Thriving amid counter-terrorism and the Prevent policy, threat and fear work as generative re-feeling devices and processes that enable 'the becoming of the future and of feeling itself' (Murphie 2018: 38). The threat (of terrorism) combined with security thinking entangle us in material, affective and sensory conditions that force us to behave in specific ways and not others. Drawing upon Christiansen (2018: 43), I suggest that threat as an affective translator works 'where sensation is displaced into the feeling of having acted'. For Christiansen (2018: 44–5) action movies can constitute a link and attunement between our feelings and how society is primed. In the context of my research, counter-terrorism and the Prevent policy alongside media affective modulations in reporting terrorist-related incidents can constitute a link and attunement between our feelings of future threat and how society is primed. Knowing and sensing the world with threat suggests 'the compositional process that bears, gestures, gestates' (Stewart 2011: 445) our lived experiences. The feelings of threat and fear engendered by terrorist attacks, counter-terrorism, the Prevent policy and 'media automatic image loops' (Massumi 2015a) pick up density in school encounters, resonating with atmospheric vibrations of threat and participating in the everyday texture of pupils' lives to enter the ecology of fear (Christiansen 2018: 44). Threat and fear can remake links between the Muslim body and terrorism, even when it seems that encounters such as being called ISIS or 'It's gonna be you next' are interpreted by Inas and Hadil (and probably other students) as jokes, and therefore seem to unmake those links.

Threat and fear de-/reterritorialised through media images and coverage of Muslim-related news and terrorist attacks enter the classroom's micro-encounters (Zarabadi and Ringrose 2018b), finding an affective timbre (James 2013) in multiple directions. The question of affective 'overcoding' (AO, 198) of the terrorism capitalist-machine is not whether threat exists or not but whether we feel that there might be a threat anywhere in the future. The 'distribution of emotions' (Bargetz 2015: 587) not only reveals who should and should not be felt to be threatening but also the emergence of Muslim missing people as new political subjects and potential terrorists. With the overcoded flows and affective agency of threat, the suspicious body of Muslim missing people is consistently 'given back' (Heath-Kelly and Strausz 2018: 63), staying in the loop of threat and security thinking, appearing and reappearing in everyday material moments and encounters. The lived feeling with threat holds the relationship between Inas's and Hadil's threatening Muslim missing bodies and threatened non-Muslim bodies. The indebtedness of Muslim missing people to security culture as the unredeemable infinite debt that it is impossible to pay off has continuously de-/reterritorialised so that they stay in affective lived threat-relations and a fantasy where they repay the security they borrowed.

The yet-to-come threat (of terrorism) and infinite debt has to be kept in touch, the feeling of being touched has to be oriented as the 'of and with' threat, 'a skin that both connects and contains' (Ahmed 2006: 551) and extends. Threat and debt as a tactile orientation bring more than one other skin surface into the terrorism capitalist-machine, producing threat-oriented subjects (Ahmed 2006: 551). To keep the terrorism capitalist-machine overcoding in flow is to keep threat as a debt, 'what is near enough to be reached' (Ahmed 2006: 552), in a contactable and reachable zone. The threat (of terrorism), counter-terrorism and the Prevent policy as a new affiliated orientation-machine place Muslim missing people as objects within reach to be monitored and controlled. For Ahmed, 'bodies tend toward some objects more than others, given their tendencies' (2006: 553); threat with the terror-ism capitalist-machine makes this toward-ness happen, Inas becoming ISIS and Hadil becoming the next Jihadi bride. Only by taking on the direction promised for social good and by returning the debt of life is this life counted as a good life, one's futurity depending on certain points reached along a life's course (Ahmed 2006: 554).

Following Seigworth's proposition that credit, or its absence, is a point of contact to be felt and accessed by touch (2016: 16), I argue that threat can work too as an affective zone for 'the sensory arrival' (Seigworth 2016: 24) of new and different relations and entanglements, and ISIS, for Inas, and Jihadi brides, for Hadil, fall into this zone. Such a haptic zone and haptic engagement (Zarabadi and Ringrose 2018b: 72) as a particular experience of tactility and touch involves not only the hands in the act of touching but eyes to see the act of touching. The tem-poral, paradoxical and indeterminate overcoding and worlding with the terrorism capitalist-machine, the imperative of the acted-upon present for the future yet-to-come threat, implies the surplus affiliated function of haptic eyes and hands that enable what Seigworth calls 'the haptic affectivity of everyday indebtedness' (2016: 24), the haptic everyday

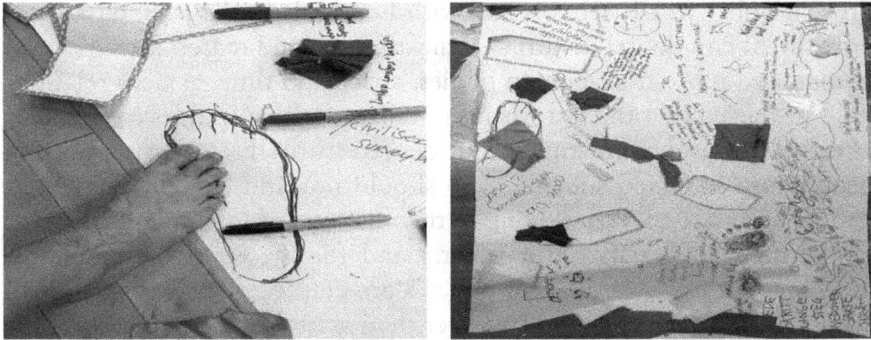

Figures 6.6–6.7 Left, the mapped foot of a past entanglement with terror (June 2018); right, the mapped foot grows into a present affective entanglement (October 2018).

becoming with the threat (of terrorism), and the haptic everyday becoming as a racialised, threatening body. Threat and terrorist assemblages braided into our everyday practices, feelings and thinking become the primary affective source by which the senses are transduced to our (shifting) places or non-places (Seigworth 2016: 24).

In the assemblages of words, feelings, sounds, space, time and colours, suddenly a foot becomes materialised in another assemblage a few months later, other feet join the walking with threat, remattered, extended, growing into a rhizome alongside the map/surface. Threat is an embodied singular engagement with a collectivity of space, bodies and feelings. Threat does things, moves and makes our lived socialities. The security messages and posters all around the London Underground are not static sounds or objects that we simply pass every day, supposedly without any intra-actions; rather we take and carry threat every time we enter the Underground and 'get into' this 'affective atmosphere' (Anderson 2009) as mapped in these images. This atmosphere is 'always already abuzz with something pressing' (Stewart 2011: 448) – threat.

Continuation: Minding the Gap

In this chapter, through ontologising the threat of terrorism as debt, I argued that the despotic terrorism capitalist-machine makes Muslim missing people indebted to the security of others. Threat as debt works as a form of control, not of fiscal relations but of bodily relations. In this affective investment what is being exchanged is not money but lived feelings and lived materialities. I engaged with various contexts of the

Prevent policy in UK schools and with London's Underground to argue how threat can de-/reterritorialise the affective and material relations of human and more-than-human bodies, space and time, as debt relations do. I proposed that the terrorism capitalist-machine enables a particular affective atmosphere of threat that de-/reterritorialises Muslim missing people into indebted subjects who should not and cannot repay their debt. They have to keep staying in the relations of infinite indebtedness in the name of security (for others) and for the terrorism capitalist-machine to move. The Prevent policy's pre-emptive logic in and beyond schools is built on potentiality rather than actual actions and, using the double conditional logic of 'would have/could have' (Massumi 2010), the future threat rather than the present. With Muslim missing people always having a potentiality for radicalisation and being seen as risky and dangerous, they have already borrowed from and are already in debt to the terrorism-capitalist-machine.

Notes

1. Channel is a multi-agency programme providing support at an early stage to people who are identified as being vulnerable to being drawn into terrorism (Channel Guidance 2015). The presence of counter-terrorism police officers on the panels has been under criticism over the past years as it has securitised what is meant to be a supportive scheme.
2. The government has launched an ongoing independent review of Prevent since 2019.
3. The revising of this chapter coincided with the Covid-19 pandemic that put the world into lockdown. UK studies showed that the BAME (Black, Asian and minority ethnic) population, particularly Bangladeshi communities, were most hit by the virus. Muslim missing people's lived socialities were represented once again by some media reports and policy discourses as entangled with being threatening and dangerous, this time in relation to a deadly virus as a new terrorism. Some scholars and activists warned that new local lockdown policies targeting BAME communities would increase ethnic segregation and inequality.
4. The UK railway station announcement is available at <https://www.youtube.com/watch?v=lC8gS3xlenI> (last accessed 15 May 2022); British Transport police, 'See it. Say it. Sorted. How you can help keep the railway safe', available at <https://www.btp.police.uk/police-forces/british-transport-police/areas/campaigns/see-it-say-it-sorted/> (last accessed 15 May 2022).
5. For more information, see <https://www.ucl.ac.uk/ioe/events/2018/jun/phematerialism-2-matter-realising-pedagogical-and-methodological-interferences-terror-and-violence> (last accessed 18 June 2022).
6. Three Muslim schoolgirls left London to marry Jihadi fighters in Syria in 2015, and were referred to in the media as 'Jihadi brides'.

References

Ahmed, S. (2006), 'Orientations: Towards a Queer Phenomenology', *GLQ: A Journal of Lesbian and Gay Studies*, 12 (4): 543–74.

Ahmed, S. (2014), *The Cultural Politics of Emotion*, Edinburgh: Edinburgh University Press.

Allon, F. (2015), 'Everyday Leverage, or Leveraging the Everyday', *Cultural Studies*, 29 (5–6): 687–706, <https://doi.org/10.1080/09502386.2015.1017140>.

Anderson, B. (2009), 'Affective Atmospheres', *Emotion, Space and Society*, 2 (2): 7781, <https://doi.org/10.1016/j.emospa.2009.08.005>.

Angerer, M.-L. (2014), *Desire after Affect*, London: Rowman and Littlefield International.

Bargetz, B. (2015), 'The Distribution of Emotions: Affective Politics of Emancipation', *Hypatia*, 30 (3): 580–96.

Berlant, L., and L. Edelman (2014), *Sex, or the Unbearable*, Durham, NC: Duke University Press.

Braidotti, R. (2018), 'A Theoretical Framework for the Critical Posthumanities Theory', *Culture & Society*, 36 (6): 31–61, <https://doi.org/10.1177/0263276418771486>.

Brennan, T. (2004), *The Transmission of Affect*, Ithaca, NY: Cornell University Press.

Campt, T. M. (2017), *Listening to Images*, Durham, NC: Duke University Press.

Channel Duty Guidance (2015), <https://www.rbkc.gov.uk/pdf/Channel_Duty_Guidance_April_2015.pdf> (last accessed 14 June 2022).

Christiansen, S. L. (2018), 'Mediating Potency and Fear: Action Movies' Affect', *Cultural Studies*, 32 (1): 43–62, <https://doi.org/10.1080/09502386.2017.1400573>.

Coleman, R. (2017), 'A Sensory Sociology of the Future: Affect, Hope and Inventive Methodologies', *The Sociological Review*, 65 (3): 525–43.

Deville, J. (2015), *Lived Economies of Default: Consumer Credit, Debt Collection, and the Capture of Affect*, New York: Routledge.

Deville, J., and G. J. Seigworth (2015), 'Everyday Debt and Credit', *Cultural Studies*, 29 (5–6): 615–29, <https://doi.org/10.1080/09502386.2015.1017091>.

Edelman, L. (2004), *No Future: Queer Theory and the Death Drive*, Durham, NC: Duke University Press.

Glissant, É. (2010), *Poetics of Relation*, Lebanon, NH: University of Michigan Press.

Graeber, D. (2011), *Debt: The First 5,000 Years*, New York: Melville House.

Halberstam, J. (2013), 'The Wild Beyond: With and for the Undercommons', in S. Harney and F. Moten (eds), *The Undercommons: Fugitive Planning & Black Study*, New York: Erik Empson, pp. 2–14.

Hall, R. (2015), 'Terror and the Female Grotesque: Introducing Full-body Scanners to US Airports', in R. Dubrofsky and S. Magnet (eds), *Feminist Surveillance Studies*, Durham, NC: Duke University Press, pp. 127–50.

Harney, S., and F. Moten (eds) (2013), *The Undercommons: Fugitive Planning & Black Study*, New York: Erik Empson.

Heath-Kelly, C., and E. Strausz (2018), 'The Banality of Counterterrorism "after, after 9/11"? Perspectives on the Prevent Duty from the UK Health Care Sector', *Critical Studies on Terrorism*, 12 (1), 89–109, <https://doi.org/10.1080/17539153.2018.1494123>.

HM Government (2021), *Revised Prevent Duty Guidance: for England and Wales*, <https://www.gov.uk/government/publications/prevent-duty-guidance/revised-prevent-duty-guidance-for-england-and-wales> (last accessed 14 June 2022).

James, R. (2013), 'Drones, Sound, and Super-panoptic Surveillance', *Cyborgology*, <https://thesocietypages.org/cyborgology/2013/10/26/drones-sound-and-super-panoptic-surveillance/> (last accessed 28 May 2019).

Joseph, J. (2011), 'Terrorism as a Social Relation within Capitalism: Theoretical and Emancipatory Implications', *Critical Studies on Terrorism*, 4 (1): 23–37, <https://doi.org/10.1080/17539153.2011.553385>.

Kundnani, A. (2012), 'Radicalisation: The Journey of a Concept', *Race & Class*, 54 (2): 3–25, <https://doi.org/10.1177/0306396812454984>.

Lazzarato, M. (2012), *The Making of the Indebted Man*, Los Angeles, CA: Semiotext(e).

Massumi, B. (2010), 'The Future Birth of the Affective Fact: The Political Ontology of Threat', in M. Gregg and G. J. Seigworth (eds), *The Affect Theory Reader*, Durham, NC: Duke University Press, pp. 53–70.

Massumi, B. (2015a), *Politics of Affect*, New York: Polity.

Massumi, B. (2015b), *Ontopower*, Durham, NC: Duke University Press.

Munoz, J. E. (2009), *Cruising Utopia, the Then and There of Queer Futurity*, New York: New York University Press.

Murphie, A. (2018), 'On Being Affected: Feeling in the Folding of Multiple Catastrophes', *Cultural Studies*, 32 (1): 18–42, <https://doi.org/10.1080/09502386.2017.1394340>.

Nixon, R. (2011), *Slow Violence and the Environmentalism of the Poor*, Cambridge, MA: Harvard University Press.

Pain, R. (2015), 'Intimate War', *Political Geography*, 44: 64–73, <https://doi.org/10.1016/j.polgeo.2014.09.011>.

Parikka, J. (2011), 'On Borrowed Time: Lazzarato and Debt', *Machinology*, <http://jussiparikka.net/2011/11/29/on-borrowed-time-lazzarato-and-debt/> (last accessed 28 May 2019).

Puar, J. (2007), *Terrorist Assemblage: Homonationalism in Queer Times*, Durham, NC: Duke University Press.

Puar, J. (2017), *The Right to Maim, Debility, Capacity, Disability*, Durham, NC: Duke University Press.

Rancière, J. (1999), *Disagreement: Politics and Philosophy*, trans. J. Rose, Minneapolis: University of Minnesota Press.

Richardson, M. (2016), *Gestures of Testimony Torture, Trauma, and Affect in Literature*, London: Bloomsbury Academic.

Saeed, T. (2017), 'Muslim Narratives of Schooling in Britain: From "Paki" to the "would-be terrorist"', in M. Mac an Ghaill and C. Haywood (eds), *Muslim Students, Education and Neoliberalism: Schooling a 'Suspect Community'*, Basingstoke: Palgrave Macmillan, pp. 217–31.

Sedgwick, E. K. (1990), *Epistemology of the Closet*, Berkeley: University of California Press.

Seigworth, G. J. (2016), 'Wearing the World like a Debt Garment: Interface, Affect, and Gesture', *Ephemera*, 16 (4): 15–31, <http://www.ephemerajournal.org/contribution/wearing-world-debt-garment-interface-affect-and-gesture> (last accessed 28 May 2019).

Springgay, S., and S. Truman (2018), *Walking Methodologies in a More-than-human World: WalkingLab*, Abingdon: Routledge.

Stewart, K. (2007), *Ordinary Affects*, Durham, NC: Duke University Press.

Stewart, K. (2011), 'Atmospheric Attunements', *Environment and Planning D: Society and Space*, 29: 445–53.

Tonstad, L. M. (2016), 'Debt Time is Straight Time', *Political Theology*, 17 (5): 434–48, <https://doi.org/10.1080/1462317X.2016.1211289>.

Vannini, A., and P. Vannini (2017), 'Wild Walking, a Twofold Critique of the Walk-Along Method', in C. Bates and A. Rhys-Taylor (eds), *Walking through Social Research*, New York: Routledge, pp. 178–96.

Whitehead, A. N. (1978), *Process and Reality*, New York: The Free Press.

Zarabadi, S., and J. Ringrose (2018a), 'The Affective Birth of "Jihadi Bride" as New Risky Sexualized "Other": Muslim Schoolgirls and Media Panic in an Age of Counter-terrorism', in S. Talburt (ed.), *Youth Sexualities: Public Feelings and Contemporary Cultural Politics*, New York: Praeger, vol 1, pp. 83–106.

Zarabadi, S., and J. Ringrose (2018b), 'Re-mattering Media Affects: Pedagogical Interference into Pre-emptive Counter-terrorism Culture', in A. Baroutsis, S. Riddle and P. Thomson (eds), *Education Research and the Media, Challenges and Possibilities*, Abingdon: Routledge, pp. 66–79.

Chapter 7

Giving Grace: Human Exceptionalism as Fascism

Patricia MacCormack

Fasces, a bundle of rods held together in unity with a binding tie. Many rods, one goal, one focus, one force. The tie that looks internally towards the rods with a vision of the homogeneity and superiority of the collective as identical in value and in drive to power. The tie that looks externally to exclusion and a distorted perspective of all outside as difference and all difference as inferior. The basic tenet of division and division alone, with the aim being that the vision of the rods is the only valid one, that the fate of the outside should be in the hands of the collective unity because theirs is not simply the superior vision but the only valid and viable one. The outside is incapable of vision. The division not of some people against others, but of the social against the natural. Humans against the world. All anthropocentrism is fascism. All human exceptionalism is fascism.

In his preface to Gilles Deleuze and Fèlix Guattari's *Anti-Oedipus*, Michel Foucault demarcates seven tenets that we must adopt in order to live a non-fascist life. All seven tenets emphasise a jubilance in the loss of both power and ego that anti-fascism affords. This directly contradicts the maxim of *Kraft durch Freude* which affiliated leisure with work for the single vision of fascism, and also shows the insipid connection between fascism and contemporary capitalism where the production of the consumer self as a leisure activity is the forced labour of modern and postmodern subjectivity, a thoroughly joyless activity. Against the excesses, or accursed share, of contemporary capitalism where too much is what drowns the individual in the misery of perpetual demands for choice in the grooming of identity and development of ego, no matter how pop or PoMo (indeed the velocity of ego-transformation is part of postmodernity's own challenge to joy), many turns to ethics are denigrated as privations denying humans their supposedly evolutionary but entirely arbitrary dominance of the Earth. From the feminist as killjoy, after Sarah Ahmed's work (2017), to the rise of abolitionism (absolute veganism that refuses all interactions with non-human animals as exploitative), it seems the awareness that the enforcement of dominating human power is unnecessary is some kind of affront to the human's undeserved place atop the hierarchical world of organisms. And to point this out is to be a destroyer of joy, where joy refers only to access to imposed power. Not strength through joy but joy through strength. This is antithetical to the creative joy of adaptive and individual localised ethical encounters and interactions as unique finite territories of creative joy.

Human exceptionalism is the most ubiquitous and insipid form of fascism that permeates the ideology of the Age of the Anthropocene, and is present in every human, no matter their status as majoritarian or minoritarian, no matter their gender, race, ability, sexuality, class or geographical location. Calling out human exceptionalism is seen as treacherous to one's species – from the majoritarian direction as a bleeding heart emotional victim of sympathy for less empowered organisms, from the minoritarian as ignoring the plight of less fortunate humans in favour of non-humans. Both directions maintain that humans somehow have a right to dominate and utilise the world at their whim, seeing their position as either an evolutionary logic in the case of the successful or an unjust problem to be rectified for the oppressed. Humans oppress humans but they also oppress the world, and while humans concentrate on humans the world is dying. Everyone wants to join the bundle of rods. Not being in the bundle seems to be the main focus of those excluded and being deservedly in the bundle the comfort afforded to the most privileged. Humans against the world. Let's make all humans equal. Let's sort out humans first, then the Earth. This is fascism. Just because the natural world isn't considered a 'problem' to be rid of, it doesn't mean it is suffering any less the fate perpetrated by fascists on their victims. In fact, the whole globe now looks like the wasteland writ large of a Nazi territory; only the identities of the victims have shifted and, in many cases, profit has become the idealised aspiration rather than some distorted fantasy of a superior being. This chapter proposes two claims: human exceptionalism is fascism and a malzoan[1] life is a fascist life. There is great joy (not privation) in abolitionist activism that can disperse the fascism of human exceptionalism.

Foucault's seven tenets for leading a non-fascist life are as follows: the freeing of political action from unitary totalising paranoia; action through (schizo)proliferation and disjunction, not hierarchy; refute the negative of segmented politics with the jubilance of metamorphic activist flows; forsake fighting fascism as a sad activity for the embrace of desire; disanchor thought leading to truth by catalysing political practices as intensifiers of thought; deindividualisation – unlike collectives rather than individual rights; 'do not become enamored of power' (AO, xiii–xiv). In Foucault's suggestions there is a clear emphasis on difference in space and differentiation over time, exploding the atrophy of fascism that absorbs the outside into it rather than metamorphosing with it. System, hierarchy, thought equalling truth, all structuring elements of anthropocentric epistemes from art to science. All belong to the Anthropocene, to the social contract, which makes the world a judiciary territory for and between humans only. Human decide what both humans and non-humans 'are' and this decision – whether claimed as scientific or moral – is mistaken for truth. The social contract, whereby the entire natural world becomes a virtualised anthropocentric version of a perceived place rather than a world of multiple material realities of diverse organisms, declares war on the natural world. Fascism leads to domination, and domination can lead to war. Michel Serres states: 'War is characterized not by the brute explosion of violence, but by its organization and legal status' (2002: 13). The world is at war but there is an operation in place whereby the enemies are not equal, the victims are victims of genocide, and the 'opposition' is the same as the invaders – those humans who fight against anthropocentric impulses so as to end the mass murder and enslavement of non-human animals are juxtaposed against those who see domination as their human right.

Carol Adams points out that conversion from a who to a what and an identity being what it does becoming what it is are two defining moments in all genocide (2014: 16–17), and we see this in operations from slaughterhouses to circuses. Unlike Adams I don't believe that witnessing the desperate existence of non-human animals as victims of genocide denigrates human victims, unless humans perpetuate the 'humans first' argument. But the horror of life for non-human animals in contemporary malzoan practices, what Marjorie Spiegel has called 'the dreaded comparison' (1997) and Charles Patterson names the 'eternal Treblinka' (2002), emphasises that the only thing we acknowledge in these comparisons is that we fear being treated as we know we treat non-humans. Adams states:

> When someone says, 'I was treated like an animal', he or she means, 'I was reduced to literal existence. I could not do; I was done to.' How are people made less human? Two of the most predictable ways are to

define them as false mass terms and to view them as animals. Acts of violence that include animalizing language transform people into false mass terms, since animals already exist in that linguistic no-man's-land of lacking a recognizable individuality. When someone says, 'I was treated like an animal', he or she means, 'I was treated as though I were not an individual.' Conditions for violence flourish when the world is structured hierarchically, in a false Darwinian progression that places humans at the top. (Adams 2014: 19)

Adams points out that there is a war, it is a war on compassion, which translates most often to a war between two human perspectives; one of compassion and grace that sees the murder and enslavement of non-human animals as its material reality, and one which, for a variety of reasons, maintains the hierarchical system of human exceptionalism. Oddly the latter attacks the former as a defensive strategy rather than actually addressing their own volitional participation in animal enslavement and murder. This lack of self-reflexivity coupled with an almost eugenic belief in human superiority enhances the fascism of anthropocentrism.

Abolitionists have no binding cord. Indeed abolitionists often loathe each other, but we are all loathed by the malzoan, just as dissidents were loathed by fascists in their diversity while the real victims were ignored, silenced, murdered. Arguments between humans are anthropocentric. Activism that refuses hierarchy, atrophy, totalitarianism (of which speciesism is the most prevalent) and the enforcement of power for its own sake is part of the often rather quiet politics of abolitionism. Tactically I use the word abstaining for the moment (inspired in part by one of the oldest abolitionist treatises, Porphyry's third century CE *On Abstinence from Killing Animals*) – how is abstaining from consuming the flesh and enslaved products of non-human animals perceived as such a radical form of aggravating activism by malzoans and even as terrorism by some governments? It is the easiest of doings because it involves not doing – not participating in exploitation and harm. Malzoans see abolitionism as a war on their rights, with the numerous arguments for exploitation ranging from the pseudo-scientific to the absurd (what's known as 'omnivore bingo' – various comparisons between humans and their similarity to lions or scenarios involving being stranded on a desert island with a pig). Abolitionists will fight the war with malzoans, and do so in their various actions from direct action to outreach. But the third party, the victim, remains silenced, in the realm of the differend – they who cannot be heard because they do not speak the language of the oppressor.

Jean François Lyotard's differend, coined originally for the absent murdered victim of Auschwitz, suggests that 'a differend is born from a wrong and is signalled by a silence' (1988: 57) where the victim cannot speak because to do so would evince them as not a victim, and where to not do so means they cannot be registered as a being. Abolitionist activism is determined to fail because it negotiates with the anthropocentric malzoan through anthropocentric malzoan means, so the victim remains silenced, but what choice if the malzoan will not listen to the screams of the non-human other? To return to the idea of abstinence, a crucial redemption may come in Foucault's demand that we embrace joy in our activism. The sadness of bearing witness to non-human suffering can become easily overwhelming. The malzoan excuse also expresses sadness in forsaking human privilege (because all excuses as to why one is not an abolitionist come down to only this one refusal to forsake). Abolitionism contrarily does not translate well into abstinence because giving up non-human flesh, secretions or entertainment involving enslavement leaves the entire world available for exploration in differing ways. New trajectories and paths unfurl. Abolition is no more abstinence than giving up/abstaining/refusing human murder, rape, or giving up/abstaining/refusing the sexism and racism that most of us are raised with. This is joy.

There is a further step in becoming anti-fascist by forsaking human exceptionalism. It comes to us as the joy of not living for ourselves (farewell wanting to be tied in the bundle with the other rods in spite our gender, race, sexuality or other alterity status) but living for the Earth, what Serres calls *biogea*, the third term independent of the war between human sides. Biogea is the Earth itself and its varied environments as well as each individual organism's life, *as* a life, not a species, a genus, but a worthy and rich independent system that deserves life not for what it is but that it is, without name and without signification of value via use capacity for the human or verisimilitude to the human (exit traditional animal rights). Abolitionism increasingly embraces anti-natalism as an inherent part of its core values of adaptive grace and decelerating care of the Earth and its occupants, of which we, according to Serres are parasites, they who take without giving and create contracts without consent. Non-humans are not oedipal substitute children, neither are they companions in a relation to which they did not agree. Further, the maintenance of a 'species' for the 'future' privileges speciesist exoticism and its purpose as entirely for human generations and progeny, not for itself and each individual organism. The entire concept of species is an anthropocentric signifying system that prevents ethics with non-human others, as clearly laid out in the brilliant work of Dunayer (2004).

Serres states, in a lengthy claim, but one which clearly shows the fascistic tendencies of anthopocentrism towards the Earth:

> A living species, ours, is succeeding in excluding all the others from its niche, which is now global: how can other species eat or live in that which we cover with filth? If the soiled world is in danger, it's the result of our exclusive appropriation of things. So forget the word *environment*, commonly used in this context. It assumes that we humans are at the centre of a system of nature. This idea recalls a bygone era, when the Earth (how can one imagine that it used to represent us?), placed in the centre of the world, reflected our narcissism, the humanism that makes of us the exact midpoint or exact culminaton of all things. No. The Earth existed without our unimaginable ancestors, could well exist today without us, will exist tomorrow, or later still, without any of our possible descendants, whereas we cannot exist without it. Thus we must indeed place things in the centre and us at the periphery, or better still, things all around and us within them like parasites. How did the change of perspective happen? By the power and for the glory of men. (Serres 2002: 33 original emphasis)

Perceiving ourselves as both the centre and the logical evolutionary zenith of earthly life and imposing the same mode of perception upon all other life forms, while simultaneously harking back to a glorious bygone time of Nature submitting to humans rather than we to Nature, both illuminate fascist tendencies. Our narcissism that leads to breeding more humans is little more than fascistic paranoia at our own mortality. Just as there is no need to exploit non-human animals, there is no need to procreate except for narcissism, and to perpetuate this master species as a master race. The cessation of the human is perhaps for some unimaginable, but the ability to imagine the future is equally impossible, so we are choosing the joy of creative differentiation in patterns of production of new modes of being, over the repetitive and reproductive (actual and perfomative) patterns of anthropocentrism which are destroying the Earth and its many other inhabitants.

Perhaps contentiously, our many and valid fights towards equality for the oppressed risk falling into an anthropocentric unitary totalising paranoia that both perpetuates the 'humans first' argument that Adams critiques, and forces the human other into bending to the very system that despises and excludes them. In many ways, wanting to be recognised as counting is succumbing to the fascist's demands. This is a thoroughly horrific impasse that has meant that many feminists have chosen the schizo-proliferative disjuncture route in seeking liberation from patriarchy over a validation as equal through performing as men in order to count as much as men, and similarly has seen what Kimberlé Crenshaw (2019) coined as intersectionality assist in the detrimental segmentation of activisms of alterity that sees white women forget all other women, towards a politics where difference within difference doesn't mean conflict or privileging one status against another. Very few feminists have embraced anti-speciesism into their intersectionality, but those who have, such as Adams, A. Breeze-Harper (also known as Sistah Vegan, 2009), Elena Wewer (2018), Tara Sophia Bahna-Jones (2011), Julia Feliz Bruek (2017) and Aph Ko and Syl Ko (2017) see it as part of a wider system of gendered, racial, class and sexual oppression without the need for hierarchy or incremental activism based on privileging anthropocentrism.

Sadly the anti-natalist aspect of abolitionist veganism has aligned itself with male hysterical existential angst movements such as efilism[2] which, in its extreme view that all life is suffering so all life on Earth should be ended through human intervention, turns anti-fascist compassion and grace into total annihilation via deliberate rather than collateral destruction of the Earth's non-human inhabitants. Like abstaining from exploiting non-humans, anti-natalism is simply abstaining from producing more humans, the production of which we *know* will cause harm to the Earth, whether through environmental impact or the deluded fantasy that the offspring will directly mirror the parent's ethical stance. There is an absurdity in lamenting the never having been.

As a queer activism, anti-natalism also delivers women from their role as reproductive vessels defined purely by their incubating capacities, a definition so beloved of fascism from its roots to the emergence of the right in countries such as Hungary, where gender studies has been shut down.[3] Anna Zsubori comments:

> The decision to ban gender studies does not come as much of a surprise to those following the rhetoric of the right-wing government. This is, however, the most significant of their many attacks on the subject in recent years. At a party congress in December 2015, László Kövér, one of the founders of the Fidesz party claimed: 'We don't want the gender craziness. We don't want to make Hungary a futureless society of man-hating women, and feminine men living in dread of women, and considering families and children only as barriers to self-fulfillment . . . And we would like if our daughters would consider, as the highest quality of self-fulfillment, the possibility of giving birth to our grandchildren.' (Zsubori 2018)

This is only one of any number of oppressive right-wing uprisings occurring globally that see the future of the human through a reimplementation of the fantasy of glory gone through the rise of difference; not necessarily through the recognition of individual groups that diverge from the majoritarian, but difference itself as the permeability and metamorphic jubilant flow of human life today. Just as anti-speciesism values non-human lives as individuals without hierarchy or species value, so too humans must fight against fascism by themselves becoming the unthinkable, perhaps forsaking their long-fought-for recognition of oppression and denial of rights. Each addition to the recognisable and valid human subject (and arguably women, whatever that means, haven't even made it into counting as valid subjects in anthropocentric perception) reiterates there are those who count and there must be those who do not. There is also a residue of obedience in this strategy of counting and a risk of atrophy of difference quickened into an icon of palatable alterity, hence the overwhelming number of white women who voted for Trump in 2016. Poststructuralist critiques of subjectivity as singular identity have been accused by equality politics as indulgent, luxurious and borne of a certain privilege that allows for experimentation. But experiments with fluid identity devalue not only the recognition but also the very possibility of being recognised and counting, repudiating the anthropocentric structuring of life itself. It is risky and it is both hard and easy, but the huge rise in minoritarian women being at the forefront of contemporary vegan feminism shows that those with the most to risk are not afraid. Foucault's call to deindividualisation is indeed a call to dehumanisation. But what has the human done for the Earth aside from decimate, enslave and corrode it?

The Anthropocene is the human Reich. It manages the conundrum of being the banality of evil of which Hannah Arendt (1964) speaks while simultaneously being a committed belief in the superiority of the human to all other life. In this sense it reflects the conundrum of the fascist operation of simultaneous signification/hierarchisation and exclusion/refusal to acknowledge. The violence perpetrated by anthropocentric signification and subsequent subjectification of organisms is double edged. To be recognised risks being placed low in the hierarchy, or to be recognised only for use, labour or other value annexed entirely against the primacy of the dominant. To be ignored can be a line of flight or it can be a literal making disappear, an operation that performs the reverse of identity politics (recognition towards inclusion) and enacts the final solution of demarcation, separation and finally execution. Anthropocentric compulsions to know come often from a motive that is seemingly benevolent – expansion of knowledge insinuates empathy while ignorance enables prejudice. The judiciary motivation of scientific knowledge which Serres sees as underpinning all social ideas independent of their relationship to truth evinces the insipid transference from knowledge as expansion to knowledge as a deferral to an immutable logic, without accounting for its inherently self-serving speculative ideology. Antonio Negri and Félix Guattari state that 'Politics today is nothing more than the expression of the domination of dead structures over the entire range of living production' (1990: 30). While it is too easy for individual humans to be defensive of their actions, the banal evil of those actions is more often a deferral to anthropocentric structures than a sensitivity to an ethical encounter which volitionally chooses violence over compassion. Non-banal active evil ironically occurs often as a reactive expression of violence towards an other when the so-called humanity of an individual is challenged, from the nostalgia of Nazism and its modern manifestations, to edgelords and Men's Rights Activists, white people blaming minorities for their own poverty or oppression, rapists and those who perpetrate animal cruelty.

I do not differentiate between active malzoan violence and banal malzoan consumption and enslavement of non-humans, because the affects are consistent and the affects are what concern the tormented other rather than the motives for anthropocentric acts of violence. However, if I am named treacherous to my species it is because I am treacherous to the many systems and dead structures to which we cling. All of these anthropocentric structures, diverse though they are, are reducible to a form of fascism because they all state 'humans first' or at the very least 'humans control who is first'. Fascism is scary from the outside, and paranoid from the inside, but we humans find ourselves even more scared by the 'what can we do?' question that seems increasingly overwhelming at each moment. The required imagination, testing, hypothesising without laying down a new atrophied structure, creativity in activism and forsaking privilege is deeply frightening, but it is also a jubilant opportunity to offer life to the world that our dead systems destroy.

Fascism imposes death but is also a dead-ing system, a structure that makes life live in a state of death through denying the unique specificity and value of every organism in what Spinoza would call each organism's own striving essence (Spinoza 1994: 75),[4] which is reason enough for its being in the world. Any new concept of communism, according to Negri and Guattari, is dependent on giving up on the deadening systems of anthropocentrism:

> We should have better defined the scope of the ecological struggle, a movement which appeared consistent with the program of proletarian liberation.

We ought to have acknowledged not only the necessity of defending nature against the menace of destruction and imminent apocalypse that hangs over it, but also the urgency of constructing new systems and conditions for reproducing the human species . . . (Negri and Guattari 1990: 155)

Anthropocentric systems deaden the world. Fascism kills, capitalism creates a zombie reality of simulacra and object orientation where even death is denied us through conservative laws on abortion, suicide and euthanasia (see Berardi 2015). The suggestion of human extinction through the cessation of actual human reproduction is not a philosophy of death. That which has not been cannot die. It is a philosophy of constructing a new system of human behaviour based on care and compassion for this world at this time to avoid an apocalypse, even though right now many non-humans, minority humans and environments are already living their own apocalypse, born to be enslaved or killed. It involves ending the death of billions of non-humans. It encourages creativity born of optimism that the Earth as a singular ecology can live and thrive because of our absence, not in spite of it. Activism becomes artistry, collectives of unlikes emerge. If it adheres to communism it is world communism, where all life is valued as equally justified in existing. But we need not reduce a repudiation of fascism to adherence to communism.

There are multiple options unthought of, unthinkable within any anthropocentric structure. To live a non-fascist life, how do we think unlike humans? How do we acknowledge our animality without fetishising and co-opting actual non-human animals? Deleuze and Guattari's becoming-animal is somewhat redeemed from the fetishism of their other becomings in this way as they never define animals. Their use is neither speciesist nor anthropocentric. It is purely about escape from the human: 'to stake out a path of escape . . . to find a world of pure intensities where all forms come undone, as do all the significations, signifiers, and signifieds, to the benefit of an unformed matter of deterritorialized flux, of nonsignifying signs' (K, 13). It is a tragic reminder of our affects towards non-humans that the default response of the other to the human is the desire to escape. It is time for humans to live that experience of perpetual aversion, both to acknowledge the wrongs we do and to force us to think without and beyond anthropocentric aims, goals, destinations. Non-humans almost certainly have their systems, but who are we to translate (thus transform) them? Why should we assimilate our versions of the world as truth when we can choose to escape from those actions of assimilation or annihilation to find ourselves on escape routes that catalyse new modes of being? The deceleration of the human species will necessitate constantly novel territories and conditions that could facilitate these escape routes, where we escape the fascism of anthropocentrism to adapt to the care of the world.

Radical compassion is an escape route which turns back to this world, now, here, and its immediate needs, via alternate sensitivity to listening to cries for care. Care, both as a feminist and as an ecosophical tactic, is becoming increasingly more viable than communism in the fight against fascism. Perhaps because it exploits the privilege humans do have, whatever kind of human we are, while embracing vulnerability and de-privileging us, our relationship with power and our place on the hierarchy. What anyone can do, what their capacity in the Spinozist sense avails them, is already enough to do. It makes radical compassion activists of us all, no matter what access we have to what powers, which will always come as unique expressive combinations. The cessation of the species is not the end of something, but the advent of care for the future of the world – turning our futurity, our 'legacy' of action, our 'what we leave behind' into what we have done now to foster greater joy, from the smallest or what Guattari would call the softest subversions, to larger collective movements. Abolitionism is not privation or denial, but the care of the world as it is today. We can live non-fascist lives in immediate and easy steps right now. But we first have to acknowledge the everyday fascism we perpetuate by clinging to human privilege and anthropocentric systems. And stop them.

Notes

1. 'Malzoan (n.): A person who condones, promotes, or actively engages in non-human animal exploitation, subjugation, reproductive abuse, torture, murder, consumption, or commodification. From Latin *malus* (bad, wrong, evil) and Greek *zôion* (animal) with the suffix -an (adhering to or following). Literally, "a person who is harmful to animals". Malzoism: the philosophy and worldview thereof. Antonym: vegan (-ism)'; malzoanism.org.
2. Efilism is the argument that all life is suffering, so life itself should be extinguished from the Earth, at least at the level of anything more complex than bacteria. The term comes from the reversal of the word 'life'. There are valuable concepts on the accountability of reproduction regarding suffering and the guarantee of joy that cannot be fulfilled by parents, as well as encouraging adoption, fostering and other anti-natalist advocacies. However, the Western adaptation of the Buddhist concept of suffering, and the omnipotent claim to know that non-humans suffer enough to vindicate their cessation through bioengineering, maintains certain power/knowledge claims that are deeply colonialist and anthropocentric.
3. Salient to this at the time of writing is the fact that in the United Kingdom, the teaching of anti-capitalism, of white guilt and of critical race studies has been made illegal in state schools.

4. In this instance, and with regard to radical compassion activism, it has been suggested that my work universalises humans into an inverse Kantianism, especially because I do not account for every instance of 'animist' societies. I do not for three reasons. First, to do so is to engage in what is known as 'vegan bingo', which are the derailing 'what about *x*' qualifiers malzoans tend to use to vindicate their own practices. Second, this critique verges on an equivalent to the 'not all men' response to feminism, which would here be 'not all humans'. Most importantly, third, I would and could not speak to, for or about animist societies, and their existence does not invalidate the mass enslavement and farming which constitutes the majority of exploitation of animals, while cultural alterity wouldn't vindicate the murder of another unless the primacy of the human was maintained.

References

Adams, C. J. (2014), 'The War on Compassion', in P. MacCormack (ed.), *The Animal Catalyst: Towards Ahuman Theory*, London: Bloomsbury, pp. 15–26.

Ahmed, S. (2017), *Living a Feminist Life*, Durham, NC: Duke University Press.

Arendt, H. (1964), *On Revolution*, London: Penguin.

Bahna-Jones, T. S. (2011), 'The Art of Truth Telling', in L. Kemmerer (ed.), *Sister Species: Women, Animals and Social Justice*, Urbana: University of Illinois Press, pp. 117–26.

Berardi, F. (2015), *Heroes*, London: Verso.

Breeze-Harper, A. (2009), *Sistah Vegan: Black Female Vegans Speak on Food, Identity, Health, and Society*, Herndon, VA: Lantern Books.

Bruek, J. F. (2017), *Veganism in an Oppressive World: A Vegans-of-Color Community Project*, London: Sanctuary Publishers.

Crenshaw, K. (2019), *On Intersectionality*, New York: New Press.

Dunayer, J. (2004), *Speciesism*, Derwood, ML: Ryce.

Ko, A., and S. Ko (2017), *Aphro-Ism: Essays on Pop Culture, Feminism, and Black Veganism from Two Sisters*, Herndon, VA: Lantern Books.

Lyotard, J. F. (1988), *The Differend: Phrases in Dispute*, trans. G. Van Den Abbeele, Minneapolis: University of Minnesota Press.

Negri, A., and F. Guattari (1990), *Communists Like Us*, trans. M. Ryan, New York: Semiotext(e).

Patterson, C. (2002), *Eternal Treblinka: Our Treatment of Animals and the Holocaust*, New York: Lantern Books.

Porphyry (2000), *On Abstinence from Killing Animals*, trans. G. Clark, London: Bloomsbury.

Serres, M. (2002), *The Natural Contract*, trans. E. MacArthur and W. Paulson, Ann Arbor: University of Michigan Press.

Spiegel, M. (1997), *The Dreaded Comparison: Human and Animal Slavery*, London: Mirror Books.

Spinoza, B. de (1994 [1677]), *Ethics*, trans. E. Curley, London: Penguin.

Wewer, E. (2018), 'Man, Animal, Other: The Intersections of Racism, Speciesism and Problematic Recognition within Indigenous Australia', *Emerging Scholars in Australian Indigenous Studies*, 2–3 (1): 24–31, <https://doi.org/10.5130/nesais.v2i1.1469>.

Zsubori, A. (2018), 'Gender Studies Banned at University – the Hungarian Government's Latest Attack on Equality', *The Conversation*, 9 October, <http://theconversation.com/gender-studies-banned-at-university-the-hungarian-governments-latest-attack-on-equality-103150> (last accessed 15 May 2022).

PART II

SITUATED FASCISMS

Chapter 8

Colonial Fascism: Redemption, Forgiveness and Excolonialism

Simone Bignall

A significant strain of contemporary Continental political philosophy takes as its point of departure the horrific fact of the Shoah under Nazi Germany and considers the conceptual origins of such political cruelty in the structuring exclusions that characterise the operation of Western sovereignty (Agamben 2005; 1999; Derrida 2009; see Bignall 2014b). Other thinkers take European fascism as an implicit horizon informing their efforts to understand how docile bodies become compliant with the powers that repress them, or to theorise creative desire as the condition of a 'non-fascist' life (see the preface in AO). Ongoing investigation and repudiation of the ideas underscoring the exclusion and attempted annihilation of Europe's *internal* others is undeniably important and prescient, especially when support for neo-fascism is swelling in many European centres. However, although Hannah Arendt (1968) points to the conceptual framework of imperialism as a source of the fascist totalitarianism that underscored the events of the Shoah and made them possible, Continental philosophers have generally been less inclined to think about the horrors Europe inflicted on its *external* others as a result of colonisation. This neglect on the part of Continental philosophy is still more troubling because the dark legacy of Western colonisation extends materially into the time of the now.

The present chapter is situated in the context of a legacy of colonial fascism in Australia, which included a formal policy of child removal that the Human Rights and Equal Opportunity Commission in 1997 identified as a settler-colonial programme of genocide. It considers the formal apology given in 2008 by the Australian government to Indigenous 'Stolen Generations', alongside the state's simultaneous disinclination to explicitly *ask for* the forg*iv*eness of Indigenous Australians. Employing a perspectival, associative and decolonising methodology that seeks points of intercultural alliance across diverse

traditions of thought, I position Indigenous conceptualisations of ontological plenitude alongside Nietzsche's thinking about the exercise of
the 'gift-giving virtue' as a mode of sovereign existence. The aim of the
discussion is to investigate the sovereign implications of the politics of
giving and receiving implicit within the acts of apology and forgiveness.
I argue that forgiveness (like apology) is a definitive sovereign act, and
therefore that the Australian government's refusal to supplicate for
Indigenous pardon is also a refusal to acknowledge Indigenous authority inherent in the sovereign capacity for forgiveness. The chapter proposes that the potential for Australian 'excolonialism' – as a creative
mode of social and political engagement that 'exits' resolutely from
entrenched colonial attitudes, behaviours and institutions – relies upon
a collaborative effort to practise the 'non-fascist life' at every level and
in every structure of existence. This potentially advances through the
mutual acknowledgement of shared sovereignty in giving and receiving
through 'excolonial' alliance, describing a creative and transformative
exchange that is at once ontological and political.

Settler-colonialism is a Type of Fascism

In settler-colonial societies, First Nations continue to assert their
unceded sovereignty but are substantively subject to foreign powers
imposed at the time of colonisation. To understand the contemporary
stakes of decolonisation and the potential for postcolonial redemption
in liberal-democratic settler-colonial societies such as Australia, it is
necessary to start by thinking about the ongoing imbrication of colonialism, fascism and neoliberal capitalism. Fascism is typically understood
as a political system based on powerful leadership, state control and
authoritarian ultranationalism with a strong racist dimension, in which
political opposition is forbidden. Fascist societies are characterised by
their fierce regimentation of values and of property and the economy;
their cultural aim is to forge national unity under strong and singular
leadership and thereby maintain an ordered society, made manifest by
the formal expulsion of contesting differences (racial-ethnic, ideological
and political). Aspiring towards this end, fascism makes use of instrumental reason and persuasive or propaganda techniques that employ
hyper-nationalism, militarism and the general glorification of violence,
the fetishisation of ideal types of individual and society, fear-mongering
through 'othering' and self-definition by opposition, mass mobilisation
towards a unified end, and the purging of dissent. Fascists typically
define themselves and the fascist system they support, and justify their

exclusionary actions against others, as a necessary and righteous means of defence against various 'social evils' and 'menaces to the nation'.

Australia is predominantly a migrant nation forged upon Indigenous lands that the British Imperial Crown declared generally non-sovereign and *terra nullius*, and therefore free for taking by colonial authorities after the first British landing in 1770.[1] The colonial (including recent contemporary) history of Australia glaringly illuminates the collusion of fascist technologies with imperial frameworks. White nationalism, the violent policing of Indigenous difference, fear-mongering through the constructed representation of unruly and anti-social indigeneity as a key element in the social imaginary, and the universal imposition of (non-Indigenous) legal, political and cultural values associated with (neo)liberal capitalism, all operate pervasively – historically and today – within Australian political society. The colonial archive is replete with disturbing examples of fascist mentality at work. For example, Natalie Harkin has detailed the extraordinary, and yet often horribly banal, documentation of her grandmother's life surveyed and administered under the 'government-orchestrated system of indentured labour' (Harkin 2020: 2). Colonial surveillance and control of Aboriginal lives began with the establishment of the South Australian colony in 1836, ramped up in the early years of the new century as demand for Aboriginal labour intensified, and reached its zenith at the height of the Assimilation era in the 1940s.[2] Harkin's research examines the 'unfolding rationale for inter-dependent policies of child-removal, institutionalisation and training, as context to the burgeoning Aboriginal domestic workforce into the twentieth century' (2020: 2). Girls, especially, were targeted for removal: not only because of the strong demand for domestic servants trained in '"civilised habits", including cooking, cleaning, washing and dressmaking' (2020: 4), but also because girls were a focus of the state's racial 'breeding' programme. The sequestering of Aboriginal girls away from their communities facilitated state control over their reproductive potential and reduced possibilities for them to 'consort' with Aboriginal partners. Indeed, the state's eugenicist 'anti-consorting' laws enforced this for Aboriginal girls, such as Harkin's grandmother, who had been granted a certificate of exemption dissolving her Aboriginal status (2020: 9; see also McConnochie et al. 1988). Harkin's research honours the histories of such Indigenous girls and women, who very often 'experienced traumatic removal from their families, isolation and alienation from white society, sexual harassment and rape'. At the same time, she celebrates these women's stories of strength, resilience and survival, and she trawls the archives for the unwitting record of their agency and voice revealed, for example, in 'vehement postal dialogue with state authorities in order to advocate, support and gain access to their children' (Harkin 2020: 12–13).

In another excavation of the colonial archive, Ali Baker writes about the reiterated violence of colonial biopolitical control that she encountered as she contended with the intimate presence – at once precious and repugnant – of her own family's traces in the imperial collections held by state institutions.[3] She writes also about the authoritative and ethical task of 'becoming human' as a way of repudiating the 'anti-memorial and absence of honouring' she found in 'the debris of documents and objects scattered throughout institutions in dark places, documents of abuse and lies' that attest to the fascist operations of colonial knowledge formation:

> When [Norman] Tindale chose to make a cast/bust of my great grandmother's head, and place that cast within the museum collection, he objectified and abjectified her within the colonial archive in perpetuity. He used her head to stabilise the colonial identity in this place. Colonial objects like head casts or photographs are re-articulated acts of violence upon us, of what has already been done to us as Aboriginal people. They contain the evidence of how we have been 'done over.' What happens then when these 'objects' of study become human? When these objects of study become scholars and artists? We become human—because while our families and elders may have been denied a humanity by the European invaders, our people never stopped being, were never frozen in time, were never plants or animals of a lower rung of a constructed false hierarchy, a hierarchy created precisely to justify the stealing of land while allowing those who benefited from the theft to feel good and righteous about it. (Baker 2018: 6)

These individual Aboriginal family histories, so beautifully reclaimed and retold by Harkin and Baker, are personalised vignettes of uneasy but graceful adjustment and of poetic resistance, situated within a vast and anonymous system of structural violence perpetrated against Aboriginal people in Australia.

Viewed from an Indigenous perspective, this colonial violence is obviously fascist: it involves the imposition of an overwhelmingly powerful system that attempts the despotic control of every aspect of Indigenous life. In this system, Indigenous political opposition is disavowed and so disallowed; Indigenous political collectives are not recognised as sovereign and authoritative. Colonial law and policy secure the normalisation of non-Indigenous social, economic and cultural values. This not only renders traditional Indigenous lands as Crown property, but also commodifies Indigenous individuals as a labouring class, sometimes indentured, in service to an imposed capitalist economy that exploits material resources extracted from Indigenous lands without consent or just recompense. The administrative consolidation and management of social hierarchy by the colonial authority was, and is, created by and designed for the majority benefit of settler society. This hierarchy was managed historically through despotic state control of (individual and collective) Aboriginal life and still today is linked functionally to authoritarian ultranationalism with a strong racist dimension. Systematic racism is evident not only in state-authored political documents but also in popular cultural artefacts such as photographs, advertisements, magazine columns and personal diaries. The colonial archive minutely details the fetishisation of ideal types of aspirational whiteness for the individual and for society, encouraging a racist national self-definition achieved in part through Indigenous 'othering' (Hage 1998). Colonisation accordingly relies upon techniques of dehumanisation including the representation of Indigenous people as 'flora and fauna' and the use of slave collars and licences of identification, along with other surveillance and penal technologies (see Harkin 2020; McConnochie et al. 1988). The overt cultural aim of the colonial 'White Australia Policy'[4] was to forge national unity and thereby maintain a stable and orderly society, made manifest by the formal expulsion of contesting differences (racial-ethnic, ideological and political). For most of the twentieth century, settler-Australia engaged in a fascist-type mass mobilisation towards the idealised end of a unified White Australia. In connection with the Aboriginal population, this was advanced initially through the purging of racial contaminants by the dispersal and internment of Indigenous families and communities in reserves and missions where it was presumed Indigenous society would decline and eventually expire; and subsequently by the assimilation and 'biological absorption' of 'half-caste' Indigenous children over many decades.[5]

The desired effect was to disable the coherent voicing of collective resistance and political dissent by sovereign Aboriginal Nations. This ambition to silence or remove the political challenge perpetually articulated by Indigenous leaders on behalf of their Indigenous Nations continues today in other ways. This is evidenced, for example, by the state's disinclination to enable an Indigenous 'Voice to Parliament' or to engage in a federal process of treaty that would require the nationwide acknowledgement of Aboriginal sovereignty in a process of equal recognition, mutual negotiation and shared agreement-making.[6] Australian Indigenous Affairs policy has often relied on militarisation, violent policing and a nationalist discourse of securitisation against the apparent threat of 'Aboriginal degeneracy'. This is the case both historically and as recently as 2007, when the federal government announced a state of emergency allowing it to suspend Australian law against race-based discrimination and so secure its policy of intervention in Indigenous communities in the Northern Territory (Altman and Hinkson 2007).

Settler-colonial Australian society has always justified its exclusionary actions and systemic violence against Indigenous peoples as a necessary and righteous means of defence against 'menaces to the [settler] nation'; spreading a defensive bulwark that was begun with colonial invasion and universally imposed at Federation in 1901, and which continues covertly today in aspects of popular media and through political discourse. Indeed, settler-colonial Australia has been built over time and legitimised only through the attempted elimination of Indigenous peoples from the political life of 'the nation' (see Wolfe 2006), an erasure made possible by excluding mention of Indigenous peoples from the founding principles and protections of the Australian Constitution. This colonial disavowal of the equal humanity of Indigenous citizens was replicated in a range of racist policies with a disempowering and often debilitating effect, ultimately reducing the efficacy of Indigenous Nations as self-governing collectives. Such fascist techniques support the settler-colonial requirement to subdue, refuse and ideally eradicate Indigenous claims to original sovereignty, which contested the legitimacy of the British legal-political apparatus imposed at the time of colonisation and continue to challenge the colonial legacy that persists in the exclusionary structures of the contemporary settler-state. They also support an expanded understanding of 'fascism in all its forms', which Brad Evans and Julian Reid (2013: 1) explain 'is as diffuse as the phenomenon of power itself'. In Australia, a form of colonial fascism lingers. It extends insidiously into contemporary operations of biopolitical neoliberalism and settler nationalism, and it corresponds with their specific modes of desire and subjectivation. The final section of this chapter will return to this issue of desire and subject-formation, to rethink the affective conditions required to observe 'the non-fascist life' in settler-colonial contexts.

And yet (of course), Australia today presents itself as a tolerant, multicultural, liberal democracy. In 2008 the Australian prime minister formally apologised to the Stolen Generations of Indigenous children, removed from their families and communities under the genocidal policies of assimilation that continued overtly into the 1970s. However, even after the apology, these extend covertly into the present: Aboriginal children today continue to be removed and placed into state custody at even higher rates than was occurring at the time of the apology in 2008.[7]

Furthermore, despite the apology and the renewed potential for post-colonial reconciliation it foregrounded, over a decade later Indigenous people in Australia continue to experience significantly lower levels of economic enjoyment, wealth, health, education, political participation and life expectancy in comparison to non-Indigenous people (see Australian Government 2019). Indigenous individuals are vastly over-represented in Australian prisons. The prominent and repetitive media exposure of police violence against Indigenous bodies – including juvenile offenders – held captive in the criminal justice system reveals in part why Australia has such an alarming and shameful level of Indigenous mortality occurring in custody, despite the recommendations made in 1991 by a Royal Commission of Inquiry into Aboriginal Deaths in Custody. What does the state's apology for colonial genocide mean in such circumstances? Is Aboriginal forgiveness for colonial genocide and institutionalised slavery even possible? If there is a potential for forgiveness in the face of such vast human cruelty and criminality, how can settler-Australians come to better understand the conditions and actions needed to enable our potential postcolonial redemption? The following section begins a response to these difficult questions.

Apology and Forgiveness: Sovereignty and the Gift-giving Virtue

When in 2008, as his first public act of leadership, the Australian prime minister Kevin Rudd *gave* an apology to Indigenous Australians for the genocidal policies of previous governments, he neglected at the same time to beg the for*give*ness of Aboriginal people. The furthest he went towards acknowledging a kind of political reciprocity was to express hope that his *gift* of apology would be *received* in the same spirit in which it was made. In fact, at the time, many Indigenous citizens were gratified by the gift of apology, which was especially moving having been withheld for more than a decade by the previous Australian leader, John Howard. The apology was also widely understood as a gift to the nation, to all Australians alike: it embodied a gesture of healing, potentially allowing us finally to take shared steps as a more unified nation, moving forward from our blemished colonial history. I do not intend to diminish the social and political importance of the prime minister's apology. But I do wish to interrogate what it means that Rudd did not explicitly ask for forgiveness. In the structure of the word 'for*give*ness', we can see that it likewise implies a gift: one for*gives* the guilty act and thereby sets the responsible person free. Rudd's failure to supplicate directly for Aboriginal pardon raises important questions about the role of power and authority implied in the acts of apology and of forgiveness; I believe a renewed attention to this issue of power might help us better attune to a hidden politics of giving, a politics of asking and of receiving, which in turn could expand our potential for transforming fascist colonial legacies.

In his meditation on *Forgiveness*, Jacques Derrida (2001) suggests that the enormity and paradoxical nature of a crime against humanity by humanity means that it becomes impossible to think about rationally, and it is equally impossible to think rationally about the possibility of forgiveness for such crimes. For instance, in many cases the individuals who originally suffered the colonial crime against their humanity are no longer alive: they expired in the poor conditions of many reserves and missions; or they were massacred on the frontier; or they were stolen from their families and institutionalised to deny and destroy their Indigenous being. They cannot forgive, because they are not here to give this gift. But by what right can today's Indigenous people forgive the violence waged upon their ancestors? Certainly, Indigenous people today bear the scars of the colonial crimes of the past, but does their potential forgiveness ever absolve these crimes? Is forgiveness for pain and trauma felt today the same thing as forgiveness for murder and theft in the past (Derrida 2001: 38)? It is not clear. The causal chain is complex and confused, and the situation does not make obvious sense. We cannot understand the conditions of forgiveness in this instance, because both the crime and the conditions of its absolution defy reason, exist beyond the usual limits of reason. Furthermore, in forgiving, we do not forgive the crime itself but, rather, the one who has committed it. We forgive the actor and not the act; we may forgive the murderer, but we cannot forgive the murder. But who is the actor in the case of colonisation (Derrida 2001: 57)? Who is to blame in the case of colonial genocide, which involved faceless bureaucracy: numberless individuals seizing countless Indigenous children from their families and homelands and at the same time working impersonally as minor cogs driving the colonial governmental machine? Who can be forgiven today for the original theft of Indigenous territories that now support the foundations of the houses that Australians live in as private property? Who exactly is responsible today for the continuing desecration of Aboriginal law and country caused by industrial activities impacting Indigenous lands and ecologies? Again, the issue of forgiveness is not clear; it makes no sense to forgive a faceless corporate bureaucracy, or a society of settlers, for a crime that is ongoing.

For Derrida, then, the magnitude and the nature of crimes against humanity – such as the crimes we see in Australian settler colonisation – are 'unforgivable'. This suggests that postcolonial reconciliation is in fact an impossibly difficult goal, which involves asking or granting absolution for something 'unforgivable'. Yet, according to Derrida, granting forgiveness for something unforgivable is a political necessity for humankind, which seems routinely to violate itself. Without the possibility of forgiveness, societies where conflicting peoples coexist remain trapped in their histories of violence and cannot move forward in peace. So, it seems *especially* where there has been an unforgivable crime waged by humanity upon humanity, forgiveness is needed if human society is to survive itself. Indeed, for Derrida, forgiveness truly takes on its most profound meaning when it is understood in relation to a crime that is 'unforgivable'. This is because, at its most profound, forgiveness is a gift that is offered regardless of an economy of exchange (Derrida 2001: 34; cf. Jankelevitch 2005). Attempts to understand forgiveness in legal terms of the requisite exchange of debt and repayment miss something vital about forgiveness, which has an unconditional aspect. In its most profound form, forgiveness cannot be measured and reduced to a matter of legal process or political recognition, but rather is a wholly gracious gift offered to the guilty as such, from the position of moral strength of the one who has been wounded. There is something fully ethical and powerful in the act of forgiveness. The one who forgives says: 'You have wounded me, diminished me; and yet I forgive you because I have the power to do so and you cannot take that away from me.' When it is offered in response to an apology for a crime that is in fact *unforgivable*, forgiveness is an act of moral strength that is virtually absolute.

The regular acts of grace and conciliation that Indigenous individuals offer to non-Indigenous society in Australia illuminate this link between forgiveness, virtue, moral strength and power.[8] It is customary for public events in Australia to be opened by an Aboriginal Elder, who is prepared to offer the participants – Indigenous and non-Indigenous alike – a 'welcome to Country'. Considered in the light of colonial fascism, it takes enormous moral and spiritual fortitude for an Indigenous Elder to offer non-Indigenous settlers a welcome to their Country,[9] which has witnessed the organised murder of Aboriginal leaders, of men, women and children; the theft of land and its parcelling up into fenced-off private property, blocking access to important cultural and sacred sites; the forced movement of Aboriginal people off their homelands, and their subsequent incarceration in reserves and institutions under strict laws that control every aspect of their lives; the deliberate attempt to eradicate Indigenous law, language and religion by forbidding their exercise; and so forth. Despite all of this, today Indigenous leaders routinely welcome settlers as visitors to their Country. I think this must be understood as a remarkable act of generosity of spirit, a superior act of forgiveness and reconciliation. At the same time, an Indigenous Elder's 'welcome to Country' is an act of sovereignty. The message of 'welcome' says: 'This remains our Country, and we have the authority to welcome you here (or not), as is our custom with strangers who come our way.' Furthermore, it is a call for responsibility, for respect, which says: 'We are welcoming you here to our lands; you ought to respect our authority, our rights, our existence, our domains, and our cultural ways while you are here.' A 'welcome to Country' is a generous gift of clemency offered authoritatively, sovereignly. In my view, non-Indigenous Australians rarely respond to this gift with the same spirit in which it is offered: settlers take it for granted that we are welcome, and typically we do not respond with the degree of respect for Indigenous authority or the cultural awareness that is asked of us.

In the face of persistent settler recalcitrance and ignorance, the inclination repeatedly shown by Indigenous Australians towards generosity and clemency can perhaps best be understood as an assertion of cultural continuity. While Indigenous peoples are diverse and cannot be defined homogeneously, there is a level of global agreement that indigeneity universally tends to share some key ontological perspectives, moral values and epistemological principles, resulting in a distinctive cultural emphasis on positive relational qualities such as 'reciprocity', 'connectedness', 'enrichment', 'generosity', 'sharing' and 'creativity'. Such qualities are discernible, for instance, in widely referenced Indigenous ontologies of consubstantial becoming and subjective plenitude associated with relational conceptualisations of self and world (Graham 1999; Rose 2000: ch. 6; 2011; Henare 2001; Marsden 2003; Rice 2005; Kuokkanen 2007; Simpson 2011). They also appear in Indigenous systems of law and justice (McCaslin 2005), and in the general principles of an Indigenous 'science of interdependence' (Cajete 2016). Giving, mutual care, restorative healing, shared responsibility of present actors to uphold the benefits of the past for the generations of the future, each are often part of a common expression by Indigenous peoples describing distinctive modes of lawful Aboriginal comportment in the world.[10]

It makes sense, then, that in the act of welcome, an Indigenous Elder's indication of a willingness to forgive the unforgivable is a deeply committed expression of Indigenous cultural life, in which values such as generosity and reciprocity have been exercised and celebrated since long before colonisation and have not been destroyed even by colonisation.[11] On the occasions when it is presented, Aboriginal forgiveness says: 'our peoples are by long tradition generous, and we offer clemency to you non-Indigenous people in the hope you can learn something from us and change your ways for the better, so that you no longer driven so completely by the desire for white possession and exclusive ownership but learn instead how to share and reciprocate'.[12]

Indeed, it is true that Western philosophical political traditions after the liberal Enlightenment tend to privilege 'possessive individualism' as an ontological framework for capitalism as the presumed 'end of history' (MacPherson 1962; Fukuyama 1992). However, it is also true that Western philosophy is diverse and cannot rightly be treated as a uniform cultural edifice: Continental European philosophy is rich with divergent conceptualisations of political ontology, social purpose and ethical potential. Minor Western traditions of socialist thought offer rich resources for understanding societal principles of non-possession and mutual aid, as well as ethical frameworks for non-imperial conduct providing scope for positive intercultural engagement. Following colonialism, it is deeply problematic for settlers to 'borrow' ideas from Indigenous philosophies and appropriate them. In my view, the only way to proceed ethically in the aftermath of empire is to situate oneself in one's own cultural and philosophical traditions and then to engage outwards to find points of sympathy and alliance with others, as respective bearers of alternative worldviews that differ in many ways but also share points of resonance, contact and overlap.[13] Over the past two decades, my work has been largely devoted to excavating buried traditions of non-imperial relationality from within Continental philosophy, as part of a strategic effort to forge decolonial conceptual alliances across Indigenous and non-Indigenous philosophies (e.g. Bignall 2010a; Bignall and Rigney 2019; Bignall et al. 2016). My hope is that this endeavour may advance the potential for intercultural mutuality in responsibly shared processes of social and political reconstruction following colonial devastation.

The work of Friedrich Nietzsche, which is in many ways marginal or slighted in the history of European thought, is a pertinent case in point: it provides settler-colonial Australians with a culturally relevant way of thinking about 'corporeal generosity' and the sovereignty of the giver.[14] Nietzsche's 'moral' philosophy is built around the idea that gift-giving is the highest virtue to which humankind should aspire. Bestowing gifts is the highest virtue, for it attests to the power of the giver (Nietzsche 1969: 99–103). For Nietzsche, individual purpose is to rise above the meaninglessness of a life controlled by outside forces one doesn't understand or consent to, by developing oneself as a self-determining power able to direct one's own path in life. This is 'will to power', as the will to exercise life in its fullness, its full power or potential. For Nietzsche, because the gift-giving virtue is an expression of sovereign selfhood, the act of giving is not well understood in terms of exchange or expectation of something in return. If one is truly sovereign, one does not rely upon the power of someone else to affirm one's authority; one simply lives and acts sovereignly.[15] Otherwise, as we see repeatedly illustrated in the early parts of *Thus Spoke Zarathustra*, the giver will be hurt perpetually by the disinclination of others to value the gift offered. For Nietzsche, the act of giving expects nothing in return. It simply gives, from a position of sovereign self-sufficiency that is not dependent upon the recognition of other powers. Importantly, however, Nietzsche considers the development of will to power to involve a reciprocal connection to the world:[16] the one who professes the gift-giving virtue is not only a giver but is also like a sponge freely absorbing the gifts offered by life and the world. This corresponds with an increase in power, enabling one to become an infinitely better giver, able to bestow gifts most freely. To receive in an unlimited way the gifts of others, or of the world, is to become full and overflowing; and to give is to have the power of giving, to be full of life and overflowing with love for humankind in relation to whom one demonstrates one's fullness of life. The gift-giving virtue is the highest virtue because it is the basis of a creative and powerful way of existing that Nietzsche claims 'may give the earth its meaning, a human meaning' (1969: 102). The gift-giving virtue is the way to redemption from nihilism, a release from the meaninglessness of life.

Its linguistic structure suggests that for*giving* is an exercise of the gift-giving virtue. We can see in its exercise how it connects with sovereignty: it asserts the independent power of the giver, who offers forgiveness from a position of moral fullness of being. The gift of forgiveness is offered regardless of a return gift in exchange, though of course it implicitly encourages a suitable response. It encourages a responsible reply of contrition and respect and changed behaviour in the future; but because it is a gift that is offered sovereignly, it is not dependent upon this response. Nietzsche thus offers settler-colonial Europeans a conceptual basis – sourced from within the Western tradition – for understanding why, when it is offered, Indigenous forgiveness is an expression of sovereign authority and continuity, which has not been destroyed by colonisation, and exists regardless of whether it is acknowledged formally by other, non-Indigenous powers. It promises a possibility of redemption from the meaninglessness or irrationality of colonialism as a human crime against humanity.

My knowledge of Indigenous law is rightly limited in detail due to its sacred nature and associated access privileges; however, it is clear that forgiveness plays a major role in Indigenous politico-legal traditions just as it does in non-Indigenous polities (McCaslin 2005). For instance, the principle of 'payback' in Aboriginal customary law serves the purpose of finishing a criminal matter and resolving disputes, enabling close-knit communities organised around kinship structures to forgive and reconcile without harbouring grudges (see Warner 1937; Gaymarani 2011; Gurrwanngu 2012).[17] In all known societies, punishment and pardon fall under the purview of a political body (not necessarily a state), which has the requisite authority to judge crimes according to the rule of the people, to decide just terms of correction, and then once justice is served, to pardon and release individuals of the burden of guilt. Forgiveness (like apology) is a definitive sovereign act, and therefore it appears that the Australian government's refusal to supplicate for Indigenous pardon – while itself making the sovereign act of apology – is a refusal to acknowledge Indigenous authority inherent in the sovereign capacity for forgiveness.

A less cynical interpretation is also possible: we might believe that the prime minister did not ask Indigenous Australians for forgiveness because he understood that colonial genocide is, in fact, 'unforgivable'. To ask forgiveness would be to ask unreasonably for the impossible. On this reading of the situation, Rudd did not ask for Aboriginal pardon because he understood that forgiveness, conceived in its most profound sense in relation to an unthinkable and unforgivable crime, is not something routinely exchanged for apology but is instead an unconditional gift that is given freely and sovereignly, from a position of absolute moral power and for its own liberating sake; or is not given at all. In other words, by not asking for a return expression of forgiveness, the prime minister implicitly acknowledged that it is the independent and autonomous prerogative of Aboriginal Australians to offer to settler society the unconditional gift of forgiveness. Perhaps Rudd recognised, then, that this is a decision that he, even as the highest representative of settler sovereignty in Australia, had absolutely no authority over and no right to ask for. Of course, the notion of a sovereign without authority over the internal affairs in its jurisdiction makes apparent the significant limitations to claims regarding the universal reach of settler sovereignty in Australia, and equally it reveals the real and continuing coexistence of plural authorities in this country (see Reilly 2012).

What, then, does the gift of forgiveness mean for the non-Indigenous recipient? According to Paul Ricoeur:

> Under the sign of forgiveness, the guilty person is to be considered capable of something other than his offenses and his faults. He is held to be restored to his capacity for acting, and action restored to its capacity for continuing [. . .] And, finally, this restored capacity is enlisted by promising as it projects action towards the future. The formula for this liberating word, reduced to the bareness of its utterance, would be: you are better than your actions. (Ricoeur 2004: 493)

On this understanding, forgiveness does not grant absolution from the 'unforgivable' fascist acts of the colonial past, but instead gives settler-colonials a release of our potential for better actions in the future. We might agree with Derrida that the gift of profound forgiveness for unforgivable crimes is necessarily unconditional, offered without reliance on a return gift to make it meaningful or genuine, since the nature of the crime and the terms of its absolution each defy reason. Nonetheless, Ricoeur's understanding of forgiveness puts an ethical imperative back on to non-Indigenous society: people like me must think responsively about what actions we can now take to show ourselves worthy of this gift of release from the contemporary burden of past colonial actions of our forebears. Here, we can see how Indigenous pardon does not respond to the already enacted better qualities of settlers (in which case, I think it would not often be given in Australian society); rather, it calls for a present and future response. It calls for settler-colonials to be better than we have been. Forgiveness is a call to responsibility, now and for the future (Ricoeur 2004; see also Hatley 2000; Banki 2018). It is up to settler society to prove itself worthy of the opportunity it is given every time an Indigenous leader welcomes non-Indigenous people to Country; and through its actions in the present and the future, to redeem itself from its crimes of the past. Only in so far as settler society acts out this promise of redemption will something like postcolonial reconciliation eventuate. Indigenous authors therefore insist that reconciliation remains an unfinished business, which waits upon settler actions of respect for, and recognition of, Indigenous sovereign authority, now and into the future (Dodson 2000; Cronin 2021).

However, we must remember that even if (or even when) non-Indigenous people start acting responsibly in respect of Indigenous authority, we cannot escape the fact that colonial fascism is an unforgivable crime. The nature of it – as a crime humanity has waged against humanity – defies reason and sense. We cannot really understand the conditions under which it can be thought of as forgiven. This makes the very idea of 'reconciliation' not only difficult to put into practice, but in fact impossible to conceive. The final section of this chapter briefly elaborates a notion of 'excolonialism', proposed as a more adequate way of understanding what happens to a society struggling to heal itself after an unthinkably violent and systemic crime has occurred. If reconciliation implies an end where painful pasts have been confronted and conflict has been resolved through the reciprocal gifts of apology and forgiveness, and everyone in the nation is united under a common civil identity, then excolonialism suggests an entirely different kind of subjective structure and an alternative type of relational and transformational process; at once more circumspect and more radical.

Excolonialism: Materialising the 'Non-fascist Life'

Signalling a process of historical discontinuity rather than a continuous and progressive movement towards a reconciled national unity, I intend 'excolonialism' to mean 'exit from colonialism'.[18] I use the prefix 'ex' in 'excolonial' in the same way that I would use it to describe an ex-partner. It connotes a former relationship from which I have extricated myself, an ex-relationship that remains an inescapable part of my personal history and which has shaped me as the character I am today, but from which I have now qualitatively distanced myself and from which I have resolutely turned away (Bignall 2014a). Excolonialism is conceived in complementary alliance with an Indigenous politics of refusal accompanying Indigenous nation resurgence, such as that described by Leanne Simpson (2017: 10) as a 'radical and complete overturning of the [settler-colonial] nation-state's political formations'. As Simpson explains, Indigenous political resurgence is necessarily and firmly rooted in unique Indigenous modes of theorising, writing, organising and thinking that do not 'belong' to non-Indigenous peoples. Settlers should take care not to covet, mine and appropriate these in an epistemological continuation of colonial histories of Indigenous expropriation (see Chandler and Reid 2019; Bignall 2022). I understand and respect the stance of Indigenous peoples who prefer to focus on their political resurgence as separate from a collaborative politics of future coexistence forged step-by-step with the non-Indigenous peoples who now occupy Indigenous ancestral territories. I also acknowledge that for some Indigenous people the continuing presence of settlers will never be welcome because of the historical trauma that colonisation has caused and the massive environmental damage that 'the extractive zone' of colonisation has wrought on aboriginal lands and lifeways (Gomez-Barris 2017). Nonetheless, excolonialism is intended as a collaborative pathway, potentially available to both Indigenous and non-Indigenous agents who believe that global histories of geographical entanglement have committed all of humanity to a conjoined future, and who are consequently seeking to work together in a transcultural production of the 'constellations of co-resistance' to settler-colonialism urged by Simpson (2017: ch. 12).[19] Excolonialism breaks with long-standing colonial habits of engagement, opening a potential for forming new styles of interaction and relationship appropriately supported by bicultural, transcultural or intercultural legal, political, economic and social institutions (Bignall 2014a; 2020; 2022). These new styles of engagement can be developed through careful conduct and respectful practices of intimacy, which may become institutionalised over time and with common determination, as the sanctioned structures of an excolonial public culture and society-to-come.

Excolonialism is not well conceived as a conclusive state of social affairs that can be realised once and for all; rather, it sets a perpetual task for postcolonial humankind, which must respond to the ever-present danger that colonial fascism will (again) take hold in relations of power. This is important because political society does not only take its ideological character from the macropolitical control exerted through the structures of government, law and policy as the institutions of sovereignty in which power is concentrated; power formations also invest the entire social field through dense networks of mobile and productive relations of struggle and subjectivation that Michel Foucault describes as 'micropolitical'. Fascism, then, is not simply imposed crudely by a governing body upon a population that receives it willingly (even fanatically), or else resists it. Rather, fascism is an affective disposition that threatens power relations wherever they appear, and whatever their scale (Evans and Reid 2013: 1–12). Furthermore, because it is an affective disposition, fascism emerges initially as a mode of desire that is then instantiated and given substance in actual practices of affective association – in power-relations – which in turn become sedimented and institutionalised as the overall set of political arrangements defining a fascist society. Resistance to fascism therefore primarily involves reflexive and critical analysis of the desires that shape subjects and their intimate relations – and ultimately invest the social field – coupled with conscientious reinforcement of associative relations (of desire and power) that materialise the 'non-fascist life'.

This is why Foucault famously commends the schizoanalytic method proposed by Deleuze and Guattari as key to combating not only historical fascism, the fascism of Hitler and Mussolini – which was able to mobilise and use the desire of the masses so effectively – but also the fascism in us all, in our heads, and in our everyday behaviour, the fascism that causes us to love power, to desire the very thing that dominates and exploits us. (AO, xiii)

Schizoanalysis investigates the different orders or qualities of desire that come to define the kinds of interactions a body is disposed to forming (AO, 277–96). In *Anti-Oedipus*, this is discussed in terms of the difference between the 'subjected-group' and the 'group subject' – a distinction which recalls Sartre's comparison of the different styles of politico-psychic organisation embodied by the 'serialised group' and the 'group-in-fusion' (AO, 64, 256, 277; see also CM; Sartre 1976; Genosko 2000; Bignall 2010c). The way desire is organised to materialise a relational entity influences the subsequent openness of that entity to forming new associations. Bodies that welcome new associations are defined by an active organisation of desire; such entities enjoy a shifting consistency organised around a core set of characteristics but are generally open to the encounters that cause modification, and they brave the risks of instability. These 'group subjects' determine their constitution through immediate and open practices of relation, rather than by establishing rules concerning membership that limit and protect a rigidly defined self-consistency. They actively engage the primary creative force of desiring-production.

By contrast, a body that seeks to preserve its established identity will prevent its own transformation by suppressing and resisting the formation of new associations with other bodies. This kind of entity is a reactive body that is restricted by the rules it enforces to protect its given identity. This method of self-preservation relies upon its defining distinction from a 'subjected-group' (or groups) that it has constructed and represented as oppositional, and it accordingly 'wards off' the transformative force of desiring-production (AO, 120). Thus, reactive bodies are themselves 'subjected-groups' characterised by the rigid control of their constitutive relations through highly institutionalised rules of passage, activity and association, such as we see in fascist formations. Reactive bodies resist the free flow of the constitutive and transformational force of desiring-production as a primary disposition towards association; this blockage can result in serial or systemic patterns of identification and controlled social organisation that discourage or exclude the possibility of interaction with alterity (see Holland 2008; Bignall 2010c).

For Deleuze and Guattari, problems of injustice, alienation and other kinds of disadvantage are developed and reproduced through structured forms of reactive desire, for example an 'oedipal' or 'imperial' coding which defines desire in relation to lack, longing and appropriative satisfaction (AO, 28; see also Bignall 2010a). Likewise, fascist social formations are produced through the reactive desires of rigid subjects who are hyper-defensive of their standing identities and the boundaries they have established and fortified in relational processes of identification, when these distribute both self and other in powerfully exclusive patterns of privilege and entitlement that benefit the fascist self. Such patterns sharpen a reactive interest in the preservation of reified identities, achieved in part through the denigration of others and the devaluation of their status as potential subjects. This helps to justify the fascist prohibition of general enjoyment of social authority and, likewise, validates the restriction of subjective security and social benefit to a privileged elite.

If settler-colonialism is a type of fascism, as was argued in the first part of this chapter, then excolonialism is its ontological, political and ethical opposite. Whereas settler-colonial Australian society is characterised by an identity politics of white hyper-nationalism, coupled with a desire to erase persistent forms of Indigenous Nationhood that challenge the security of the settler nationalist identity and its claims to unimpeded enjoyment of the uniform sovereignty imposed at colonisation, excolonialism calls for a different mode of desire enabling an alternative style of identification and association (Bignall 2020). Specifically, it calls for an active, open and affirmative mode of desire that joins partners in mutually beneficial relations that enhance their affective potentiality, enabling each to become more complex and dynamic in their activities of relational self-constitution. Excolonial desire supports the self-in-fusion of a 'nomadic' group subjectivity (Braidotti 2002; 2006; 2011), which is produced through – or 'between' – affective processes of becoming-otherwise as complex orders meet in constitutive relations with others and with the world (TP, esp. Plateau 10). An excolonial Australian group-subject will be formed by 'the resonance of disparates' as diverse cultural societies seek to combine productively and respectfully through complex processes of composite engagement (DI, 94–116; see Bignall 2019). Excolonial partners will join carefully in piecemeal and selective encounters that aim for mutual enhancement at recognised sites of shared agreement, while respecting resilient differences that define the specificity or uniqueness of each party and should not be denied, erased or coerced into submissive sameness (Bignall 2010b; 2014a; 2019).

Accordingly, whereas settler-colonialism proceeds through the fascist-type dehumanisation of a subjected Indigenous class and the institution-alisation of a regime of inhumane political technologies of segregation and racist assimilation, excolonialism depends upon shared resistive processes of 'becoming-human' through processes of ethical engagement (Bignall 2020). However, excolonialism does not seek for 'becoming-human' to reinstate the version of humanism connected with anthro-pocentric European modernism and associated imperialist programmes of global 'civilisation'. Excolonialism is best considered in terms of an intercultural framework that brings together Indigenous philosophical perspectives of 'more-than-human' existence and ontological plenitude with non-Indigenous frameworks of Continental 'posthumanism', such as we see elaborated by Rosi Braidotti (2006; 2009).[20] That is, excolo-nialism is an intercultural ethical perspective for guiding positive trans-formations in complex affective orders that are fundamentally open and dynamic, formed through expansive relations and more-than-human agencies that both constitute and bind subjects in shifting structures of mutual interdependency, subjectivity and sociability (Bignall 2014a; 2022).

Importantly, then, whereas Australian settler-colonialism relies upon the erasure or dismissal of the sovereignty of First Nations peoples, excolonialism proceeds in terms of mutual regard for the sovereign capacity of each to exercise an active 'will to power': to enter actively into constitutive relations of understanding and agreement that are affirming and enhancing. At the same time, excolonial relations acknowledge the sovereign right of each partner to refuse those aspects of engagement that threaten to harm or diminish them. In this way, excolonialism incorporates a 'politics of refusal', such as that celebrated by Indigenous critical theorists and activists (A. Simpson 2017; L. Simpson 2017; Birch 2018). Excolonial relations can accommodate both agreement and disagreement simultaneously, because excolonial subjects understand each other as complex and multi-dimensional groups-in-fusion; they interlace 'bit by bit' in piecemeal and selective encounters, and not in their respective entireties (EP, 237–43; TP, 504; Bignall 2014a; 2019). In view of the long history of colonial entanglement that Indigenous and non-Indigenous societies have endured and through the experiential knowledge they have accrued as a consequence, their respective peoples can now be judicious as partners in an excolonial relationship. Engaged communities can learn to appreciate and affirm those aspects of their coexistence that bring mutual benefit (even if these are overall or by comparison very few or minor in nature), and to avoid those aspects where disagreement is trenchant and irresolvable. From selectively positive and affirmative engagements that bring positive affections in shared enhancement, further joys may be formed actively over time. An excolonial approach to identity as open, complex and shifting – and to social relations as partial, selective and piecemeal – gradually enables the incremental transformation of widespread hostility born from colonial fascism towards more amicable forms of sociability (Bignall 2014a).

This future possibility requires that social partners have sound knowledge of self and other, so that they can effectively decide how their relationship can best be orchestrated to bring mutual benefit and avoid those aspects of their involvement that they can predict will diminish or destroy one or both. For Indigenous peoples whose social structures and organs of self-governance have in many instances been devastated by colonisation, processes of Indigenous nation-rebuilding are a crucial step towards identifying, organising and acting once more as sovereign entities (Cornell 2015; see also Jorgensen 2007). As future partners in a potential excolonial relationship, it is fitting that settler-colonial governments should responsibly support Indigenous Nations as they strive to reclaim their sovereign capacity as a prerequisite condition for active engagement in excolonial relations (Vivian et al. 2017). Indeed, Australia has recently taken some first hesitant steps in this direction: some state jurisdictions have begun to institute policy that recognises and supports the self-governance capacity of regional Aboriginal Authorities, and others have commenced treaty discussions; of course, treaty can proceed legitimately only through the mutual affirmation of signatories as respective sovereign powers.[21]

This chapter has argued that the potential for Australian excolonialism – as a creative mode of social engagement that 'exits' resolutely from entrenched colonial attitudes, behaviours and institutions – relies upon a collaborative effort to practise the 'non-fascist life' at every level and in every structure of political existence. I have suggested that this may advance through the mutual acknowledgement of shared sovereignty in giving and receiving through excolonial alliance, describing a creative and transformative exchange that is at once ontological and political. Excolonialism makes a break with the past for the sake of the future; but it does not claim that the past can be surpassed (Bignall 2014a). Australians – Indigenous and non-Indigenous – will carry colonialism with us forever; the best we can do is to create our futures on the basis of a different set of power relations. As a positive form of shared future after colonialism, excolonialism requires Indigenous and settler Australians to begin to materialise a different method and style of engaged coexistence. Excolonialism calls for collaboration through complex sets of affective interactions in accordance with a political ontology that preserves difference and diversity as a creative condition of a genuinely shared social life, produced ethically as an equitable outcome of plural sovereign engagements. While this is a task barely begun, it is not impossible or utopian; excolonial-type engagements already exist, dispersed throughout the socius; discernible, for example, in the multiple acts of collaborative partnership currently being formed between Indigenous and non-Indigenous agents of social and environmental governance (see Langton et al. 2004; Hemming et al. 2011). Enacting excolonialism – through the conscientious exercise of the non-fascist life in shared relational practices repeated over time – encourages a different set of power relations to emerge and become institutionalised. With vigilance and sustained effort into the future, this may eventually enable partners in postcolonial political society to affirm that we have moved beyond fascist colonialism, such that it no longer defines settler-colonial Australian ways of being and relating. Our potential for postcolonial redemption rests upon this possibility; ultimately, whether the release of forgiveness can be granted for the unforgivable crime of colonial genocide is a sovereign matter for Indigenous Nations to decide.

Acknowledgement

I am grateful for the helpful feedback given by an anonymous reviewer and for the advice given by Alison Vivian and by Steve Hemming, especially on the subjects of Aboriginal law and customs of giving and forgiveness.

Notes

1. An exception to this general rule was made in South Australia, which King William IV established as a colony in 1836 by Letters Patent that formally recognised Indigenous occupation and ownership of land and associated rights to the undisturbed enjoyment of property and its benefits. However, the original recognition of Indigenous rights was quickly ignored and conveniently forgotten by colonial settlers in this jurisdiction. This forsaken promise to honour Aboriginal rights remains a 'burning issue' for Indigenous South Australians. See Berg 2010, and especially the 'Preface' by Indigenous leaders Trevorrow, Trevorrow and Rigney. The general presumption of *terra nullius* applied to the other Australian states and territories and was famously overturned by the Australian High Court in its 1992 decision of *Mabo v Queensland (no.2)*. However, whereas the court recognised original native title, it did not extend its recognition to Aboriginal sovereignty and law as a source of such title. For discussion, see Strelein 2006.

2. Harkin elaborates: 'The core legislative framework controlling and enabling surveillance of my own family during this time included the *Aborigines Act 1911* (SA) and the *Aborigines Act 1934–1939* (SA). These Acts governed the Aborigines Protection Board (1939–1962), which assumed legal guardianship of all Aboriginal children. The Board had powers to remove Aboriginal people to reserves, and to transfer control of Aboriginal children to the Children's Welfare and Public Relief Board. In addition, the *Aborigines (Training of Children) Act 1923* (SA) also enabled the transfer of control of Aboriginal children to the State Children's Council [. . . which could . . .] remove children on the claim of "destitution" or "neglect", regardless of their family circumstance' (2020: 7).

3. Baker's research highlights how colonial 'data collection' contributed to the 'categorisation of racialised ideas about Aboriginal people and was part of a global movement of analysis using the ideologies of eugenics . . . concerned with racial purity, blood quantum, and hierarchies of race' (Baker 2018). Norman Tindale was an anthropologist, linguist and ethnographer who worked for the South Australian Museum from the early 1920s to the 1960s. Baker explains how Tindale's casting of her grandmother Gumillya Boxer's head, without her family's knowledge or consent, was made in the 'scientific' service of phrenology: that is, the bogus 'science' of measuring intelligence through the scale and shape of a person's head.

4. As Evan Smith (2017: 379) notes, the British Union of Fascists 'pointed to the "White Australia Policy" and the treatment of the Indigenous population as examples of the hierarchical racial politics that could support the maintenance of both Empire and fascism'. Formally titled the Immigration Restriction Act (1901), the 'White Australia Policy' was the first legislative Act of the new Australian Commonwealth. The Attorney-General Alfred Deakin explained in 1901: 'That end, put in plain and unequivocal terms . . . means the prohibition of all alien coloured immigration, and more, it means at the earliest time, by reasonable and just means, the deportation or reduction of the number of aliens now in our midst. The two things go hand in hand, and are the necessary complement of a single policy – the policy of securing a "white Australia"' (Commonwealth of Australia 1901). The Immigration Restriction Act remained in place until 1966, when Australia became a signatory to the UN Convention on the Elimination of all forms of Racial Discrimination and it became apparent that Australia's new international commitments were vastly at odds with its internal system of racist policy. Australia ratified the Convention in 1975.

5. In a report handed down in 1997, the Australian Human Rights and Equal Opportunities Commission found that Australia's institutionalised programme of Indigenous child removal and racial assimilation amounted to genocide, according to the definition given in the Geneva Convention (HREOC 1997).

6. See the Uluru Statement from the Heart at <https://ulurustatement.org/the-statement/view-the-statement/> (last accessed 15 May 2022). Although some regional state jurisdictions including Victoria and the Northern Territory have recently initiated treaty processes with local Indigenous groups, Australia remains the only settler-colonial federation never to have negotiated a treaty with First Nations peoples. The Australian Constitution makes no mention of Indigenous peoples. On July 30, 2022, Prime Minister Anthony Albanese took a long-overdue first step toward a referendum that would rectify this absence and enshrine an Indigenous Voice to Parliament in Australia.

7. In 2007 there were 9,054 Indigenous children in state care. By 2016 this figure had increased to 16,816 (see Behrendt 2017).

8. I am *not* suggesting that Indigenous Australians have accepted the fact of colonisation (which would be absurd), nor that they should (which would

be presumptive); I am merely noting that signs of clemency are frequently expressed in the Australian polity by Indigenous authorities advancing a potential for Australian healing. I am also arguing that such signs should be understood as sovereign acts. For a discussion of Indigenous refusal to forgive as an alternative strategy of anti-colonial resistance, see Flowers 2015.

9. Aboriginal Country is an interconnected life ecology, involving the land, water, air, animals, ancestral spirits, and the bodies and minds of the Aboriginal citizens of that Country (see Rose 2000). Aboriginal self-governance requires that leaders 'speak *as* Country' (see Hemming et al. 2011). In offering a 'welcome to Country', an Elder is therefore offering an invitation to a widely relational engagement with themselves and interconnected aspects of their existence.

10. For the Ngarrindjeri people, for example, these principles are referenced in the story of Thukeri. See Bell 2014; Ngarrindjeri Nation 2007. My thanks to Steve Hemming for this point. For another example, see Deborah Bird Rose's (2011) meditation on 'the beginning law' that is the story of the 'wild dog dreaming'.

11. Although beyond our immediate concern, it is worth noting that many Indigenous people have found a cultural resonance in some Christian values and the doctrine spread through the evangelical work of colonial missionaries. For some, the coercive imposition of Christianity supplanted ancestral beliefs, but for others Christianity provided a framework for mending the traumatic effects of colonisation and materialising core Indigenous values in another guise. For a comprehensive account of the mixing of Indigenous and Christian traditions of spirituality and ethics by Aboriginal communities living on missions, see Harris 2013.

12. See Aileen Moreton-Robinson (2015) for an analysis of 'white possession'. Whereas she tends to treat possessiveness as a natural quality of 'whiteness' and the Western subject, my own view is that subjectivity (including the subject of whiteness) is inessential in its properties and with respect to its agencies of being and becoming. For me, this is the basis of ethics and provides permanent scope for the (imperial European) subject to be-and-act otherwise and so seek forgiveness for harms caused. Relatedly, I also consider the philosophical tradition that informs the self-concept of Western subjectivity to be highly diverse, including significant narratives of non-possession, mutual aid and interdependency or reciprocal being. For more on this, see Bignall 2010a.

13. For a similar view expressed by the Chikasaw philosopher Jodi Byrd, see Byrd 2011: xxxiii.

14. The reader might note the irony of my choice of Nietzsche in this context, considering the misuse of his ideas by the Third Reich in the service of German fascism. For discussion of 'corporeal generosity' in the Continental tradition including Nietzsche, see Diprose 2002.

15. This, indeed, is a guiding principle of Indigenous nation-building as a platform for reclaiming self-governance and sovereignty after colonisation, to which I will return in the final section of this chapter.

16. This message is especially clear in Book 2 of *The Genealogy of Morals* (Nietzsche 2009).

17. Though beyond our immediate concern, it is worth noting here that the Aboriginal legal principle of 'payback' is at times materialised in practices of violent retribution such as spearing or beating, and so is commonly cited as evidence of the inability of the Australian common law to recognise and accommodate Aboriginal customary law as being consistent with its own precepts. In reality, Aboriginal customary law persists alongside the Australian common law introduced with colonisation, and is in fact the primary legal framework referred to by Aboriginal peoples living in more remote regions of Australia

such as the Northern Territory. For considerations of legal pluralism in this context, see Williams 1987; Rose 1996; Sutton 2006.

18. This term was first coined and defined in my essay on 'Collaborative Struggle' (Bignall 2014a). On discontinuous history as a continuous process of exit, see Bignall (2010a: ch. 6) and Foucault's (1984; 1986) writings on Kant and Enlightenment.

19. Indigenous peoples who prioritise 'separatism as a mode of relations' (Maddison 2020) may therefore have no need per se for a formulation of 'excolonialism' as a collaborative platform for the transformation of settler-colonial systems. However, some Aboriginal leaders consider the prospect of 'exit from colonialism' vital and inspiring for the political work of nation resurgence, and make frequent and extensive use of the concept in their resistance strategies (Dennis Eggington, pers. comm.). As a framework of general responsibility (including settler-colonial responsibility) for directing Australian society towards an 'exit from colonialism', I am also encouraged by how well Indigenous colleagues regard it as 'an opportunity for a valued and sustained shift' (Birch 2018: 12).

20. Regarding the potential for an intercultural alliance of posthumanism with Indigenous philosophies of more-than-human being, see Bignall and Rigney 2019; Bignall et al. 2016.

21. A postcolonial treaty process is long overdue in Australia, which remains the only British/European settler-colonial nation that has never negotiated a settlement with First Nations as original sovereign powers.

References

Agamben, G. (1999), *Remnants of Auschwitz: The Witness and the Archive*, trans. D. Heller-Roazen, New York: Zone Books.

Agamben, G. (2005), *State of Exception*, trans. K. Attell, Chicago: University of Chicago Press.

Altman, J., and M. Hinkson (2007), *Coercive Reconciliation*, North Carlton: Arena Publications.

Arendt, H. (1968), *The Origins of Totalitarianism*, Orlando FL: Harcourt.

Australian Government (2019), Department of Prime Minister and Cabinet, *Closing the Gap Report*, Canberra: Australian Government Press.

Baker, A. (2018), 'Camping in the Shadow of the Racist Text', *Artlink*, 38 (2), <https://www.artlink.com.au/articles/4674/camping-in-the-shadow-of-the-racist-text/> (last accessed 2 April 2019).

Banki, P. (2018), *The Forgiveness to Come: The Holocaust and the Hyper-Ethical*, New York: Fordham University Press.

Behrendt, L. (dir.) (2017), *After the Apology*, <https://au.demand.film/after-the-apology/>.

Bell, D. (2014), *Ngarrindjeri Warruwarrin: A World that Was, Is, and Will Be*, North Melbourne: Spinifex Press.

Berg, S. (2010), *Coming to Terms: Aboriginal Title in South Australia*, Adelaide: Wakefield Press.

Bignall, S. (2010a), *Postcolonial Agency: Critique and Constructivism*, Edinburgh: Edinburgh University Press.

Bignall, S. (2010b), 'Affective Assemblages: Ethics after Enjoyment', in S. Bignall and P. Patton (eds), *Deleuze and the Postcolonial*, Edinburgh: Edinburgh University Press, pp. 78–103.

Bignall, S. (2010c), 'Desire, Apathy and Activism', *Deleuze Studies*, 4: 6–21.

Bignall, S. (2014a), 'The Collaborative Struggle for Excolonialism', *Journal of Settler-Colonial Studies*, 4 (4): 340–56.

Bignall, S. (2014b), 'Postcolonial Redemption', *Concentric: Literary and Cultural Studies*, 40 (2): 29–54.

Bignall, S. (2019), 'The Obscure Drama of the Political Idea: Postcolonial Negotiations, Deleuzian Structures and the Concept of Cooperation', *New Formations*, 93: 101–21.

Bignall, S. (2020), 'Colonial Control', *Coils of the Serpent*, 6: 111–28.

Bignall, S. (2022), 'Colonial Humanism, Alter-Humanism and Ex-colonialism', in S. Herbrechter, I. Callus, M. Rossini, M. Grech, M. de Bruin-Molé and C. Müller (eds), *Palgrave Handbook of Critical Posthumanism*, Basingstoke: Palgrave, <https://doi.org/10.1007/978-3-030-42681-1_55-1>.

Bignall, S., and D. Rigney (2019), 'Indigeneity, Posthumanism and Nomad Thought: Transforming Colonial Ecologies', in R. Braidotti and S. Bignall (eds), *Posthuman Ecologies: Complexity and Process after Deleuze*, London: Rowman and Littlefield, pp. 159–82.

Bignall, S., D. Rigney and S. Hemming (2016), 'Three Ecosophies for the Anthropocene: Environmental Governance, Continental Posthumanism and Indigenous Expressivism', *Deleuze Studies*, 10 (4): 455–78.

Birch, T. (2018), 'On What Terms Can We Speak? Refusal, Resurgence and Climate Justice', *Coolabah*, 24–25: 2–16.

Braidotti, R. (2002), *Metamorphoses: Towards a Materialist Theory of Becoming*, Cambridge: Polity.

Braidotti, R. (2006), *Transpositions: On Nomad Ethics*, Cambridge: Polity.

Braidotti, R. (2009), *The Posthuman*, Cambridge: Polity.

Braidotti, R. (2011), *Nomadic Subjects: Embodiment and Sexual Difference in Contemporary Feminist Theory*, 2nd edn, New York: Columbia University Press.

Byrd, J. (2011), *The Transit of Empire: Indigenous Critiques of Colonialism*, Minneapolis: University of Minnesota Press.

Cajete, G. (2016), *Native Science: Natural Laws of Interdependence*, Santa Fe, NM: Clear Light.

Chandler, D., and J. Reid (2019), *Becoming Indigenous: Governing Imaginaries in the Anthropocene*, London: Rowman and Littlefield.

Commonwealth of Australia (1901), *Parliamentary Debates, Immigration Restriction Bill, Second Reading*, 12 September.

Cornell, S. (2015), 'Processes of Native Nationhood: The Indigenous Politics of Self-Government', *The International Indigenous Policy Journal*, 6 (4), <http://ir.lib.uwo.ca/iipj/vol6/iss4/4> (last accessed 15 May 2022).

Cronin, D. (2021), *Trapped by History: The Indigenous–State Relationship in Australia*, London: Rowman and Littlefield.

Derrida, J. (1992), *On Cosmopolitanism and Forgiveness*, trans. M. Dooley and M. Hughes, London. Routledge.

Derrida, J. (2009), *The Beast and the Sovereign*, trans. G. Bennington, Chicago: University of Chicago Press.

Diprose, R. (2002), *Corporeal Generosity: On Giving with Nietzsche, Merleau-Ponty and Levinas*, New York. SUNY Press.

Dodson, P. (2000), 'Beyond the Mourning Gate: Dealing with Unfinished Business', Wentworth Lecture, Canberra, Australian Institute for Aboriginal and Torres Strait Islander Studies.

Evans, B., and J. Reid (2013), *Deleuze and Fascism: Security, War, Aesthetics*, Abingdon: Routledge.

Flowers, R. (2015), 'Refusal to Forgive: Indigenous Women's Love and Rage', *Decolonization: Indigeneity, Education & Society*, 4: 32–49.

Foucault, M. (1984), 'What is Enlightenment?', in *The Foucault Reader*, ed. P. Rabinow, London. Penguin, pp. 32–50.

Foucault, M. (1986), 'Kant on Enlightenment and Revolution', *Economy and Society*, 15 (1): 88–96.

Fukuyama, F. (1992), *The End of History and the Last Man*, New York. Free Press.

Gaymarani, G. P. (2011), 'An Introduction to the Ngarra Law of Arnhem Land', *Northern Territory Law Journal*, 1 (6): 283–304.

Genosko, G. (2000), 'The Life and Work of Félix Guattari', in F. Guattari, *The Three Ecologies*, trans. Ian Pindar and Paul Sutton, London: Athlone Press, pp. 106–59.

Gomez-Barris, M. (2017), *The Extractive Zone: Social Ecologies and Decolonial Perspectives*, Durham, NC: Duke University Press.

Graham, M. (1999), 'Some Thoughts on the Philosophical Underpinnings of Aboriginal Worldviews', *Worldviews: Global Religions, Culture, and Ecology*, 3 (2): 105–18.

Gurrwanngu, J. (2012), 'Ngarra Law: Aboriginal Customary Law from Arnhem Land', *Northern Territory Law Journal*, 2: 236–48.

Hage, G. (1998), *White Nation: Fantasies of White Supremacy in a Multicultural Society*, London: Routledge.

Harkin, N. (2020), 'Whitewash-Brainwash: An Archival Poetic Labour Story', *Australian Feminist Law Journal*, 45 (2): 267–81, <https://doi.org/10.1080/132 00968.2019.1757935>.

Harris, J. (2013), *One Blood: 200 Years of Aboriginal Encounter with Christianity – A Story of Hope*, Adelaide: Australians Together.

Hatley, J. (2000), *Suffering Witness: The Quandary of Responsibility after the Irreparable*, Albany, NY: SUNY Press.

Hemming, S., D. Rigney and S. Berg (2011), 'Ngarrindjeri Futures: Negotiation, Governance and Environmental Management', in S. Maddison and M. Briggs (eds), *Unsettling the Settler State: Creativity and Resistance in Indigenous Settler-state Governance*, Sydney: Federation Press, pp. 98–113.

Henare, M. (2001), 'Tapu, Mana, Mauri, Hau, Wairua. A Maori Philosophy of Vitalism and Cosmos', in G. Grim (ed.), *Indigenous Traditions and Ecology*, Cambridge, MA: Harvard Divinity School, pp. 197–221.

Holland, E. W. (2008), 'Schizoanalysis, Nomadology, Fascism', in I. Buchanan and N. Thoburn (eds), *Deleuze and Politics*, Edinburgh: Edinburgh University Press, pp. 74–96.

HREOC (1997), *Bringing Them Home. Report on the National Inquiry into the Stolen Generations*, Canberra. Human Rights and Equal Opportunities Commission.

Jankelevitch, V. (2005), *Forgiveness*, trans. A. Kelley, Chicago: University of Chicago Press.

Jorgensen, M. (2007), *Rebuilding Native Nations: Strategies for Governance and Development*, Tucson: Arizona University Press.

Kuokkanen, R. (2007), *Reshaping the University: Responsibility, Indigenous Epistemes and the Logic of the Gift*, Vancouver: UBC Press.

Langton, M., M. Tehan, L. Palmer and K. Shain (2004), *Treaties and Agreements with Indigenous Peoples*, Melbourne: Melbourne University Press.

MacPherson, C. B. (1962), *The Political Theory of Possessive Individualism*, Oxford: Oxford University Press.

Maddison, S. (2020), 'Separatism as a Mode of Relations: Practicing Indigenous Resurgence and Nationhood in the 21st Century', in S. Maddison and S. Nakata (eds), *Questioning Indigenous–Settler Relations. Indigenous–Settler Relations in Australia and the World*, Singapore: Springer, vol. 1, <https://doi. org/10.1007/978-981-13-9205-4_10>.

Marsden, M. (2003), *The Woven Universe*, ed. C. Royal, Otaki: Estate of Rev. Maori Marsden.

McCaslin, W. D. (2005), *Justice as Healing: Indigenous Ways*, St Paul, MN: Living Justice Press.

McConnochie, K., D. Hollinsworth and J. Pettman (1988), *Race and Racism in Australia*, Redfern: Social Sciences Press.

Moreton-Robinson, A. (2015), *The White Possessive: Property, Power and Indigenous Sovereignty*, Minneapolis: University of Minnesota Press.

Ngarrindjeri Nation (2007), *Yarluwar-Ruwe Sea-Country Plan*, Murray Bridge: Ngarrindgeri Regional Authority.

Nietzsche, F. (1969 [1883]), *Thus Spoke Zarathustra*, trans R. J. Hollingdale, London: Penguin.

Nietzsche, F. (2009 [1887]), *The Genealogy of Morals*, trans. H. B. Samuel, Oxford: Oxford University Press.

Reilly, A. (2012), 'Sovereign Apologies', in J. Evans, A. Genovese, A. Reilly and P. Wolfe (eds), *Sovereignty: Frontiers of Possibility*, Honolulu: University of Hawaii Press, pp. 196–219.

Rice, B. (2005), *Seeing the World with Aboriginal Eyes*, Winnipeg: University of Manitoba Press.

Ricoeur, P. (2004), *Memory, History, Forgetting*, trans. K. Blamey and D. Pellauer, Chicago: University of Chicago Press.

Rose, D. B. (1996), 'Indigenous Customary Law and the Courts: Post-modern Ethics and Legal Pluralism', Discussion Paper No. 2, Canberra: Australian National University.

Rose, D. B. (2000), *Dingo Makes Us Human: Life and Land in an Australian Aboriginal Culture*, Cambridge: Cambridge University Press.

Rose, D. B. (2011), *Wild Dog Dreaming: Love and Extinction*, Charlottesville: University of Virginia Press.

Sartre, J.-P. (1976), *Critique of Dialectical Reason: Volume 1*, trans. A. Sheridan, Atlantic Highlands, NJ: Humanities Press.

Simpson, A. (2017), 'The Ruse of Consent and the Anatomy of "Refusal": Cases from Indigenous North America and Australia', *Postcolonial Studies*, 20 (1): 18–33.

Simpson, L. (2011), *Dancing on our Turtle's Back*, Manitoba: Arbeiter Ring.

Simpson, L. (2017), *As We Have Always Done: Indigenous Freedom Through Radical Resistance*, Minneapolis: University of Minnesota Press.

Smith, E. (2017), 'The Pivot of Empire: Australia and the Imperial Fascism of the British Union of Fascists', *History Australia*, 14 (3): 378–94.

Strelein, L. (2006), *Compromised Jurisprudence: Native Title Cases Since Mabo*, Canberra: Aboriginal Studies Press.

Sutton, P. (2006), 'Customs Not in Common: Cultural Relativism and Customary Law Recognition in Australia', *Macquarie Law Journal*, 6: 161–75.

Vivian, A., M. Jorgensen, A. Reilly, M. McMillan, C. McRae and J. McMinn (2017), 'Indigenous Self-Government in the Australian Federation', *Australian Indigenous Law Review*, 20: 215–42.

Warner, L. (1937), *A Black Civilization: A Social Study of an Australian Tribe*, New York: Harper and Brothers.

Williams, N. M. (1987), *Two Laws: Managing Disputes in a Contemporary Aboriginal Community*, Canberra: Aboriginal Studies Press.

Wolfe, P. (2006), 'Settler-Colonialism and the Elimination of the Native', *Journal of Genocide Research*, 8 (4): 387–409.

Chapter 9

Escaping Pro-life Neo-fascism in Italy: Affirmative and Collective Lines of Flight

Angela Balzano

Introduction

Pro-life neo-fascists have returned to Italy; or have they always been there?

Beginning from the idea that the rise of pro-life neo-fascism in Italy did not begin with the last national political elections, this chapter attempts to show how neo-fundamentalist and misogynist fascism is rooted in a network of associations and movements that have operated for years, including in collaboration with the supposedly leftist governmental coalition. To pursue this aim I adopt the ever-effective methodology developed by Donna Haraway in *The Promises of Monsters* (1992). To move through neo-fascism to *non-fascist life* I use her 'travel machine that also functions as a map' (Haraway 1992: 304): the Greimas semiotic square. My semiotic square is titled 'The uprising of bodies: through pro-life neo-fascism to *non-fascist life*'. In the first quadrant of the square, 'Neo-fascism against Women', I begin with an initial snapshot: the huge poster hung up on Gregorio VII Street in Rome by the organisation Pro Vita. Moving to quadrant B, 'Fascism against Feminism', I offer a second snapshot: the parade maxi-banner that Forza Nuova hung up outside the International Women's House. In quadrants A and B we see how fascists and neo-fundamentalist movements opposed to abortion converge in attacking sexual and reproductive rights, only recently and partially obtained. The two snapshots are emblematic of this inauspicious convergence and help us to delve into the dynamic core of the issue at stake: *our bodies/ourselves*. In quadrant C, 'Nation-state Reproduction', I scrutinise the Fertility Plan campaign and conscientious objectors to abortion with the aim of highlighting how institutional politics are contributing to disseminating microfascist attitudes. Finally, I outline some of the affirmative politics that might

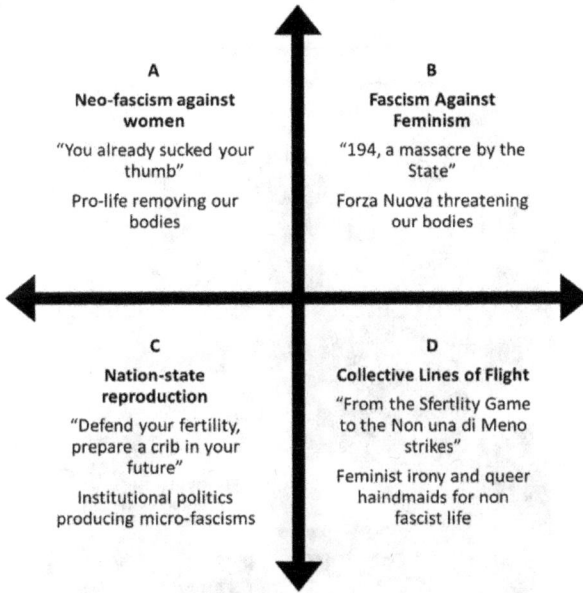

A
Neo-fascism against women

"You already sucked your thumb"

Pro-life removing our bodies

B
Fascism Against Feminism

"194, a massacre by the State"

Forza Nuova threatening our bodies

C
Nation-state reproduction

"Defend your fertility, prepare a crib in your future"

Institutional politics producing micro-fascisms

D
Collective Lines of Flight

"From the Sfertlity Game to the Non una di Meno strikes"

Feminist irony and queer haindmaids for non fascist life

Figure 9.1 Greimas semiotic square: 'The uprising of bodies: through pro-life neo-fascism to non-fascist life'.

constitute non-fascist lives. In quadrant D, 'Collective Lines of Flight', I explore the practices recently developed by feminist movements in Italy, such as the Sfertility Game created by the Favolosa Coalizione in 2016 and the protests and performances staged by Non Una di Meno in 2018. It is my hope that herein we will find actions in motion that resemble an uprising of bodies.

Neo-fascism against Women

On 3 April 2018 Pro Vita hung a huge poster up on Gregorio VII Street in Rome. The poster (Figure 9.2), measuring 7 metres wide and 11 metres high, depicts a human embryo; the press release accompanying the poster offers this paradoxical description: 'The image of a child in the mother's womb, to raise consciousness.'[1] The text on the poster is even more mystifying:

> You were like this at 11 weeks. All your organs were present. Your heart had already started beating from the third week after conception. You already sucked your thumb. And now you're here because your mother did not have an abortion.

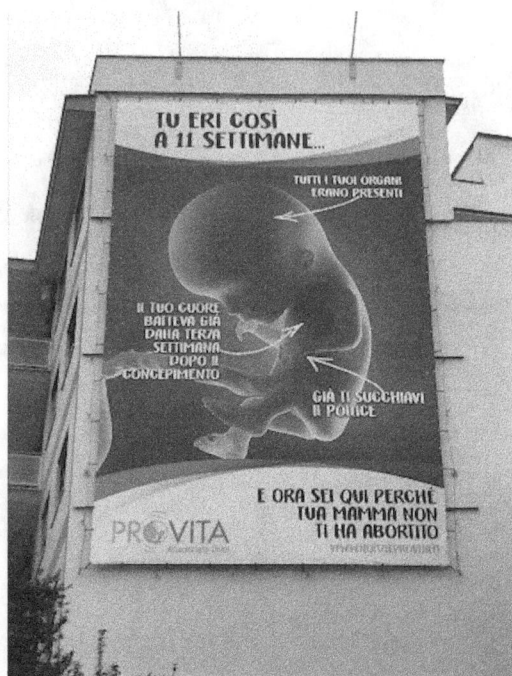

Figure 9.2 Pro Vita poster against abortion, Gregorio VII Street, Rome, 2018.

This poster was the first part of a multifaceted strategy launched for the 40th anniversary of Law 194, passed on 22 May 1978, the Italian legislation that regulates access to the voluntary termination of pregnancy (*Norme per la tutela sociale della maternità e sull'interruzione volontaria della gravidanza*). According to Pro Vita, Law 194 'allows the suppression of unborn children' and must be amended to increase protection for the embryo and the value of maternity, at the expense of women's self-determination.

To pursue their ideological beliefs, pro-life activists[2] led by Pro Vita and its president Toni Brandi also put out a petition. A brief analysis of the call for signatures makes evident the new strategy adopted by pro-life militants. They no longer attack women's freedom of choice, nor does the title refer explicitly to embryo protection. They changed key words in order to appeal to a broader base of supporters. As Carlo Casini, former president of Movimento per la Vita (Movement for Life, MpV, the oldest Italian pro-life organisation) clearly explained in an interview, 'to save children, we need women's cooperation'.[3] Pro Vita has embraced Casini's suggestion and titled the petition: 'For women's

health: Sign to inform them about the physical and psychological consequences of voluntary abortion'.[4] This is an example of a wrongful
appropriation: the feminist stance in favour of women's health has been
turned into a well-organised political trap. The text of the appeal continues in this rhetorical vein. It does not begin by asserting that 'the
embryo is one of us', as in other international pro-life campaigns.[5]
Pro Vita prefers to say that 'Abortion damages multiple people: not
only the children but also mothers, fathers, siblings and grandparents.'
The petition has the purpose of asking the Ministry of Health to dis-
seminate information about the damage that abortion can cause to
women's health; it aims to transmit legislative proposals to the Health
Commission in Parliament to ensure that women in public hospitals are
made aware of the consequences of abortion.

Comparing Pro Vita to previous pro-life campaigns can help us to
understand how the rhetorical expedient fails to conceal the misogynist
and conservative content of Pro Vita's appeals. In the end, these asser-
tions coincide with the purposes laid out by MpV. Although Pro Vita
and MpV use different communication strategies, both have the ultimate objective of entering into the space of public hospitals to intercept
women seeking abortion services with the intention of making them
change their minds about pregnancy termination. There is nothing new
except for the language, and the medium remains the same: utilising
the law itself to prevent women from choosing. Let me outline how this
project unfolds.

MpV was founded in 1975 with the explicit aim of countering pro-
choice struggles and of operating on the political and social level to
follow the doctrine of the Catholic Church, as laid out in *Humanae
vitae*, the encyclical written by Pope Paul VI in 1968. After abortion
was legalised, in 1981 MpV organised a referendum to repeal Law 194,
but it was rejected by the electorate. Since the failure of the referendum,
MpV has opted for a more accommodating strategy, in 1985 creating
the Centres of Life Aid, structures through which they promote the use
of natural contraceptive methods and try to convince women, through
volunteers as well as material aid,[6] not to abort. As Carlo Casini makes
clear, pro-life activists learned a lesson from the referendum's failure:
'Those who want to defend life must look at reality, today it is not possible to change Law 194, we have to work with what we have.'[7] This is
why pro-life activists are using article 2 of Law 194: in this way, they
can sign specific agreements with regional governments, secure public
funding and gain authorisation to open their centres in public hospitals
and clinics.[8]

The recent petition by Pro Vita does nothing more than retrace the aims formerly laid out by its predecessors, merely reformulating the communication strategy to make it more attractive especially to women and younger generations. This does not mean, however, that Pro Vita treats women as key actors; rather, women remain one of their targets. As with the MpV campaigns, the Pro Vita poster does not depict any women. Their cultural propaganda is focused on images of the foetus from 11 weeks, because earlier there is no way of identifying similarities with a new-born child. Their communication strategy removes the woman who is carrying on the pregnancy, preferring to foreground only the product of conception. This move to abstract the foetus from the woman's body is explained by the need to define the embryo as 'human life'. When placed alongside a woman, the embryo would not stand the test of the definition of 'human life'. Women have communicative faculties, memories, experiences, relationships, social roles; above all women do not depend on anyone else to live: women are autonomous subjectivities. The embryos removed during pregnancy termination procedures today are, in most cases, eliminated during the first weeks and before the third month, when they do not display any of the traits found in women, especially considering that they would never be able to autonomously sustain life: without a placenta, umbilical cord and a woman's desire to carry on with the gestation, the unborn would never be born.

The conservative position of pro-life activists abstracts the issue from this materialistic conception of bodies and subjectivities. It removes any reminder of women's bodies in the effort to enhance life 'from conception'. Since the late 1980s pro-life movements have repeated the same propaganda-type rhetoric that was recently confirmed by the Pro Vita poster. They employ an imaginary of extra-terrestrial space to represent the foetus. As Haraway noted, the use of the image of an astronaut (a man) swimming in space, floating free, tied only by the umbilical cord to the spaceship, has served precisely to spread a belief throughout the social body that a foetus can have an independent life, that it does not need a woman to live. There is no mother in the Pro Vita poster. In her place, all around the foetus, there is only empty space. As if the poster were not expressive enough, the text describing Pro Vita's mission is even more direct. Here the group's true political stance is made clear: 'the value of life and of natural family are essential for the future of humanity. Thus, Pro Vita exists and operates in the name of those who cannot speak.'[9] Ironically, it is possible to misunderstand this sentence: how many men have spoken for women? The list would be long and ongoing, but this is not a case of speaking for or about women. Pro-life activists are not speaking for women; they have elected themselves to speak for the unborn. Haraway's question, *who speaks for the foetus?* (1992: 311), would be promptly and eagerly answered by the Catholic neo-fundamentalist coalition: 'We speak for the foetus, but we do even more than that!'

It is not only a political semiotics of representation that we find ourselves dealing with. Contemporary pro-life movements have learned how crucial it is to combine communication campaigns with legal and political initiatives. My aim here is to analyse this complex strategy in order to highlight the *neo* of neo-fascist pro-life movements. Of course, their desire to represent the unborn is linked to the fascist social construction of women and families. Nevertheless, pro-life organisations today are advancing fascist tactics not only by unjustly appropriating feminist language and struggles but also by colonising the human rights debate with their request to extend the legislative protection of life to embryos. As Foucault wrote: 'it is true that the old banners were raised, but the combat shifted and spread into new zones' (1992: xii). Pro-life movements have begun to build networks with even more reactionary political forces and in the last decade they have begun to block legal amendments that would increase women's self-determination.

Fascism against Feminism

The huge poster by Pro Vita was removed a few days after it appeared thanks to feminist protests. However, four days later, on 7 April, another semiotic attack took place in Rome, this time resembling a threat. This brings us to the second snapshot. Somewhat shocked, we look at the large-format parade banner hung by Forza Nuova[10] just outside the International Women's House in Rome (Figure 9.3) and read the slogan it bears: '194, a massacre by the state' (*194 strage di Stato*).[11] First Catholic pro-life movements, then fascists: expressions of a country that is struggling to resist violently conservative political forces. The Pro Vita poster constructs ideological propaganda while Forza Nuova's enormous parade banner adds a threat, typical of fascist squads, that outlines the terms of the conflict. It is no coincidence that the fascists displayed this banner outside the International Women's House: they chose this site with the aim of specifying their enemy: feminism.[12]

The war conducted around women's wombs is ongoing. In the crusade against abortion, MpV and Pro Vita have allowed fascists to participate on a more explicit level. While neo-fascist pro-life discourse mystifies the issues at stake by invoking women's health and human rights,

Figure 9.3 Forza Nuova parade banner against abortion outside the International Women's House, Rome, 2018.

traditional fascists are conducting an even more appalling attack against women's self-determination and all forms of feminism. They did not choose the Ministry of Health or a hospital. Why? Because the object of their obsession goes beyond the struggle to make abortion illegal; more broadly, they are obsessed with the possibility that women might choose not to perform any reproductive work at all. When fascists say 'Law 194 is a massacre by the state', they are saying that 'women cannot be free, they must be bound to the reproductive order of the nation'. It is a message for all feminists, considering that the International Women's House has been a landmark safe space for feminists from different countries and generations since 1983. It is a political threat given that the mission of the International Women's House openly states: 'The priorities of the International Women's House are tied to issues related to self-determination and to free reproductive health choices.'[13] Moreover, the fascists' assertion is patently untrue, if we consider the data gathered by the Italian Ministry of Health to be reliable. In its report on Law 194, the ministry specifies that the abortion rate has decreased since the law's approval.[14] It is untrue because the law has granted more women the possibility of avoiding death as the result of an unsafe abortion.

Fascists have deliberately ignored the reality of unsafe abortions caused by banning such procedures, because they have always considered the reproduction of the nation a key value, more important that women's health and autonomy. This is a matter of fact and historical record: until the approval of Law 194, abortion remained illegal in Italy, because article 546 of the fascist penal code, known as the Rocco Code, was in effect. The abortion ban was inserted in book II, title X, the section punishing 'Crimes against the integrity and health of the race', and stated: 'Whoever provides for, with her consent – a woman's abortion, will be punished with imprisonment from 2 to 5 years. The same punishment will be applied to the woman who consented to the abortion.' No punishment is established for men, only for women and physicians. On the one hand, this can be explained as reflecting the intrinsic sexism of fascist legislation; on the other hand, it expresses the need to control women's wombs in order to preserve the biological reproduction of the population and to bind women to the reproductive roles required to sustain a welfare state based on heterosexual, nuclear families. This article was applied until 1975 when the Italian Constitutional Court declared it unconstitutional by virtue of its conflicting with article 32 (the Republic safeguards health as a fundamental right of the individual) and moreover because 'the mother's health and life and the foetus's health and life are not on the same level'. Thus, as early as 1975 pro-life activists and fascists had their answer: a ban on abortion is unconstitutional, women and foetuses are not comparable. Nevertheless, after forty years they are gaining influence in Parliament and increasing their numbers in public hospitals and their visibility in media and social networks. This would not be a real concern if the persistence of their activism was not so effective in the legal arena and in women's lives, as we see in quadrant C.

Forza Nuova is not the only fascist organisation that is combating women's freedom of choice, it is merely the most conservative and tied to the ancient imaginary of the decades of fascist rule. Fascist organisations opposed to abortion in Italy also include Comitato no194, a group that continues to call for the repeal of Law 194 and to organise marches and prayer sessions outside public hospitals. Pietro Guerini, president of Comitato no194, has declared that the fight against abortion is an anti-communist one, in perfect harmony with fascist politics. In his words: 'Historically and objectively, no fascist dictatorship has ever legalized voluntary abortion (not in Italy, nor in Spain, nor in Chile, nor elsewhere), the MSI voted against 194 in 1978 in Parliament and in 1981 invited its voters to speak up calling for the law to be repealed.'[15] Most frightening, however, is the fact that the Italian government (Lega and Cinque Stelle) has created a Ministry of the Family and assigned this office to Lorenzo Fontana, a member of Comitato no194, who declared his intention to repeal Law 194. In addition, Fontana participated in a pro-life demonstration that ended in a debate with the leader of Forza Nuova, Roberto Fiore, and his son Alessandro, himself a leader of Pro Vita.[16] We only have to connect the dots to answer this chapter's opening question: pro-life fascists have always been here, and they are trying to renew their tactics in order to deal with the present landscape.

Beyond Forza Nuova and Comitato no194 there is CasaPound, which has yet another strategy, one that does not directly oppose abortion rights but insists that women must be mothers in order to be fully realised. The historian Elia Rosati describes CasaPound as a neo-fascist organisation, noting that since 2008 it has brought about a new fracture in public space thanks to 'its abilities with new media and new forms of activism, characterized by a much more visible capacity to appeal to the young' (Rosati 2017). However, the members of CasaPound define themselves as 'third millennium fascists' and, apart from these new communication strategies, their political beliefs and myths remain unchanged from the fascism of the past. Furthermore, CasaPound and Forza Nuova share the same enemy (the term used by CasaPound in its manifestos): feminism. Where Forza Nuova hangs banners, CasaPound organises seminars and campaigns under the title 'Time to be a Mother'. These 'third millennium fascists' wrote a draft bill titled 'National Natality Allowance', which excludes non-Italian children and parents, Gypsy people and unemployed persons, thus perversely combining racism, sexism and classism (Rosati 2018: 162–3).

Having arrived at the end of quadrants A and B, we can proffer an analytical suggestion following the path charted by Cooper in *Life as Surplus*. Pro-life movements together with new and old fascist organisations have been working for a long time against women and feminism, sharing political objectives while using different tactics. All of these reactionary and conservative groups could be included in Cooper's category of neo-fundamentalism, an informal coalition that began to arise in the late 1970s and is characterised by a compulsive focus on the 'sexual arena and family values' (Cooper 2008: 169). In Cooper's words, neo-fundamentalists had to face 'new left political demands, from feminism to gay rights' and they 'gave voice to a newfound nostalgia – one that obsessed over the perceived decline of the heterosexual, male-headed, reproductive white family' (2008: 169). At this point, let us examine how some of the neo-fundamentalist groups' favourite political arguments reappear in national institutional politics.

Nation-state Reproduction

In the last decades, there has been obsessive attention to reproductive and sexual issues in Italy across the institutional political spectrum, from the leftist coalition to right-wing parties. For our purposes, it suffices to begin quadrant C with the National Fertility Plan (NFP), launched in 2016 by Beatrice Lorenzin, the minister of health under the Renzi government.[17] The plan was introduced with the slogan 'Defend your fertility, prepare a crib for your future!', and was accompanied by 12 posters that were widely disseminated through social networks and new media outlets. The plan itself is not a programmatic document, but a rhetorical pamphlet. It does not contain indications regarding social services, welfare infrastructure or basic income support, measures traditionally considered crucial to sustaining women and encouraging them to choose maternity. The minister eliminated any doubts on this point beginning with the first page of the document: 'The aim of the Plan is to inform citizens about the role of Fertility in their lives, its duration and how to protect it by avoiding behaviours that can put it at risk' (fertility is capitalised in the original text). *The Guardian* did not hesitate to publish an opinion piece about this campaign titled 'Italy's fertility day posters aren't just sexist – they're echoes of a fascist past' (Coppolaro-Nowell 2016).

Figure 9.4 Italian Ministry of Health, National Fertility Plan (NFP) posters, 2016. Source: Italian Ministry of Health.

One of the best-known and most hotly debated posters shows a young woman holding an hourglass and saying: 'Beauty is ageless. But fertility is not.' The slogan 'Prepare a crib for the future!' is positioned over a woman's uterus, while fertility, which should be a realm of private life rooted in an individual's bodily self-determination, is violently displaced: at a time when even natural resources are being privatised, fertility has been transformed into a common good depicted as being equivalent to water. The Italian flag and the appeal to the Constitution are the icing on the cake that renders the Fertility Plan's warning real: 'In Italy, the population's replacement rate is too low to ensure generational changeover. This causes a progressive ageing of the population' (Ministero delle Salute 2016: 138). Lorenzin's own statements indicate more clearly that the issue at stake is the reproduction of the nation-state:

> In 2026 less than 350,000 children per year will be born in our country, 40% less than 2010. An apocalypse. We will be finished from an economic point of view, and in terms of our vital capacity. This is the true Italian emergency. If we tie all this to the increase in the elderly and chronic diseases, we have the portrait of a dying country.[18]

Evoking a fascist scenario – the idea of a nation that must defend itself to survive the apocalypse – the NFP invites women and men to police their reproductive organs and gametes using new health technologies and devices of the self. It suffices to look at one poster targeting men. Depicting a hand holding a cigarette, it says: 'Don't let your sperm go up in smoke.' Another poster including both women and men (Figure 9.5) shows the intrinsic racism of the plan. The appropriate 'good habits to be promoted' are represented by four white, smiling people shot close-up, while the 'bad company to avoid' is represented by five dark-skinned people, all of whom are smoking, some of them depicted close-up and others further in the background. Here it is essential to grasp the *neo* aspect of this fascist imaginary. Since the NFP is positioned in the biopolitical era, it operates through a biomedical approach by focusing more on the self-management of individual/private health than on welfare structures: *do not smoke, defend your fertility!* Indeed, the NFP appears to be an injunction to *our bodies/ourselves*, one that aims to convince us that we ourselves must control the proper functioning of our reproductive systems.

The biomedical realm is currently the political arena *par excellence*, the highly contested space in which neo-fundamentalists try to install their biopolitical devices even while women try to exercise

Figure 9.5 Italian Ministry of Health, National Fertility Plan (NFP) poster, 2016. Source: Italian Ministry of Health.

their reproductive and sexual freedom. It suffices to point out that the percentage of conscientious objectors to abortion among physicians in Italy is high to demonstrate that clinics and hospitals have become a conflict zone, a crucial arena in which to influence and police women's bodies. As the data show, the national incidence of conscientious objectors is over 70 per cent, rising to a dangerous high of nearly 90 per cent in several regional districts and cities (Sicily, Marche). On the one hand, the reasons behind this threatening rise can be found in the history of Law 194 and the limitations of its text; on the other hand, the political tactics of neo-fundamentalist movements have also contributed.

Law 194 was the result of a decades-long struggle by feminist and social movements, but the text of the law was not written following a referendum. In 1976 President Leone's government decided to dissolve Parliament in order to avoid holding a referendum that might lead to a more radical, feminist law. The law was thus written by a governmental coalition including Catholic and reactionary parties as well as socialists, communists and liberals. The resulting text falls short of recognising the principle of women's self-determination even while it seems to embrace their right to health. Telling the truth about Law 194 would mean admitting that access to safe abortion procedures had not been accepted as a full right for every woman in every case. In 1978, rather, abortion was seen as a concession that the state made in relation to some women and in particular circumstances. As specified in article 4, abortion is allowed only for health, economic or social reasons or when the life of the child and/or mother is at risk. Article 5 introduces another limit on women's self-determination, a limit embodied by physicians: 'If termination is not found to be urgently required, the physician shall request her to reflect for seven days. After seven days have elapsed, the woman may take the document issued.' As if it were not enough to have rendered women so inferior that they are considered incapable of making their own decisions, the law also provides a way not only for physicians but also neo-fundamentalists to wholly deny women's freedom to choose: the option of conscientious objection as laid out in article 9. According to this clause, physicians can refuse to perform abortions and they are not asked to perform any other kind of work instead. The law does not put any limit on the percentage of physicians who can choose this option, a fact that seems to have produced the national rate of 70 per cent as a logical consequence. The path available to neo-fundamentalists now becomes clearer: they do not need to repeal the law in order to prevent abortions, they only need to enter into an alliance with physicians. This alliance was signalled on 15 November 2014 when Pope Francis participated in the anniversary of the Association of Catholic Physicians and invited the 7,000 association members to undertake 'brave choices such as conscientious objection [. . .] because, for the Catholic Church, abortion is a scientific problem'.[19]

Collective Lines of Flight

While for neo-fundamentalists abortion became a 'scientific problem', for feminist movements it has been and perhaps always will be a political struggle. Especially since the late 1960s, the realm of reproductive and sexual choices has been a starting point for creating alternative ways of life, non-fascist forms of collective regeneration. The feminist movements of the late 1960s had long-term consequences on women's lives, giving rise to slow but truly effective changes in terms of culture and behaviour. When Pro Vita launched its campaign against abortion and Forza Nuova hung its banner against Law 194, when the NFP was unveiled and Pope Francis invited physicians to engage in conscientious objection, women in Italy were already living non-fascist lives even without full political awareness.

Let me clarify this point. All of these neo-fundamentalist political tactics can be read as a reaction to the spread of women's self-determination. It is indeed true, as Lorenzin warned, that women in Italy are reproducing less and less. From a feminist point of view, however, this is not an apocalypse but rather a positive effect of the long-term revolution that began in the late 1960s. It is not possible to explain the low birth rate in relation to the economic crisis alone; there are also cultural reasons underlying women's choices not to become mothers. If we look at the Eurisko research focusing on the non-reproductive choices of women, we discover that the majority of women without children have a medium-high level of education, medium-to-high incomes and skilled jobs. The picture that emerges shows women with 'a life full of interests and objectives: freedom from duties, professional aspirations, commitment in the cultural sphere'. Women often reported that they chose not to reproduce for mere pleasure and fun. The research results highlight that these women have substituted traditional 'family values' with an alternative set of ethics that 'would seem to be inspired by a personal ethical code that includes the values of ecology, caring for the environment and environmental sustainability'. These women are 'more oriented toward the outdoors and do not have family life or the home as a main focus, preferring to invest in external and extra-domestic activities'.[20] This shift therefore represents a non-fascist way of life, one that began to spread silently, in a molecular manner and on an individual level, to then explode loudly on the molar and public scale. Women are already choosing not to reproduce the nation-state, although this choice does not always reflect politically organised and oriented approaches.

The trend not to reproduce is not confined to national borders; it involves all of Europe, as is evidenced by the total fertility rate of 1.6 live births per woman in 2016, a rate that continues to come in under 'the 2.1 live births per woman that is considered to be the replacement level in developed countries: the average number of live births per woman required to keep the population size constant in the absence of migration'.[21] It is no coincidence that Eurostat, in comparing data across years, notes that 'Fertility rates steadily declined from the mid-1960s.' This seems to confirm our hypothesis: something in our sexual and reproductive behaviour has deeply changed following the impact of feminist movements for freedom of choice and the right to health.

At the same time, in recent years feminist activists have been more successful in organising protests and spreading new forms of life, making individual choices more visible and powerful and transforming them into collective lines of flight, potential escape routes from neo-fundamentalists' reactions and attacks. Let us begin our journey through these multiple feminist, non-fascist practices with the Sfertility Game, created in 2016 in Italy by the Favolosa Coalizione. To explain what the Sfertility Game is, I quote from the text written by this transfeminist network:

> On 22 September 2016 the Italian Minister of Health launched the first Fertility Day to disseminate the National Fertility Plan: a political project that rereads, in a neoliberalist key, the fascist imaginary of women as producers of children for the nation-state and that reimposes the primacy of heterosexual reproduction. The Favolosa Coalizione, a network of feminist and queer subjectivities based in Bologna, has for the occasion created the Sfertility Game, a crazy board game that, with irony and a spirit of desecration, subverts the governmental logics that attempt to reduce our bodies to gametes, nullifying self-determination, denying any conscious, non-reproductive choice. The Sfertility Game is the result of a collective effort that coalesced around the illustrations of the artist Percy Bertolini, a political practice of activism that is highly creative, communicative and participatory.[22]

The aim of the game is to underline that women have already become uncontrollable subjectivities, that our sexual desires and reproductive choices are already branching off in different directions as compared to the diktats of the NFP. Nevertheless, being a self-managed subjectivity entails facing many obstacles, obstacles concretely identified in several spaces on the board. A player who lands on space number 17 (Figure 9.6), for instance, meets a woman who had an unsafe abortion

Figure 9.6 Favolosa Coalizione, Sfertility Game, 2016. Courtesy of Percy Bertolini and Favolosa Coalizione.

Figure 9.7 Favolosa Coalizione, Sfertility Game, 2016. Courtesy of Percy Bertolini and Favolosa Coalizione.

and, due to a recent civil law, has to pay a fee of €10,000; if the player cannot afford this amount, she or he must go to prison.

Furthermore, the game seeks to highlight the material difficulties of parenthood in a country such as present-day Italy, the price that women pay when they choose maternity. For instance, let us look at spaces 9, 10 and 11 (Figure 9.7). In space 9 we find a woman who gave birth to two children but did not succeed in keeping her job: she has to go back one space. In space 10 we meet a mother of two children who is still very productive for her company: she can go ahead three spaces. In space 11, however, the same women who was doing a perfect job of balancing familial and professional life experiences a nervous breakdown: she must drop out for a round to seek treatment. At the end of this queer board game we found ourselves both laughing and thinking, which is why the Sfertility Game seems to embody Haraway's statement that 'Irony is about humor and serious play. It is also a rhetorical strategy and a political method' (1991: 150).

The year 2016 also made a strong impression because it was when Lucia Perez, a 16-year-old girl, was held against her will, raped and murdered in Mar del Plata, Argentina. The fact that three men were arrested for this crime did not stop the rage that spread among women and feminists. In Argentina, they reacted by asserting that male and gender violence could not be effectively handled using the instruments of the state. Preferring the path of self-management, they decided to organise a general assembly in Rosario attended by more than 100,000 activists, establishing the global network known as *Ni Una Mas* and launching the women's strike on 8 March. The first Italian assembly of Non Una di Meno was held on 27 November 2016 and followed by a national demonstration involving more than 250,000 people protesting male and gender violence, held in Rome on 26 November.[23] Since that time, Non Una di Meno has organised two strikes and disseminated a political plan that was developed, through a collective writing experiment, over the course of several national assemblies and countless local meetings. On

Figure 9.8 La Mala Educación and Non Una di Meno, Handmaid Performance, 26 May 2018, Bologna. Courtesy of La Mala Educación and Non Una di Meno.

the molecular scale, the scale of daily involvement in a local yet public space, it is interesting to note how feminists have been able to use their own bodies to create and communicate non-fascist ways of life. Keeping in mind the Pro Vita manifesto in quadrant A, it is important to consider the different approach to the anniversary of Law 194 embraced by Non Una di Meno. For this occasion, the feminist network organised local demonstrations to call attention to the perilously high percentage of conscientious objectors. Without having planned it, the local feminist networks of Non Una di Meno in both Milan and Bologna decided to occupy public space with a 'Handmaid Performance'. In Bologna, the performance took place during a demonstration on 26 May 2018, when the feminist students of La Mala Educación dressed themselves as Handmaids from Margaret Atwood's novel and later TV series *The Handmaid's Tale* (Figure 9.8).

Their wrists chained together, they walked through the historic city centre in silence and, on arriving in the intersection that hosts a huge outdoor market, they broke the chains and threw their red robes on the ground to the accompaniment of 'La Rage' by Keny Arkana, showing that bodies are always capable of revolting even when they may seem docile and subjugated. As Foucault stated: 'There are two meanings of the word "subject": subject to someone else by control and dependence; and tied to his own identity by a conscience or self-knowledge' (1982:

Figure 9.9 La Mala Educación and Non Una di Meno, Handmaid Performance, 26 May 2018, Bologna. Courtesy of La Mala Educación and Non Una di Meno.

781). On their skin several slogans were written: 'pro-life means no choice', 'we want more than Law 194' and 'repeal conscientious objection'. As a final gesture, the activists chose to form a line blocking city traffic, standing side by side with their raised hands forming the shape of a triangle, the global, transgenerational symbol of women's freedom of choice (Figure 9.9).

Perhaps '[t]hose who would preserve the pure order of politics and political discourse' (Foucault 1992: xii) might criticise the Handmaid performance, arguing that it is nothing more than a way of increasing the visibility of non-fascist forms of life and does not constitute a tool capable of obtaining 'rights'. From the perspective adopted in this chapter, however, the creative process of performance is considered an affirmative political practice in and of itself. It is indeed true that the main feature of this performance is non-oppositional. Rephrasing Foucault, we could say 'It is not enough to say that this is anti-authority struggle' (1982: 780). It is more appropriate to describe it in terms of a struggle capable of opening up new spaces of counter-subjectification. In fact, the feminist activists who organised the Handmaid performance do not 'expect to find a solution to their problem at a future date'; instead their aim 'is the power effects as such'. They criticise the medical profession not 'because it is a profit-making concern but because it exercises an uncontrolled power over people's bodies, their health, and their life and death' (Foucault 1982: 780).

The Handmaid performance was the result of several meetings organised by the group La Mala Educación at the University of Bologna, the wired product of collective knowledge-building. It would not have been possible without the inspiration provided by two key feminist thinkers: Rosi Braidotti and Donna Haraway. In choosing the soundtrack, the activists embraced the suggestions that Braidotti makes in her book *Per una Politica Affermativa*: 'We entered the feminist posthumanism era, the hyper-accelerated time of a feminism transmitted in rhyme to the notes of a postindustrial strongly antiracist rap' (2017: 40). The decision to subvert the plot of *The Handmaid's Tale*, rewriting its ending in a public space, came from a collective reading of *A Cyborg Manifesto* and *The Promises of Monsters* by Haraway: 'the boundary between science fiction and social reality is an optical illusion' (1991: 150).

It should be noted that the performance was not followed by a void. Activists created a public, self-managed sexual and reproductive consultation service devoted to young people, La Mala Consilia, located in the university neighbourhood. This service is more than a way of making up for the absence of state health and reproductive facilities; it is a meeting place for all the subjectivities who seek freedom of choice. It functions as such because Foucault's admonition – 'do not demand of politics to restore the rights of the individual' (1992: xiv) – is truer than ever. Thus, the way in which contemporary feminists shape their activism appears to closely resemble 'an opposition to the effects of power which are linked with knowledge, competence, and qualification'. In other words, feminists today still struggle 'against the privileges of knowledge' (Foucault 1982: 781). In so doing, feminist activists seem to suggest that in the contemporary context, it is more effective to learn how to self-manage our own health, to establish networks among women and scientists, to circulate marginalised or underground cultures, rather than asking for governmental recognition. Positioning themselves at the crossroads of knowledge production, science-fictional subversion and reproductive medicine, contemporary feminists seem to be aware of Haraway's warning: 'The stakes in the border war have been the territories of production, reproduction, and imagination' (1991: 151).

It is here, at this crowded and conflictual crossroads, that we can find feminists engaged in making non-fascist lives, committed to Foucault's heritage, struggling against 'the fascism in us all' and the 'love for power' (AO, xiii). Feminists are desiring and experimenting with a future in which sexual and reproductive behaviours that diverge from the heterosexual norm can join a safe space of self-determination. This future is the present built every day in women's centres, feminist libraries, shelters and associations fighting male and gender violence, in schools, universities and all the other on- and offline locations where the aim is never the reproduction of sameness but rather the regeneration of an *inappropriate/d* kind of otherness (Haraway 1992; Minh-ha 1986).

Notes

1. <https://www.notizieprovita.it/attivita/maxi-manifesto-provita-a-roma-no-all-aborto/> (last accessed 22 April 2019). Since 2014 Pro Vita has organised an annual March for Life. It operates 'in defence of children' and 'of life from conception to natural death', supporting 'the family founded on marriage between a man and a woman'. As non-profit organisation Pro Vita is focused on content dissemination, it has an editorial publishing house and a newspaper. It seems that the relationship between Forza Nuova and Pro Vita has a long history, including funding. See <https://www.corriere.it/extra-per-voi/2017/07/06/tutti-legami-pro-vita-forza-nuova-0f71ba70-6254-11e7-84bc-daac3beed6c1.shtml> (last accessed 15 May 2020).
2. The following associations have also promoted the petition: AIGOC, Comitato Difendiamo i Nostri Figli, Non si tocca la famiglia, Vita è, Ora et Labora in Difesa della Vita, Human Life International, AiBi Amici dei Bambini, Movimento con Cristo per la Vita Schio, La Nuova Bussola Quotidiana, il Tavolo Permanente per la Famiglia con la Regione Veneto, Libertà&Persona, Papa Giovanni XXIII, Movimento dell'Amore Familiare and Generazione Voglio Vivere.
3. See the video interview with Carlo Casini in *Così è (se vi pare). Il movimento per la vita in Italia*, documentary, directed by Irene Dionisio. Italy: Consulta Torinese per la Laicità delle Istituzioni, Fluxlab, 2012.
4. <https://www.notizieprovita.it/petizioni/per-le-donne-firma-perche-siano-davvero-informate-sullaborto/> (last accessed 22 April 2019).
5. <https://oneofus.eu/> (last accessed 22 April 2019).
6. <http://www.mpv.org/progetto-gemma/> (last accessed 22 April 2019).
7. *Così è (se vi pare). Il movimento per la vita in Italia*, 2012.
8. Article 2 of Law 194: 'For the purposes of this Law, the counselling centres may make use of voluntary assistance, on the basis of pertinent regulations or agreements, from appropriate basic social welfare organisations and voluntary associations, which may also assist mothers in difficulties after the child is born.'
9. <https://www.notizieprovita.it/missione/> (last accessed 22 April 2019).
10. From its website, one can learn that Forza Nuova is 'a political movement founded on 29 September 1997, under the patronage of San Michele Arcangelo, by Massimo Morsello and Roberto Fiore'. Forza Nuova shares online its political agenda, namely the *Eight Programmatic Points for National Reconstruction*, which has as first point the repeal of Law 194. The fascist connotations of this organisation are easily recognisable; among the other features of its political agenda are an immigration ban, the 1929 state–Church agreement's restoration, and an increase of population based on natural and heterosexual family. See <http://www.forzanuova.eu> (last accessed 22 April 2019).

11. In a country such as Italy, using the expression 'massacre by the State' (*strage di Stato*) means referring to a highly conflictual and violent period characterised by collaboration between the main political party in Parliament and the main autonomous fascist political organisations. If there are proponents and perpetrators of massacres in Italy, it is precisely among the fascist organisations that one must look for them. It may help to remember Piazza Fontana, the Years of Lead and the massacre at Bologna railway station.
12. The International Women's House in Rome was established in 1983 for social purposes, particularly with regard to women's citizenship. The priorities of the International Women's House relate to self-determination and reproductive justice, but also gender violence and international cooperation.
13. <http://www.casainternazionaledelledonne.org/index.php/it/chi-siamo/who-what-we-are> (last accessed 22 April 2019).
14. <http://www.salute.gov.it/imgs/C_17_pubblicazioni_2552_ulterioriallegati_ulterioreallegato_0_alleg.pdf> (last accessed 22 April 2019).
15. <http://no194.org/wp-content/uploads/2015/05/194art85.pdf> (last accessed 22 April 2019). MSI is an Italian political party founded by fascist veterans.
16. <http://espresso.repubblica.it/attualita/2018/10/08/news/dal-ministro-fontana-a-forza-nuova-le-mani-sulla-194-1.327598> (last accessed 22 April 2019).
17. <http://www.salute.gov.it/imgs/C_17_pubblicazioni_2367_allegato.pdf> (last accessed 22 April 2019).
18. <https://www.repubblica.it/politica/2016/05/15/news/beatrice_lorenzin_rischiamo_il_crac_demografico_serve_agire_ora_o_sara_troppo_tardi_-139852112/> (last accessed 22 April 2019).
19. <http://press.vatican.va/content/salastampa/it/bollettino/pubblico/2014/11/15/0853/01821.html> (last accessed 22 April 2019).
20. <https://www.west-info.eu/it/non-voglio-figli-perche-sono-lunadigas/gfk-eurisko-lunadigas-profilo-donne-italiane-18-55-anni-senza-figli-in-famiglia-che-dichiarano-di-non-volere-figli-2015/> (last accessed 22 April 2019).
21. <https://ec.europa.eu/eurostat/statistics-explained/index.php/Fertility_statistics#live_births_per_woman_in_the_EU_in_2016> (last accessed 22 April 2019).
22. <http://www.bilbolbul.net/BBB16/?p=907> (last accessed 22 April 2019).
23. <https://nonunadimeno.wordpress.com> (last accessed 22 April 2019).

References

Balzano, A., and C. Flamigni (2015), *Sessualità e riproduzione. Due generazioni in dialogo su diritti, corpi e medicina*, Turin: Anake.

The Boston Women's Health Book Collective (1971), *Our Bodies, Ourselves*, New York: Simon and Schuster.

Braidotti, R. (2017), *Per una Politica Affermativa: Itinerari Etici*, Milan. Mimesis.

Cooper, M. (2008), *Life as Surplus: Biotechnology and Capitalism in the Neoliberal Era*, Seattle: University of Washington Press.

Coppolaro-Nowell, A. (2016), 'Italy's Fertility Day Posters Aren't Just Sexist – They're Echoes of a Fascist Past', *The Guardian*, 5 September, <https://www.theguardian.com/commentisfree/2016/sep/05/italys-fertility-day-posters-sexist-echoes-of-fascist-past> (last accessed 22 April 2019).

Cossutta, C., V. Greco, A. Mainardi and S. Voli (2018), *Smagliature Digitali: Corpi, Generi e Tecnologie*, Milan: Agenzia X.

Foucault, M. (1982), 'The Subject and the Power', *Critical Inquiry*, 8 (4): 777–95.

Foucault, M. (1992), 'Preface', in G. Deleuze and F. Guattari, *Anti-Oedipus*, Minneapolis: University of Minnesota Press, pp. xi–xiv.

Grandi, F. (2014), *Doveri costituzionali e obiezione di coscienza*, Naples: Editoriale scientifica.

Hanafin, P. (2007), *Conceiving Life: Reproductive Politics and the Law in Contemporary Italy*, Aldershot: Ashgate.

Hanafin, P. (2014), 'Law's Nomadic Subjects', in B. Blaagaard and I. Van der Tuin (eds), *The Subject of Rosi Braidotti*, London: Bloomsbury, pp. 214–19.

Haraway, D. (1991), *Simians, Cyborgs and Women: The Reinvention of Nature*, London: Free Association Books.

Haraway, D. (1992), 'The Promises of Monsters: A Regenerative Politics for Inappropriate/d Others', in L. Grossberg, C. Nelson and P. A. Treichler (eds), *Cultural Studies*, London: Routledge, pp. 295–337.

Haraway, D. (1997), *Modest_Witness@Second_Millennium. FemaleMan©_Meets_OncomouseTM*, London: Routledge.

Minh-ha, T. (1986), 'She, The Inappropriate/d Other', *Discourse*, 8: 11–38.

Ministero della Salute (2016), *Piano Nazionale di Ferilità*, <http://www.salute.gov.it/imgs/C_17_pubblicazioni_2367_allegato.pdf> (last accessed 22 April 2019).

Rapp, R. (2001), 'Gender, Body, Biomedicine: How Some Feminist Concerns Dragged Reproduction to the Center of Social Theory', *Medical Anthropology Quarterly New Series*, 15 (4): 466–77.

Rosati, E. (2017), *Presente! La Trincea della Memoria Storica del Neofascismo Italiano. Il caso Sergio Ramelli*, Zaprauder, <http://storieinmovimento.org/wp-content/uploads/2018/04/Zap42_4-Zoom3.pdf?fbclid=IwAR37HmAV2xriDOJVJvApxeY3yFn79a0r4wllGT63OQbhwObpyEtzEF97xAs> (last accessed 22 April 2019).

Rosati, E. (2018), *CasaPound Italia. Fascisti del Terzo Millennio*, Milan: Mimesis.

Chapter 10

Nomadism Reterritorialised: The Lessons of Fascism Debates in Korea

Woosung Kang

Fascism in Deleuze and Guattari

Despite the modest excuse that 'schizoanalysis *as such* has strictly no political program to propose' (AO, 380), two volumes of Deleuze and Guattari's *Capitalism and Schizophrenia* definitely belong to the theoretical and practical speculations on political philosophy. Theoretical in the sense that they, reassessing Spinoza and Nietzsche in their own way, create philosophical smooth spaces which ultimately lead to what might be called the ontology of power (*pouvoir*); practical not because they insist on the radical politicality of desire itself or the task of politicising molecular desire, but because they keep suggesting ways to prevent lines of flight being blocked off and turning on themselves. Their work is, in short, 'not so much pro-revolution as it is anti-counterrevolution' (Buchanan 2008: 117).

A lot of scholars have, however, been very much sceptical of the politicality of Deleuze and Guattari's philosophical thinking, arguing that their politics enjoys no specific significance as a domain of thought comparable to aesthetics and philosophy and that they 'subscribe to violent anti-historicism that leads [them] to insist more and more on the distinction between history and becoming' (Patton 2011: 115–16). Critics also point out that Deleuze and Guattari's political thought, if there is any, is focused more on individual and collective forms of desire than on the structural capture of state power, thereby reducing all politics to micropolitics.

Indeed, Deleuze and Guattari are not particularly inclined to refer directly to the political categories that traditional Marxist class politics favours; they rather insist that 'the impetus for social change was provided by movements of deterritorialization and lines of flight' (Patton 2011: 116), new 'geographical' concepts that illustrate what they call

'revolutionary-becoming' (D, 111). The reason why they seem consistently critical of Marxist politics in general relates to their political
diagnosis that classical Marxism failed to understand the micropolitical
movement of May '68. For them, May '68 in France was a molecular
event in Alain Badiou's sense, making what spurred it all the more
imperceptible if solely approached from the viewpoint of macropolitics.

> The politicians, the parties, the unions, many leftists, were utterly vexed;
> they kept repeating over and over again that 'conditions' [of revolution]
> were not ripe. It was as though they had been temporarily deprived of
> the entire dualism machine that made them valid spokespeople. Bizarrely,
> de Gaulle, and even Pompidou, understood much better than the others.
> A molecular flow was escaping, minuscule at first, then swelling, without,
> however, ceasing to be unassignable. (TP, 216)

For Deleuze, especially after his encounter with Guattari, traditional
Marxism is one of the primary instances of macropolitics that does not
catch 'something that flows or flees, that escapes the binary organisations, resonance apparatus, and overcoding machine: things that are
attributed to a "change in values", the youth, women, the mad, etc' (TP,
216). Indeed, they insist that 'everything is political' and at the same
time that 'every politics is simultaneously a *macropolitics* and a *micropolitics*' (TP, 213). As Ian Buchanan succinctly states, '*Anti-Oedipus*
is a polemic against both the cynicism of the right and the defeatism
of the left' (Buchanan 2008: 117). These remarks do not mean that
the micropolitics of molecular desire of 'superstructures' carries more
importance than macropolitical change in the 'base'. Nor do they denote
that the individual flow of desire has 'a relative autonomy' from 'structural determination' by the state and infrastructural economy. Rather,
the difference lies not between the social and the individual (or inter-
individual), but between 'the molar realm of representations, individual
or collective, and the molecular realm of beliefs and desires', since 'flows
are neither attributable to individuals nor overcodable by collective
signifiers' (TP, 219). In this respect, the *différance* of micropolitics in its
complex connection and conjugation with macropolitics in Deleuze and
Guattari designates what I would like to call the 'affective assemblage'
of a segmented socius, which makes macropolitical representations possible and at the same time impossible.

The complex relationship between macropolitics and micropolitics
in Deleuze and Guattari, therefore, resembles neither that in Hegelian
dialectics between essence and phenomena nor that of cause and effect in
Althusserian Marxism. The two realms do not constitute any 'expressive'

relationship; they are either connected or conjugated with each other according to tangential, contingent assemblages of desire in a given socius, distinguishable only in terms of degree and tendency, speed and intensity. Hence Deleuze and Guattari's constant warning against the theoretical confusion which tends to put macropolitical change at the social level over the micropolitical escape of flows. For them, political struggles are always engaged criss-cross-wise; they do not take place between rigidly segmented or supple lines that tend to reterritorialise decoded flows and various lines of flight that always escape striated spaces in the abstract machine of the state. These antagonistic systems of opposition are, in a sense, in inverse relation to each other, by which mutant flow constantly eludes rigid and supple lines while the latter constantly try to arrest the former. Fascism is none other than the name of this molar as well as molecular reterritorialisation of 'fixation opposed to the fluidity of desire' (Holland 2012: 76).

For this connection with fascism, Michel Foucault's famous remark in the preface of *Anti-Oedipus* sounds all the more urgent. Foucault, describing *Anti-Oedipus* as 'an Introduction to the Non-Fascist Life', pinpoints three adversaries of the book, the major representative of which is, along with old leftist politics and psychoanalysis, fascism.

> And not only historical fascism, the fascism of Hitler and Mussolini – which was able to mobilize and use the desire of the masses so effectively – but also the fascism in us all, in our heads and in our everyday behavior, fascism that causes us to love power, to desire the very thing that dominates and exploits us. (AO, xiii)

Undoubtedly, what Foucault attempts to emphasise here is the resilience of fascism and the concomitant difficulty in actualising the task of ridding 'our speech and our acts, our hearts and our pleasures' of the 'slightest traces of fascism' (AO, xiii), which tends to result in 'a petrification of desire's movement by the paranoid fixation on social aims and goals' (Hristov 2016: 168). Moreover, the danger of microfascism gets serious when we believe ourselves 'to be a revolutionary militant' (AO, xiv); political resistance is not entirely free from microfascism, a blockage of desiring-production which is immanent in molecular assemblages themselves. According to Guattari, 'fascism seems to come from the outside, but it finds its energy right at the heart of everyone's desire' (CS, 171). Despite the fact that 'Deleuze and Guattari isolate the fascist moment as something over and done with' (Protevi 2000: 186), microfascism is not a thing of the past because 'new forms of molecular fascism are developing' (CS, 163). What must not be dispensed with, therefore, is the analysis of the constant evolution of microfascism, that is, a critical attention to its sheer resilience: 'what fascism set in motion yesterday continues to proliferate in other forms, within the complex of contemporary social space' (CS, 163).

Thus the task of molecular analysis is neither to recognise that the desire for fascism is an outcome of ideological illusion or bad faith nor to repeat that the masses are easily deluded by political power. It rather requires an undaunted search for the genealogy and mechanism of fascism in which the 'machinic composition of totalitarian powers is the indispensable corollary of a micropolitical struggle for the liberation of desire' (CS, 164). As Deleuze and Guattari underscore, 'the masses were not innocent dupes; at a certain point, under a certain set of conditions, they wanted fascism, and it is this perversion of the desire of the masses that needs to be accounted for' (AO, 29). Molecular analysis or schizoanalysis has to confront this micropolitical power of fascism in the masses and to find an answer to the question why desire desires its own repression.

> The masses certainly do not passively submit to power; nor do they 'want' to be repressed, in a kind of masochistic hysteria; nor are they tricked by an ideological lure. Desire is never separable from complex assemblages that necessarily tie into molecular levels, from microformations already shaping postures, attitudes, perceptions, expectations, semiotic systems, etc. Desire is never an undifferentiated instinctual energy, but itself results from a highly developed, engineered setup rich in interactions: a whole supple segmentarity that processes molecular energies and potentially gives desire a fascist determination. (TP, 215)

It is certain that Deleuze and Guattari's political interest lies elsewhere than in the Marxist critique of ideology, which operates at the level of molar opposition between the dominant and the dominated in terms of class politics. The masses are not passive recipients of macropolitical determinants, and political decision making always involves a descent into 'a world of microdeterminations, attractions, and desires, which [the masses] must sound out or evaluate in a different fashion' (TP, 221). Obviously, their concept of desire decisively differs from that of psychoanalysis, which overcodes individual desire with notions of the death drive and masochism. Because of the inherent danger that disables the masses from pursuing lines of flight and reterritorialises everything available for retrieving molar security, desire as assemblage cannot be uniformly ensconced within the individual psyche. The molecularisation of fascism feeds not only on the active self-repression of the masses' desire but also on the uncanny reterritorialisation of desire according to the logic of 'pure destruction and abolition' (TP, 230).

Fascism, in its micro-formation and as a bizarre totalitarian machine, is doubly problematic not simply because it perversely blocks off and reterritorialises the flow of desire but also because it amounts to 'a peculiar kind of acceleration of desire' at the molecular level (Holland 2012: 76). This explains why the revolutionary-becoming in Deleuze and Guattari involves more than just a deterritorialisation of the death drive or the liberation of desire from the repressive force of fascist macropolitics. If the masses actively desire, at a molecular level, the repression of desire itself, and if this constitutes the catastrophic danger of the evolution of fascism in global capitalist society, what is urgently needed in acting out the non-fascist way of life is something like a Nietzschean will to power that obviates and wards off the reterritorialisation of molecular assemblages of desire in the very spaces of deterritorialisation.

What, then, exactly is the assemblage of desire that actively produces microfascism? What kinds of assemblages are there in global capitalism where, after the demise of historical macrofascism, it becomes alluring for us to be 'trapped in a thousand little monomanias, and self-evident truths, and clarities that gush from every black hole and no longer form a system' (TP, 228)? When Deleuze and Guattari contrast fascism with totalitarianism, the difference lies in the mediatory role of the state and its peculiar involvement with the war machine. Indeed, the war machine, originally a nomadic decoding force of lines of flight opposing state power, is the very agential assemblage that facilitates the paradoxical evolution of historical macrofascism to the microfascism of global capitalism. As is explicated in Axiom II of the 12th Plateau, 'Treatise on Nomadology – the War Machine', the war machine was the invention of nomads, who operated 'exterior to the State apparatus and distinct from military institution'; 'nomad existence necessarily effectuates the condition of the war machine in space' (TP, 380). Though the nomadic war machine 'does not necessarily have war as its object', despite its negative implication of physical violence, we are immediately told that 'war and the battle may be its necessary result (under certain conditions)' (TP, 416). What is the war machine after all?

> We define 'war machine' as linear assemblages constructed along the lines of flight. Thus understood, the aim of war machine isn't war at all but a very special kind of space, *smooth space*, which they establish, occupy, and extend. *Nomadism* is precisely this combination of war machine and smooth space. We try to show how and in what circumstances war machines aim at war (when the State apparatuses take over a war-machine

that's initially no part of them). War machines tend much more to be revolutionary, or artistic, rather than military. (PP, 33)

The war machine, initially created by nomads outside the state, has nothing to do with war itself; it transgresses the territories of the state and violently debilitates the striated sedentary spaces of settlers. But it is destined to be captured, at certain historical moments, by the state and employed to facilitate the reterritorialisation of smooth spaces back into striated ones. The war machine is, by definition and in essence, a sort of space machine which attempts to create smooth spaces outside the state's territories or transforms striated spaces into smooth spaces where nomadic assemblages may further extend movements of lines of flight. Nomadism in Deleuze and Guattari epitomises the operational process of securing smooth spaces by means of the insecure war machine: the war machine is not always identical with the nomadic people's military way of subjugating the striated territories of the settled residents of the state. If the war machine has any political or historical associations with war, it must be either because the occupation of smooth spaces often necessarily involves violent struggle against state power or because it is extremely vulnerable to the capturing power of the state machine, as we witnessed, for instance, in the 'barricades' of May '68.

Deleuze is keenly aware of such a tactical contamination of the war machine when he adds that 'we can't assume that lines of flight [of nomad war machines] are necessarily creative, that smooth spaces are always better than segmented or striated ones' (PP, 33–4), as he illustrates in the case of a nuclear submarine which results in establishing a smooth space devoted to war and terror. In as much as the war machine, as space machine, has anything to do with the collision and confrontation with the state for its annihilation, the violence of war necessarily accompanies the function of the war machine, it being neither the condition nor the object of the war machine itself. To borrow a term from Jacques Derrida, 'war is the "supplement" of the war machine' (TP, 417). This explains why Deleuze and Guattari persistently call this nomadic space machine a war machine, despite the possible (mis)identification of the war machine with war and violence. As they point out that the 'war machine has an extremely variable relation with war itself' (TP, 422), Deleuze and Guattari not only emphasise, by this scandalous term, the paradox that the nomadic securing of smooth spaces is not possible without the destruction of the state and its rigid segmentarity, but also insist on the fact that the state apparatus, a striated machine initially lacking any objective of war, comes to take war for its primary goal precisely after it appropriates the war machine, thereby changing its nature and function while mobilising it against nomads themselves and other states. In short, the war machine becomes war itself with its capture by the state, which then actively transforms its nomadic, supplementary function into something entirely different: a cancerous destroyer machine. The tactical relation of war with the war machine in nomadism turns into a strategic one by the state.

It is precisely in terms of this strategic appropriation of the nomadic war machine by the state that fascism differs from totalitarianism and military dictatorship. Fascism, not a state *de jure*, is able to build itself into a de facto state of totalitarian drive by appropriating the war machine, thereby transforming both the nature of the totalitarian state itself and the war machine. For Deleuze and Guattari, when fascism 'builds itself a totalitarian State, it is not in the sense of a State army taking power, but of war machine taking over the State'; fascism, unlike the classic totalitarian state which attempts to repress all possible lines of flight, 'is constructed on an intense line of flight, which it transforms into a line of pure destruction and abolition' (TP, 230). Indeed, fascism is a sort of 'realised nihilism' in the sense that it is the peculiar combination of the totalitarian macro-formation of the state equipped with the belligerent war machine as its weapon with the micropolitical intensification of the masses' desire into a will to total destruction.

To imagine and realise the non-fascist way of life, therefore, warlike struggles at both macro- and micro-levels must be waged simultaneously and on all fronts. On the macropolitical level, the revolutionary-becoming has not only to transform, as old Marxists did, the repressive state apparatuses of coercive totalitarianism into democratic ones, but should also work for the total abolition of fascist forms of the suicidal state itself by opposing any kind of idea of total war. At the micropolitical level, emphasis must be put not merely on challenging the fascist war machine's mass intensification of lines of flight into the destructive will, but also on driving out of ourselves 'the will to wager everything you have every hand, to stake your own death against the death of others' (TP, 230). Here lies the reason why Foucault calls *Capitalism and Schizophrenia* 'a book of ethics' (AO, xiii). It is for this danger of the fascist appropriation of the war machine and of the state with its intensification of lines of flight that Deleuze and Guattari insist on the significance of 'infrastructural' micropolitics in an age of global capitalism or 'liberal fascism' (Evans and Reid 2013: 3), the sixth variant of the war machine.

The First Debate on Fascism in Korea

The contemporary formation of microfascism differs from the historical one in that it is no longer based on the conjugation between state power and the war machine. Today, the global capitalist war machine takes over the state as its constituent, in consequence of which the state is 'serving merely as a variable model of realization for capitalist axiomatization' (Holland 2013: 129). After the collapse of historical fascism with its idea of total war and the war economy, war ceases to be the materialisation of the war machine. According to Deleuze and Guattari, there no longer remains, especially after the Second World War, a need for macrofascism combining the totalitarian state with the destructive war machine. Instead, fascism becomes a matter of microfascism in the form of the automatisation and axiomatisation of the world economy. The capitalist war machine, the most recent mutant of fascism, comes to reign over the entire axiomatic space and to 'put all the parts of the universe in contact' (TP, 476). Due to the globalisation of capitalist accumulation, whether in the form of neoliberalism, the welfare state or the military-industrial complex, the world is entirely turned into a flat smooth space over which 'reigned a single war machine, even when it opposed its own parts' (TP, 476). The capitalist war machine of the 'new world order' overtakes what nomads did earlier with the war machine: creating smooth spaces out of the striated spaces of the state. The original function of the state – vanquishing nomadism and controlling migration by the striation of smooth spaces – becomes useless, if not obsolete, since capitalist processes of axiomatisation, no longer dependent on the state, work much more swiftly and flexibly than the overcoding and striating procedures of the state, even if it still needs the state as the 'reterritorializing moment of its axiomatic' (Holland 2013: 129). No wonder global capitalism appears to function, at least in its deterritorialisation of state-driven striated spaces, just like nomadism.

But the similarity is neither real nor constitutional. Inasmuch as the capitalist axiomatic appropriates the state for its reterritorialisation of deterritorialised nomadic spaces, its seemingly nomadic production of smooth spaces ultimately serves for the intensification of worldwide capitalist accumulation. A striking case in point of mistaking this illusory similarity for a real one is the first fascism debate that happened in Korean intellectual circles around 2002. Since the 1990s, Korean society has witnessed the peculiar proliferation of discourses on nomadism, which associate nomadism with whatever has a tinge of postmodern urbanity, from a neoliberal, easy-going lifestyle to unconstrained identity politics, in so far as it claims the value of constant mobility and unsolidi-fied fluidity. Taken out of context, nomadism symbolises political and cultural frivolity in Korea, which tends to defy the boundaries of existing norms. Especially, nomadism in Korea highlights a pro-technological and consumer-friendly cultural trend derived from the benefit of speedy online access to global virtual spaces, which the most wired country of the world can easily provide.

In fact, what is called 'digital nomadism' in Korea has a closer connec-tion with the ideas of Jacques Attali and Michel Maffesoli than those of Deleuze and Guattari: digital wandering, spiritual hedonism, a quest for immediate pleasures and a fetishistic addiction (Young-Joo Choi 2010: 392–6). The popular reference to nomadism is highly insensitive to their differences, as a journal columnist argued that 'it is doubtful whether Deleuze and Guattari's nomadism is actually far from that of Attali' (Park 2010: 109). It was in the middle of this conundrum and with the timely publication in 2002 of *Nomadism* in two massive volumes by a prominent Korean sociologist Jin-Kyung Yi that the first debate on fascism occurred. The debate itself actually involved a leftist critic and a Deleuzean philosopher. Jong Young Lee, an editor-in-chief of *The Radical Review in Korea*, mercilessly attacked, in a controversial article entitled 'Fascists Talking about Anti-fascism: A Critique of Deleuze and Guattari' in the liberal journal *Literature and Society*, what he calls 'a theoretical fascism' (Jong Young Lee 2002: 764) of Deleuze and Guattari as well as academic scholars who he thinks uncritically uphold and mystify their apolitical idea of nomadism. In the next issue of the same journal, Jae-Yin Kim, a young Deleuzean philosopher, simply dis-missed Lee's argument as nonsensical in his rebuttal, 'How Deleuze and Guattari are Stigmatized as Fascist and Non-humanist', accusing Lee of blind obscurantism.

Lee claims to have discerned three serious theoretical mistakes that Deleuze and Guattari (and their Korean followers) committed: 1) a misunderstanding of the Freudian concept of desire and schizophrenia in *Anti-Oedipus*, 2) a careless blindness towards the actual fascist impli-cations of the theoretical concept of the war machine in *A Thousand Plateaus*, and 3) an overall lack of any category of viable political sub-jectivity. His critique seems to be entirely based on traditional Marxist political philosophy in which, he argues, any political theory, without conceptualising revolutionary subjectivity and a practical programme, would ultimately 'sponsor a clandestine fascism in the guise of anti-fas-cism' (Jong Young Lee 2002: 763). It turns out that Lee has no knowl-edge of Deleuze and Guattari's problematisation of Marxist political philosophy and its model of class revolution, which is epitomised in their notions of the 'mass' and the 'war machine', since Lee basically regards concepts such as 'desiring-machine', 'molecular lines of flight' and 'nomadism' as identical with the 'free floating signifiers' of capitalist postmodernity. Lee's argument basically resonates with the spirited indictment of nomadism on the Korean left: for them nomadism means a cultural malaise which 'exists only for "hyper-nomads" like CEOs, experts, tourists, professionals, and capitalists; nomadism is denied to "infra-nomads" who could not help but cross borders in order to survive as a free worker-slave' (Park 2010: 110). No wonder Lee's 'symptomatic misreading' of Deleuze and Guattari's 'discrepancy between theoretical position and practical stance' (Jong Young Lee 2002: 781) abruptly leads him to a Habermasian, if not a Kantian, accusation that 'Deleuze and Guattari's nomadism lacks universal appeal. Subscribed to instrumental understanding, nomadism as a practical discipline, unable to imagine a revolution which presupposes the recognition of human equality and individuality, cannot even eke out a conspiracy theory or a political *coup d'état*' (Jong Young Lee 2002: 779). For Lee, Deleuze and Guattari's gesture of political intervention into the microfascist war machine of global capitalism does not matter at all; he associates fascism with historical macrofascism, identifying the revolutionary politics of Deleuze and Guattari's nomadic war machine with the postmodern apolitical philosophy which is, for him, ultimately subservient to global capitalist accumulation. A bizarre mixture of old Marxism, Kantian universalism and the aesthetics of erotic subjectivity in Herbert Marcuse and Slavoj Žižek, Lee's critique of Deleuzean nomadism as fascism represents the populist, anti-intellectual hostility of Korean leftist activists towards what he calls 'the blind pursuit of lines of flight without any idea of actual revolutionary subjects and their solidarity' (Jong Young Lee 2002: 772).

On the other hand, Jae-Yin Kim's rebuttal focuses less on the direct theoretical confrontation with Lee's 'molar misunderstanding' of Deleuze and Guattari than on the 'ethics' of critique and the chronic anti-intellectualism of the so-called progressive activists in Korea. First of all, Kim thinks Lee's critique amounts to a 'defamation' of Deleuze and Guattari: it simply 'went too far' (Jay-Yin Kim 2002: 1222), unable to distinguish its target; his critique should have been directed not at 'Deleuze's political philosophy itself' but at 'the Deleuze phenomenon in Korea' (Jay-Yin Kim 2002: 1224). For Kim, it is useless and almost impossible, if not meaningless, to point out and correct all the distorted conceptual misunderstandings because Lee's critique is based on a cursory, careless misreading of Deleuze and Guattari's original texts via bad translations. He regards Lee's argument as a typical example of anti-intellectual snobbery in Korea.

> People used to say, often quoting Deleuze, that practical application is more important than the rightful understanding of concepts. But it is impossible to imagine that Deleuze recommends the random use of his concepts. Deleuze made the remark in the context of criticising a predominantly scholastic philosophical milieu in French academic circles, exhorting the suspension of empty conceptual debates. In Korea, this was wrongfully accepted to mean that any subjective application of concepts, even if out of context, is allowed as long as it meets popular political expectations. It is indeed deplorable since such an abuse of concepts often resorts to the very philosophical authority of Deleuze himself. I would like to call it an authoritarian application of concepts, which has plagued the Korean public sphere. (Jae-Yin Kim 2002: 1224)

Simply put, Lee's disoriented accusation, for Kim, merely repeats 'the popular prejudices in Korea concerning Deleuze and Guattari', showcasing an uncanny combination of bigoted hostility, dependent upon equally authoritarian figures, towards non-Marxist theoretical authorities with a lack of intellectual rigour in the 'general reception of Western theories in the Korean soil' (Jay-Yin Kim 2002: 1238). What is worse, the first Korean translation of *Anti-Oedipus* from which Lee amply quotes, published in 1991 by a scholar of Greek philosophy and later completely retranslated by Jae-Yin Kim himself in 2013, has been notorious among scholars for its overall lack of command and for arbitrary misinterpretations of Deleuze's key concepts, let alone stylistic negligence regarding Korean prosody. Kim flatly dismisses the validity of the first Korean edition of *Anti-Oedipus* as unfit for intellectual debate, proclaiming that 'whoever boasts their understanding of Deleuze after having read this translation is as much as admitting to their own stupidity' (Jay-Yin Kim 2002: 1225). And to back up his dismissal, Kim selects for example one of the passages from the 1991 translation and takes issue with it, accusing Lee of 'careless recourse, without any direct reference to original texts, to bad translation which is fraught with popular prejudices and imaginary assumptions' (Jay-Yin Kim 2002: 1235).

Unfortunately, the first fascism debate in Korea concerning Deleuze and Guattari's concept of nomadism was not followed by subsequent polemics. Lee quit the dispute, accusing Kim of being 'a Deleuze epigone' who uncritically idolised the original texts of a Western philosopher within the narrow field of academia, while Kim only responded that it was not worth a debate if Lee's unethical attitude remained unchanged.

An isolated event as this is, this intellectual episode showcases the typical pattern of subsequent debates concerning the issue of the general reception of Western theories in Korean soil and the particular political implications of a specific philosophy. At first, an activist from the left mounts a premature political critique on a specific Western theory that is favourably circulated among intellectual scholars and then popularised in public sectors, without sufficient knowledge and professional rigour. To this, an expert in that theory takes issue with the lack of understanding of philosophical concepts and the irresponsible ethics of politicised attack. Then the debate veers, via strong rebuttals from intellectuals, towards the problem of Korean translations of original texts and the competition around the authority of 'correct' translations. And then the self-claimed activist 'whistleblower' typically declares the debate meaningless, labelling it a toy of intellectual theorists devoid of real political implications. Finally, what could have been a productive exchange in the public sphere becomes an acute confrontation between popular 'uninformed rejection' and professional 'scholarly speculation', each side antagonistically blaming the other for liberal elitism and anti-intellectual snobbery, respectively. The debate cannot be qualified as an example of what Deleuze calls 'legitimate misrepresentation' because both fail to have an 'immediate relationship with the outside', with the otherness of their polemic (Deleuze 1985: 144–6).

Undoubtedly, not merely a practical political signification but also a rigorous understanding of the text is required in order to problematise the potential fascist implications of any given theory, especially one that attempts to envisage the possibility of a non-fascist way of life in terms of a detailed re-examination of historical fascism as well as the microfascism of the global capitalist war machine. As Deleuze and Guattari emphasise again and again, 'smooth spaces are not in themselves liberatory', and there is a high risk of falling again into the trap of re-striated spaces of the capitalist war machine, since in the globalised economy 'the striation and the smoothing are precisely the passages or combination' (TP, 500). Their lesson is that the critique of microfascism must involve the difficult and unending task of finding nomadic smooth spaces in the most striated spaces, while avoiding the capture of reterritorialisation.

Still, there must be a good reason why popular sentiment in Korea towards 'nomadism' in 2002 took the shape of unbridled consumerism and why the left activists mistakenly identified this capitalist power of the ruthless molecularisation of desire with Deleuzean ideas of microfascism and the nomadic war machine. My interest is neither to endorse the practical validity of Lee's misinformed theoretical critique itself nor to take sides with Kim's unwavering belief in the intactness of original texts. Far from it. For me, what is at stake is the possibility of collaborative cultural critique which can raise the question as to why and how in Korea a certain theory so easily becomes an object of fierce political confrontation, having been summoned for either unconditional authority or irremediable stigmatisation. From this perspective, anti-intellectualism and elitism coexist like flip sides of the same coin.

The Second Debate on Nomadism in Korea

It is not easy, as was indicated at the outset, to pinpoint the ground zero from which one can configure the political implications of Deleuze and Guattari's theoretical intervention into global reality. Deleuze started his career as a post-'68 intellectual and his philosophical ideas are the outcome of a consistent pursuit of explicating the failure of the May revolution, thereby coming to enjoy a special status as a new materialist thinker, especially after the demise of actual socialism in 1989 and the subsequent decline of Western Marxism. In Korea, Deleuze was initially introduced as part and parcel of a bundle of 'post-Marxist theorists' who are believed to be the liberal proponents of micropolitics. Ironically, the first translation of *Anti-Oedipus* in 1991 contributed to strengthening the popular prejudice about Deleuze's schizoanalysis, fixing his image as a postmodern thinker whose concepts, such as 'desiring-machine' and 'Body without Organs', are easily identified with those of post-Lacanian psychoanalysis. A case in point is the translator's note on the meaning of *Ça*, which Jae-Yin Kim thinks is 'a main culprit that misguides the entire reading of *Anti-Oedipus* and Deleuze's philosophy' (Jae-Yin Kim 2002: 1226). According to Kim, despite Deleuze's clear warning, 'what a mistake to have ever said *the* id' (AO, 1), the Korean translator's note explains that 'This term, put into a Korean *Gkot* [It] here, corresponds to *Ça* in the original French. In English translation, *It* is interpreted as *Id*, and as *Es* in German, both of which mean the Freudian term *Id*' (Myung-Kwan Choi 1991: 13). *Ça* connotes something entirely different from Freud's Id, implying as it does an assemblage of unconscious desires or what Deleuze conceptualises under the new notion of 'machines' in the plural. (Deleuze's apostrophe on '*the* id' also indicates the multiplicities of *Ça* as irreducible to a single unity or a Freudian Id.) Of course, it is too much to single out this mistake as condemning *Anti-Oedipus* to be popularly misread in Korea as a book of psychoanalysis, but Kim's complaint deserves more serious attention.

The popular misuse of the term nomadism partly showcases the peculiar destiny of Deleuze and Guattari's philosophy in Korea: nomadism was widely adopted, especially in commercial advertisements and technological sectors just before the national financial bailout in 1997, to mean the urge to enjoy a free, unfettered lifestyle with the consumption of high-tech products and a cultural obsession with acquiring self-management skills that global neoliberal capitalism upholds. Without an immediate vision of political revolution at hand amid the national campaign for speedy globalisation and the concomitant decline of Marxism as a political theory, leftist activists such as Lee were desperate to find a scapegoat on which to vent their frustration. And they suspected that Deleuze and Guattari's nomadism, with its unflinching critique of old Marxist politics, was in close connection with the Attali–Maffesoli pair in their complicit relationship with, if not direct sponsorship of, neoliberalist drives of mobility and fluidity under the guise of an anti-fascist theoretical mask. But the blame should have been placed somewhere else than on nomadism.

It was none other than Deleuze and Guattari who diagnosed the inherent risk of molecular micropolitics and the molar axiomatisation of global capitalism as well as the molar macropolitics of old Marxism: 'The administration of great organized molar security has as its correlate a whole micromanagement of petty fears, a permanent molecular insecurity, to the point that the motto of domestic policy makers might be: a macropolitics of society by and for a micropolitics of insecurity' (TP, 216–17). For them, global capitalism and Marxist political organisation both feed on people's fear of insecurities, having in common the idea of the micromanagement of conscious individual subjects. Deleuze and Guattari's schizoanalysis is fundamentally different from other theories of the political left or of postmodern 'ethics of the other' because they clearly discern 'something unaccountably escaping' (TP, 216), something that cannot be entirely captured by macropolitical power centres and the micropolitics of insecurity and fluidity in global capitalism. In this respect, more sinister still in the Korean context is the negative effect of scholarly simplifications of Deleuze's philosophy. No wonder the second debate revolves around the question as to whether nomadism deserves the central place in Deleuze's political philosophy and whether his entire philosophy, by extension, could possibly be represented by it.

This time it was a debate between two scholars concerning the 'correct' translation of Deleuze's key concepts. In 2001 Jae-Yin Kim, then a PhD candidate who was in the last stage of his dissertation on Deleuze's ontology, printed the first Korean translation of *A Thousand*

Plateaus with a small publisher. Due to financial pressures to meet the deadline for funding, the publisher replaced, without Kim's knowledge, some chapters, especially chapters of 11–13 in which Deleuze and Guattari deal with ritornello, nomadism and the capture of the state, with manuscripts translated from the English edition by an anonymous translator. Despite this scandalous nonsense, the overall quality of the translation, except for those three chapters, deserves special attention. Kim made great efforts to explicate, with superb annotations, Deleuze's concepts, minutely speculating on the original implication of the French text and at the same time coining theoretical terms more palatable to the Korean context and prosody. He also collaborated with other scholars by continually posting his manuscripts online on his own homepage in order to reflect suggestions and comments from the public.

Jin-Kyung Yi, who was then writing his sensational book *Nomadism*, made a critical comment on Kim's translation three years later on the website of a scholarly community of which he is one of the leading organisers. Yi claimed that Kim's Korean translation of some key concepts such as *agencement* (assemblage), *ligne de fuite* (line of flight) and *plan de consistence* (plane of consistency) did not deliver the original meaning due to the uninformed misunderstanding of the philosophical context. He suspected that Kim depended heavily on idioms from German and Japanese translations.

> I would like to add that some key concepts of Kim widely differ from my own. Especially, to render *agencement* [*baechi*] as 'assemblages' [*baechimul*] rather than 'arrangement' clearly demonstrates his lack of knowledge of the concept of *agencement*, and his term, segmentarity [*jôlpyônsong*], for *segmentarité*, which is closer to 'line segmentality' [*sônbunsong*], must be borrowed from the Japanese translation which also ignores the mathematical implication of line segment in Deleuze's conceptual terrain. Kim offers a term 'surface flatness/evenness' [*gornpan*], which has only a geological meaning, for *plan de consistence*; 'compositional consistency' [*gudoeui ilgwansong*] would be a better choice, which is completely missed in Kim's translation for its possible reference to the German term *Konsistenzplan*. (It seems that German and Japanese scholars also did not yet properly understand the meaning of the concept.) But above all, Kim's word 'flight' [*doju*] rather than 'escape' [*talju*] for *fuite* rings much too passive and negative, unable to contain the active implication of creatively getting away from the striation. This might be a tactical choice to simply show himself off, nullifying the movement of active escaping which makes people get away from the world by reducing it to a mere passive flight. (quoted in Jae-Yin Kim 2004: 441)

For Yi, who was also circulating his own manuscript of a Korean translation of *Nomadism*, Kim's work falls far short of scholarly expectations. Yi thought it unwise to seriously consider Kim's challenging postures towards established academia, so he completely dismissed Kim's rebuttal in a critical review of the book in a literary journal, simply adding in an interview later that Kim's translation and polemical review deserve no theoretical debate since they are the work of a graduate student. Kim's argument, however, appears as much informed as, and often more pointed than, that of Yi. Specifically taking the issue of Yi's term 'escape' (*talju*) and its active drive, Kim argues that what matters is not the preference for a certain term over another, acknowledging the practical usefulness of Yi's word. But Kim later attacks Yi's translation of *fuite* into 'escape' for its flat denial of Deleuze's sense of passivity and danger inherent in the movement of flight itself, since *talju* assumes that the destructive tendency and the danger of annihilation 'only come from the outside' (Jae-Yin Kim 2004: 51). This might constitute a critical point concerning the imagination of a non-fascist way of life and its viability.

As Deleuze and Guattari repeatedly warn against the 'false impression' which ignores that 'lines of flight, for their part, never consist in running away from the world but rather in causing runoffs, as when you drill a hole in a pipe' (TP, 204), *ligne de fuite* does not just mean an active escaping from the dangerous world but a way of making the world derail itself by making a hole in the system, which is immanently destructive and creative. It has nothing to do with imagining a new subject outside the world order, who can discover weapons after the escape. As it is, 'it is on the line of flight that new weapons are invented, to be turned against the heavy arms of the State' (TP, 204). As Deleuze and Guattari point out concerning the four dangers of power in 'Micropolitics and Segmentarity', lines of flight are not 'good by nature and necessarily' (TP, 227), and it would be an oversimplification to 'attribute to them the movement of the arrow and the speed of the absolute' because lines of flight themselves 'emanate a strange despair, like an odor of death and immolation, a state of war from which one returns broken; they have their own dangers' entirely distinct from the ones coming from the possibility of being 'sealed in, tied up, re-knotted, reterritorialized' (TP, 229) by the capture of the state. And this explains why the non-fascist way of life, for them, does not merely involve resisting the striating capture of the state but also concerns preventing lines of flight from '*turning to destruction, abolition pure and simple, the passion of abolition*' (TP, 229), that is, from our becoming a 'realised nihilism' of the molecular war machine in its microfascist formations.

As de Vries succinctly sums up, the problem is 'how to govern or resist if the chances are rife that one may end up in a black hole or on a line of destruction' (2013: 133). Because there is a high possibility of the 'conversion of the risk of micro-fascistic destruction into the certainty of macro-fascistic segmentation' (de Vries 2013: 140), we constantly find, but also have to create, ourselves on uncertain grounds in a continuous and intangible play between macro- and microfascisms. In this respect, Kim's idea makes much more sense than Yi's, since the inherent risk of lines of flight is not the difficulty of getting out of, and resisting, capture without contaminating oneself with the regime of power, but the uncertainty as well as unpredictability of the positive orientation of the line of light itself due to its immanent negativity. Because it would be untenable 'to think that it is sufficient, in the end, to take the line of flight or rupture', and there lurks the danger of the line of flight's 'turning into lines of abolition, of destruction, of others and of oneself' (D, 105), what we need should never be an active acknowledgement of the 'haecceities' of the escape itself.

Another point of interest in the second debate between Yi and Kim is the question concerning the significance of Deleuze's idea of nomadism in his entire political philosophy and its actual implications in Korean society. How central is the concept of nomadism in Deleuze and Guattari's philosophy? For Kim, however, the question would rather be how critical is Deleuze and Guattari's nomadism for Yi's politics? For the purpose of explicating, or popularising for that matter, Deleuze and Guattari's nomadism, Yi deliberately associates nomadism with familiar concepts with similar implications. He says at one point that 'nomadism has a sense of the absolute, but strangely enough it also has close affinity with *atheism*' (Yi 2002, 2: 381). And he also connects the concept of the war machine with Nietzsche's *agon*, which means, for him, 'the way of outwitting the opponent without antagonism (*antagon*), presenting a better wisdom to the counterpart' (Yi 2002, 2: 298). The war machine becomes a positive ethics of mutual recognition without unnecessary antagonism in a fierce masculine confrontation like a sword fight between Japanese samurais (Yi 2002, 2: 423). Finally, in the last chapter of *Nomadism* symptomatically titled 'A Philosophy of Non-I and Commune-ism', Yi virtually identifies Deleuze's 'active' nomadism of escaping with a Taoist notion of 'inaction' or a version of Jean-Luc Nancy's idea of *communauté désœuvrée* (inoperative community).'

How difficult it is to accept objects as they are without any pre-given distinctions! And how thrilling it is to imagine it and its possible realization!

To take the world or objects or events as 'what they are', to accept them as they come and go. Indeed, 'a mountain is none other than a mountain, and water water', as they said. The 'affirmative philosophy' of Spinoza and Nietzsche would be just like this! Isn't it just like what Lao Tzu said: 'the philosophy of *akarma* (inaction)'? (Yi 2002, 2: 724)

Here Deleuze's idea of nomadism, shorn of any negative implications of destructive fascism and the war machine, turns into a positive ethical philosophy of affirmation and inaction.

For Kim, such a symbolic affiliation appears very much symptomatic, if not pathetic. According to Kim, Yi 'tends to understand nomadism much too metaphorically'; it showcases 'the most nihilistic and negative way of interpreting the affirmative philosophies of Spinoza, Nietzsche and Deleuze' (Jae-Yin Kim 2004: 457). Yi's identification of Deleuze and Guattari's nomadism with the philosophy of inaction reminds us of Nietzsche's critique of Buddhist nihilism, according to which human beings are inclined to desire *Nothing* rather than not desire at all. Not without reason, we are here also reminded of Giorgio Agamben's appropriation of Melville's figure of Bartleby as a symbolic manifestation of potentialities for non-action against the capitalist system of alienation (Kang 2020: 58); Bartleby's 'politics of im-potentiality' is nothing other than an appeal to an individual ethics of persisting 'to be one's own lack, to be in relation to one's own incapacity, to not being in actuality' (Agamben 2000: 182). De Vries is certainly right to suggest that with Deleuze and Guattari, 'one can only become yet never be free from fascism: the non-fascistic life exists only in becoming' (2013: 146). One cannot, in the same vein, simply escape and arrive at a life beyond fascism, whether in the form of a nomadism of *agon* or a philosophy of *akarma*; one is only able to create, again and again, and this creation will remain uncertain and unpredictable.

The Third Debate on Nomadic Imperialism

It is not an accident that the second debate did not end as a mere scholarly altercation over the correct translation of the original text. Kim's critique of the author of *Nomadism* could easily be extended to other figures who tend to tailor the political philosophy of Deleuze and Guattari for their own relish, and at the same time to those who appropriate theoretical speculations for their own practical agenda. Right after the second dispute, an active ecologist, Kyu Seok Chun, who has long been committed to nationwide 'grassroots movements' in rural areas in Korea, published a controversial book, *Nomadism as Aggression*, with a leftist press. The book caused a sensational impact in the Korean public sphere. He severely criticised, like Jong Young Lee, the Korean advocates of Deleuzean nomadism for their unashamed justification of what he calls 'the discourse of market imperialism and neo-aggression disguised as neoliberalism' (Chun 2006: 7). But the main target of his critique on nomadism turns out to be Deleuze and Guattari: 'Deleuze and Guattari's unconditional sponsorship for a schizo and a nomad amounts to nothing less than the expression of paranoid phobia which unduly identifies individual identity, rationality, and reflexivity with social totalitarianism and oppression' (Chun 2006: 241). Resorting to his own historiographical research on nomad tribes, the author specifically pinpoints the danger of the concept of the war machine, vehemently observing that 'the real wars carried out by the nomadic war machine, however positively it is philosophically implicated and embellished as a new paradigm, were as cruel as, or even bloodier than, other wars of aggression' (Chun 2006: 233).

As in the first debate on Deleuze's fascism, Chun, as a leftist activist, pours out uninformed accusations against proponents of nomadism. In response to this, Jung-Woo Lee, a philosopher and independent scholar, immediately rebutted in a review, with the authority of a professional expert, that Chun's tremendous ignorance of philosophical knowledge was based on careless misreading and irresponsible distortion, and deserved no serious consideration. Indeed, Chun confesses his insufficient understanding of *A Thousand Plateaus* since, as he describes it, 'it was full of clever sophistries and pedantries, worse than any other philosophical books to understand' (Chun 2006: 214). Lee, dissuading himself from proving that Deleuze's nomadism is *not* aggression, simply dismisses Chun's book as worthless, recommending that the author 'painstakingly reread the original text or find a better translation' (Jung-Woo Lee 2006). For Lee, Chun's book is unethical and preposterous since it falls far short of a critique in any possible sense because of its serious breach of basic codes of discussion.

As the publisher acknowledged in an online explication to the reviewer, Lee's rebuttal makes sense because Chun's notion of nomadism as aggression has nothing to do with that of Deleuze and Guattari. But the publisher also points out that Lee should have known better, as an expert, than to simply dismiss the book and should have asked why the author was so emotionally hostile to cultural nomadism in Korea and what was symptomatically lurking behind such a furious critique. As it stands, Chun's book is neither the result of rigorous speculation nor of theoretical reflection; he might have thought it necessary to warn against what he regarded as the general profligacy among the Korean public, which was thoughtlessly pursuing a frivolous capitalist way of life in the name of nomadism. Thus considered, the real enemy of Chun's book on nomadism cannot be Deleuze and Guattari themselves but the former activist turncoats who, in order to justify their compromises, have recourse to nomadism as their theoretical frame of reference. With the early recusal of the author from further altercation, the third debate, potentially a restaging of the first one between elitism and anti-intellectualism, actually follows the second path of internal polemic among academic scholars, most of which is not elaborated here in detail. (For further references, see Hong 2006; Woo 2006.)

The one thing that almost no participant paid close attention to is the fact that Chun's misunderstanding of Deleuze's nomadism does not solely come from his lack of knowledge of Deleuze and Guattari's original texts. Curiously enough, Chun consistently quotes and requotes, throughout the entire second part of the book where he engages his critique on nomadism, from Jin-Kyung Lee's *Nomadism*, rather than directly referring to Jae-Yin Kim's new translation of *A Thousand Plateaus*. Why did he do this and what does it mean? As another philosopher participating in the debate suggested, the question to be asked is: 'why does "nomadism" in Korea get entangled in this confusion?' (Jinsok Kim 2006). Deleuze and Guattari themselves are certainly not responsible for this; they have been duly appreciated among scholars and at the same time widely misunderstood as postmodern thinkers or even dismissed as fascist collaborators among leftist activists, while being generally unknown to the public precisely for want of direct accessibility to their texts. Everyone talks about nomadism but nobody wants to read Deleuze and Guattari, or else they read them from bad translations or through a popularised intellectual guide. Who is responsible for this conundrum? Upon closer inspection, it appears ironic that Jung-Woo Lee's dismissal of Chun's book for ignorance of Deleuze's philosophy proves wide of the mark. Indeed, Chun seems as conceited and learned as any other thinker about nomads and nomadism, because what he understands as Deleuze's nomadism mostly comes from Jin-Kyung Yi's *Nomadism*.

What Chun was really ignorant of, however, is the fact that *Nomadism* appears not to be, as Jae-Yin Kim already suggested, an authoritative study of Deleuze's political philosophy per se, though it is a tolerably good guide for a popular understanding of nomadism in Korea. Being an outcome of public lectures, *Nomadism* is essentially a book of cultural or sociological reinterpretation of various forms of nomadism for a Korean audience, utilising Deleuze and Guattari as a conceptual guide. It does not focus on delving into what de Vries calls the *problématique* of Deleuze and Guattari's nomadism: why the war machine as space-creating machine, referring neither to historical nomads nor to an ethics of inaction, takes the central place in their concepts of nomadism and revolutionary-becoming. Heavily influenced by the tendentious reading of *Nomadism*, Chun mistakes Deleuze and Guattari's nomadism for something entirely different, a secularised positive signifier of an easy-going lifestyle or an ethics subservient to global capitalism. He could not fathom why Deleuze and Guattari take great pains to secure the possibility of 'Nomadology', not nomadism, as a new science of creating smooth spaces via the war machine, nor why they stick to the concept of the war machine despite its negative connotations. In this respect, Jinsok Kim is absolutely right when he diagnoses that 'those who talk about Deleuze and "nomadism" in Korea have been relatively reticent about the "war machine" while specifically emphasising the capture of the state apparatus', and that this particularly 'contributes to the general prejudice about nomadism as a romantic or anarchic practice which appears highly vulnerable to recapture by digitalised consumerism or an evasive strategy of simply running away from the state itself' (Jinsok Kim 2006).

Such a romanticised and anarchic version of nomadism is precisely the 'image of thoughts' through which nomadism in Korea has been reterritorialised, that is, stigmatised, by Korean leftist thinkers and activists such as Chun; *Nomadism as Aggression* relies heavily upon the prejudiced identification of Deleuze and Guattari's nomadism with the violence of the historical nomad's war machine on the one hand, and upon the lack of imagination which fails to connect the state-driven war machine with the reterritorialising power of global capitalism. Such a premeditated notion of nomadism appears again and again in Chun's book, especially when he predominantly relies on the authority of Yi's book. For example, Chun takes issue with Deleuze and Guattari's 'complimentary appraisal' of Genghis Khan.

> In this way, they [the Mongolian nomads] were able to establish a giant 'empire' that dominates and 'appropriates' the various state apparatuses while continuing to remain a war machine without necessarily forming new sedentary state apparatuses. *Deleuze and Guattari show their complimentary appraisal for this manoeuvre.* 'The reason why Genghis Khan and his followers were able to hold out [their system] for a long time is that they partially integrated themselves into the conquered [state] empires,

while at the same time maintaining a smooth space on the steppes to which the imperial centres were subordinated. That was their genius, the *Pax Mongolica*.' (Yi 2002, 2: 457–8, italics added)

A chain reaction happens here. Yi quotes from the 'Nomadology' plateau of *A Thousand Plateaus* the paragraph where Deleuze and Guattari explain how the Mongolian empire temporarily succeeded in solving the fatal danger inherent in subjugating the state by the nomadic war machine; they also stress that the conquest of the state apparatuses has the high risk of the war machine's being recaptured by the conquered state. Judging from the whole context, it is clear that Deleuze and Guattari have no intention of praising the *Pax Mongolica* itself as a viable political option, simply indicating the exceptional but temporary success of Genghis Khan's war machine (TP, 418). But Yi's *Nomadism* simply 'overcodes' their idea, if you will, by adding the unnecessary explanation that 'Deleuze and Guattari show their complimentary appraisal for this manoeuvre.' This unnecessary intervention, in turn, leads Chun to unduly accuse Deleuze and Guattari of endorsing the cruel aggression of the Mongolian empire in the name of the nomadic war machine. No wonder Chun confuses Deleuze and Guattari's analysis of historical nomads, who invented the war machine, with their concept of the war machine, which is essentially a machine for creating smooth spaces. In the same vein, it is also hardly a coincidence that Chun identifies the consumerist symptoms of the global capitalist war machine with the essential characteristics of nomadism, and by extension with what he calls aggression in the nomadic war machine.

The Lessons of the Debates

No scholar in Korea can possibly deny the intellectual perseverance and tremendous genius that Jin-Kyung Yi demonstrates in his *Nomadism*; he contributes immensely to the advancement of the Korean ecosystem of knowledge distribution. *Nomadism* is indeed a superb example of original intelligence and synthetic thinking; a critical and 'nomadic' appropriation of Deleuze and Guattari's political philosophy in the heterogeneous context of the Korean cultural milieu. His book, in two massive volumes of over 1,500 pages, attempts to explicate in detail the gist of two quintessential books of Deleuze and Guattari's collaboration. Credit must go to him for fertilising our intellectual sphere and for enhancing popular accessibility to difficult philosophical texts. It is, indeed, as rare an achievement as the two translations of *Capitalism and*

Schizophrenia into Korean. Without *Nomadism* and the timely publication of Jae-Yin Kim's Korean translations, these intellectual debates would not have been possible.

Yi's *Nomadism*, however, unwittingly orientalises, if not romanticises, Deleuze and Guattari's philosophical manoeuvre by exteriorising the immanent negativity of the war machine and at the same time softening their philosophy as an ethics of the Oriental virtue of inaction, thereby provoking the general, especially in the leftist camp, prejudice concerning the frivolity of nomadism. People like Jong Young Lee and Chun could never sensibly differentiate the molecular movement of the global capitalist war machine from the revolutionary possibility of the nomadic war machine, identifying micropolitics against microfascism with fascism itself and confusing nomadism with historical nomads. In short, *Nomadism* contributes to the ossification of the popular image of nomadism, either romantic or anarchic.

The issue demanding further critical examination concerns Yi's scandalous connection of Deleuze's nomadism with the ethics of 'inaction'. Certainly, there is a strong ethical drive in Deleuze and Guattari's political concept of nomadology, but its implication differs widely from the recourse to individual ethics, such as a Foucauldian 'care of the self' or a postmodern work ethic of 'self-management' in global capitalism's molecular spaces. Their ideas are inseparably connected to collective efforts to create the possibility of revolutionising what they call the politics of minorities who 'do not become revolutionaries' (D, 111), and their work 'provokes and sustains the critique of dominant visions of the subject, identity, and knowledge, from within one of many "centers" that structure the contemporary globalized world' (Braidotti 2011: 7–8). Yi's *Nomadism* does not aim to provide a handy manual for such revolutionary politics in Korea; there is no doubt a high risk that such a move would be recaptured by the molecular, discursive micro-formations of the global capitalist machine. Yi's notion of nomadism is fundamentally based on the idea of the theoretical deterritorialisation of dominant knowledge-producing systems which drive us back into an identity politics of 'ethical perseverance to synthesise "transdisciplinary" researches against the encyclopaedic systematisation of knowledge' (Yi 2004: 55–6). Behind Chun's condemnation of nomadism lurks Yi's idea of nomadism as an ethics of inaction, which effectively reterritorialises nomadism as one without the violence of the war machine. As Evans and Reid warn, sometimes the worst forms of fascism arise 'in response to problems that are poorly understood, on the back of trite if well-meaning solutions' (Evans and Reid 2013: 3).

The series of debates on fascism and nomadism in Korea lost much of what they achieved. More than a dozen years have passed since the last debate, but there has been no sign of further public debate on Deleuze and Guattari or any new discussion of other thinkers of their calibre. Fierce as they were, the way past debates ended left deep scars on each participant and in the entire environment of the Korean public sphere. For one thing, when it comes to the matter of understanding original texts as faithfully as possible, we still do not have a consensus on the basic principle that what is most needed is a third party authority that determines, once and for all, winners and losers. Debates on fascism and nomadism in Korea completely failed to reach the point of intellectual collaboration. One lesson of these fierce debates would be that a critique of the political implications of a theory should not be equated with that of a theorist's political stance. The real lesson, however, might be that we have good reason to study and speculate further on Deleuze and Guattari's philosophy. As Deleuze and Guattari argue in *What is Philosophy?*, the task of critical thinking always already involves creating new concepts, which amounts to creating smooth intellectual spaces from striated abstract machines.

As one of the reviewers of Chun's book suggests, to imagine a non-fascist way of life is unthinkable if we cannot answer the question whether 'nomadism' is immanently subservient to the capitalist war machine or whether capitalism in Korea is agile enough to spur the swift reterritorialisation of nomadism (Jinsok Kim 2006). Chun is likely to say yes to the first question based on his cursory understanding of nomadism obtained from Yi's book; Jae-Yin Kim would probably reply that the question itself is false. As bigoted and misinformed as it is, Chun's radical stance ironically showcases Deleuze and Guattari's warning that the war machine is inherently in danger of reterritorialisation, even in intellectual polemics. Perhaps what we have to learn from these debates might paradoxically be a Spinozan wisdom that sometimes 'inadequate ideas can be made to give rise to adequate ideas' (Buchanan 2000: 5). The danger of reterritorialisation in the era of neoliberal capitalism is immanent, as Deleuze and Guattari keep warning us, but we should not stop imagining and creating molecular lines of flight from the global capitalist war machine and its possibility of fascism. We definitely need a lot more from Deleuze and Guattari's philosophy in our path of 'mak[ing] thought a war machine, a nomadic power' (Deleuze 1985: 149) towards the non-fascist way of life.

References

All the English translations from Korean texts were made by the author.

Agamben, G. (2000), *Potentialities: Collected Essays in Philosophy*, trans. D. Heller-Roazen, Stanford: Stanford University Press.
Braidotti, R. (2011), *Nomadic Subjects: Embodiment and Sexual Difference in Contemporary Feminist Theory*, New York: Columbia University Press.
Buchanan, I. (2000), *Deleuzism: A Metacommentary*, Edinburgh: Edinburgh University Press.
Buchanan, I. (2008), *Deleuze and Guattari's Anti-Oedipus: A Reader's Guide*, New York: Continuum.
Choi, M.-K. (1991), *Anti-Oedipus*, Seoul: Minumsa.
Choi, Y.-J. (2010), 'Reception and Comprehension of Nomadism in Korea', *Journal of French Studies in Korea*, 52: 385–437.
Chun, K. S. (2006), *Nomadism as Aggression*, Seoul: Shilchonmunhaksa.
Deleuze, G. (1985), 'Nomad Thought', in David B. Allison (ed.), *The New Nietzsche*, Cambridge, MA: MIT Press, pp. 142–9.
De Vries, L. A. (2013), 'Politics on the Line', in B. Evans and J. Reid (eds), *Deleuze and Fascism: Security, War, Aesthetics*, London: Routledge, pp. 126–47.
Evans, B., and J. Reid (2013), 'Fascism in all its Forms', in B. Evans and J. Reid (eds), *Deleuze and Fascism: Security, War, Aesthetics*, London: Routledge, pp. 1–12.
Holland, E. W. (2012), 'Schizoanalysis, Nomadology, Fascism', in I. Buchanan (ed.), *Deleuze and Politics*, Edinburgh: Edinburgh University Press, pp. 74–97.
Holland, E. W. (2013), *Deleuze and Guattari's A Thousand Plateaus: A Reader's Guide*, London: Bloomsbury.
Hong, Y.-K. (2006), 'Fascism and the Right to Philosophy', *Hwanghae Review*, 51: 216–44.
Hristov, D. (2016), 'Fascism in the Works of Deleuze and Guattari', *STVAR: Journal for Theoretical Practices*, 8: 161–73.
Kang, W. (2020), 'Bartleby and the Abyss of Potentiality', *Concentric: Literature and Cultural Studies*, 46 (2): 37–61.
Kim, J. (2006), 'Philosophers Selling Nomadism', *Kyosu.net*, 1 May, <https://www.kyosu.net/news/articleView.html?idxno=9651> (last accessed 14 June 2022).
Kim, J.-Y. (2002), 'How Deleuze and Guattari were Stigmatized as Fascist and Non-humanist', *Literature and Society*, 15: 1221–41.
Kim, J.-Y. (2004), 'From *A Thousand Plateaus* to *Nomadism*', *Literary Community*, 39: 439–72.
Lee, J. Y. (2002), 'Fascists Talking about Anti-fascism: A Critique of Deleuze and Guattari', *Literature and Society*, 15: 763–81.
Lee, J.-W. (2006), 'The Courage of Ignorance or Intellectual Misunderstanding', *Kyosu.net*, 3 April, <https://www.kyosu.net/news/articleView.html?idxno=9436> (last accessed 14 June 2022).
Park, M. Y. (2010), 'The Ideology of Nomadism and the Debilitation of Social Critique', *Inmulgwasasang (Persons and Thoughts)*, 125: 102–19.
Patton, P. (2011), 'What is Deleuzean Political Philosophy?', *Critica Contemporánea*, 1: 115–26.
Protevi, J. (2000), '"A Problem of Pure Matter": Deleuze and Guattari's Treatment of Fascist Nihilism in *A Thousand Plateaus*', in K. Ansell-Pearson and D. Morgan (eds), *Nihilism Now! 'Monsters of Energy'*, Basingstoke: Palgrave Macmillan, pp. 167–88.

Woo, S. H. (2006), 'Korean Capitalism and Nomadism', *Green Review*, 88: 19–28.

Yi, J.-K. (2002), *Nomadism*, 2 vols, Seoul: Humanist.

Yi, J.-K. (2004), 'A Crisis of Human Science and Nomadism', *Sôgang Humanities Journal*, 18: 31–56.

Chapter 11

Cancerous Silence and Fascism: The Spanish Politics of Forgetting

Mónica Cano Abadía

Introduction

This chapter navigates the possibilities of explaining the Spanish (post-) Franco experience through Deleuze and Guattari's idea of microfascism as a cancerous Body without Organs (BwO). Its aim is also to advocate the need for a micropolitics to dislodge trauma and face the challenge of creating another political framework in Spain. Although there is still an ongoing debate about whether Franco's regime was actually fascist (Hadzelek 2012), this chapter will use the denomination of fascism to refer to Francoism.

During the Franco dictatorship and even after its end, during the so-called Transition, a dangerous repetition of the same codes led to a lack of recoding that constituted cancerous strata in Spain. Understanding fascism as sets of codes that fix subjects in rigid systems of thought and desire, I suggest that silence is the most appalling characteristic of the fascist Spanish rigid system. During the civil war and the dictatorship, opinions were violently silenced; afterwards, even nowadays, the fascist processes of silencing opinions have in turn been silenced.

The processes of intergenerational transmission of the trauma of political violence have been shaped in Spain by a crushing silence that has left an unhealed wound embedded in our (political) subjectivities. The lack of decoding and overcoding, the crippling silence, meant the impossibility of healing the wounds, the impossibility of reparations (especially since the desire for silence led to the juridical erasure of Franco-era crimes), and the impossibility of embracing our potentialities. It meant immobility, as individuals were oriented to unity and molarity.

Against this politics of silence and forgetting, an overcoding labour of remembrance should be done at frequencies that are maybe differently audible. The political framework in Spain still does not permit a different decoding and overcoding that allows dealing with trauma. How can we create cracks in this fixed framework and enable critical thinking towards a micropolitics of transformation in Spain against very ingrained, old and new fascist flows?

The Franco-era dictatorship is a historical manifestation of macrofascism. Nevertheless, in this chapter, I am more interested in explaining the Spanish rigid system of codes as microfascist phenomena and in shaking off our transgenerationally transmitted political trauma through a labour of remembering against fascist molarity. In order to do so, this chapter is divided into four parts. The first part will try to understand the concept of the cancerous and fascistic BwO; the second will propose an understanding of Spanish fascism as a cancerous BwO animated by silence; in the third part, the transmission of intergenerational trauma through silence will be analysed; finally, the fourth part will show how the fascist cancerous strata are still enabling the repetition of fascist codes in Spain; nonetheless, these codes do not remain unchallenged and cracks appear in the shape of a politics of remembrance as resistance that has been done through testimonies.

Fascist Desire

In the first part of this chapter, I would like to outline the concept of fascism as a cancerous BwO, a concept that will then be used in the second part to understand fascist desire in the micropolitical setting of Franco-era and even post-Franco-era Spain. In 'Micropolitics and Segmentarity', Deleuze and Guattari claim: 'What makes fascism dangerous is its molecular or micropolitical power, for it is a mass movement: a cancerous body rather than a totalitarian organism' (TP, 215). This statement goes in the direction of pointing out what I consider, with Holland (2008: 75), to be their major contribution: providing tools to understand how the masses desire fascism. In the words of Deleuze and Guattari: 'Only microfascism provides an answer to the global question: Why does desire desire its own repression, how can it desire its own repression?' (TP, 215). The main question that I would like to elucidate in this first part is: What do they mean with this characterisation of fascism as a cancerous body? What does it imply to understand fascism as a tumour?

In *Anti-Oedipus*, Deleuze and Guattari considered fascist desire as a fixation of the social representations that registered on the Body without Organs, understood as the locus of social investments. The more fixed these representations, the more paranoia there would be, and the more fascistic the tendencies would be as well. Fascism is, then, according to this idea, a freezing of desire; a paralysing movement that adversely affects the fluidity of desire. The fascist desire is paranoiac, reactionary and molar, whereas the revolutionary desire is molecular.

Nonetheless, their conceptualisation of fascism in *A Thousand Plateaus* undergoes a conceptual change. While in *Anti-Oedipus* fascism was a catatonic movement that led to immobility, in *A Thousand Plateaus* fascism is linked to acceleration. In this sense, fascism is desire that accelerates and moves too fast. Also, in this second volume of *Capitalism and Schizophrenia*, they introduce the concept of a cancerous BwO. A BwO refers to 'a substrate that is also identified as the plane of consistency (as a non-formed, non-organised, non-stratified or de-stratified body or term)' (Message 2010: 37). It is linked to the virtual dimension of reality in general, to the plane of immanence, to a common plane for all bodies, minds and individuals. A BwO is non-stratified, unformed, intense matter; a matter of intensity. It is a full egg before the extension of the organism and the organisation of the strata (TP, 153); but *before* does not mean chronologically prior: it is adjacent to the organism, engaging continually in the process of constructing itself. A BwO is always swinging between the surfaces that stratify it (and potentially capture it in a cancerous movement of self-replication) and the plane of consistency that sets it free and allows it to reach its full potential as a BwO (TP, 161).

In this movement, 'the BwO is desire; it is that which one desires and by which one desires' (TP, 165). Desire is connected to complex and multilayered assemblages that go into molecular levels: postures, attitudes, perceptions, etc. Desire should be able to circulate through the BwO but it can develop fascistic features: 'Desire itself results from a highly developed, engineered setup rich in interactions: a whole supple segmentarity that processes molecular energies and potentially gives desire a fascist determination' (TP, 215). How then can desire become fascist? By falling 'into the proliferation of a cancerous stratum' (TP, 165). Desire becomes fascist through the cancerous repetition of the same codes; through a stagnant repetition and proliferation of the same strata. Processes of stratification 'may (or may not) lead to our rejection of a unifying subjectivity and embrace instead the forever-formative Body without Organs' (Message 2010: 272). In the case of excessive, accelerated proliferation of the same strata, desire becomes a prisoner of the tumorous strata.

Nonetheless, although fascism is trapped into cancerous strata, it is still desire: 'Even fascism is desire' (TP, 165). Desire can then pertain to the construction of the plane of consistency and lead to the formation of a full BwO, or it can pertain to stratic proliferation that leads towards cancerous and fascistic BwOs that constitute 'terrifying caricatures of the plane of consistency' (TP, 163).

When a BwO gets caught in the strata and enters a loop of malignant self-replication that makes it unable to reach its full potential, that BwO is considered cancerous. As Deleuze and Guattari point out: 'If the strata are an affair of coagulation and sedimentation, all a stratum needs is a high sedimentation rate for it to lose its configuration and articulations, and to form its own specific kind of tumour, within itself or in a given formation or apparatus' (TP, 163). The excessive stratification in which the cancerous BwO gets caught makes it become 'organized, signified, subjected' (TP, 161).

A cancerous BwO is caught in a pattern of endless reproduction of the self-same pattern. It does not allow potential movements of decoding and overcoding, as it is excessively coded. Desire is coded when it is restricted to certain activities and ends, when it is not free to achieve its full potentialities and is trapped in repetition and too similar strata. Fascist desire is also coded in the sense that it enters certain definite relations. In this manner, fascist desire is trapped in tumorous rigidity and its ability to explore alternatives by movements of decoding and overcoding is severely restricted.

Fascist desire is, then, trapped in same-like stratification. The intensities and singularities are locked in a system of redundancy that is stuck in a continuous loop of repetition. A cancerous BwO has too much sedimentation and insufficient overcoding. As John Protevi wrote in his entry for fascism in *The Deleuze Dictionary*: 'By endlessly repeating the selection of homogenized individuals in a process of "conformity" the cancerous BwO breaks down the stratum on which it lodges: social cloning and assembly-line personalities' (Protevi 2010: 103). Microfascism, then, is a cancer of the stratum. It is a set of rigid, tumorous codes and systems of thought and desire. As the only thing that the cancerous Bwo admits is more cancer, the endless repetition of the same, the cancerous BwO can only lead towards molarity and conformity. It is accelerated sameness, proliferation of the same codes that potentiates an inability to overcode.

The plane of consistency to which the BwO is connected also opens the possibilities for new understandings of the world. In *Spinoza and Us*, Deleuze insists on the idea that we should follow Spinoza when trying to understand any body. A body can be anything: an animal, sounds, an idea, a social body, a linguistic corpus (S, 127). Understanding a body in a Spinozist manner implies paying attention to its latitude and longitude. Latitude is conceptualised as the relations of speed and slowness that compose its infinite particles. Longitude, on the other hand, is conformed by its sets of affects; it would be the anonymous force that comprises its 'capacity for affecting and being affected by other' bodies' (S, 123).

I will argue in the next section that the longitude of Spanish fascism would be affected by cancerous proliferation and excessive, stratified speed, whereas the force that animates Spanish fascism would be silence. Silence, then, will be considered as the force that shaped (and still shapes) Spanish affects.

Cancerous Silence

In this second part, I would like to navigate the possibilities of explaining the Spanish Civil War and post-civil war experiences through Deleuze and Guattari's idea of microfascism as a cancerous BwO. As suggested in *A Thousand Plateaus*: 'For each BwO we must ask 1) What type is it, how it is fabricated, by what procedures and means (predetermining what will come to pass)? 2) What are its modes, what comes to pass, and with what variants and what surprises, what is unexpected and what is expected?' (TP, 152).

The type of BwO that the fascist desire constitutes in Spain is a cancerous type that is fabricated through silent stagnation. The repetition of the same through the silencing of potential or actual dissidence caused a cancerous proliferation of the same fascistic set of codes. This predetermines what will come to pass: the silencing of certain sets of codes rendered them invisible; at the same time, it legitimised only the audible ones: the stagnant, recurring ones. Desire cannot flow here; the unexpected is blocked. What can be expected in this fascistic context is only sameness. Taking all this into account, I argue that in Spain there was (and perhaps still is) a rigid system of thought and desire, ruled mainly by a crushing silence that has trapped Spanish desires in endless repetition of codes, in molarity and conformity.

Silence can be considered one of the fundamental parts of the process of codification of desire in Spain. This process of codification governed by silence has been shaped by exercises of forgetting. A politics of forgetting has been installed in Spain as a crucial part of national identity. As Leela Fernandes defines it (2014: 2416), a politics of forgetting is a political and discursive process in which specific marginalised groups are invisibilised and forgotten by the hegemonic political culture. The hegemonic political discourse in Spain since the civil war considers the political left as 'the Reds': an almost caricaturesque pejorative term (but often also used to self-identify) used by the Nationalist faction to refer to Republicans, including supporters of the government, far-left communists and anarchists who were against the military coup. Anybody who was against the fascist military rebellion was considered a Red, anyone who had any kind of what was considered anti-fascist thought was considered a Red. This political enemy was rendered invisible through various acts of violence. They were invisibilised in a physical way because they were removed from everyone's sight: they were forced to leave the country, forced into exile; they were forced to go into hiding; they were killed. Also, they were invisibilised in a symbolic way: their political discourse, the political discourse of the left, was silenced. It was risky to voice anti-fascist opinions that went against the fascist, hegemonic discourse. Silencing certain discourses goes hand in hand with creating hegemonic discourses: eliminating the possibility of different exercises of overcoding, eliminating difference and the possibility of finding new lines of flight is necessary to constitute the molarity of the status quo that fascist regimes seek.

Forgetting has been used in Spain as a collective act in the creation of rigid sets of codes that involve a shared identity and a hegemonic narrative. As Ernest Renan argues in 'What is a Nation?', the essence of a nation is that all the members have a great deal of things in common, and also that they have forgotten many things. Forgetting, then, can be seen as a condition for the formation of frameworks of mutual recognition. Following this idea, I believe that after the civil war the Spanish population that remained in Spain (those who were not killed or exiled) was forced to forget certain things in order to construct the victors' narrative. They were forced to forget their anti-fascist views and opinions, and their anti-fascist practices. For instance, it has almost been forgotten that there were numerous anarchist communities in Aragón, Catalunya and Asturies (Casanova 1987; Barrio Alonso 1988). Also, the innovative pedagogy of the Republican schools was repressed and persecuted, the teachers (mostly women) were attacked and punished. The Spanish population was also forced to forget their anti-fascist political culture, which conformed to the Republican values of the 1931 Constitution: freedom, equality and fraternity, democratic values of radical equality and social justice, including a special consideration of the equal role of women in society, in a clear attempt to overcome the inequality and discrimination that women faced in other earlier times.

Furthermore, the Spanish population was forced to forget their family members who were killed or exiled or, even worse, were hiding in the maquis. The maquis were guerrillas who hid in the country and fought against Francoist Spain. They were often supported by their families and neighbours, who gave them food and supplies. This practice was highly dangerous for everybody involved and was surrounded by silence. These people did not exist any more in the public sphere, and their existence was known only to those who directly helped them; for the rest of the people, they were forgotten (Sorel 2002; Moreno Gómez 2006).

Anti-fascist thoughts and practices were rendered invisible, while Francoists shaped the hegemonic political narratives. In this sense, Franco's 'manipulation of Spanish history aimed to confuse and obscure the facts about the Civil War' (Encarnación 2014: 42), and the victors' discourse was then transmitted to the Spanish population through indoctrination, extensive use of propaganda, and the silencing of certain facts and opinions (Richards 1998).

During the Franco era, the Spanish people were intimidated into not expressing their opinions. People are still nowadays traumatised into not being noticed by neighbours, even regarding the tiniest apolitical aspects of life. Under this freezing and rigid set of codes, the Spanish population has been led to believe that if they are not noticed, if they do not express their opinions out loud and keep quiet, they will not end up as a name on a purge list. Indeed, the entire population was scrutinised, house by house, family by family. The Franco regime committed exemplary murders and repressive practices of various kinds: threats, detentions, beatings, rapes, persecutions, executions, etc. These practices provoked so much fear that a thunderous silence was imposed for decades; a silence that affected individual and collective behaviour. Republicans were forced to keep silence in order not to be noticed. And their silence has been kept silent.

Franco died in his bed in 1975. After that, both leftist and right-wing parties decided not to challenge the status quo and to keep difficult questions silent for fear of endangering national reconciliation. The transition to democracy, the restoration of liberal democratic freedoms, was seen by many as a moment in which the Francoist structures could be finally challenged. Nonetheless, the pact of forgetting required people to forget about the past and to look together into the future. This was an invitation to avoid dealing with the legacy of Francoism. This meant suppressing painful memories derived from the past civil war division of the population into victors and vanquished (Preston 2012). The memories were also suppressed in the collective political discourse:

The 'pact of forgetting' reached by political elites during the transition and accepted by the majority of Spaniards was mirrored in the extensive academic literature spawned by Spain's democratization, which almost completely ignored questions about the legacy of widespread and systematic human rights abuses for the new democracy. (Davis 2005: 859)

There was a forgiving gesture that accompanied the politics of forgetting of the pact of silence: 'The legal codification of this act of forgetting was the Amnesty Law of 1977, which encompassed acts of political violence committed during the civil war and the forty-year Franquist dictatorship that followed' (Boyd 2008: 135). There was no prosecution of war criminals and fascist criminals, and there was a full amnesty that led to politically induced amnesia about fascism. In the context of the so-called Transition to Democracy, 'those who had been obliged to be silent for nearly 40 years were once again required to accept that there would not be public recognition of their past lives or memories' (Graham 2004: 30). The public and collective reprocessing and overcoding of trauma was prohibited, and all the painful memories of those who suffered under the fascist regime were expected to be kept, once again, in private. Thus, this pact of silence perpetuated Franco's presence in the public sphere. Although memorials to victims of fascism hardly exist, statues of Franco and other fascist imagery are still visible. The silencing process only silenced some people's stories and memories and perpetuated the victors' narrative that stated that Franco saved Spain from the clutches of 'the Reds'.

Through this silencing, national reconciliation was staged during the transition to democracy, but political structures and legal mechanisms from the dictatorship were kept in place, thus legitimising them. Therefore, this process of silencing has led to processes of conformity in Spanish society that imply the repetition of the same fascistic codes over and over again. There was a forced conformity of opinion, as dissidents were either killed, exiled or terrorised into silence. This caused a lack of decoding and overcoding, a cancer of the Spanish strata that were (and I believe still are) too sedimented and difficult to overcode. The politics of forgetting and amnesia have damaged the democracy they were intended to fortify (Boyd 2008: 143). As Vicenç Navarro says: 'There cannot be an authentically democratic culture in Spain until there is an antifranquist culture, for which we need a vivid historical memory' (Navarro 2001).

The political stagnation that was produced by this forced silence results in the impossibility of healing the wounds caused by the civil war and Francoism. It also leads to the impossibility of embracing the full potentialities of Spanish society, as desire is stuck in too much stratification. Spanish society is still ruled by cancerous strata inherited from this politics of silencing. As a result, Spain is incapable of over-coding this rigid system of thought and desire, and is thus oriented to molarity, to unity. It is comprised of rigid strata; it is homogeneous and standardised because of the endless non-productive repetition of the non-different.

Silent Transmission of Trauma

There has also been a desire for silence, a desire for keeping things as they are, a fear of change. The cancerous BwO does not allow desire to desire otherwise. Within this molecular silence that impregnates every aspect of our lives, it is not easy to see this fascist inside that desires stagnation and immobility. Also, silence has been a mechanism of stratification of desire. Silence has been used to force the repression of thoughts, practices and memories that could lead to desiring otherwise. The transmission of the molar narrative has benefited from the silencing of discourses that were demonised and persecuted. That forced repression has led to a traumatic stratification.

According to Michelle R. Ancharoff (1998), silence is one of the mechanisms of transmission of trauma, along with excessive openness, identification and repetition. For Ancharoff, social and family silence is probably the most common way of transmitting war trauma. Silence transmits norms, myths and metamessages without the possibility of questioning them, leading to molarity, unity and the rigidity of systems of thought and desire. Rosental and Volter (1998) analyse, in the context of trauma caused by Nazism, how silence and family secrets are the most effective mechanisms of ensuring the continuity of trauma. Survivors learn that questions should not be asked, and their fantasy then creates the answers. Silence also isolates survivors and impedes their processing of trauma and grief (Danieli 1998).

Following Marianne Hirsch's theory of intergenerational transfer of traumatic memories (Hirsch 2002), it can be said that if a society does not address the traumas caused by political violence in the past, its nega-tive effects interfere with future generations and there is a pathological repetition across generations. Can desire desire otherwise when it is stuck in endless repetition of the same? These negative effects, Hirsch says, tend to repeat the same violent codes, such as the need to have enemies, polarisation, victimism, shame or fear of questioning power.

In the case of the Spanish Civil War, psychiatrist Armañanzas Ros (2009) reports the case of a patient who constantly mentioned the civil war and spoke about how his father, who endured it, never said anything about it until he was 70 years old. This was not an isolated case. Armañanzas Ros often had patients who claimed that their parents never said anything about the war. Survivors were unable to explain what they experienced, which speaks of the 'untranslatability of their story' (Hirsch 2002: 80). Armañanzas Ros considers that even mental health professionals have participated in the pact of silence by not addressing the frozen grief, the PTSD, the guilt, the shame or the fear of their patients.

Post-war generations are brought up in a silence that only gives an idea about the violence that their parents and grandparents endured during the war and the political repression they suffered. As Volkan states (2004), post-war first generations are charged with certain tasks that involve keeping alive the memory of the trauma, grieving the losses, and fighting for reparations and transitional justice. How is this possible when silence is so thick that it literally buries even deeper the more than 114,000 who disappeared under Franco's rule? In silence, political mourning cannot be possible. Mourning and grief are frozen and do not disappear – they are melancholically incorporated. In the case of the Spanish state, there was an implicit demand for oblivion from the institutions. It was forbidden to mourn publicly, and the safety of the whole family depended on this silence.

As a granddaughter of the civil war, my generation has inherited and absorbed political trauma through non-verbal communication. The wound of the horrors of fascism remains open and unaddressed because of the stagnant repetition of the same. It is difficult for us to address this issue because we do not have a direct connection with what happened, and we inherited only amnesia. At the same time, we will be the last generation who can speak with the survivors and encourage them to break their silence and unearth memories that are buried deep under strata of silence. We have not heard the stories of fascism in Spain. Our families still have stories that have been kept untold, forced to be kept silent. It is time to listen to them if we want to shake off our political trauma.

Coding and Overcoding Fascism

The tension between fascist silence, fascist uproar and anti-fascist contestation is always palpable in Spain. In recent times, two fascist and two anti-fascist events have come to my attention as opposing ways of unearthing fascism, with very different aims and objectives. Regarding the fascist events, we witnessed the return of outspoken and activist fascism in two key moments: the conflict around the exhumation of Franco's remains, and the far-right party VOX winning seats in Andalusia for the first time after a very long socialist regional government. The anti-fascist moments that I would like to highlight are both linked to the unearthing of historical memory: the publication of two books that narrate the testimony of victims of fascism.

Fascist Backlash

The Historical Memory Law passed in 2007 was a first step towards the unearthing of political memory and towards breaking the silence. As Aleksandra Hadzelek summarises, this law

> condemns Franco's regime, recognises all victims of the war and violence on both sides of the conflict, annuls prior legislation, offers government assistance in identifying victims buried in clandestine mass graves, prohibits political events at Valle de los Caídos [Valley of the Fallen, the burial place of Franco and a monument to nationalist soldiers who perished in the war], and grants Spanish citizenship to descendants of Republican exiles from the Civil War, as well as surviving members of the International Brigades. (Hadzelek 2012: 153)

The Historical Memory Law drew the line at altering monuments of historical significance, such as El Valle de los Caídos [por Dios y por la Patria] (The Valley of the Fallen [for God and the Fatherland]): the monumental Catholic basilica under which Franco's remains are buried and that constitutes the only monument to fascism in Europe. The construction of El Valle de los Caídos was commissioned by the dictator himself. Its construction was carried out mainly by political prisoners, many of whom died there due to forced labour (González-Ruibal 2009). The decision to leave monuments to fascism unaffected by the Historical Memory Law reflected the attitude of the public at the time, when a majority opposed tinkering with the Franco memorial in any major way. This hesitation reflected a considerable lingering ambivalence about Franco.

In June 2018 the socialist president Pedro Sánchez announced his intention to exhume Franco's remains from El Valle de los Caídos and transform the monument from a shrine to Francoism into a memorial for the victims of fascism. Explaining his decision, Sánchez insisted:

'Something that is unimaginable in Germany and Italy, countries that also suffered fascist dictatorships, should also be unimaginable in our country.'[1] The fascist uproar at this was loud, and a sour debate was sparked in Spain. Those who considered this a profanation organised a movement called 'El Valle no se toca' ('Don't Touch the Valley') that describes itself as a movement whose objective is to save Spain, and that consists of a group of Spaniards who have decided to resist the intentions of the government to desecrate the Valley of the Fallen.[2] They organised protests at which they waved the Spanish Francoist flag, showed fascist imagery such as the Falange's yoke and arrows, and performed the Nazi salute.

One of the political groups behind this movement is VOX, a far-right party that won 10.26 per cent of the votes in the general elections held in 2019 and entered the Congress of Deputies for the first time with 52 seats, making it the third largest force. They opposed the exhumation of Franco's remains and have the objective of derogating the Historical Memory Law which, they believe, indoctrinates the Spanish population with leftist propaganda. VOX is a split-off from the most extreme parts of the Popular Party, and in December 2018 broke new political ground after winning 12 seats in a regional election in Andalusia. The leadership of VOX has been in contact with Steve Bannon, and France's far-right leader Marine le Pen toasted VOX's success on Twitter, so this movement should also be seen in the broader context of the rise of far-right movements in contemporary politics.

VOX's proposals are sifted through a thick layer of Spanish ultra-nationalism with an authoritarian national-Catholic matrix (Valencia-García 2018), which is reflected in their territorial claims in relation to Gibraltar, the nostalgic support for the Franco dictatorship, the iron fist against Catalan independence, the repeal of the Law of Historical Memory and the centralisation of the state and the liquidation of the autonomy of the regions.

Reading VOX's electoral programme, one can easily see that it may contain traces of Francoism. They advocate the unity of Spain, placing themselves in clear opposition to the Catalan or Basque pro-independence movements. VOX emphasises the importance of the family, defined by the traditional Catholic values espoused by Francoism. They intend to fight against fundamentalist Islam by regaining control over Spain's borders, detaining and deporting fundamentalists, and opposing Turkey joining the EU. Of course, they fight against what they call 'gender ideology', a term often used by the Church hierarchy and ultra-Catholic groups. In this sense, they advocate the derogation of the Law against

Gender Violence, as, for them, it clearly leads to discrimination against men because of their sex, causing juridical inequality and fostering false accusations by women about sexual violence. They also plan to remove abortion from public health care, since they defend life from conception to natural death. Finally, VOX is against the recognition of certain LGBT rights, such as marriage, because they consider that their union denaturalises marriage.

The ghost of Franco seems to be reappearing in Spain – but was it ever really gone? The politicians who form VOX nowadays are not new to the political arena: they were part of the Popular Party, the right-wing party that has been sharing power with the socialists for the last forty years. In this sense, we can understand a saying that is common in Spanish, and that talks about unaddressed labours of remembrance: 'From that dust we get this mud.' From the dust that we have inherited from the cancerous strata of Francoism, we get this muddy 'new' fascist movement.

When Remembering is Resisting

In 2018 two very interesting books were published: texts that can help us overcome and shake off the silence that surrounds fascism in Spain. A labour of remembrance against the replication of fascism through silence and silencing is needed nowadays in Spain. Breaking the pact of silence is fundamental in order to create and organise a struggle against forgetting, against the erasure of the past.

The Historical Memory Law was a first step in this direction, but it is not enough. Against the inherited politics of silence and forgetting, a labour of remembrance should be done. The stories are there, they are lived somehow, they are embodied in people's lives. They are just not heard. Have we lost the ability to hear each other? We may have to learn to listen to them, to look at our surroundings with a renewed will to overcome our past (and present) experiences of internalised and normalised fascism.

These are efforts made to recover memories that were taken from us, in line with the activist work against forgetting that has been present in Spain since the transition to democracy and especially since 2000, when the Association for the Recovery of Historical Memory was founded. Despite the molarity of fascism, the lines of flight persevered and might find a way to break down the cancerous strata. The Association for the Recovery of Historical Memory works to recover oral and written testimonies of political repression. Their most visible labour of remembrance is done by excavating the physical strata that cover the unmarked grave-yards that still plague the Spanish territory. They unearth and identify the corpses, thus giving families solace and the opportunity to bury and grieve for their disappeared loved ones. Their research to find mass graves involves interviewing locals and reading historical archives – archives that Mariano Rajoy, the (Popular Party) president of Spain between 2011 and 2018, refused to open so that information could be studied and disseminated.

I will mention here two different kinds of testimonies that I believe are relevant to unearthing the horrors of fascism. The first was written by Enesida García Suárez, who was a child during the civil war. The second is by journalist Cristina Fallarás, whose grandfather was killed during the war and whose family kept it a secret for decades.

Enesida García Suárez was eleven years old in 1938 when Francoists killed her parents and sister because her parents were giving food to her uncles, who were hiding from Francoist soldiers in the mountains. Her family was killed along with eleven other families in a small village called Tiraña. Enesida, as she explains herself, needed more than forty years to be able to write in her notebook about what happened; her testimony, one of the few intact ones, was only published in 2018.

Enesida gives an account of the silence that was installed in Tiraña after the massacre: it was deep and long-lasting. Even after Franco died in 1975, the silence was unbearable. On 1 November 1978 there was the first official homage to the victims in a public memorial that took place at the cemetery of Tiraña. The windows and doors of the houses surrounding the cemetery were kept closed, as if the inhabitants of those houses were afraid even of seeing what was happening during the memorial.

Cristina Fallarás wrote about her family story in *Honrarás a tu padre y a tu madre* (Honour thy Father and thy Mother). The aim of her book was to break the silence that has run through generations in the Spanish state: 'My name is Cristina and this is the story of a family and its silences. The story of how silence spreads, crosses generations and ferments' (Fallarás 2018: 34, my translation). This is the story of her family, a story buried in silence. On 5 December 1936, Félix Fallarás, 35 years old, married with two children, was shot at the Torrero cemetery in Zaragoza (my hometown), where the earth was soaked with blood. He was not known as a political activist. At that time, one of those in charge of the firing squads was Pablo Sánchez, who collaborated with the Gestapo and ended up reaching the rank of colonel in Franco's army. In 1957 he went to the bank accompanied by his daughter María Jesús. They were introduced to a new employee. He was the youngest son of Felix Fallarás. Ten years after that meeting he married Maria Jesús. Within a year of the wedding their daughter Cristina was born.

Cristina Fallarás was brought up not knowing anything about her paternal grandfather. He simply was not there. As Fallarás says: 'Even his death they made disappear. I did not meet Felix. His story does not exist. Even that was denied to him' (2018: 33, my translation). Her paternal grandmother never spoke about the war or about her murdered husband. The other part of the family, however, was proudly fascist: her maternal grandfather even spoke proudly about people he killed. And one of the people he killed was his son-in-law's father. Cristina's parents never spoke about the war either: they needed that silence to overcome the horror of what had happened in and to the previous generation. In her own words: 'Questions are not asked because they would break the silence. And everything ends and begins with silence' (Fallarás 2018: 40, my translation).

But she felt the need to start asking questions, to start breaking the silence. She says that they cut off a part of your memory, and that changes you; recovering it changes you a second time. She started a journalistic and personal journey to look for her dead. She tried to look for her dead in order not to kill herself (Fallarás 2018: 11). Unearthing the memory of the dead during the war was now a matter of survival. She tries to invoke her dead, to initiate a dialogue with her dead.

Both Enesida and Cristina made an effort to navigate through their pain and tell the stories of their dead. This labour of remembering has to honour the efforts of those who survived hunger, pain, loss, persecution, institutional mistreatment, stigma and oblivion. It has to honour the people, especially women, who have quietly been remembering the dead for decades and bringing flowers to the ditches where their loved ones are buried. Moreover, it takes distance from the idea of an invulnerable, resilient subject who just, somehow, overcomes the trauma and moves on. It is a way of connecting with our political wounds and embracing our radical vulnerability as political and affective beings.

As Fallarás states, the wounds ferment with silence. Silence in the Spanish state speaks about the pain, anger and sadness of a whole generation of survivors, and shows how the next generations have been brought up in that same breeding ground. It is us, who are alive now, who must raise our voices and create places where we can share our frozen pain, where we can listen to the unearthed words of the dead.

Conclusion

This chapter has defended the idea that we can understand the fascist Spanish phenomenon as a cancerous BwO: as repetition of the same codes, as lack of decoding and overcoding, as stagnant reiteration of the same. Silence has been the motor of this stagnation: political silence that was forced on the Spanish population after the civil war and during Franco's dictatorship and that led to cancerous proliferation of fascistic desire.

The final aim of this chapter has been to raise the question: How can we create cracks in the fixed, fascistic Spanish framework and enable a micropolitcs of transformation against old and new fascist flows? In order to do so, this chapter has pointed out how it is necessary to fill the gaps in Spanish political memory about fascism in order to overcome the trauma that was channelled through silence and perform an over-coding labour of remembrance. In this sense, remembrance is resistance. Breaking the pact of silence, making audible the stories of the victims, are the tools proposed to dislodge the political trauma caused by silent fascism. Making audible the memories of those who endured political repression could break the strata that now only allows more fascism, that stagnates desire into same-like codifications.

Through a politics and labour of remembrance we could overcode the cancerous strata and create cracks in this fixed, cancerous, fascist framework. This would enable critical thinking towards a micropolitics of transformation in Spain against very ingrained, old and new fascist flows.

Notes

1. My translation. See <http://www.rtve.es/noticias/20180618/entrevista-pedro-sanc hez-exclusiva-para-rtve-directo/1752454.shtml> (last accessed 15 May 2022).
2. See <https://www.facebook.com/pg/vallenosetoca> (last accessed 15 May 2022).

References

Ancharoff, M., et al. (1998), 'The Legacy of Combat Trauma: Clinical Implications of Intergenerational Transmission', in Y. Danieli (ed.), *International Handbook of Multigenerational Legacies of Trauma*, New York: Plenum Press, pp. 257–78.

Armañanzas Ros, G. (2009), 'Transmisión transgeneracional del trauma de nuestra guerra civil', *Norte de Salud mental*, 8 (34): 44–51.

Barrio Alonso, A. (1988), *Ángeles. Anarquismo y anarcosindicalismo en Asturias (1890–1936)*, Madrid: Siglo veintiuno editores.

Boyd, C. P. (2008), 'The Politics of History and Memory in Democratic Spain', *The ANNALS of the American Academy of Political and Social Science*, 617 (1): 133–48.

Casanova, J. (1987), 'Anarchism and Revolution in the Spanish Civil War: The Case of Aragon', *European History Quarterly*, 17 (4): 423–51.

Danieli, Y. (ed.) (1998), *International Handbook of Multigenerational Legacies of Trauma*, New York: Plenum Press.

Davis, M. (2005), 'Is Spain Recovering Its Memory? Breaking the "Pacto del Olvido"?', *Human Rights Quarterly*, 27 (3): 858–80.

Encarnación, O. G. (2014), *Democracy without Justice in Spain: The Politics of Forgetting*, University Park, PA: University of Pennsylvania Press.

Fallarás, C. (2018), *Honrarás a tu padre ya tu madre*, Madrid: Anagrama.

Fernandes, L. (2014), 'The Politics of Forgetting: Class Politics, State Power and the Restructuring of Urban Space in India', *Urban Studies*, 41 (12): 2415–30.

García Suárez, E. (2018), *Mi infancia en el franquismo. Tiraña, Asturies, 1938*, Oviedo: Cambalache.

González-Ruibal, A. (2009), 'Topography of Terror or Cultural Heritage? The Monuments of Franco's Spain', in N. Forbes, R. Page and G. Pérez (eds), *Europe's Deadly Century. Perspectives on 20th Century Conflict Heritage*, Swindon: English Heritage, pp. 65–72.

Graham, H. (2004), 'Coming to Terms with the Past: Spain's Memory Wars', *History Today*, 54 (5): 29–31.

Hadzelek, A. (2012), 'Spain's "Pact of Silence" and the Removal of Franco's Statues', in D. Kirkby (ed.), *Past Law, Present Histories*, Canberra: Australian National University, pp. 153–76.

Hirsch, M. (2002), 'Marked by Memory: Feminist Reflections on Trauma and Transmission', in N. K. Miller and J. Tougaw (eds), *Extremities: Trauma, Testimony, and Community*, Champaign: Illinois University Press, pp. 71–91.

Holland, E. (2008), 'Schizoanalysis, Nomadology, Fascism', in I. Buchanan and N. Thoburn (eds), *Deleuze and Politics*, Edinburgh: Edinburgh University Press, pp. 74–97.

Jerez-Farrán, C., and S. Amago (2010), *Unearthing Franco's Legacy: Mass Graves and the Recovery of Historical Memory in Spain*, Notre Dame, IN: University of Notre Dame Press.

Juliá, S. (2006), *Memoria, historia y política de un pasado de guerra y dictadura. In Memoria de la guerra y del franquismo*, Madrid: Taurus.

Message, K. (2010), 'Black Hole', in A. Parr (ed.), *The Deleuze Dictionary Revised Edition*, Edinburgh: Edinburgh University Press, pp. 33–5.

Moreno Gómez, F. (2006), 'Lagunas en la memoria y en la historia del maquis', *Hispania Nova: Revista de historia contemporánea*, 6: 463–89.

Navarro, V. (2001), 'Los costes de la desmemoria histórica', *El País*, 16 June.

Preston, P. (2012), *The Spanish Holocaust: Inquisition and Extermination in Twentieth-century Spain*, London: Harper Collins.

Protevi, J. (2010), 'Fascism', in A. Parr (ed.), *The Deleuze Dictionary Revised Edition*, Edinburgh: Edinburgh University Press, pp. 103–4.

Renan, E. (1995 [1882]), 'What is a Nation?', in S. Woolf (ed.), *Nationalism in Europe*, London: Routledge, pp. 54–66.

Richards, M. (1998), *A Time of Silence: Civil War and the Culture of Repression in Franco's Spain, 1936–1945*, Cambridge: Cambridge University Press.

Rigby, A. (2010), 'Amnesty and Amnesia in Spain', *Peace Review*, 12 (1): 73–9.

Rosental, G., and B. Völter (1998), 'Three Generations within Jewish and Non-Jewish German Families after the Unification of Germany', in Y. Danieli (ed.),

International Handbook of Multigenerational legacies of Trauma, New York: Plenium Press, pp. 297–314.

Sorel, A. (2002), *La guerrilla antifranquista: la historia del Maquis contada por sus protagonistas*, Tafalla: Txalaparta.

Valencia-García, L. D. (2018), 'VOX and the Return of the Radical Right in Spain', *Centre for Analysis of the Radical Right*, 7 December, <https://www.radicalrightanalysis.com/2018/12/07/4022/> (last accessed 29 October 2020).

Volkan, V. D. (2004), 'Traumatized Societies and Psychological Care: Expanding the Concept of Preventive Medicine', in D. Knafo (ed.), *Living with Terror, Working with Trauma: A Clinician's Handbook*, Lanham, MD: Jason Aronson, pp. 479–98.

Chapter 12

The Wounds of Europe: The Life of Joë Bousquet

Rick Dolphijn

Figure 12.1 Joë Bousquet in his room around 1940, photographer unknown.

> My wound was there before me, I was born to embody it.
>
> Joë Bousquet quoted in LS, 174

The Time of Surrealism

At the tender age of 18, philosophy student Ferdinand Alquié became acquainted with the writer Joë Bousquet, who was then just in his thirties but already much more advanced in life. Alquié was born in Carcassonne, a fortified city in the south of France, and had not left the city yet. Near the end of the First World War, Bousquet came to live in that town too, to reside with his sister, in a room with the shutters permanently closed. The friendship between Alquié and Bousquet lasted for the rest of their shared lives, and can be felt still in the published letters Bousquet wrote to him over the years. There are letters from the early 1930s, in which Bousquet asks the young and eager Alquié to be cautious with regard to the Russian communist party and to notice how their ideas differ from what Marx actually had to say. In other letters, Bousquet tells Alquié to pursue his interests in Descartes and Spinoza, of whom he, already as a young man, could talk so vividly. Intelligent and eloquently written letters they are, in the topics discussed but also in those left out. Only rarely do they mention the horrors of their times, the way in which, after the Great Depression hit the European continent, the 1930s became the time when the sun would finally go down on Europe. After the great nineteenth century in which Europe had given birth to its prodigy child modernism, as well as to nationalism, racism and sexism, Europe now introduced its people to its final beastly offspring: fascism. After its working classes were ruined by the financial crises, a venomous nihilism overtook Europe again (as Nietzsche had already foreseen) and was making people, more than ever, celebrate the death of Otherness, *knowing damn well* that this would eventually also kill themselves.

Alquié and Bousquet lived through these times very consciously. Yet in their correspondence they prefer not to analyse these matters. Bousquet writes a lot about the music of Beethoven and is keen to share with Alquié many of the wonderful books he has read over the years. In one of his last letters, when writing about how the work of Sartre incorporates the techniques of a symphony, he comes to talk of the necessity of writing – which obviously is a love that the poet and the philosopher both share – and its importance for life, and he concludes:

> The art of writing does not gain anything by complicating its techniques . . . It is an art form which is born poor and revolutionary, and which grows by reducing itself to the satisfaction of an elementary need. (Bousquet 1969: 252, my translation)[1]

In his book *The Philosophy of Surrealism*, published in France in 1955 after Bousquet had died, Alquié, by then a professor of philosophy at the Sorbonne in Paris, notes that it was in Bousquet's room that he first discovered Surrealism. A year later the book was reviewed by the young Gilles Deleuze, Alquié's student since 1945, who noticed immediately that Alquié's philosophy of Surrealism was entirely a philosophy of life

(LO, 111–15). This room in Carcassonne, where Bousquet had spent his life writing (poor and revolutionary), was a place where many of the Surrealist writers and painters were received. Here, the young Alquié met Elsa Triolet, Simone Weil, Jean Ballard and notably Max Ernst. The walls of this room were covered with paintings by friends such as Tanguy, Ernst, Masson, Dalí and Miró, if they were not loaded with books on art and philosophy, collections of poetry and novels. There was also a bust of Seneca, the Stoic philosopher, who told us that life was a choice, a very personal choice.

However, the situation described above came about because of a tragic event.

On 27 May 1918 Lieutenant Joë Bousquet was severely wounded at the battle of the plateau of Brenelle, south of Vailly (during the offensive of the Chemin des Dames), while he was executing an order to drive the enemy back beyond the Aisne. A German bullet struck his spine and paralysed him from the chest down. After a long period of hope of healing (much of which was spent in intensive care in the military hospitals of Ris-Orangis, Toulouse and Carcassonne), at the end of 1924 the doctors concluded that Bousquet would not be able to use his lower limbs any more. This meant that he would remain bedridden for the rest of his life, that he would rarely leave his room at 53 rue de Verdun (note the bitter irony in the name of the street). The bullet never left his body. Before he was wounded, it was said that Bousquet was rather a *beau vivant*. He was fond of alcohol, had a series of affairs with married women, and was surely not impressed by the powers that determined the war. There are rumours still that Bousquet was wearing shiny red boots in and outside the trenches, only to provoke the German enemy. Never afraid of death.

Of course, everything changed the moment he was wounded.

'Can Bousquet be called a Surrealist?' Alquié asks us. Bousquet lived in this room for over thirty years, until his death in 1950, well after the Second World War had ended. The room was a Surrealist paradise, it was the ideal inner world, of which Breton so often fantasised (see Mical 2005: 4), filled with dreams and drives and far removed from the horrors that dominated the outside world, yet at the same time somehow reflecting it, inextricably connected with it, resonating it creatively. But obviously, to ask whether Bousquet himself was a Surrealist is a very different question. Apart from the room, Alquié believes that Surrealism is practised in the fiction that Bousquet wrote. He recalls *Rendez vous d'un soir d'hiver* (1933). The protagonist of this story, Annie, seems to express herself not solely through language, which would make her character essentially discursive, Alquié claims. Rather,

her character moves with the world, a world that Bousquet has to give a voice. The stories told have to be accompanied by the stories untold, by the undercurrents that accompany the here and now. With Bousquet, Alquié claims, language is not telling us everything that happened. With Bousquet, language negates, it intends to intervene, but the world of love, the world of matter, is at hand in Annie. With Annie, what speaks is the body and all of its drives, conflicting, disoriented and chaotic as they are, and the world they give rise to.

That is very much what Surrealism was about, Alquié stresses in the rest of the book: Surrealism's interest in dreams, in the darkest of drives, in nature unforeseen is a move away from the expressed, the knowable. But this is by no means an idealist claim. Breton, with a background in medicine and psychiatry, had served in a neurological hospital where he practised Freudian theories treating patients suffering from shell shock. Mapping the wounds that marked their environments *and* them, Breton was interested in mapping the undercurrents that did not accept Cartesian or Kantian dualisms that separated the mind from the body and the subject from the object. In that sense, Breton seems to follow the same path that Lucian Freud, painter and grandson of Sigmund Freud, followed many years later, as Adrian Searle reads his paintings: 'Hell isn't only other people. One must include oneself and one's body in this comedy of errors and terrors and that's what Freud does' (Searle 2019).

The errors and terrors incorporated, the visible and invisible wounds that not so much limit one's being but make it possible, that's what Breton was interested in. From the start this meant that Surrealism (like Dada) was doing serious social criticism. Apollinaire's play *The Breasts of Tiresias*, written in 1903 but staged (with the subtitle 'a Surrealist musical') only in 1917, thereby introducing the term 'Surrealism', proves that provocative and creative interventions in pacifism and the critique of hierarchy (patriarchy in this case) had been at the root of Surrealism from the start. Lee Miller's entire oeuvre, including the iconic picture of herself taking a bath in Adolf Hitler's Munich apartment (while he killed himself in Berlin), with her boots filthy from a visit to the Dachau concentration camp dirtying his bathmat, is perhaps the best example of the provocative and creative interventions that are key to Surrealism.

Thus, when André Breton claims that 'derealisation' is central to the Surrealist project, it makes good sense for Alquié to stress that Breton is not interested in 'escaping' the real. On the contrary; Surrealism, he claims, is about not being fooled by the realities of the day, about realising the unforeseen that may appear in our dreams, in the margins of the everyday, obscured by the present. Derealisation, for Breton, though very much making use of irony and keen for the absurd (a different tone), is unmistakably focused on what matters today. Or as Alquié puts it:

> Breton, rejecting dualism, cannot go outside the world to find the nonlogical Being to which he aspires. He must discover it in this very world, which forbids him to preserve the solidity and structure of the knowable world. (1969: 71)

Concluding from this, Alquié, the philosopher, claims that the prodigies of surreality must therefore be searched for *within* the knowable and the given. But for Breton and the other Surrealist (artistic) thinkers, this is obviously not a category to begin with: to them, the known is necessarily indistinguishable from the unknown, language is indistinguishable from all the rhythms and the resonances that happen, the event is indistinguishable from the people living it ... For Breton and the other Surrealists therefore, living in the interbellum, witnessing how nihilism – the eternal disease of Europe – got hold of Europe and the suicidal regimes this gave birth to, derealisation was about critiquing the presence of fascism on the rise. Derealisation 'illuminates', as Alquié puts it further down the page, as it moves away from the dominant discourse and is interested in other forms of expression.

Interestingly enough, Alquié himself, in his life as a professor of philosophy, would in the end be a fierce advocate of Cartesian dualist thinking (he was known for having long and lively debates with Spinozist Martial Gueroult, who favoured monist thinking). So, it is all the more surprising that his influential book *The Philosophy of Surrealism* defines Surrealism as monist. Its emphasis on derealisation, on radically critiquing the economic, social and political realities of the day, does not allow any binary opposition. Not so much emphasising or recognising the differences that mark an event, the Surrealist actually refuses to accept these, and instead searches for ways to offer us a whole, to include the dream, the non-human, the desires that refuse to be told, giving us a 'philosophy of the event' which explores a stream of consciousness *and* unconsciousness, the organic and the inorganic, involving mind and matter. And indeed, that is what happens in his stories. Bousquet himself puts it as such: 'The truth may announce itself in language, it needs to be framed in the entirety of life to reveal it' (Bousquet 1967: 25, my translation).[2]

Realism and the Imagination in Twentieth-century Literature

In his recent book *The Great Derangement*, Amitav Ghosh notices how especially twentieth-century fiction, as an art form, was dominated by dualism, anthropocentrism and the progress narrative. By analogy with scientific innovations (or 'discoveries' as progress narratives prefer them to be called), so important for realising human exceptionalism and alienation from the world, fiction played a key role, he claims, in actually *creating* these dualisms, recognising the hierarchies that run them and internalising them with the general audience. Not only in Europe and the US but throughout the world, Ghosh sees that the authors of the twentieth century, whether true to existentialism, structuralism, post-modernism or postcolonialism, have practised these dualist ideas of modernity, as we can call this form of thinking. For although modernity was anticipated throughout the nineteenth century (with its inventors, its philosophers, its statesmen), it was in the twentieth century that the naturalism (German Romanticism, for instance) that had dominated (fiction) writing before was replaced by a human sociology.

Marcel Proust perhaps shows us better than anyone else how, after the First World War, when capitalism quickly erased nobility, the social struggle became the dominant perspective from which the human analysed the Great Outside. In *In Search of Lost Time* (1913–27), the first book shows us young Marcel reflected in a series of relations that mark Combray, the village where he spent his holidays. In part one he notices the big church that summarised and embodied the city, the two staircases (of his family's house and of the house of his neighbour, M. Charlus) that summarised the plot, the hawthorn and its pink flowers with the same rhythm as some musical ensembles and reminding him of the pompoms on a rococo shepherd's staff. It is only through these meticulous observations of worldly resonances that we get a glimpse of little Marcel and upper-class life. Little Marcel is fully entangled in the village and its surrounding forests, filled with all sorts of non-human life forms which he keenly observes. How different is this in the final book of this project, *Time Regained*, in which only the humans (dead or alive) seem to remain, in which the environment has been reduced to the *mise en scène*, the decorum, for the Prince de Guermantes, Mme de Forcheville, Mme de Saint-Loup, Mme de Farcy, Oriane, Odette and so many others who are fighting for attention on all four hundred pages. How different these first serene explorations of the silence and softness of the earth are, compared to the endless conversations and conflicts with which the series ends.

Ghosh claims that the twentieth century was the time when the human being only had eyes for itself, when human (formalised) language defines the truth, and when an idea of 'realism' dominates the discourse in such a way that spaces for creativity and imagination have practically disappeared:

> Thus do sincerity and authenticity become, in politics as in literature, the greatest virtues. No wonder, then, that one of the literary icons of our age, the novelist Karl Ove Knausgård, has publicly admitted to 'being sick of fiction.' As opposed to the 'falsity' of fiction, Knausgård has 'set out to write exclusively from his own life.' (Ghosh 2016: 128)

Let us be clear about this: Ghosh is very critical of the idea that authors limit their perspectives to 'their own lives', practising the humanism that has not just been dominant in European and American fiction, but that especially during the twentieth century has been taken up by authors in Asia, Africa and the Arab world, who have followed this modernist trend, as he puts it, for fear of the stigma of 'backwardness' (as it is progress that matters). Ghosh concludes that, as writing had become more and more caught up in the human and all-too-human perspective, it simply *forgot about the earth*, placing the human being under a bell jar, stewing in its own sour air. Collectively submerged into this 'vulgar realism', he concludes that this narrative is a formula for 'collective suicide' (Ghosh 2016: 128), which is reflected in the ecological state of the world today.

I agree with Ghosh that twentieth-century literature, in general, has focused an awful lot on humans, and thereby has forgotten about the earth. And perhaps the state of literature at the start of the twenty-first century is even worse (Where has the experiment gone? Why are whole genres such as science fiction being 'expelled' from the contemporary literature sections?) The idea of writing down one's own life, as Knausgård proposes it, is suicidal. I even agree that we can use a term such as 'modernity' to pinpoint what alienation is all about. However, I also agree with Jean François Lyotard who said that postmodernity is an epoch not so much situated 'after' modernity but that is concerned with the ongoing rewriting of the modern project. Similarly, posthumanism, at least for me, is concerned with an interest in rewriting humanism.

In the light of this, I want to return to one of those icons of modernity, Marcel Proust, who gives us a firm critique of the humanism Knausgård proposes:

> Through art alone are we able to emerge from ourselves, to know what another person sees of a universe which is not the same as our own and

of which, without art, the landscapes would remain as unknown to us as those that may exist on the moon. Thanks to art, instead of seeing one world only, our own, we see that world multiply itself and we have at our disposal as many worlds as there are original artists, worlds more different one from the other than those which revolve in infinite space, worlds which, centuries after the extinction of the fire from which their light first emanated, whether it is called Rembrandt or Vermeer, send us still each one its special radiance. (Proust 2000: 254)

Surrealism and the Anti-fascist Life

Whereas Ghosh places Surrealism with the other movements that, after the First World War, agreed with modernist ideals and embraced humanism in all of its (pseudo-fascist) forms, Alquié, rightly so, stresses that especially in its early days, with Apollinaire, Breton, Weil even, and especially Bousquet, Surrealism did the exact opposite. Beginning with Apollinaire's abovementioned rereading of Tiresias, Surrealism, *from its very start*, was searching for a way to deal with the new rigid modernist (and capitalist) realities that had become all too real especially after the war. Or, as Alquié puts it:

> To liberate man was always the aim of surrealism. Is it necessary to add that with Nazism menacing, in the midst of an oppressed France, the problem of man's liberation could not be resolved by automatic writing, but in a manner more precise, urgent and pointed, by taking a political position and by a call to arms. (1969: 163)

So interestingly enough, whereas Ghosh claims that now is the time to break with realism, to free the imagination from the conditions of truth, Alquié says that this is exactly what the agenda of Surrealism was.

In the time of fascism, Surrealism set itself to live the anti-fascist life, not to be suffocated by the intricate systems of control that, for instance, Antonio Gramsci wrote about, but by preferring imagination, to search for a way out. Alquié offers us a fascinating perspective on what Surrealism was doing and why. Especially today it is of the greatest importance to understand *how* Surrealism was deeply political, to understand how, in contrast to, for instance, existentialism, where there was an all too obvious political stance present in the writing, Surrealism (and Dada as it preceded it, in many ways) chose *not* to take the critical stance. Why? Because critique necessarily involves engagement, or, as Michel Serres puts it: 'An idea opposed to another idea is always the same idea, albeit affected by the negative sign. The more you oppose one another, the more you remain in the same framework of thought' (Serres with Latour 1995: 81). Surrealism refuses to subject itself to the logic of humanism, fascism and nationalism. Very much rooted in the contemporary, it closes the shutters, feels the outside, but demands the imaginary take over.

The famous, negative, historical illustration of Surrealism rejecting fascism is, of course, the moment Salvador Dalí was expelled from Surrealism by Breton because of his Hitler fascination (and because his work turned quite commercial, and for even more uninteresting reasons). A much more telling, affirmative and imaginative illustration (and certainly the illustration Alquié would favour) was the special friendship that Joë Bousquet developed with Max Ernst, the German Surrealist painter (1891–1976). A lieutenant in the German artillery, Ernst was actually part of the battalion that Bousquet was ordered to repel when he received the bullet that crossed his lungs and hit his spine: 'If Max Ernst, who was to become my best friend, saw dead coming out of Vailly, they were mine', confided Bousquet in a letter to Maurice Nadeau. 'If he saw soldiers carrying off their officer, he attended my rescue.'[3]

In his letters to Ernst, Bousquet often reflects on that moment in history that they did not share but that did bring them together:

> My wound, Max, is not too heavy a ransom for my pride at having known, at twenty, such moments . . . If I write one day about the war, it will be to say the opportunity it has been for me to know the Germans, to understand them, to admire them. (Bousquet 1969: 170, my translation)[4]

I don't want to end up in too much of a historical analysis here, but there is so much going on along these lines. It is not known when these letters were written or sent but probably around 1943/1944 when Ernst had already fled fascist Germany and was living in New York.

In the quote above, Bousquet says 'if I write one day about the war', but of course he never actually wrote about the war. He did write endlessly about the wound that not so much took his life but that gave him life. It was because of the wound that he had to write, it was because he lived his wound that he understood that the wound was not just part of him but just as much of Max Ernst, and of France, and of Germany, of the bodies and the bullets that had been lost at Vailly. In his correspondence with Simone Weil, Bousquet takes a similar position. Infuriated by the horrors on the battlefields of the Second World War, Weil, the activist, has a plan to work as a field nurse and to make an impression on the enemy soldiers. Women who wanted to join her should agree never to be released from duty, she insisted. Bousquet noted the idealist and romantic nature of this project and proposed a more materialist approach.

Anyone reading his *Philosophy of Surrealism* will note that, although Alquié became familiar with many Surrealist artists and thinkers, it is in the last section, solely dedicated to Joë Bousquet, that the true spirit of the book reveals itself. Very much inspired by Breton, Apollinaire and others, it was in the end because of Bousquet that Alquié was able to develop the first and last *complete metaphysics* of Surrealism. Written with passion and rigour, it is through Bousquet that Alquié showed us that Surrealism was the philosophy worthy of its time.

According to Alquië it is because of the wound that Joë Bousquet is the true philosopher of Surrealism. Because of the wound, because of how the wound mattered, Bousquet understood that it was *not* reason or language that literature had to stick to. Bousquet found out, the hard way, that is was because of the wound that *life as a whole* had to be put on the agenda. If we are to overcome the horrors of the present, we have to understand the wound affirmatively, we have to search for ways to live it. And this is why Alquie, and Deleuze after him, would in the end insist that although Bousquet should be seen as the philosopher of the Surrealists, he himself is actually a Stoic. Because of the wound, because he lives the wound, Bousquet, throughout his life, is able to be untouched by the passions of fascism (the most passionate regime of all). Because of the wound, Bousquet is able to live his life beautifully, in pain, and on his surreal, posthuman conditions.

Alquié sums this up beautifully:

He has no destiny, for he is his destiny. He has not been injured, for he is his injury. I do not call him stoic, wanting what he is, but one, being what he is. Nothing is more laughable than the opinion that he is a 'modern' author for no one is less than he of this idiotic age ... Bousquet has no system. The system is born from seeking in objects a unity that the self does not discover in itself. Bousquet is one; his wound has made him invulnerable, incomprehensible. (1969: 167)

Stoicism, Europe and Living the Wound

Living with the wound, living with the presence of his own death, which was also the death of Europe, Bousquet was in search of ways to live his wound 'most beautifully', devoting his life to profound thinking, to writing brutally and spontaneously 'before language', as Jean Paulhan put it (Bousquet 1967: 14).[5] Facing death, and not afraid to keep on facing death as it kept staring him in the eye, Bousquet lived the non-fascist life by embracing joy and avoiding sadness. In line with a long tradition of free spirits before him (Spinoza, Nietzsche, Proust and Woolf), Bousquet imagined himself a life at the margins, in search of the Great Health that would make his wounds livable, that gave him just enough breath to scream.

Half a century later, Deleuze's awakening as a philosopher came in 1968, when the student protests turned the French intelligentsia upside down and gave it a new university (Paris 8), where Deleuze himself would spend the rest of his professorial life. But 1968 was also the year he met Félix Guattari, with whom he would write four books, *and* it was the year in which Deleuze, always of fragile health, became terminally ill (he had to live on one lung for the rest of his life). It is no coincidence that, in his 1969 book *The Logic of Sense*, on which he had been working during the preceding years next to his dissertations, he turns to Joë Bousquet. Being a student of Ferdinand Alquié since 1945, as mentioned, publishing reviews of his two major works (see LO), and choosing Alquié as the supervisor for his second thesis on Spinoza (EP), Deleuze was familiar with the work of Bousquet, and as he had just found his wound (the manifold wound we could call 1968), or better, the life he was about to explore, it was in this new book that Bousquet played a crucial role.

It is no coincidence that, as well as being the book that reveals his interest in Bousquet for the first time, *The Logic of Sense* is also the book in which Deleuze writes about Stoicism most elaborately, and he notably defines the Stoic according to Bousquet and the life that he lived. Stoicism, he claims, is a concrete or poetic way of life that is characterised by the most personal relation with a wound. Note that he talks of *a* wound, not 'the' wound or 'one's' wound. Stoicism is about realising a life that lives the way *a* wound is incarnated or *actualised in everything*; one's body, one's mind, the objects according to which this life is given form, the ideas accompanying them . . . A wound is necessarily expressed in many different/contradictory voices, but more often unheard. This is because the accident causing the wound necessarily happens before humanity begins, that is, its cracks do not follow human reasoning, humanist organisation, modernist dualisms, but rather brutally and violently tear open the (unknown) surfaces of reality. A wound itself is never limited to an individual, but, more likely, traverses an entire continent; its human and its non-human realities, its material and immaterial flows. It is at work everywhere, yet it surfaces wherever things get fragile.[6]

Fascism is certainly a European wound, which sometimes cracks into other parts of the world (and into the political system as such), but that realised a deep and groundless nothingness through the entire Old Continent, cracking up entire national systems, institutions, people and cultures from the 1920s. Entangled with modernism, colonialism, racism and sexism, with which it eagerly defined concepts such as 'progress', fascism has proved itself a threat to the political process as a whole up until today. Emphasising various forms of 'hope' (hope for better times, for a 'pure' society, for the restoration of an order that benefits all, and that never existed), the roots of fascism run deep into European history. But fascism did not just start in the nineteenth or early twentieth century. Félix Guattari was right when he stressed that 'The Inquisition had already put together a type of fascist machinery which kept developing and perfecting itself up to our own time' (CS, 162). Of course, it goes back much further than that, and there is good reason to see these echoes of 'hope' (the key concept of fascism) in European Christianity and Platonism (the philosopher/king is about to save you from the misery of the cave).

Times have not changed, fascism still lurks everywhere. In a magnificent text entitled 'Everybody Wants to be a Fascist', Guattari shows us how 'microfascism' is ready to realise itself any time soon:

> I repeat: what fascism set in motion yesterday continues to proliferate in other forms, within the complex of contemporary social space. A whole totalitarian chemistry manipulates the structures of state, political and union structures, institutional and family structures, and even individual structures, inasmuch as one can speak of a sort of fascism of the superego in situations of guilt and neurosis. (CS, 163)

Guattari summarises what has been the core of Deleuze and Guattari's reading of fascism since 1968, which is that fascism, especially today, in our globalised world, is at the heart of *everyone's* desire. Thus, it is too easy to be 'against' fascism, just as it is too easy to simply oppose modernism, racism or sexism. Europe was built on this, our lives were built on these passions, this resentment.

To live the anti-fascist life means to face what threatens it constantly. It takes constant practice to live *another* life, to explore the alternative. And to face one's biggest fears, to not have 'hope' that things will eventually improve, but to actively choose a different life, to imagine a life that does not allow fascism to happen, is exactly the kind of life that Stoicism proposes to us. Stoicism has always encouraged us to look for the alternative, to walk the non-fascist walk of life, to look fascism in the face in order to keep reminding ourselves to take the other route. Absolutely key is, then, the building up of the most personal relation with the wounds that have marked our lives since the beginning. To explore these wounds, to love them, is the only way to realise what an anti-fascist life is all about. And this is precisely what Bousquet did when he lived his wound. To use his own words: 'Become the person of your misfortunes; learn to embody their perfection and brilliance' (Bousquet quoted in LS, 149).

Nearing the end of his life, unable to talk and hardly able to move by himself, Deleuze returns to Bousquet in his final publication, *Immanence . . . a Life*. A swan song, filled with concepts that were dear to him and his philosophy; the plane of immanence upon which life takes place; the virtual as the eternal truth that may not have a present, but that is real in all of its consequences . . . And then he returns to Bousquet, to the wound:

> A wound is incarnated or actualized in a state of things or of life; but it is itself a pure virtuality on the plane of immanence that leads us into a life. My wound existed before me: not a transcendence of the wound as higher actuality, but its immanence as a virtuality always within a milieu (plane or field). (PI, 31–2)

Joë Bousquet, the poet, the thinker, the correspondent, the friend, led a beautiful life in pain, amid the horrors of fascism. Guided by unbounded imagination, he became a crucial figure in Surrealism, living the idea central to it, always practising another derealisation from the fascist realities that wounded his era, that wounded him. Derealisation is not an aesthetics but a philosophy, it is not a choice but a necessity. Deleuze's last reference was to Bousquet, only a few months before he, in the proper Stoic fashion, chose to end his own life, as this was no longer the life he chose to live.

In his biography, René Nelli, lifelong friend of Bousquet, stated that although he was definitely intrigued by Surrealism in the early years, especially because of how it was liberating us from the (fascist) present, Bousquet was in the end much more of a 'realist' or a 'materialist' (in the Spinozist sense of the word) than Breton and the others.[7] Dreams are interesting in his view, but for how they are practices of the imagination, how they function as embodied and lived realities, how they question and the ideas they generate. Experience things until we forget who we are, as he writes in *Le livre heureux*; by which he means forgetting our individualities and understanding how our lives, upon our wounds, are not limited to our bodies, but are in every way engaged with the matters of the earth.

Alquié agrees with Nelli as he concludes, at the end of his book, that Bousquet was a much more radical thinker than Breton, especially when it came to his negation of transcendence. 'Bousquet tries to reduce himself entirely to events' (Alquié 1969: 168). To liberate man is, in the end, not just to free oneself from the fascist Other, but also from the fascism within, the fascist self. 'Bousquet's genius was [. . .] to understand that by the effects of his wound separation had become his essence' (Alquié 1969: 170). Only by starting from the wound, by always facing the fascism cracking through the earth, the Surrealist room, the event, through every essence, Bousquet did not propose to us anti-fascist being or existence, but life.

Notes

1. 'L'art de écrire ne gagne rien a compliquer ses techniques . . . C'est un art né pauvre et révolutionnaire-né et qui grandit en se ramenant à la satifaction d'un besoin élémentaire.'
2. 'La vérité ne peut qu'être annoncée dans le langage et il lui faut tout le cadre d'une vie d'homme pour se révéler.'
3. 'Si Max Ernst, qui devait devenir mon meilleur ami, a vu des morts en sortant de Vailly, ils étaient des miens', my translation. See <https://www.ladepeche. fr/article/2000/10/01/92086-comment-le-mourant-d-une-guerre-a-invente-une-poesie.html> (last accessed 5 November 2019).
4. 'Ma blessure, Max, n'est pas une rancon trop lourde pour l'orgueil que je porte d'avoir connu, a vingt ans, j'ai mérité de jouer dans leur admiration le rôle qu'ils ons joué dans la mienne. Je ne peux te dire cela qu'à toi. Si j'écris un jour sur la guerre, ce sera pour dire l'occasion qu'elle a été pour moi de connaître les Allemands, de les comprendre, de les admirer.'
5. Paulhan wrote these words to introduce *Lettres à poisson d'or*, which contains the love letters Bousquet wrote to Germaine, the woman he loved from 1937 until he died. The letters to his first love, Fany, were collected in the book *Un amour couleur de thé*.
6. For more on the wound and on woundedness, see Dolphijn 2021: 91–103.
7. It was in 1932, in a letter to Alquié, that Bousquet said he felt 'completely separated' from the Surrealists, who (he claims) consider music mere movement, whereas he is convinced that music is able to reveal that the human being is a wound (a gap) in time, a wound for their self (Bousquet 1969: 204–5).

References

Alquié, F. (1969), *The Philosophy of Surrealism*, Ann Arbor, MI: Ann Arbor Paperbacks.
Bousquet, J. (1933), *Rendez vous d'un soir d'hiver*, Paris: René Debresse.
Bousquet, J. (1945), *Le médisant par bonté*, Paris: Gallimard.
Bousquet, J. (1967), *Lettres à poisson d'or*, Paris: Gallimard.
Bousquet, J. (1969), *Correspondance*, Paris: Gallimard.
Bousquet, J. (1984), *Un amour couleur de thé*, Paris: Verdier.
Dolphijn, R. (2021), *The Philosophy of Matter: A Meditation*, London: Bloomsbury.
Ghosh, A. (2016), *The Great Derangement*, Chicago: University of Chicago Press.
Mical, T. (ed.) (2005), *Surrealism and Architecture*, Abingdon, Routledge.

Nelli, R. (1975), *Joë Bousquet, sa vie, son oeuvre*, Paris: Albin Michel.

Proust, M. (2000), *In Search of Lost Time*, London: Vintage. Translation of *A la recherche du temps perdu*, Paris: Gallimard, 1913–27.

Searle, A. (2019), 'Lucian Freud: The Self-Portraits Review – menacing, elusive . . . orgasmic?', *The Guardian*, 22 October, <https://www.theguardian.com/artand design/2019/oct/22/lucian-freud-the-self-portraits-review-royal-academy-london (last accessed 26 May 2022).

Serres, M., with B. Latour (1995), 'Third Conversation: Demonstration and Interpretation', in *Conversations on Science, Culture, and Time*, Ann Arbor: University of Michigan Press, pp. 77–124.

Chapter 13

Fascistophilic Epidemics: Transpositions on the Shiite Medico-Religious Imagination

Arash Ghajarjazi

Introduction

In early 2020, when the news broke that the first confirmed cases of Covid-19 in Iran had occurred in the city of Qum, the paranoid religious state dispatched a special task force armed with tear gas and armoured fighting vehicles to suppress the epidemic's growth in the country.[1] Browsing through the state-sponsored media, one could hear them thinking, 'How could this horrible biological disaster befall the city of Qum, the most sacred and holiest place in Iran, the centre of Shiite scholarship and the backbone of the Islamic Revolution?' The threat posed by the epidemic was already unsettling, to say the least, for a regime facing protracted issues relating to security, legitimacy and power. In the months preceding the Covid-19 pandemic, a series of crises had ravaged the Islamic Republic. It was barely surviving the economic sanctions imposed by the United States and domestic public protests that broke out periodically around the country. Moreover, it lost its most important military commander, Qasem Soleimani, who had been in charge of the regime's military operations in Syria and Iraq. Soleimani's assassination led to the most astonishing turn of events. In perhaps the darkest comedy of the century, in avenging its commander's death, the regime's revolutionary guards shot down a passenger aeroplane, killing all of the 176 people on board, 167 of them Iranian citizens. This led to more protests and more crackdowns. It was in the wake of these events that Covid-19 visited the country.

By sending riot control units to Qum, instead of mounting a medical response, the regime treated pestilence as protest. Still, a few months later, once the disease had been declared a pandemic, the coronavirus began working to the advantage of the state. It might even be called a non-human ally. This was because the virus deterred protests, safeguarding the Islamic State, at least for a while. Entertaining a broad conception of fascism, it might be said that we are dealing here with an entanglement between a fascist religious state and a viral disease. As previous epidemics in human history testify, viruses and bacteria have an affinity with fascist machines. One can think of the typhus epidemic that took hold of fascist Italy during the Second World War (Wheeler 1946), the plague in the fascist state (*avant la lettre*) of the Ottoman Empire in the sixteenth and seventeenth centuries (Bulmus 2005) and cholera pandemics in the proto-fascist Victorian age (Afkhami 2019; Morris 1976). I am tempted to call them fascistophilic agents. Indeed, viral and bacterial epidemics are attracted to fascist complexes.

There is something more than mere politics at work when pandemics fall upon a society, which conjoins the biological, political and religious spheres in a single entangled ecology. In this chapter, I move towards understanding fascism in Iran as the formation of a certain semiotics in the Shiite epidemic-ridden medico-religious imagination. I unpack this Shiite fascism through a transpositional analysis, which moves between two key theoretical objects from Iran: a short demonological discussion on epidemics in a sixteenth-century medical treatise and a drawing of a mass protest during a severe cholera pandemic in 1892. I begin my discussion of each case by describing the context in which it appeared before focusing on the objects individually. In analysing the first object, I work with Reza Negarestani's concept of the cyclone to develop a concept of fascism that is specific to the Islamic milieu. Further on, feeding this concept into my examination of the second object and drawing on Deleuze and Guattari's notion of faciality, I argue that Shiite fascism evolved in two stages, moving from a pre-facial diagrammatic phase to a facialised political state.

Given the immense amount of work that has been done on early twentieth-century fascism in Europe, in the mental ecology of today fascism is no longer just a historical term. It is also a dense philosophical concept, the contemporary relevance of which has never been more stark. This has been especially so over the past decade, during which the uneasy historical echo of fascism has caused much alarm in Euro-American media and academic communities. Despite the concerted research into and debates over fascism's contemporary manifestations in Europe, the same urgency is alarmingly absent in discussions about the Middle East. This is profoundly unnerving. Never before has the Middle East been embroiled in such grave sociopolitical turmoil. Never before has it experienced ethnic and gender discrimination, economic corruption and systematic violence against human and non-human ecologies on such a scale.

Whereas Western(ised) scholars and analysts seem comfortable using the term fascism in relation to the rise of nationalist movements across Europe and the US, they largely shy away from making the same connection in relation to the Middle East. The current US administration and comparable governments across Europe are readily criticised on account of their variously implicit or outright fascisms, at least rhetorically. At the same time, it is almost unthinkable that one might use the same term in criticising, say, the much more ruthless, discriminatory and violent regime of Iran. By thinking fascism, the present essay makes a modest conceptual incursion into the field of Middle Eastern and Islamic studies so as to make this unthinkable connection.

Fascisms are not political aggregates found in dictatorial or totalitarian regimes. They are not molar, Deleuze and Guattari remind us, but molecular. Fascists are not, or at least not primarily, dictators, ruthless rulers, monarchs or politically agitated imams – although fascist machines can very well generate such figures. They are far more clandestine and inconspicuous. I understand fascism as a mode of functioning in the world that can be activated in any human ecology, given the proper biocultural content. It is not – or at least not primarily – an ideological, political or economic construct. It is not 'of ideology but of pure matter, a phenomenon of physical, biological, psychic, social, or cosmic matter' (TP, 165). Fascism may become molar in the later stages of its development.

In this essay, the concept of fascism works as a deliberate anachronism, a theoretical abstraction, which probes nineteenth-century Iran, a time and space that is seemingly different from the historical fascisms of the Euro-American milieu. By analysing the two theoretical objects that I have mentioned above, my aim is to point to the historical moment in which Shiite fascism found its first form of expression – a fascism more universal and abstract than historical fascism per se, yet concrete enough to continue operating on a global scale to this day.

Historical Context: An Epidemic Stage for Modernity in the Nineteenth Century

The main scene of this essay is set in the mid-nineteenth century, around the time when the first polytechnic institute of education in the Middle East was established in Tehran, the Chamber of Technique (Dār al-Funūn). The prime minister at the time, Mīrzā Taqī Khān Farāhānī, better known as Amir Kabir, hired a handful of European professionals to revolutionise the entire system of higher education in Iran. These

European teachers offered designed courses that ushered in a new disciplinary regime in the Middle East (Menashri 1992; Ringer 2001). Medicine, mineralogy, military engineering, physics and chemistry were among the new disciplines, which at the time were termed the 'new sciences' (Gurney and Nabavi 1993). Of the disciplines taught at the institute, medicine was unique and perhaps the most socially influential, for it directly affected people's daily lives. It was especially crucial, though, in the light of the recurring cholera epidemics. These not only struck Iran but were part of the wider cholera pandemics that also periodically took hold of Europe and America between 1852 and 1893. (Barua and Greenough III 1992). Of the six pandemics that occurred in the nineteenth century, however, five hit the Persian territories. Accordingly, Iran became a contested space among a range of physicians, politicians and religious figures (Ebrahimnejad 2004; Afkhami 2019). Just as Covid-19 spread across the globe in just a few months, in the nineteenth century cholera travelled rapidly between cities over land and sea. Much like the current pandemic, cholera was not an isolated episode, but part and parcel of the global order.

This bacterial era was especially critical for regions lying between Bombay and Baghdad, which were riven by social and religious unrest, British colonial encroachments, episodic conflict with Russia and administrative corruption. Leading scholarship in the field of Middle Eastern studies has largely mapped out the historical context in which these cholera pandemics were embedded (Algar 1980; Amanat 1989). What remains little examined, however, is how cholera as a biological force contributed proactively to the formation of Shiite global power and its fascist development. Keeping this in mind, it is possible to see a moment of historical resonance at which the paranoid Islamic Republic initially sent its armed forces to Qum to face Covid-19, only for the disease to become an ally to the regime. As the vanguard of Shiite clerical power in the twenty-first century, the Islamic regime remembered, as it were, the cholera pandemic that its forerunners had had to deal with a century before.

Cholera provided the *ulama* with a condensed semiotic locus from which to derive meaning, for it was the periodical event in the century that resisted and challenged epistemic efforts to apprehend it. Much like Covid-19, nineteenth-century cholera remained a medical mystery for most of the period.

That Obscure Object of Epidemics

Recent epidemiological studies have shown that cholera is caused by toxigenic bacteria. In epidemiological terminology, they are known as *V. Cholerae*. These bacteria colonise the intestines and incite the rapid degeneration of the organs, which results in severe diarrhoea and dehydration. 'A distinctive epidemiological feature of cholera', writes one team of biologists, 'is its appearance in a regular seasonal pattern in areas of endemic infection and in explosive outbreaks' (Faruque, Albert and Mekalanos 1998: 1301). Moreover, they suggest that despite 'numerous studies over more than a century, the epidemiology and ecology of cholera remain mysterious and challenging to investigators in the field' (1998: 1309). According to the latest research in epidemiology, Faruque, Albert and Mekalanos observe, the biological causes of cholera remain uncertain. Of course, the actual bacterial agent has been microscopically observed as playing the central role in epidemics around the globe. Strictly speaking, however, the pathology of cholera has not been yet scientifically determined. What can be said with certainty is only that certain microscopic agents operate in an outbreak. However, exactly how these agents function during an epidemic, their patterns of dissemination and their ecology have not yet been recorded in detail – one wonders if it is possible that they ever will. Moreover, at least from a theoretical point of view, the bacteria themselves are ecologically distinct from a cholera epidemic. There is a conceptual difference between choleric bacteria and cholera as a disease – in the same way that coronavirus SARS-CoV-2 is not Covid-19. The latter is a complex arrangement of different bacteria (viruses) with a varied range of symptoms *and* different ecological conditions.

Given this distinction, it can be said that whereas viruses and bacteria – that is, their genetic codes, DNA footprints or chemical structure – can be definitively detected and identified, their pathologies – their prognostic behaviours, symptoms and manifestation as disease – remain rather obscure. With this in mind, in further unpacking interrelations between fascism and epidemics in the following two analyses, I borrow the concept of 'indeterminacy' as taken up by Rosi Braidotti and Karen Barad. Whereas Braidotti uses the term 'sexual indeterminacy' (Braidotti 2011: 78) and Barad refers to 'ontological indeterminacy' (Barad 2007: 116), I adopt the concept of 'pathological indeterminacy' in the context of medicine.

First Object: Fascistophilia in Islam

The pathological indeterminacy of cholera epidemics has been a recurrent issue in older medical paradigms, whether Galenic, medieval Islamic or the clinical medicine of the nineteenth century. Before clinical medicine became the norm in Iran, epidemics were understood in light of Galenic humoralism. As one of its derivatives, medieval Islamic medicine associated cholera and other epidemic diseases with air putridity, a large-scale phenomenon that could be triggered by celestial movements, the accumulation of dead bodies or rotten fruits in one place and seasonal changes.

In the sixteenth century, however, a new medical trend developed in the Shiite medical context. This turning point is exemplified in *Naṣīḥatnāmay-i Sūlaymānī* (NS), a medical treatise that I have taken as a point of departure for this analysis. Written by a religious physician named Muḥammad Ḥakīm Ibn Mubārak (d. 1566), the novelty of this medical text resided in how it infused medical discussions about cholera with demonological theories. Ibn Mubārak wrote this treatise during the Safavid era, paying special attention to cholera among other epidemics. The text was sent as a gift to the Persian Shah's adversary in the Ottoman Empire, who was fleeing the cholera outbreak that hit his capital of Istanbul at the time.

As part of the newly emerging practice of 'prophetic medicine' in the period (Shoja and Tubbs 2007; Pormann and Savage-Smith 2007), NS reintroduced the *jinn* into discussions on the aetiology of cholera.[2] Subsequently, the *jinn* came to be seen as one of the most powerful causes of air putridity and thus an active component of cholera outbreaks. This development was part of a broader discursive transformation in Shiite medical history. Up until the period in which Ibn Mubārak wrote his text, Galenic miasma theories remained standard, with minor revisions and updates being made by a range of scholars, from Avicenna in the tenth century to Ibn Ilyās in the fourteenth. Around 1500, however, medical thinkers began to systematically inject Islamic theology into the older medieval humoralism. In this new medicine, the *jinn* crept into pathological discussions. This was a period in which medicine started taking Islamic demonology more seriously.[3]

In certain formal manifestations, *jinn* (as Ibn Mubārak presents them) are able to putrefy the air. He explains the process in the following way: when *jinn* get into a fight, they become blasts of wind, which blow from different directions. At the confluence of these winds, a cyclone appears. Thus, this figure of the cyclone, Ibn Mubārak suggests, is a combination of 'many winds, each of which on their part stands before one another'. From 'the encounter and meeting of these winds with each other', he goes on, 'a cyclone emerges' (Ibn Mubārak 2007: 513). This cyclonic pattern furthermore putrefies the air, which in turn triggers an outbreak.

Etymologically, the word *jinn* comes from the Arabic root *j-n-n* meaning to conceal. Throughout most of Islamic demonological history, these existents were thought to have been concealed from human senses, although reincarnated as *jinn* they could be seen, heard and touched. They were reportedly capable of changing forms; as such, they were corporeally indeterminate. They belonged to a cosmic force able to launch radical interventions in earthly affairs. Their manifestation as cyclones, however, only became pronounced in later periods. Cyclonic fights were one of the ways in which the *jinn* could intervene on earth. In this mode, the wind became their climatological expression and the cyclone their mode of operation, the means through which they precipitated calamities such as epidemics. Ibn Mubārak's invocation of cyclones as a model for the *jinn*'s performances on earth was not a literary metaphor but a historically grounded discursive choice. It was no coincidence that the *jinn*'s corporeal indeterminacy dovetailed with cholera's pathological indeterminacy in the minds of Muslim scholars.

Browsing through primary sources in this period and comparing this treatise with earlier materials indicates how the figure of the cyclone as a demonological form has resurfaced in Islamic medico-religious imagination on many occasions. Descriptions such as Ibn Mubārak's appear, for example, in the encyclopaedic works of the seventeenth-century scholars Muḥammad Baqir Majlisī (d. 1699) and Muḥammad Hashim Fuzūni Astarābādī, as well as in the writings of the nineteenth-century Muslim physician Mūsā Ibn Sāvūjī. In contrast, the image of *jinn*-as-cyclones is nowhere to be found in earlier sources, such as the Quran. Hence, it can be observed that between the late fourteenth century (when prophetic medicine superseded medieval humoralism) and the mid-nineteenth century (when European clinical medicine reformed medical praxis in Iran), the cyclone continued to serve as the model for *jinn* activities on earth. In this imagination, then, if *jinn* took actions that had biological consequences on earth, then they would take the shape of a cyclone.

In his debut theory-fiction *Cyclonopedia*, Reza Negarestani has radically dehistoricised the concept of the cyclone by expressing it mathematically as 'feedback spirals', defined as 'fields of operation for everything that emanates from the Middle East' (Negarestani 2008: 34). He recognises two principal forces at work in cyclones: 'divergent' and 'integrating'. Whereas one force moves away from the vertical axis of the cyclone, the other is drawn towards the centre. One force is centrifugal, the other centripetal; one exerted radially, the other vertically. The main fascination of cyclones resides in the simultaneous operation of these two opposing forces. In a cyclone, one is both drawn towards the centre and pushed away from it at the same time. According to this formula, Negarestani has his protagonist theorise, '[a]n entangled mess of vortical and corkscrewing motions, the structure of the middle-eastern political formations is a cyclone armed with a drilling and extracting instrumentality; it is a cyclone and an oil drill used for extracting un-heard-of political and power formations' (2008: 36).

Reappropriating Deleuze and Guattari's concept of the war machine, Negarestani speculates that cyclonic activities can become fascist if they are forced into ceaseless activity, if they are not allowed to rest or to stay inactive. Or, according to the vertical and radial functions of cyclonic logic, cyclones may become fascist or fascistophilic if they are forced to work along the vertical axis with only minimal divergences or radial activity. On this view, if war machines continue interminably on high alert and 'exclude peace, silence and inactivity', they become fascist machines (Negarestani 2008: 126). On Negarestani's view, therefore, Islamic radicalism is not fascist. This is because it draws on the very well-known practice of *taqiyya*, whereby a Muslim jihadi conceals themselves as a peaceful and passive citizen while waiting for the right opportunity to go on the offensive and detonate their explosives. One must look elsewhere, then, to find Islamic fascism.

Negarestani presents his cyclone-formula as a model upon which Middle Eastern petrology and petropolitics are based. That said, the image of the cyclone can also be traced back to the discourse surrounding cholera epidemics. These connections, perhaps, are more concrete than those made in Negarestani's speculative universe. Exploring them involves pursuing further the microbiological implications of cyclones' conceptual presence in medical discussions about cholera. What if the dual vectors of Negarestani's cyclone can be activated in thinking about cholera epidemics? And is it possible to find a way towards understanding how epidemics can become fascistophilic?

Pathways to Fascism: Choleric Microbiological Tactics

Despite the pathological indeterminacy that has characterised the epidemiology of cholera, both historically and today, innovative research has established how choleric bacteria behave under different ecological conditions. In astonishing detail, certain studies have shown exactly how these bacterial agents manage to stay alive in the face of human medical endeavours and harsh ecologies. This line of research has provided detailed knowledge of how the bacterium of *V. Cholerae* survives the very epidemic to which it belongs.

In their contribution to a collection of scientific essays titled *Epidemiological and Molecular Aspects of Cholera*, Anwar Huq, Chris J. Grim and Rita R. Colwell distinguish two distinct tactics adopted by the bacterium. Through controlled experimentation with the bacterium, in which they observed how it coped with both harsh and favourable environments, they have successfully recognised and described these tactics in detail (Ramamurthy and Bhattacharaya 2010: 311–39). The first is performed in unfavourable conditions, such as those in which the bacterium has little or no access to nutrients. Under these conditions, the bacterium becomes dormant and no epidemic can be detected. In order to stay alive, *V. Cholerae* enters a semi-active but non-operative state. To be able to survive in this state, each bacterium undergoes a process called 'rounding up' in which the cell loses its flagellum (that is, its tail) while maintaining the 'integrity of its membrane' (Ramamurthy and Bhattacharaya 2010: 315). In this way, the bacterium protects 'its internal environment against the surroundings, keeping its genetic material (DNA) intact, and at the same time having its metabolic activity at the lowest rate but enough to promote the uptake of nutrients via appropriate transport systems when these substrates become available again in the environment' (Ramamurthy and Bhattacharaya 2010: 316). These processes of rounding up have been visualised in microscopic images (Figure 13.1) in another epidemiological study (Baker et al. 1983: 932–4).

In a study by Mohammad Sirajtur Islam, Bohumil S. Drasar and R. Bradley Sack (1994), this same tactic of choleric rounding up has been examined using different methods. These provide more detail on the process. For the bacterium to manage its transformation and maintain a stable state of roundedness, this study shows, it needs to *camouflage* itself by blending into the skin of another cell, thus sustaining itself in hostile environments. In a word, the bacterium *masks* itself as a legitimate member of the environment. It becomes an undercover agent in an unfavourable host ecosystem. This 'epibiotic' tactic, in which it lives on the surface of another organism, makes it possible for *V. Cholerae* to survive until the right moment arrives for it to become operative. And when it does, the cell performs its second tactic: reoperationalising itself.

This second tactic involves a bacterium first growing its flagellum back, allowing it to mobilise its mass on the surface of its host cell. Once

Figure 13.1 A *V. Cholerae* bacterium in its active mode, with a fully grown tail. Source: Baker et al. 1983: 936.

the flagella have reached their operational potential, each bacterium initiates a process whereby it connects with other bacteria, with which it forms 'coordinated' links. This process, which is known as 'biofilm formation' in microbiology, allows the bacteria to become offensive once more.[4]

Choleric bacteria, then, have two functional modes. Whereas in one they stay inactive but alive, in the other they are operational and epidemic. When in the state of rounding up, bacteria can remain inactive and silent – or, to use Negarestani's terms, indulge in 'divergent activities' (Negarestani 2008: 126). In the active mode, in contrast, they are militarised and forced to work vertically, that is, to target host cells and drill through human digestive canals.

The first tactic, epibiotic camouflage, is strikingly similar to *taqiyya*, which has proven especially dangerous in the hands of modern Islamic radicalism. All recent terrorist attacks in European territories have been direct outcomes of successful *taqiyyas*. According to Negarestani's succinct definition, in its modern sense '*taqiyya* deals with concealing one's belief by undertaking the belief or the practice of the Other, so as to provoke the enemy society or hostile Whole, in its search for the true believers, to react against its own population and entities' (2008: 124). In this mode, however, there is no fascism, for the war machines, jihadis or bacteria stay silent and inactive.

It is precisely because of this ability to round up and camouflage itself amid peaceful organisms that Western countries have not dubbed Islamic radicalism fascist. The term fascism becomes relevant only in case of full militant commitment and blatant activities. It is only as the second tactic comes into effect, then, that cholera epidemics become facsistophilic and display affinities with fascist machines. This has happened on a large scale in the course of Islamic history, in ways that are too blatant to be ignored.

Fascisms in Islam: Semiotics of Monomania

Fascism is often immediately linked to megalomania. The figures of fascism – that is, the actual human faces of certain political leaders – are often imagined as megalomaniac people, who are obsessed with and deluded by their perceived grandeur. This psychological effect, however, is only a later development in a much more fundamental psychosocial and biosocial formation.

Monotheism had long laid down the necessary schemata for this very specific effect. Is it no accident that both fascism and monotheistic religions, to quote Georges Bataille, have a 'tendency toward concentration' (Bataille 1979: 76). Is this not evident in the symbols called to mind when fascism is mentioned? An axe wrapped up in a bundle of sticks, a crooked or standard cross, or the vertical middle L of the word Allah. Before developing into a megalomaniac figure, a fascist must first have a propensity towards *monomania*: the semiotic monomania of the one and only God. The global ambition of fascism comes only after this monomania takes form – Deleuze and Guattari call this later development the 'postfascist' figure (TP, 421). It is in this sense that Bataille characterises fascism in terms of 'a foundation that is both religious and military, in which these two habitually distinct elements cannot be separated' (1979: 81). I have already shown that the fascist mode of operating, in Negarestani's formulation, inhered in the vertical axis of the cyclone, according to which fascist agents are fully committed to militant action and cannot rest, diverge or stay silent. Interestingly, Bataille observes that this religio-military binding, this axial monomania, had taken place in the formation of the first Islamic caliphate: a historical instance in which a proto-fascism forms without there being any state structure in place. This fascism forms 'from the bottom up – starting, as it were, with nothing' (Bataille 1979: 80), uniting the paramilitary desert nomads with a newly devised Islamic paradigm. At this point, *taqiyya* was as yet unknown to Islamic traditions.

I am dealing here with the semiotics of monomania. It is important to note that efforts to adapt the concept of monomania from psychology should in no way be understood as an attempt to frame fascism as a psychological phenomenon. I use monomania to refer not to a psychological condition, but a semiotic process. At stake here are the ways in which monomania functions in the world. On this point, diagnostics and treatment are irrelevant.

On this view, the fascist moment comes about as the direct consequence of one single decision, a decision made to ensure the absolute security and immutability of a single sign. This paranoid, monomaniac act is one of excluding not only other possible signs, but also other semiotic possibilities. A given formation is fascist immediately after a series of war machines either fixate on one sign – 'the face of the despot or of god' (TP, 116) – or, to use Negarestani's account, are forced to stay in the active mode at all times.

Ibn Mubārak's invocation of *jinn* and cyclones was among the first discursive moments in the formation of Shiite fascism, in that the affinity between cholera and the *jinn* was expressed in terms of cyclonic behaviour. In Ibn Mubārak's medical imagination, the cyclone was conceived as a semiotic diagram, according to which Islamic monomania could be exercised and extended. In elaborating on how exactly fights between *jinn* lead to an epidemic, Ibn Mubārak explained that *jinn* activity derives from any 'movement and stasis against the Islamic law (*shar*ʿ)' (Ibn Mubārak 2007: 517). Addressing the Ottoman king (to whom his treatise is dedicated), Ibn Mubārak claims that this is why Istanbul had been hit by cholera. What he termed movement and stasis (*ḥarkat va sukūn*) was a formulation of the *jinn*'s cyclonic belligerence, which could incite deadly epidemics. Through this formulation, Ibn Mubārak laid a clandestine foundation for an Islamic fascism to come.

Second Object: Shiite Fascism Facialised

This monomania did not remain within the confines of Shiite medico-religious discourse. It also propagated in the public sphere and was enacted sociopolitically. It is encountered in the Tobacco Protest of 1892 – a significant historical episode in the late nineteenth century. This protest was ignited by one of the concessions that the Iranian state made to Britain, on which it bestowed a full commercial monopoly over tobacco crops in Iran. This decision allegedly outraged local merchants, who joined forces with Shiite clerics for the first time. The result was the issuing of a religious decree (*fatwā*) against the consumption of tobacco.

Figure 13.2 The Tobacco Protest at the royal palace in Tehran. Anonymous artist, drawing printed in *The Graphic*, February 1892.

What is more, these religio-political developments took place against the backdrop of one of the most brutal cholera epidemics in the century, the outbreak of 1889 (Afkhami 2019: 52). Coming as the state was failing to manage the epidemic, the concession over tobacco commerce catalysed the Tobacco Protest.

An anonymous eyewitness took a snapshot of this protest by making a drawing on 4 January 1892. In February of that same year, the sketch was published in *The Graphic*, a newspaper that circulated weekly in England (Figure 13.2). The image, which Amir Afkhami reproduces in his book, shows a few clergymen leading a large crowd to the entrance of the Royal Palace in Tehran. Whereas the ordinary people in the central mass have their backs to the viewer, the clergymen face in the opposite direction, towards the viewer. Their right hands are all raised and their faces are drawn in much more detail than the few visible profiles of the ordinary protesters.

This was a formative moment for the clerical order, for it was the first time that clerics had successfully steered the masses towards a clear goal in a unified protest. Afkhami compares the significance of this protest for the ongoing epidemic with similar situations in Europe:

Rising discontent and fear among Europe's underprivileged during outbreaks often resulted in urban riots and insurrections. The Iranian experience with the 1889 cholera epidemic, on the other hand, was class blind and revealed the singular role of Shiite Islam in directing the currents of social unrest that emerged in its wake. (Afkhami 2019: 52)

It was in this protest that Shiite fascism was practically expressed for the first time. Never before had clerics been so close to the public, having the power to incite and mobilise them en masse.

Attending to the image, viewers can distinguish a semi-spiral movement among the raised hands and sticks. The spiral begins with the most distinguishable figure, just to the lower left of the centre of the image, and proceeds through the lower and middle right of the drawing, all the way to the upper-right corner. The Western observer who drew the image somehow captured this Middle Eastern cyclonic behaviour. This image brought everything together in one percept: the cholera epidemic provides the context, the Shiite clerical monomania is in the foreground and a cyclonic mass protest spirals towards the royal palace. At last, the figure of the cyclone was given actual political expression and became fascist in effect.

The protest represented in the image is discernibly target-oriented. The mass is gravitating towards a point in that people are being encouraged to actively move towards the palace gate. This is no peaceful protest; no one is allowed to rest and diverge. We are not dealing with a diffuse protest populating a space without direction. There is a clear 'integrating' movement running from the periphery to the centre, that is 'drilling' its way to the heart of the state.

What is more, this spiral movement is now facialised. If the *jinn*'s cyclonic performance remained faceless in Ibn Mubārak's medico-religious imagination, the Tobacco Protest (as visualised in Figure 13.2) attained a facial aspect. It was no coincidence that the draughtsperson paid attention to the mullahs' faces. For this Western observer, they were evidently the Face of the crowd. In this snapshot, the monomaniac semiotics (which, thus far, I have only shown operating covertly in the Shiite medico-religious discourse) was acquiring facial traits. Looking closely, it becomes clear that the only visible faces are those of the mullahs.

These faces were not necessarily personal, in that they were not representative of certain individuals. They were *the Face of the people*, not merely faces among them. The mullah-figure *was* the Face: turban on top and beard at the bottom. This face does not belong to a person's body; rather, this is the Face of the cyclonically drilling mass. As Deleuze and Guattari elaborated in their theory of faciality,

the face is a map, even when it is applied to and wraps a volume . . . The head, even the human head, is not necessarily a face. The face is produced

Figure 13.3 The face of the mullah, which was said to have been spotted on the surface of the moon during the first few years after the revolution.

only when the head ceases to be a part of the body, when it ceases to be coded by the body . . . when the body, head included, has been decoded and has to be *overcoded by* something we shall call the Face. (TP, 170).

In this sense, the mullah-figure became precisely the Face of the people by wrapping around the body of the mass, a map that guided and coded both the crowd and the Western observer's gaze. The becoming-facial of the Muslim mass was therefore a formative stage in the development of Shiite fascism. The centripetal forces of the cyclone found their facial expression in the figure of the mullah. This is where one encounters Islamic fascism proper, in which no concealment, no strategic camouflage (*taqiyya*), no silence or inactivity is allowed.

From this point onwards, the face of the mullah, with its beard and turban, became the key signifying force in Shiite culture. The face of the 1979 Islamic Revolution, Ruhollah Khomeini's, was the most evolved figure of this fascist machine. It can still be found sprayed on walls in Iranian cities; some even say that they have seen it on the surface of the moon in the form of a highly abstracted figure in which the turban and beard stand out clearly (Figure 13.3).

Epilogue

The Islamic regime that rules over contemporary Iran is the culmination of at least two centuries of fascistophilic thought and practice. This force, however, has been losing face over the past decade. If cholera intensified the monomaniac semiotics inherent in Shiite religious

Figure 13.4 Iranian supreme leader Ali Khamenei in the state mourning arena in August 2020. Source: Khamenei.ir.

discourse and ultimately led to the mullahs' facialisation in the late nineteenth century, the novel coronavirus has defacialised the clerics of the Islamic Republic.

A photograph of the Iranian regime's supreme leader, Ali Khamenei, published on his official webpage shows this defacialisation in its most literal sense (Figure 13.4). The photograph was taken in August 2020, when Iran was struggling with an uncontrollable surge of Covid-19 cases around the country. This surge came in the month of Muharram, the most ritually significant time of year for Shiite Muslims. Khamenei ordered that Shiite mourning rituals had to be observed and performed across the nation. To evidence his personal commitment to the rituals in the face of the pandemic, he organised a mourning session at the state arena, involving one reciter and one participant, himself. The photograph shows him sitting on a chair in the empty mourning area with a hygienic mask partially covering his face. In previous years, every high-ranking official was obliged to take part in this event, joining the leader in mourning the death of his imam. In 2020, however, the ritual turned into a lonesome, faceless performance.

The face mask defines the image, more than any of the other visual signs that it contains. The turban and beard are visible, certainly, though they are obscured by the superimposition of the mask. The mask reminds the viewer of the epidemic's power over religion – the same religion that, despite the cholera epidemics of the late nineteenth century, took to the streets and staged a grand protest against the state. Today, however, that religion has been overpowered by the Covid-19 pandemic. The fascism of the Shiite religion, which, over the course of two centuries, has evolved into a state facialised by the figure of the mullah, is now facing a crisis of faciality. Whereas cholera epidemics created a biosphere in which the Shiite religion could practise axiality and militancy in the nineteenth century, the coronavirus pandemic is now creating divergent forces that are throwing its monomania off course. If the Shiism of the nineteenth century could subordinate the cyclonic savagery of the *jinn* to its vertical agenda and attain faciality in its fascist formation, then the Islamic regime today has lost face in the swirl of the coronavirus pandemic.

Notes

1. The state's response can be seen in this video: <https://www.youtube.com/watch?v=RLYS9l7XFHA> (last accessed 15 May 2022).
2. I use the same word *jinn* in both the singular and plural senses, avoiding the word *jinns*. In so doing, I refer to *jinn* as a generic category in Islamic demonology, using the definitive article with the term. This usage has been adapted from Amira El-Zein and Simon O'Meara, among others (El-Zein 2009; O'Meara 2015).
3. The idea that the *jinn* were the force behind epidemics was not entirely new and can be traced to earlier sources. That said, this demonological argument was confined to jurisprudential and popular discourses and had been kept methodically separate from medical debates. Hence, although discussion about the *jinn* appeared here and there in narrative and legal medicine, their role in epidemics had never been explicitly mentioned, let alone theorised. With NS and contemporaneous medical texts, however, these two bodies of knowledge began to merge.
4. The term biofilm refers to a process whereby multiple microorganisms form a consistent biological membrane.

References

Afkhami, A. A. (2019), *A Modern Contagion: Imperialism and Public Health in Iran's Age of Cholera*, Baltimore, MD: Johns Hopkins University Press.

Algar, H. (1980), *Religion and State in Iran, 1785–1906: The Role of the Ulama in the Qajar Period*, Berkeley: University of California Press.

Amanat, A. (1989), *Resurrection and Renewal: The Making of the Babi Movement in Iran, 1844–1850*, Ithaca, NY: Cornell University Press.

Baker, R. M., F. L. Singleton and M. A. Hood (1983), 'Effects of Nutrient Deprivation on Vibrio Cholerae', *Applied and Environmental Microbiology*, 46 (4): 930–40.

Barad, K. (2007), *Meeting the Universe Halfway: Quantum Physics and the Entanglement of Matter and Meaning*, Durham, NC: Duke University Press.

Barua, D., and W. B. Greenough III (1992), *Cholera: Current Topics in Infectious Disease*, New York: Springer.

Bataille, G. (1979), 'The Psychological Structure of Fascism', trans. Carl R. Lovitt, *New German Critique*, 16: 64–87.

Braidotti, R. (2011), *Nomadic Theory: The Portable Rosi Braidotti*, New York: Columbia University Press.

Bulmus, B. (2005), *Plague, Quarantines and Geopolitics in the Ottoman Empire*, Edinburgh: Edinburgh University Press.

Ebrahimnejad, H. (2004), *Medicine, Public Health, and the Qājār State: Patterns of Medical Modernization in Nineteenth-Century Iran*, Leiden: Brill.

El-Zein, A. (2009), *Islam, Arabs, and the Intelligent World of the Jinn*, Syracuse, NY, Syracuse University Press.

Faruque, S. M., M. J. Albert and J. J. Mekalanos (1998), 'Epidemiology, Genetics, and Ecology of ToxigenicVibrio Cholerae', *Microbiology and Molecular Biology Reviews*, 62 (4): 1301–14.

Gurney, J., and N. Nabavi (1993), 'Dār Al-Funūn', in *Encyclopaedia Iranica*, ed. Ehsan Yarshate, New York: Bibliotheca Persica, vol. 6, pp. 662–8.

Ibn Mubārak, M. Ḥ. (2007), *Naṣīḥatnāmay-i Sūlaymānī*, ed. Ḥ. R. Burqaʿī, Ganjīnay-i Bahāristān.

Islam, M. S., B. S. Drasar and R. B. Sack (1994), 'The Aquatic Flora and Fauna as Reservoirs of Vibrio Cholerae: A Review', *Journal of Diarrhoeal Diseases Research*, 12 (2): 87–96.

Menashri, D. (1992), *Education and the Making of Modern Iran*, Ithaca, NY: Cornell University Press.

Morris, R. J. (1976), *Cholera 1832: The Social Response to an Epidemic*, London: Croom Helm.

Negarestani, R. (2008), *Cyclonopedia: Complicity with Anonymous Materials*, Melbourne: re.press.

O'Meara, S. (2015), 'From Space to Place: The Quranic Infernalization of the Jinn', in C. Lange (ed.), *Locating Hell in Islamic Traditions*, Leiden: Brill, pp. 56–73.

Pormann, P. E., and E. Savage-Smith (2007), *Medieval Islamic Medicine*, Washington, DC: Georgetown University Press.

Ramamurthy, T., and S. K. Bhattacharya (2010), *Epidemiological and Molecular Aspects on Cholera*, Cham: Springer Science & Business Media.

Ringer, M. M. (2001), *Education, Religion, and the Discourse of Cultural Reform in Qajar Iran*, Costa Mesa, CA: Mazda Publishers.

Shoja, M. M., and R. Shane Tubbs (2007), 'The History of Anatomy in Persia', *Journal of Anatomy*, 210 (4): 359–78.

Wheeler, C. M. (1946), 'Control of Typhus in Italy 1943–1944 by Use of DDT', *American Journal of Public Health and the Nations Health*, 36 (2): 119–29.

Chapter 14

An Athens Yet to Come

Stavros Kousoulas

Architectural Technicities

Michel Foucault asks us to consider technology in a much broader sense, one that is not confined only to what can traditionally be called the 'hard sciences' but wishes to encompass a population of practices, including institutions and practices of governance (Foucault 2000: 364). Foucault advances a concept in which technology is understood as any practical rationality governed by a conscious goal: *techne* (Foucault 2000: 364). If an artefact and its capacity for niche construction is conceptualised with a focus on its interventive and manipulative agency, then the very concept of technology – the production and control of artefacts – can surpass the binaries between social and material, human and non-human. In Foucault's words, 'if one placed the history of architecture back in this general history of *techne*, in this wide sense of the word, one would have a more interesting guiding concept than by the opposition between the exact sciences and the inexact ones' (Foucault 2000: 364).

Gilbert Simondon shares similar concerns: at the heart of one of his most important books, *On the Mode of Existence of Technical Objects* (1958), lies the conflict between culture and technology. According to Simondon, this conflict is based on a fundamental misunderstanding of technology which, at least in cultural terms, positions it as a foreign reality (Simondon 2017: 134). For that reason, Simondon proposes the term 'technical culture', suggesting a way of thinking which surpasses that conflict. The point of departure for a way of thinking which no longer considers technology and culture apart is a shift of focus from the usage and utility of technical objects. Aiming to provoke an awareness of the modes of existence of technical objects, one should instead focus on the genesis of the objects themselves (Simondon 2017: xi).

Simondon does this by developing the concept of technicity. For Simondon, technicity is fully relational, abductive and deals with a constant becoming. If one aims to avoid reductionism, then, Simondon advises us, one should also study beyond the technical objects to the technicity of these objects as a mode of relation between human and world (Simondon 2017: 162). The autonomy of each technical object – or better said, each technical individual – lies in its relational technicity, since 'technical objects result from an objectification of technicity; they are produced by it, but technicity is not exhausted in objects and is not entirely contained in them' (2017: 176). In this sense, one could move from architectural objects to an architectural technicity which operates in terms of reticularity: located within assemblages, reticularity is the immediate relation of events and actions that occur in a given structure which, however, is understood in terms of its potentials for action, not in its extensive and formal outlines, and has to be studied in etho-logical, that is affective, terms. If becoming, according to Simondon, is defined as the operation of a system possessing potentials in reality, then it is the disruptive agency of these potentials that pushes future states of the system into being (2017: 169). Therefore, understood as a population of technicities, architectural practices engender a par-ticular mode of architectural reticularity by relating them to their own future.

Generalisation and Concretisation

Nonetheless, what does a technicity consist of? In his book *Gesture and Speech* (1964), anthropologist André Leroi-Gourhan examines the anatomical technicity of the human hand, positing its development within the reticularity of the body and the environment. Focusing on the discovery of fossils of the *Zinjanthrope* in Kenya in 1959, Leroi-Gourhan claims that the necessary condition for language is biped-alism. Bipedalism frees the hands from walking and simultaneously enables the mouth to speak, creating a new form of anatomical tech-nicity, composed of new relations of speed and slowness, movement and *stasis* in the animal itself, altering radically the ways it relates with its environment. The hand can make and manipulate artefacts, relating now not only to the surface of the earth but to *any* surface. The amplification in the degrees of freedom of the limb-now-known-as-the-hand is an example of what Leroi-Gourhan names generalisation or de-specialisation, which one can also find under the Deleuzian term of deterritorialisation (Altamirano 2016: 134). While early humanoids used their stone tools in a similar fashion as animals use their claws, humans nowadays use their tools at both a spatial and temporal distance. This is what Leroi-Gourhan has in mind when he uses the concept of generalisation: while other animals followed an evolutionary path that was highly specialised and, essentially, internal, humans evolved by externalising through technology.

Complementing Leroi-Gourhan, Simondon approaches the genesis of an object as a process of refinement, which nevertheless should not be examined in terms of usefulness or profitability since such external criteria do nothing more but obscure the technicity of the object itself (Chabot 2013: 12). Simondon advances a process of examining the evolution of technical objects which is internal: what is broadly called refinement is in fact a process of concretisation. While human evolution involves a constant generalisation via the external de-specialisation of the species through its technicities, the technical objects, assisting in that generalisation, follow a process of a perpetual – yet peculiar – specification. What Simondon is claiming is that any technical object is located between an unstable event – the coming together of parts – and a consistent, stable structure – the parts when in operation. Different objects possess different degrees of concretisation, the levels of which determine the technicity of a given technology. The degrees of concretisation are themselves composed out of the relations of the parts which constitute the technical object.

Taking this into account, let us briefly focus on the Athenian urban unit, the *polykatoikia*. The *polykatoikia* is found throughout Athens, usually three to six floors tall, with multiple apartments on each floor and residents of diverse origin and income. Once the abstraction of the *polykatoikia* is there, we can examine each of the elements that it is made of: the structural parts, bricks, concrete and slabs that hold it together, the networks of pipes which transfer energy and water through it, the openings in its surfaces, its doors and windows. It goes without saying that I do not aim to provide an evolutionary account of each of these elements, and that is precisely the point: each of the elements that this abstract urban unit consists of has its own independent history, its own genealogy that needs to be unravelled. In other words, even in this abstract version of the urban unit, each of its parts fails to explain their coming together when examined in isolation. Technological, and consequently architectural, invention involves formulating a consistent and coherent system from disparate parts. The *polykatoikia* that emerges from the combination of these disparate elements is an example of concretisation. As Simondon claims, the principle of this process is effectively the manner in which the object causes and conditions itself in its functioning and in the reactions of its functioning on its utilization; the technical object, issued forth from the abstract work of the organization of sub-systems, is the theatre of a certain number of reciprocal causal relations. (Simondon 2017: 32)

The relationships of reciprocal causality that Simondon mentions are in fact the operational modes of reticular technicity: *techne* in action. It is not a matter of how useful a technological object can be – for whom is an immediate question, much more complex than it initially appears – but rather a question of an immanent consistency, a faithfulness to the operation of an abstract machine. This faithfulness is the reason that Simondon claims that technical evolution is no different than biological. In this respect, the moment when a technical object reaches a high level of concretisation is the moment when it affords multi-functionality.

The *polykatoikia*, at the beginning of the twenty-first century, is concretised precisely due to its ability to present such a complex level of abstraction. In its own right, this level of abstraction is a result of the multi-functionality of all the other technical objects that compose the *polykatoikia*: the pipes through which warm water runs, the dinner that is being prepared on the stove, the windows that allow visual but not thermal contact. It is not only the urban unit that becomes multi-functional, each of these elements become so too. A wall supports loads, protects from the outside, connects appliances to networks of electricity and communications while being a blank canvas for its resident's interventions. In other words, the affective capacities of the urban unit, its potentials to affect and be affected, have been amplified to such a degree that one can speak of a high-level Athenian technicity – and this is why any technicity is primarily an affective one. To put it succinctly, the effects of the *polykatoikia* exceed by far and in ways never imagined the initial problems that they were meant to confront.

In the case of Athens, the *polykatoikia* was the formation in which libidinal desire was invested. The housing unit, in its structures and operations, produced a lack on the libidinal level not due to its failure, but rather due to its immense success as a means of urban individuation. In the Athenian urban environment – or, better said, the Athenian urban ecologies – and in the gradual and intense involution by means of the *polykatoikia*, the desire for a radical becoming-other was produced precisely because the *polykatoikia* was working well. This is almost obvious at the level of political economies: for them to be productive, the technical individuals that form them should not be out of order. Therefore, for the desires of a generalised subject to be individuated, there was the need of a concretised object that would assist the emergence of a lack. In its high-level technicity, the *polykatoikia*, decoded and multi-functional, has equally amplified its affects, so much as to produce a lack in the Athenian subject: what if I were to take my housing unit away from the rest, what if I were to stand apart? The moment, therefore, that the generalised Athenian subject and the concretised *polykatoikia* became aware of their affects was the moment that allowed for a direct perception of all the environmental choices available, which consequently brought forth the actualisation of active changes in the urban environment itself. In other words, it was the moment when the Athenian milieu – interior, exterior, membrane and energy – would no longer need the *polykatoikia* as its point of convergence, but would need to, literally, fold upon itself. Through the territory of the housing unit and through the territory of the whole Attica basin, Athens could not only be at once and everywhere, but crucially, could become at once and everywhere.

In this sense, during the years before the Olympic Games of 2004, a dual process was at play. On the one hand, the intense construction activities throughout Attica; on the other, the stratification of multiple micro-desires, in the form of overcoded rhetorics and practices regarding Greece's assumed economic and geopolitical role. It was in 2001, when Greece entered the European monetary union, that a long-lasting quest seemingly ended. Greece was now officially part of the West; expressed in both minor and major modes, an ongoing process of modernisation that started at the formation of the Greek state was now declared successful. Greece was financially growing while its capital could prove itself capable of hosting the most popular event in the world. New metropolitan infrastructures were under construction. At once and everywhere in the basin of Attica, Athens wished even to cross its territorial limits; the basin itself. In the years just before the Games, many masterplans, conferences and actual real-estate values were intent on dictating the same thing: Athens no longer needed to be constrained by the mountainous volumes that form the basin. Envisioned as a coastline metropolis, Athens would cease its inward development and would open to the sea that surrounds it, both north and south, east and west. Therefore, all the Olympic constructions had to be placed accordingly. Dispersed throughout Attica, not only in the basin, the now deserted buildings and infrastructures of the Olympic Games are indeed an Athens that never came.

What did come, nonetheless, would alter profoundly the Athenian technicities. Ever since the emergence of the *polykatoikia*, the logics of the Athenian involution were individuating in a relative continuity.

After the turn of the century, a radical dephasing would occur, a bifurcation that would reorganise the diagram of the Athenian urban ecologies. Due to its complexity, one needs to approach this shift from multiple points of view. In doing so, a bold claim will also start to emerge, one that brings ostensibly different – for some directly opposite or even clashing – Athenian instances together.

Urban Black Holes

Since 2003 and continuing until now with varying intensity, hundreds of thousands of refugees from Asia have arrived in Greece, most of them settling in Athens. While the first group of immigrants, those coming mainly from Albania or the countries of Eastern Europe, would be assimilated into the Greek population relatively easily (common religion and traditions were crucial in this), this time the situation would be different. In all its variations over the past two decades, the arrival of refugees from Asia was never close to the slow and steady influx that occurred after the fall of European communist regimes. As a result either of conflict (Afghanistan, Iraq, Syria), political persecution (Egypt, Lebanon, Palestine) or ongoing political and economic instability (Pakistan), massive numbers of people have arrived on the Greek coast, only to be gathered and left in Athens. While for most the ambition was to secure entry into the European Union, the very migration policies of the EU do not allow them to move further than Greece. In this respect, and similarly to what has occurred and continues to occur in other Mediterranean countries over the past two decades, an entire population is found in a continuous transitional limbo. Most of them have dispersed to various neighbourhoods of Athens, residing in empty apartments. Simultaneously, an exodus from the centre of Athens is occurring, encouraged by both a strengthened economy and the ongoing infrastructure construction throughout Attica, the concretised *polyka-toikia* and the generalised Athenian subject.

The new wave of refugees would assist in the further individuation of the Athenian technicities. However, in its coupling with other structures and operations that emerged during the years after the Olympic Games, a radical bifurcation would occur in the technicities themselves. In order to approach this bifurcation, this dephasing of the Athenian diagram, we will examine the structural couplings that produced the germs of this, most recent, disruption in the metastable field of the Athenian urban ecologies. At the same time, another coupling will come to the fore: that of Athens and its own futurity.

Found in a position of extreme poverty, the majority of refugees would be forced to share basements and lower-floor apartments in huge groups. Twenty to thirty people would live together in spaces of sixty square metres, with rent being paid not per apartment but per head and per day. It is an operation that continues, one that is largely overlooked in accounts of the recent urban history of Athens, even though, as I will claim, it assisted in the most radical bifurcation of the Athenian technicities. Its effects were almost immediately visible in the public spaces of the centre: thousands of people, not able to afford to spend any time in their apartments except during their sleeping hours, would spend most of the day in the streets, squares and parks of Athens. Following specific agreements, the residents of each apartment would roughly spend one third of their time working, one third sleeping and the rest in public spaces, taking turns so as to fit as many people in as possible. Even at the level of its micro-architectures, the *polykatoikia* no longer regulated urban involution. Interior, exterior, their reversals and the energy exchanged among them was now regulated by the human body itself. To live in Athens was no longer determined by what was singular for the *polykatoikia*: apartment sizes, floor plans, pavements and stairs all became suddenly irrelevant and insignificant. What determined the centre of Athens, in its micro-architectures, was how much a body could afford and how many bodies it could afford. For the thousands of refugees arriving in Athens, the question was how many days and with how many others they could afford in an apartment. For the apartment owners, the question was how many refugees they could fit in without irreversibly damaging their property while assuring the maximum profit from it. A micro-management of the breathing body, a micro-architecture of instant profit; both, the first whispers of a black hole.

One could claim that this shift in the Athenian technicities was only relevant for a small percentage of the population of Athens: refugees seeking housing and apartment owners who could take advantage of this. However, the importance of a singularity is not to be measured by the amount of ordinary points that it relates to; on the contrary, a singularity appears as such by its capacity to affect other singular points – that is, to reorganise the continuum. In this sense, the absolute deterritorialising and decoding of the housing unit that emerged in these years is not to be approached in terms of how it relates to an established past but, rather, in its composability with a futural urban ecology. The prosperity and capital accumulation of the first decade of the century would result in the establishment of an advanced private banking system that was practically absent from Greece in previous years. For the first time, housing loans on a massive scale and in an accessible form were available. Athens could individuate beyond the limits of its overcoded and informal building constructions and operations. In an environment that facilitated quick and carefree access to bank loans, there was no longer any need for all the nuances of a technicity that had developed in order to overcome the absence of an extended banking system. The ties between landowners, constructors and apartment owners were no longer compossible with what, simply, worked faster: a loan for buying a plot, a loan for constructing a *polykatoikia*, a loan for buying parts of it. Soon the structure of the *polykatoikia* would transform as well, from the decoded and adaptable housing unit of previous decades, to an overcoded expression of each owner's financial status, preferably in the up and coming new suburbs. A black hole starts to vibrate.

So far we have been examining two parallel individuations, one at the centre of Athens and the other in its suburbs. In their coupling they start to potentialise the total and radical dephasing of the most dominant Athenian technicity, that of the *polykatoikia*. At a level that involves the micro-architectures of the city, the *polykatoikia* would face its absolute decoding and deterritorialisation, both in the city centre where rents would be now operating in an even more generalised fashion, as well as in the new suburban constructions where bank loans would bypass the *quid pro quo* land allowance operations. In both cases, the result was a gradually growing incompossability of the Athenian technicities of the time with the ones to come. The technicities would fully bifurcate when coupled with the effect that the Olympic Games had on the involution of Athens.

Aside from functioning as attractors to newly developed areas of Athens, the infrastructure and large-scale constructions of the Olympic Games would also alter the Athenian ecologies in a more profound manner. The preparation and construction process for most of the Olympic facilities was largely serendipitous, initially coordinated by the Greek state but with a growing involvement of the private sector, especially as the deadline for the Games was approaching (Phokaides et al. 2013: 95) The 'urgency' of fulfilling a desire that traversed multiple assemblages (of different populations and of different interests) justified the development of mechanisms that could bypass legislative frame-works and bureaucracies as well as any reactions to them. If this was a common and successful operation until that moment, it was because of the fact that it involved the quasi-crystallisation of an economy of agglomeration: a commonly beneficial technicity of proximal distances, of shared knowledge and of the capacity to auto-regulate land, building and rental prices through a non-centrally controlled relation between offer and demand; these were some of the elements that made the involution *qua* the *polykatoikia* so successful.

By contrast, from the state of exception that the Olympic Games imposed – or, better said, from the desire for it – emerged the formation, for the first time in Athens, of economies of scale in the construction sector: not a shared technicity, but rather the internalisation of a technicity within a large private investor, maximising profit by minimising costs due to the fully centralised control of massive construction projects. Growing large due to their involvement in the Olympic Games, these newly formed construction companies would start to operate in the housing market as well. Needing to use their personnel and equipment after the Games, they would focus on both real-estate and housing constructions throughout Attica, albeit deploying a technicity that had nothing in common with that of the *polykatoikia*: large-scale capital investments, massive land acquisitions and the construction of whole city blocks instead of housing units (Issaias 2014: 145). In the structural coupling of these three individuations (from the deterritorialisation and decoding of the *polykatoikia*, to the bank loans substituting for its operations and the formation of economies of scale), the germ that would reorganise the Athenian ecologies emerged: an absolute retreat to the private, understood not in financial or market terms but in terms of stratification and rigidification. Never being a matter of decision but always the effect of a contingent technicity, the Athenian ecologies up to that point were always operating and structuring themselves in terms of a continuous modulation. More than being positioned between built forms and construction operations, the modulatory processes that transductively propagated in the Athenian milieu demanded the reticular formation, investment and involvement of an extended assemblage that would allow the co-determinable establishment of multiple alliances. This is why, despite its modulations, the *polykatoikia* had never been operative as a means of separation; it constantly resolved any disparate tensions on a level that negotiated between micro- and macro-architectures.

What seemed the erosion of the *polykatoikia*, an absolute porosity of it at the level of a meso-modulation, was in fact the opposite. Any informational and energetic exchange within the Athenian milieu was becoming more and more incompossible with the futurity of an urban ecology that was retreating to segmentarity. The Athenian subject was gradually becoming what philosopher Quentin Meillassoux calls a *reactive* one (Meillassoux 2007: 99). A reactive subject undergoes a line of becoming which actually consists of a constant retreat, a reassurance of its own supposed givens and limits, a perpetuation of modes of thinking and practices which are never to deviate from its own immediate and short-term interests. It is a form of subjectivity shielded behind its own stubbornness, operating in terms of 'idiocy'. Interestingly, the noun 'idiot', when examined etymologically, derives from the Greek ιδιώτης: a private citizen, the one that has no interest for the commons, enclosed in herself, refusing any opening to anything exterior. Therefore, with the particles of Athenian involution shifting towards an absolute and enclosed interior, an absolute privacy, there was no regulation of any informational or energetic exchange in a trans-affective manner. Consequently, in the plane of a shared urban becoming, both the interior and the exterior became redundant: everything and nothing was possible, everything and nothing was crucial. The informational values that the Athenian milieu was producing became significant in as much as they referred to the possibility of a privately consumable future, and not to the virtuality of a co-determinable futurity. Another whisper of a black hole.

How can one, therefore, speak of an Athenian futurity, of an Athens yet to come? In both architectural and urban theory, when it comes to speaking of the future, the dominant approach is that of a vast array of exclusive disjunctions: either this possible future or that one. Exclusive disjunction is an application in futural terms of what philosophically is known as the law of the excluded middle. The law of the excluded middle presupposes that a statement is either true or false. Nothing can simultaneously be both, as it would violate the very law itself. It is also what characterises modernity's relations with futurity; deeply rooted in its propositional logics and representational means, modernity assumes a possible future and not a futural future. In other words, not a future based on virtuality, but a future based on possibility. For that possible future to come, either a set of rational rules and propositions will be applied or we 'may have the impression of something akin to a nightmare' (Le Corbusier 1986: v). As philosopher Claire Colebrook claims,

> exclusive disjunction operates with an 'either/or' while . . . it allows the subject the somewhat good conscience of compromise . . . It precludes any future that is not ultimately subjective . . . As long as there is a subject, a being for whom the world exists as a historical entity with decisive outcomes, a subject who deems himself to be the outcome and agent of history, then there will be 'a' future that will emerge from an interpreted line of time. (Colebrook 2017)

A future that is governed by exclusive disjunctions is a future of a reactive subject: either this or that future for either us or them. In the past two decades in the Athenian urban ecologies there have been three major instances when a future was abruptly brought forth. I will not examine each of them in detail since this exceeds the scope of my argument. What will become obvious through them is that in all cases, it was a future that was attempted to be brought into the present from a realm of possibilities. In other words, in all these opposing moments, the Athenian subjects that dreamed of an Athens yet to come did so from a point of view that was fundamentally uninterested in anything that did not appeal to its segmentarity; a point of view that constantly shrinks, uninterested in anything that implies an affective transformation, invested solely in securing a rigid self-referential stability. In 2004, 2008 and 2011, a black hole was formed in Athens, one that still attracts anything that is captured by it.

Athens beyond Us and Them

If in the case of the Olympic Games we have already examined the proliferation of a desiring-machine that wished and managed to transform the Athenian technicities accordingly, then what remains is to highlight how these desires individuate into what for many has been positioned in the exact opposite political field: the youth uprising of December 2008 and the Squares Movement of the summer of 2011. Let us briefly examine each of them. As architect Stavros Stavrides summarises,

> on 6 December 2008, a police car was passing in front of one of the coffee shops where young people meet . . . What a few boys did was to yell at these policemen . . . But the policemen in the car did something so disastrous that it immediately triggered a huge youth outburst. They parked their car and they returned armed to respond to the insult. One of them took out his gun, aimed at one of the 15-year-old students and shot him. The boy died on the pavement. (Stavrides 2010: 132)

On the same night, an almost immediate wave of rage swept through the city – massive clashes between protesters and the police, hundreds of shops attacked and destroyed, as well as numerous public buildings. In the days that followed, many public buildings were occupied in various areas of Athens and were temporarily transformed into organisational centres for all the different aspects of an ongoing urban unrest. To name a few examples, the National Opera was occupied by artists and became a centre of artistic experimentation, the building of the General Confederation of Workers was transformed into an information centre for any form of protest, while a huge, empty, central plot was transformed into a communal park. Interestingly, throughout the uprising there was no specific political or organisational centre, but rather a number of them, most of the time with opposing assumptions, goals and practices. What bound them together was an abstract request for an upcoming social and urban justice, one that would be achieved either by massive demonstrations, building occupations or riots and looting. In all cases, a supposedly repressed subject was opposed by its repressive counterpart, demanding its right to the city. However, the issue with any demand to a given urban right is precisely that this right is given, either as an allowance from an equally abstract subject in power or as a generality that, instead of explaining anything, sums up the complexity of an urban ecology in the form of a reified vagueness. The December uprising ended as suddenly as it started; ironically, the Christmas break was meant also as a break from urban struggle.

Only a couple of years later, Greece and its capital would spiral into a debt crisis. The bailout package of 2010, as well as all the ones that followed, composed of various transnational agreements between Greece, the Eurozone and the IMF, had severe effects. The Squares Movement in Syntagma, the most central square of Athens, was a direct result of this. Lasting for about two months, throughout the summer of 2011 almost 2.6 million Athenians either protested, occupied, discussed or passed regularly through the square (Leontidou 2012: 306). Contrary to the 2008 uprising, the square was clearly the physical centre of opposition to the economic policies of the Greek government and the European Union. Nonetheless, in the square itself, one could witness two parallel dynamics: that of its upper part, almost next to the Parliament building, where anger and resentment prevailed, and that of the lower part, where leftists would debate 'the preconditions of direct democracy, organised self-help, mutual aid, solidarity and collective action' (Leontidou 2012: 306).

Chronologically, the rise of neo-fascist political parties in Greece coincided with the events of the Squares Movement. However, could one speculate on a more complex relation between the two – while avoiding the naïve error of equating them? If its leftist part was debating direct democracy, controlling and forbidding the presence of any official political organisation in the square, in the upper part of Syntagma hatred was growing: the ones in the Parliament, they are the thieves, they are responsible, they should pay. Therefore, a dual process of segregation was at play. On the one hand, we who will construct an alternative model of life; on the other, they who are responsible and have to pay for their actions. When in August 2011 the Squares Movement dispersed, its effect would be a radicalisation of segmentarity: while the December uprising produced the very technicities of a renewed yet still uncontrolled segregation, the Squares Movement rigidified a fundamental exclusion, an 'either/or' who claims the right to both an urban subject and to its enunciations, to both the 'good/bad' historical agents, the 'good/bad' interpretations of a temporal line and to both 'good/bad' possible futures. The black hole is formed.

In their involution, the Athenian technicities were eventually internalised as an absolute informational proliferation that made information itself valueless. In this regard, they assisted in the formation of an infinity of subjects that at once desired their becoming-other, without, however, any affective interest in anything-other. In its deterritorialisation, any subject that can dislocate itself from itself in order to formulate novel assemblages can always become something less than what it was: becoming is not progress, individuation is not fine-tuning. Due to the technicities we have been examining, or to be more precise, due to the individuation of the Athenian technicities and their bifurcations, equally radical bifurcations occur on the level of any Athenian subject. In this sense, a black hole is nothing else but a failed line of flight (Message 2010: 34). Therefore, a black hole in a process of individuation is always a potential outcome, caused either by a threshold crossed too quickly or by an intensity that becomes destructive precisely because it is no longer bearable (Message 2010: 34).

In the case of Athens, both causes apply. Until the beginning of the twenty-first century, the Athenian technicities were individuating by means of a continuous prolongation of their own singular points. The germ that at once deterritorialised and decoded the *polykatoikia* and its operations, while simultaneously informing any individual as the particle of urban involution qua loaning, marks both a rapid crossing and an unbearable intensity. There is no longer a co-determination that is affectively shared and constantly bootstrapped, but rather the exchange between a molar economy and a molecular particle of urbanity that depends solely on its molar counterpart and not on its affective, technical alliances. Before the formation of molar fascist assemblages in the Athenian urban ecologies, there was the formation of infinite microfascisms: one for every body, for every *polykatoikia*, for every loan granted and every debt still owed, for every immigrant and every other, for all of us and all of them. As Deleuze and Guattari put it, micro-fascisms have a specificity of their own that can crystallise into a macro-fascism, but may also float along the supple line on their own account and suffuse every little cell ... Interactions without resonance. Instead of the great paranoid fear, we are trapped in a thousand little monomanias, self-evident truths and clarities that gush from every black hole and no longer form a system, but only rumble and buzz, blinding lights giving any and everybody the mission of self-appointed judge, dispenser of justice, policeman, neighbourhood SS man. (TP, 228)

Any fascism, any black hole, be it in molar or molecular desires, be it still at the level of the libidinal or the political, does not emerge out of an ideological nowhere; it emerges precisely in the in-between of the reticularity of any technicity. To avoid any misunderstanding, what in the case of Athens is conceived as the proliferation of infinite micro-fascist subjectivities is none other than the emergence of infinite reactive subjects out of the Athenian urban ecologies and their technicities themselves. If any environmental manipulation affords its individuation without the reticular manipulation of the subject that attempts it – if in other words transformation occurs only on the extensive level (by means of a debt attributed to the supposedly powerless from the supposedly powerful) and not reticularly on the intensive level (as a co-determining affective amplification via the individuation of shared technicities) – then any present and any future are always fundamentally exclusive. The question, therefore, is how can one escape a black hole, not by creating another – that of a grand narrative of an alternative possibility, left or right – but through the very technicities that made it emerge in the first place?

For the Athenian urban ecologies, the fact is that both the housing market and the construction sector – the particles of the Athenian involution for almost two centuries – have now collapsed. In a decline that exceeded all expectations, especially after 2010, Athens is no longer individuating in any way that even barely resembles its past. Another fact, nonetheless, is that Athens is still individuating; that is precisely why it is both necessary and timely to thoroughly examine what are the current Athenian technicities. More than simply identifying them, one needs to reveal the spatial and temporal nuances of both their structures and their operations, in order to extrapolate from the urban ecologies that they form. Such a task exceeds the scope of this chapter. However, it bears the promise of an extrapolation on the future of Athens that would not be based on any possibility – architectural, urban, economic, social, political – but rather on the virtuality of its current technicities at play, those that we have examined individuating, reorganising the Athenian metastable field, producing subjects and objects that are reticularly producing them anew. In addition, it is an extrapolation from the current affective repertoire of Athens and its multiple assemblages, those of both micro- and macro-architectures, molecular and molar architectural technicities. To affectively attune oneself with the current Athenian technicities does not involve the production of yet another narrative (of urban change, social justice or political emancipation) but rather the affirmative production of a futurity through the actual and virtual potentials of an environmental manipulation that occurs 'here and now' while aiming at a 'not-here-and-not-yet'.

In this sense, to examine the Athenian technicities and out of them extrapolate on the futurity of their urban ecologies is deeply political. However, it is political in a fundamentally non-subjective sense; to be more precise, it involves the political enunciation of a subject that no longer remains reactive and captured by the attractive allure of any microfascist lines, but rather catalyses the reorganisation of an active subjectivity. Contrary to a reactive subject, an active subject follows a becoming that connects it to the becoming of a world – or, the becoming of the urban ecologies it produces and is produced by. It is a subject that has no interest in maintaining its stability just for the sake of existing, but instead wishes to actively seek the violence of the encounter with the technicities that manipulate it and its environment. Following Meillassoux, an active subject that is attuned in the affective amplification of its manipulative repertoire is

> capable of an innovative, inventive becoming . . . Its increase of force does not come from an autonomous decision of a constitutive subject, but from an experience that is always undergone, an affective test in which a radical exteriority gives itself, an exteriority never felt before as such. (Meillassoux 2007: 101)

In this respect, diagramming the current Athenian technicities can separate the political from the personal, the collective assemblages of micro- and macro-architectures from the segmentarity of a reactive subject. As philosopher Brian Massumi underlines,

> personalising narratives actually occlude this affirmative power of resistance, because they are focused first on defining the present event in terms of the individual's past, and only then look to opening the collective future in a break from narratives from the past . . . We live toward the future transindividually, in excess over our personhood. The political is not coming home to a familiar face. The political is estrangingly intensive. It is rewilding. In its movement, we are stranger to ourselves . . . The political acts in the

name of a life we have not lived. It acts for the life we have yet to live. (Massumi 2017)

Consequently, if the political is collective, then the future it produces is collective as well. However, it is a collective future in a dual sense: it is both a future of multiple assemblages and their structural couplings, as well as a multiple future itself. Not this or that, not a future for either us or them, but a future for us and them: a future which we co-determine, trans-individually and trans-affectively, through the technicities that we produce. At the same moment, the future itself determines who, when, where and how we are: the ways we structure and operate the manipulations of an urban ecology, how we modulate it and ourselves, how we individuate alongside that which individuates us. The Athenian technicities, therefore, do not only manipulate an actual space, they manipulate a virtual future, they mediate between the uncertainties of a futurity and the certainties of an actuality. In other words, collective futures pass through the technicities that potentialise them, a way of conducting the present into the future, the actual into the virtual: any technicity is a way of ordering time and events through micro- and macro-alliances, aberrant nuptials between the molecular and the molar. If one affirms the present of Athens via the technicities that individuate it, then the issue of its futurity is no longer that of a radical temporal break, but rather an issue of collective affectivity and the manipulative means that amplify it or diminish it. No longer a line of time which is to be broken, but rather bifurcations; intensive thresholds of fundamental qualitative change. In other words, not an Athenian future to choose from, but an Athenian futurity that chooses us.

References

Altamirano, M. (2016), *Time, Technology and Environment*, Edinburgh: Edinburgh University Press.

Chabot, P. (2013), *The Philosophy of Simondon: Between Technology and Individuation*, trans. A. Krefetz, London: Bloomsbury. Translation of *La philosophie de Simondon*, Paris: Vrin, 2003.

Colebrook, C. (2017), *Futures*, <www.academia.edu/21696436/Futures> (last accessed 15 May 2022).

Foucault, M. (2000), 'Space, Knowledge and Power', in J. D. Faubion (ed.), *Power*, New York: The New Press, pp. 349–64.

Issaias, P. (2014), *Beyond the Informal City: Athens and the Possibility of an Urban Common*, Delft: TU Delft.

Le Corbusier (1986), *Towards a New Architecture*, trans. F. Etchells, London: Architectural Press. Translation of *Vers une architecture*, Paris: Les Éditions G. Crès, 1927.

Leontidou, L. (2012), 'Athens in the Mediterranean "Movement of the Piazzas":

Spontaneity in Material and Virtual Public Spaces in City', *City*, 16 (3): 299–312, <https://doi.org/10.1080/13604813.2012.687870>.

Leroi-Gourhan, A. (1993), *Gesture and Speech*, trans. A. B. Berger, Cambridge, MA: MIT Press. Translation of *Le Geste et la Parole*, Paris: Editions Albin Michel, 1964.

Massumi, B. (2017), 'Histories of Violence: Affect, Power, Violence – The Political is not Personal', interview with B. Evans, *Los Angeles Review of Books*, 13 November, <lareviewofbooks.org/article/histories-of-violence-affect-power-violence-the-political-is-not-personal/#!> (last accessed 15 May 2022).

Meillassoux, Q. (2007), 'Subtraction and Contraction: Deleuze, Immanence, and Matter and Memory', in R. Mackay (ed.), *Collapse*, vol. 3, Falmouth: Urbanomic, pp. 63–107.

Message, K. (2010), 'Black Hole', in A. Parr (ed.), *The Deleuze Dictionary Revised Edition*, Edinburgh: Edinburgh University Press, pp. 33–5.

Phokaides, P., I. Polyzos and L. Triantis (2013), 'Reconsidering the Greater Urbanism Agenda: Crisis, Planning and Architecture in Metropolitan Athens', in B. Upmeyer (ed.), *Monu: Greater Urbanism*, vol. 19, Rotterdam: Board Publishers, pp. 94–9.

Simondon, G. (2017), *On the Mode of Existence of Technical Objects*, trans. C. Malaspina and J. Rogove, Minneapolis, MN: Univocal. Translation of *Du mode d'existence des objets techniques*, Paris: Aubier, 1958.

Stavrides, S. (2010), *Towards the City of Thresholds*, Trento: Professional Dreamers.

PART III

PATRIARCHAL FASCISM

Chapter 15

Fascism and the Entangled Subject, or How to Resist Fascist Toxicity

Christine Daigle

LP MOBILE hier [15 March 2019] 06:26
Attaque dans deux mosquées en Nouvelle-Zélande: 49 morts, un tireur
australien identifié comme un extrémiste de droite arrêté.

RC INFO hier [15 March 2019] 05:21
'C'est une attaque terroriste', déclare la première ministre de la Nouvelle-
Zélande, Jacinda Ardern, alors qu'au moins 49 personnes ont été tuées
dans deux mosquées

RC INFO hier [15 March 2019] 03:49
Massacre en Nouvelle-Zélande: Des tueries commises vendredi dans deux
mosquées ont fait au moins 40 morts et une vingtaine de blessés

LP MOBILE jeu. [14 March 2019] 22:29
Nouvelle-Zélande: fusillade dans une mosquée, plusieurs victimes d'après
les médias sociaux

RC INFO jeu. [14 March 2019] 22:17 [Eastern Standard Time]
Une fusillade a éclaté vendredi après-midi à proximité d'une mosquée de
Christchurch en Nouvelle-Zélande

Above is the feed of news alerts that I woke up to on 15 March 2019.
Before drifting into sleep the night before I had heard the alert vibrations on my phone which was lying beside my pillow. I did not check
the phone at the time and chose sleep. Waking up to this was brutal.
Yet another mass shooting. Another act of white supremacy, targeting the Muslim community this time. Despicable violence and hatred
perpetrated against a community that has been consistently and increasingly demonised since 9/11 and more so since the election of the 45th
president of the United States.

I began reading the details. A white supremacist perpetrator. An elaborate plan. Semi-automatic weapons. A manifesto published online the

day before, promising a live streaming of the attack. A GoPro camera. Almost 17 minutes of Facebook live streaming. The gunman leaving his car, exclaiming: 'Let's get this party started.'[1] Chilling.

As outrage and debate unfolded, the same questions were recurring. Shouldn't powerful media enterprises such as YouTube, Twitter, Facebook and any other similar platform automatically remove material propagating hatred against groups and showing the actual killing of humans? Why have the algorithms of filter tools failed and what are the potential outcomes of this? What can its ripple effects be? CNN correspondent Anna Coren, visibly shaken, described the video and her own reaction to it, saying: 'It is one of the most horrendous things that I have ever seen in my entire career.' She added, 'It was like watching a video game' as the shooter proceeded systematically to ensure each person was dead, shooting them point blank.[2] A still image on the internet matches Coren's description, an image I choose not to reference here. It is very much like any image one might see in a first-person shooter video game where the player assumes the position of a combatant holding a weapon and searching for targets to shoot. Again: chilling.

Fascist modes of thinking and their concrete political materialisations have been spreading at an alarming rate. Whether one lives in or next to a fascistic regime geographically has become irrelevant due to the virtual spaces in which we all exist – sometimes very intimate spaces such as the space beside my pillow. Our mediatic virtual selves[3] are, whether we seek it or not, constantly exposed to the many expressions of ultranationalism, racism, sexism, trans- and homophobia that fascistic regimes support and champion along with an ever-increasing tendency to further concentrate the means of power in the hands of the very few. We all suffer from this since there is no space where we can escape the pervasive reach of fascism.

As a posthumanist material feminist thinker, I conceive of the human being as a radically entangled being, subjectively and materially. As such, we are vulnerable to the toxicities of the world, be they material – such as pollutants and heavy metals – or immaterial – such as hate speech which, inevitably, ends up taking violent material form through the actions it precipitates and encourages, as in the case of the Christchurch massacre. When faced with an incessant barrage of violence and hatred, one reaction might be to retreat from the social and virtual spheres, weave for oneself a little cocoon of isolation to lick one's wounds and be safe from any further harm. Exposing oneself to the pervasive onslaught of the media can be absolutely overwhelming. This desire to retreat, however, is as dangerous as it may be tempting. First, as the entangled beings we are, such a retreat is impossible: we cannot disentangle our-selves from our manifold relations. Second, even if it were possible it would be undesirable, as disengagement gives more clout to fascist modes of thinking as it further isolates us, as I argue below. We must resist this desire and continue to engage or else we might contribute to our own demise.

I understand all beings as radically entangled and propose that we are transjective beings; that is, we are concomitantly trans-subjective and trans-objective. We are always caught up in a field of tensions and forces, being done and undone, both by ourselves and by other beings we are entangled with, doing and undoing them as well, both subjectively and materially. Our bodies are enbrained and our minds are embodied, to use a phrase put forward by Rosi Braidotti (2018). We are assemblages of experiences, consciousness, materiality and so forth, and we exist on an ontological plane in which agency is attributed to all beings – thereby eliminating human exceptionalism. We are bundles of multiple agentic capacities, some intentional – such as the choices we make – but many more the expression of the intentless direction that biochemical processes provide at the foundation of life and upon which we make our choices (Frost 2016). We are not the individuals closed upon themselves, autonomous, and separate from other beings that the humanist tradition has proposed. We are permeable 'dividuals', our skin, orifices and porous mucous surfaces allowing for the transit and transfer of cells and substances that sustain and alter our lives. No traffic through membranes, no life. No intermingling with one's habitat, no life. These processes are material, through and through, and entangle-ment is fundamental to life processes (Frost 2016: 145).

Each person is an assemblage of effervescent agency or, as Bennett would put it, an 'interfolding network of humanity and nonhumanity' (2010: 31). We are dividuals whose bodies and overall beings vibrate along with all material and immaterial agencies: assemblages that operate within congregational assemblages. With Alaimo, we can refer to ourselves as transcorporeal beings. This 'entails a rather disconcerting sense of being immersed within incalculable, interconnected material agencies' (Alaimo 2010: 17). We are 'the very stuff of the messy, contin-gent, emergent mix of the material world' (Alaimo 2010: 11). As porous beings we are speared by the materiality surrounding us at the same time that we seep into that materiality. This all means that we are toxic bodies with exceedingly leaky borders. We are exposed subjects, 'penetrated by substances and forces that can never be properly accounted for' (Alaimo 2016: 5). Alaimo's focus is on the various ways in which our bodies are rendered toxic because of how we have disrupted and polluted our environment. Because we are transcorporeal and exposed, we are vulnerable in our materiality. I add to this that we are even more vulnerable in that we are not only transcorporeal, but also trans-subjective.

I have explained in some detail elsewhere how trans-subjective operations function.[4] Language, discourse, social imaginaries, ideologies, discussions with friends or non-friends, readings, viewings: all the phenomenological experiences we have in this shared world are equally constitutive of our selves. That self-constitution occurs in an entangled fashion with our material constitution and is not always conscious. In fact, a lot of the trans-subjective constitution of ourselves occurs at a pre-reflective and non-conscious level and is as potent, if not more, than conscious processes of self-constitution. The operations of power so well described by Foucault – or the ways in which women come to interiorise their own oppression as described by Beauvoir – are examples of this, as are the operations of the media on viewers and how being exposed to ideas – directly or indirectly – may shape our subjectivities in ways we are often unable to even acknowledge. While some experiences may allow us to see the impact in a most vivid manner, with traumatic experiences for example, I argue that every experience, even the most mundane, has constitutive impact.

Therefore, just as much as we are permeated by the toxicity of the polluted ecosystems and habitats in which we live, as trans-objective beings, we also suffer from the toxicity of the trans-subjective realms in which we navigate. The transjective being is vulnerable materially and subjectively. It is exposed to a manifold of toxic entanglements, including the toxicity of fascist modes of thinking that permeates us in multiple ways.[5] The amount of exposure to toxicity of my transjective being increased dramatically as I read the thread of news alerts in my feed that morning of 15 March. The sudden exposure to the rhetoric and politics of hatred and its violent manifestation that day in the mass killing, an exposure not only experienced by those in the close vicinity of the massacre but by everyone who encountered it via news feeds as well as still and moving images, contributed to the spread of the fascist mode of thinking that motivated the perpetrator. Fascism spreads like a virus: sometimes violently but more often insidiously.[6] As mentioned above, Alaimo claims that we are toxic bodies since we are permeated by toxic substances that penetrate our bodies through the various porous membranes that constitute us. Just as much as we cannot control or escape this process – indeed, we live in the Anthropocene epoch wherein the human impact has left a trace on a global scale and in the most remote locations – we also cannot control or escape the processes whereby the ambient political dystopias permeate us. As the transjective beings we are, the various dystopias in which we exist permeate us. We are rendered toxic materially and subjectively.[7]

The contemporary human in developed countries is exposed in one day to the same amount of information it would have taken a medieval human a lifetime to be exposed to.[8] Media, especially digital and social media, have contributed to this fantastic acceleration. Some would lament that while each individual has access to this great amount of information,[9] they do not have either in-depth or sometimes any understanding at all of many issues. The act of scrolling through news feeds on Facebook, Twitter, Instagram or one's favourite news outlet's app provides one with snippets of information through headlines, but rarely does one click on an item and read a whole article. Long articles tend to be skimmed through or only read partially even when the person clicking on the link has a high interest in the issue. The overload of information therefore does not translate into a better-informed citizenry.

One must add to this the important phenomena of information bubbles and echo chambers.[10] Beyond self-selecting our preferred media on traditional analogue platforms such as newspaper, television and radio, which creates its own set of information bubbles, algorithms track our various clicks and the time we spend reading any item we encounter on the web. Just as algorithms ensure that the shoes or dresses you shopped for using your browser propagate adverts in your Facebook or Instagram feed, algorithms monitor what type of information you are interested in and the sources they come from and populate your various feeds with similar items. This generates information bubbles which isolate individuals from one another due to their own individual browsing histories. My news is not the same as my neighbour's news. We may partake in some of the same bubbles if we have the same kind of political leanings and other cultural, religious and social beliefs and interests such as cute kittens. However, I do not get exposed to news originating in far-right information outlets or websites because algorithms know I have no interest in these. Nor do far-right adherents get exposed to information originating from moderate or left-leaning sources that I regularly consult. Navigating the information bubbles and associated echo chambers – we comment and respond to posts from authors/news personalities/Twitter activists/friends and acquaintances with whom we mostly agree – we find an echo of our own beliefs that serves to reinforce those beliefs and positions we hold, our worldview. We can no longer talk to one another once we become a part of radically separate bubbles.

This is how affective polarisation is reinforced in our contemporary context. Analysing Canada's particular situation as next-door northern neighbour to the United States, Stephen Marche argues that the civil war had already started to unfold, well before the election of Donald J. Trump, and that Canadians have to figure out how to handle this. He explains that American political life has been polarised since the 1970s and that the phenomenon has accelerated since the mid-1990s. This affective polarisation of politics is now at an all-time peak.[11] It has arrived at the point where many people would not want their children to marry someone who is a partisan of the other party, and where trans-partisan Thanksgiving dinners, that is, dinners at which family members are from both the Republican and Democratic parties, last on average 50 minutes less than mono-partisan dinners.[12] Given the importance accorded to Thanksgiving in American culture, this is not a banal difference.

The fact that we cannot communicate across divides, that our worlds look so radically different depending on which bubbles we call home, allows for damaging political ideologies to creep in. When individuals are isolated and populations fragmented and divided in a way that posits the other as a threat, fascistic modes of thinking can thrive. In the conclusion of her powerful book *The Origins of Totalitarianism*, Hannah Arendt explains

> The ideal subject of totalitarian rule is not the convinced Nazi or the convinced communist, but people for whom the distinction between fact and fiction (i.e., the reality of experience) and the distinction between true and false (i.e. the standards of thought) no longer exist. (1966: 474)

It is not hard to see that the information bubbles and echo chambers in which we exist have blurred the distinction between fact and fiction for a significant number of people. The increase in conspiracy theories along with growing scepticism towards science, which makes room for anti-vaxxers and flat earthers, provides fertile ground for the creation of heightened numbers of individuals who become susceptible to fascistic modes of thought. Adding to her key insight about ordinary persons and their vulnerability to totalitarianism,[13] Arendt expresses an important worry which emerges when individuals experience solitude and isolation. 'Totalitarian government, like all tyrannies, certainly could not exist without destroying the public realm of life' (1966: 475), she says. The destruction of the public space, the agora, may lead to the emergence of totalitarian regimes. The notion that spaces such as social media are providing us with a missing 'real-life' agora is easily challenged. That space provides opportunities for ideas to be expressed and to collide, for thinking and exchange to unfold and for discussion and argumentation. Isolated in our bubbles, however, we only ever encounter the same ideas we already have. Caught in this loop, there is no generative encounter of ideas.[14]

Fascism thrives on such terrain where the collective is weakened due to the isolation of individuals who live under the illusion that they have more interactions and an increased social existence due to the proliferation of virtual spaces. What is fascism and how does it operate? Just like ordinary sexism, there is such a thing as ordinary fascism. The imposition of moral and social rules in the most mundane choices and behaviours are the expression of a microfascism that Deleuze and Guattari identify in their work. According to them, microfascism is as damaging as macrofascism, especially when it aligns with the latter to foster the loss of critical reactivity to one's political entanglements. In fact, microfascism prepares the ground for macrofascism. Deleuze and Guattari note that 'What makes fascism dangerous is its molecular or micropolitical power, for it is a mass movement: a cancerous body rather than a totalitarian organism' (TP, 215). Every instance of microfascism is like a cancerous cell, ready to multiply and infect the social body. As transjective beings isolated in our bubbles and exposed to this toxicity, we may be scooped up by fascist modes of thinking and movements.

Reflecting on his youth in fascist Italy, Umberto Eco describes fourteen characteristics that make a political regime fascist. What he is describing is 'Ur-fascism', or eternal fascism. Eco argues that one is dealing with fascism when a regime displays one or more of these characteristics. They are: a cult of tradition, anti-modernism, championing action for action's sake, considering disagreement as treason, displaying a fear of difference, appealing to a frustrated middle class, obsessing with a plot (which often includes thinking of oneself as besieged), shifting the rhetoric about enemies (construing them as both too weak and too strong), considering pacifism as trafficking with the enemy, displaying contempt for the weak, educating to become heroes, machismo, selective populism and using Newspeak – making 'use of an impoverished vocabulary, and an elementary syntax, in order to limit the instruments for complex and critical reasoning' (Eco 1995). The Italy of Eco's youth displayed many of these characteristics to various degrees, as did other European authoritarian regimes between the two world wars and after. Eco concludes his essay with a warning: 'Ur-Fascism can come back under the most innocent of disguises.' This means for him that 'Freedom and liberation are an unending task.'

We should take Eco's warning to heart since many contemporary political movements and an alarmingly growing number of regimes are displaying fascistic characteristics. The other – be they other because of their religion, ethnicity, gender, sexual orientation, language, geographical origin – is demonised, barriers and walls are erected to prevent their mobility between countries and continents, or they are left drifting and drowning at sea. The others are constrained to neighbourhoods in certain urban and suburban settings, they are imprisoned for the smallest deed or they are shot on their way to a convenience store. The disintegrating social climate in the US allows for certain groups to fuel and feed off the discontent of particular classes of citizens. The use and abuse of social and traditional media to initiate suspicion of the liberal and critical media – labelling it as 'fake news' – and to ostracise certain groups – through actions taken by individuals in positions of power, including the most powerful individual who occupied the presidency from 2017 to 2021 – has brought up the resurgence of 'Newspeak'.[15] Rallies and public speeches by 45[16] are perfect examples of the use of impoverished language that Eco identifies as a major characteristic of Ur-fascism. Populism is on the rise around the world, creating an unstable social and political climate. Our environment is toxic no matter how we look at it.

As a consequence, we all suffer from various degrees of post-traumatic stress disorder (PTSD). Doug Specht (2018) and Anthony Feinstein (2017) in their respective columns explore the impact violent news and their associated images have on journalists. Feinstein explains that the adverse psychological effect of working in war zones has now expanded to newsrooms where journalists are on the receiving end of user-generated content. The war zone enters the newsroom at the other end of the world with one click, as citizens take their own pictures or videos and forward them to journalists. Sorting through these images to decide what is 'newsworthy' can cause great anxiety and trauma. With this in mind, Specht argues that journalism schools need to better prepare future journalists to face the violent images they will be confronted with in the newsroom on a daily basis. According to him, journalists need to be better prepared and have access to better support. The problem, however, is that this is not only true of journalists but of anyone with access to a news feed, be it traditional and analogue or social and digital. We are constantly immersed and exposed in a world gone mad, and following this state of affairs puts us closely in contact with the worst and the horrible. One in fact need not even be following the news to be exposed in this way, since an accidental click while scrolling online or seeing a friend's post on their wall can have the same impact if it conveys such material.

One cannot 'unring a bell'. Once an experience has been had, its impact is inscribed in the assemblage we are as transjective beings and leaves a trace that cannot be erased. Leigh M. Johnson discusses Werner Herzog's experience of listening to the audio recording of Timothy Treadwell and Amie Huguenard's gruesome deaths from a grizzly bear attack in his documentary *Grizzly Man* (2005) and later remarking to a friend of Treadwell's: 'You must never listen to this' (Johnson 2015). Herzog regrets having listened. The audio's trace will stay with him well beyond its disappearance from material soundwaves, just as the images from the Christchurch attack seen by Anna Coren will stay with her. Multiple images have left their traces in my transjective being because I follow activist and journalist Shaun King on Twitter (@shaunking), who relentlessly exposes racist injustice and attacks on black people in the US and has successfully launched many internet searches for guilty parties. How many innocent black persons have I seen punched, stabbed, shot at? Gut-wrenching experiences of witnessing violence and hatred. When I see a tweet that starts with 'All hands on deck!' – King's way of capturing attention and launching a search for culprits on Twitter – I often have a wish to skip because I do not want or need to see yet another act of senseless violence to know that this is happening. And yet there is a duty to bear witness, not in a voyeuristic sense, but to take on the suffering, to acknowledge that the violence happens and, in bearing part of the trauma, to vow to work towards changing the world for the better.[17] A difficult task if ever there was one.

It has been argued that despite the fact that millennials are a major political force, they are reluctant to use their power. Beyond the apathy people are too quick to project on to them, they often experience sentiments of hopelessness and helplessness.[18] Many feminists are beginning to feel the same way. Despite the #MeToo movement and what one thought would be a defining moment from which one could not come back, Brett Kavanaugh was still appointed to the Supreme Court of the US even after Christine Blasey-Ford was heard as a witness on 27 September 2018 by the special committee of Senate and was deemed a credible person by members of that committee. The toll this has taken on her is quite unimaginable. The toll it has taken on millions of citizens, in the US and abroad, is also hard to measure. Whoever spent hours with her, bearing witness to her incredible act of courage and hoping, if only for a minute for the most cynical like me, that this would change the course of things has suffered an incredible blow. On social media that day, after having been mesmerised for hours by Blasey-Ford but completely unable to watch the live streaming of Kavanaugh's response – I caught up with excerpts later in the day – I posted on social media that we – 'we' being the people in my media bubble composed of feminists and liberal-minded people – were so outraged only because we knew this would all be for naught. I hate that it turned out that I was right when Kavanaugh's nomination was later confirmed, but there was really no other explanation for the collective anger that was felt and expressed since, if we truly believed the hearing would change anything, we would have been hopeful rather than bitterly angry. I was infected by the affective overload of this, the toxicity experienced as Blasey-Ford was viciously trashed in the media and as senators exercised high levels of bad faith and hypocrisy. I was sick for a good three weeks thereafter, needing antibiotic treatment. It was not the flu, it was not a cold, just a virus and me needing to rest. Perhaps my transjective body's way of saying enough of this toxicity.

I reiterate my earlier question: What ought one to do? Weave for oneself a cosy cocoon and prevent the toxicity from reaching us? Desensitise ourselves to it maybe? What is there to do when fascist modes of thinking launch attacks on profound values in ways that erode even the best-intentioned human's stamina and capacity to act and counter damaging modes of thinking and propaganda? As the interconnected transjective beings we are, we face an unprecedented connection via the internet and social media. We are immediately confronted with the racism, phobias, violence and conflict occurring in the world via those platforms. The barrage from far-right regimes of all stripes that seem to busy themselves with the dismantling of any kind of social progress accomplished in the last decades is disheartening. The staunchest activists feel as though they are running out of steam and the energy levels are at their lowest, faced with the inexplicable continued success of populist regimes that are nationalist, racist, sexist, homo- and transphobic and religiously intolerant. It feels as though all the gains made through hard-won battles to make the world a more inclusive space and efforts to ensure that all are allowed to thrive are being attacked and eliminated one by one.[19]

We are faced with important risks. Just like bacteria that are becoming more and more resistant to antibiotics, fascistic modes of thinking look as though they are becoming more and more resistant to critical scrutiny. But more importantly, we run the risk of becoming desensitised, of being complicit when our energy levels are so depleted because the barrage of bad to worse news never stops. We risk becoming more resistant to evil. By being repeatedly exposed to it, do we run the risk of banalising evil? Of becoming Eichmann? Yet another mass shooting. Yet another bombing. Yet another black male slaughtered by US police because they were wearing a hoodie. Exposure to these images via one's Facebook or Twitter feed or any other source is constant. The barrage of images that angers also desensitises. It is a very fine line between this anger and desensitisation. In an interesting piece on the necessity to fight detachment, Alex Bond explains that a detached point of view is impossible for a scientist. As a pollution researcher working with birds, he engages in collecting beached birds to inquire into the impact of plastic and its ingestion. He says:

> Anyway, you work all through the day, cutting open dead birds, hauling out plastic. If you don't take time at the end of the day, or take a day off, to just process and talk about what you go through, it's not very healthy at all. I am convinced that there's a case to be made for symptoms similar to PTSD, such as a reticence to discuss some of the events, and thoughts that result from them, in conservation scientists. (Bond and Liboiron 2018)

He adds: 'I think if you shut off emotions, if you're not careful, you lose part of your humanity. If offing a beached bird becomes normal, there's something wrong.' I agree with Bond.

The power of fascist modes of thinking and the use of media by its proponents are such that it is easy to feel depleted and worn down, to start thinking 'this is normal'. Such a response is worrisome as it may allow those fascist modes of thinking to spread even further. Yet we can resist fascist toxicity precisely by understanding, embracing and championing ourselves as entangled. The entangled being that gives in to fascist modes of thinking gives in to its own demise as it allows for more toxicity to unfold and affect itself and the world. If anger is the driver of political action, of resistance to fascism, we have a duty to remain enraged. My grandmother was a wise person. As the impatient and easily angered teen that I was, and puzzled at her cool-headedness and lack of anger, I asked her one day how she managed never to get angry at things. Her answer was stunning in its simplicity: 'It is too hard to make oneself un-angry again.' I dutifully remind myself of this whenever I lose my cool and ruin my day because the toaster burned my bread, traffic has made me late, or a customer service representative has got my request wrong, again. Taking my grandmother's answer as a piece of advice is good for everyday frustrations. It has the added advantage of allowing one to save one's energy to be angry at what matters, not waste time on trivial annoyances. We have a duty, more than ever, to stay angry at the state of the world and to fight worldviews that isolate and disconnect us, that infect us with their toxicity. We must not become un-angry.

This anger, however, ought to – perhaps paradoxically – take the form of an affirmative empathy. Brigitte Bargetz argues that new materialisms are efficient tools to address contemporary political issues and the associated risk of depoliticisation. She sees new materialism's approach, one I embrace as a posthumanist material feminist, as extremely potent since it resists melancholia or paranoia in creating and inventing new political horizons. It allows for combating widespread feelings of depletion, powerlessness and despair

> through developing a politics that call for a performative tactics of counter-feelings. They produce a space of counter-manifestation, and thus express an emphatic and optimistic longing and search for a new or renewed politics and agency. They signal 'wrestling with despair' (West 2008: 216), a despair that is widely felt within the political and theoretical present. (Bargetz 2018: 191)

As transjective beings, we are entangled with all other beings, big and small, material and subjective, concrete and abstract. If we come to embrace ourselves as such and champion entanglement rather than attempting to guard ourselves against it, we will engage in affirmative empathy towards others and towards ourselves. This requires opening ourselves to the potential violence, to the toxicity we are surrounded and permeated by, suffering from it, suffering along with others – human and non-human alike – to bear witness and keep one's anger alive so that we can resist and subvert damaging fascist modes of thinking and what they advance. It is the only way to fight toxicity.

Acknowledgement

This chapter draws on research supported by the Social Sciences and Humanities Research Council of Canada

Notes

1. As reported in this article from *The Washington Post*: <https://www.washingtonpost.com/local/lets-get-this-party-started-new-zealand-gunman-narrated-his-chilling-rampage/2019/03/15/fb3db352-4748-11e9-90f0-0ccfeec87a61_story.html?utm_term=.e5b95e81ce85> (last accessed 15 May 2022).
2. The whole segment where Anna Coren discusses this can be seen at <https://www.cnn.com/videos/world/2019/03/15/new-zealand-mosque-shooting-video-description-coren-sot-vpx.cnn> (last accessed 15 May 2022).

3. Those parts of ourselves that are entangled with media and virtual spaces such as the internet.

4. See Daigle 2017. At the time of writing that essay, I had not decided on the term 'transjectivity' to convey how both types of constitution are intermingled and inseparable.

5. Insofar as fascist modes of thinking cause damage to human societies – which I doubt is debatable – they can be labelled as toxic. Something can be deemed toxic when it is extremely harmful or malicious and this is the case with fascist thinking. Toxicity is also a matter of degree. Some substances can be neutral or even beneficial when ingested in the right doses, but harmful or even deadly when ingested in doses that are too high. Such is the case with water. It may very well be that one needs to expose oneself to small doses of toxic discourses and worldviews to at least be able to grasp them and fight them effectively. I come back to ways to resist the toxicity of fascism towards the end of the chapter which involve exposing oneself to it.

6. Finalising this essay during the Covid-19 pandemic gives this statement even more potency. We have learned – and continue to learn – how the virus spreads in many different ways, and how the amount of disruption it wreaks is distributed on a wide scale from asymptomatism to death. The same can be said about fascism, depending on a number of factors.

7. In addition to the multilayered anxiety derived from the various toxicities permeating us, we may also suffer from environmental anxiety. As entangled transjective beings, we are part of the affective fabric through which we may feel the immense pressures that other species and the natural world are facing. In addition to our own extinction, which is ever more imminent, we have contributed to degrade the Earth-system and brought to extinction an inordinate number of species. We are thereby toxic in two ways: first, by being permeated by the toxicities – material and subjective – in which we exist and, second, by acting in the world in a way that refuses to acknowledge our own entanglements, positing ourselves as exceptional and entitled and proceeding to extract and consume other beings as resources rather than embracing them as instances of entangled life. Empathic beings who see themselves as entangled and kin to all life suffer anxiety in partaking in a species that is so damaging. Others, perhaps more selfishly, suffer anxiety in their mourning the extinction of their own species as well as some preferred other species due to human action. The level of distress and despair that the Anthropocene epoch and its environmental crisis generates adds to the toxicities that permeate us in a significant way.

8. In an essay published by the BBC, Gaia Vince (2013) discusses cities and how urban life has changed us. Contrasting the virtual urban spaces generated by the likes of Facebook, Twitter and Grindr, she points out that the virtual is both local and global. One has access to local and global information just as easily. 'The virtual city does have a more problematic side, however. Never has there been so much information about so much of our lives in such an accessible form. In the course of a day, the average person in a Western city is said to be exposed to as much data as someone in the 15th century would encounter in their entire life.' There are many sources discussing the notion of 'information overload'. Many challenge the supposed newness of this phenomenon, pointing to the fact that even pre-printing press scholars complained about being overloaded with information. That the phenomenon has been exacerbated by the printing press and then by the digitisation of information is not questioned, however.

9. Granted, this access is universal only as a potential. In reality, many individuals do not have wide access to information due to the circumstances in which they live or sometimes, albeit more rarely, by choice.

10. There is a lot of information about these phenomena available on the web. The following link provides a succinct overview: <https://fs.blog/2017/07/filter-bubbles/> (last accessed 15 May 2022); see also Sadagopan 2019. For a more in-depth analysis, see the work of Wendy Hui Kyong Chun. In her *Updating to Remain the Same* (2017), she investigates what she calls the 'creepiness' of new media and such phenomena as networks, internet friending and outing. Networks are formed through algorithmic analysis of various engagements by users – liking or disliking content, for example – leading to the formation of 'neighborhoods [which] are forms of voluntary segregation – that YOU reside with people "like YOU", whose actions preempt and shape YOUR own' (Chun 2017: 120). She opens her later essay 'Queerying Homophily' by pointing out that homophily is 'the axiom that similarity breeds connection [and] grounds contemporary network science'. She emphasises that 'homophily, love as love of the same, closes the world it pretends to open; it makes cyberspace a series of echo chambers' (Chun 2018: 60). Furthermore, 'networks perpetuate identity via "default" variables and axioms' (2018: 61) and their homophily thereby naturalises discrimination (2018: 81). She calls for a reprise of theory in order to do away with the identity politics at the heart of networks.

11. See Marche 2019. Marche's essay is a combination of anticipation fiction and essay on the state of affairs in American politics and how it may affect Canadians. He says that Canadians have one job: figuring out what will happen in our neighbour's country and how it will impact us. The question for Canadians is: 'What do we do if the US falls apart?'

12. Marche discussed the phenomenon of affective polarisation and this piece of information on the CBC radio show *The Sunday Edition* with Michael Enright on 29 October 2018. The segment where he discusses this starts at 6:18: <https://www.cbc.ca/radio/thesundayedition/the-sunday-edition-october-28-2018-1.4877630/what-should-canada-do-if-there-s-a-civil-war-in-the-u-s-1.4877641> (last accessed 5 April 2019).

13. Her attention to the non-committed, the non-extremists here, is reminiscent of her interest in Adolf Eichmann. Confronted with this criminal at his trial – a man she expected to exude moral vileness but who, instead, came across as an insignificant, banal office clerk who was just 'doing his job' – allowed her to coin the concept of the 'banality of evil' (Arendt 2006). Evil that is banal is in some ways more horrendous than evil that is not. Its insidiousness makes it more difficult to unearth and fight.

14. I would not want to argue that such spaces are completely ungenerative. For example, use of social media and virtual spaces contributed to the Arab Spring in significant ways that helped the movement achieve the proportions that it did. While the full impact of this movement is difficult to assess, some positive, generative outcomes certainly unfolded.

15. Eco claims that certain uses of language contribute to making people susceptible to fascist control. I see an interesting phenomenon to which I do not have a full explanation. In recent years, we have seen an increased sanitisation of language driven by a concern for acceptance, de-stigmatisation and inclusivity. The use of 'n-word', 'r-word', 'f-word' is meant to produce a more civil society, and yet there is increased ostracisation, racism, ableism, sexism. Our societies seem less and less civil. Might the use of sanitised language be an instance of Orwellian doublethink and Newspeak?

16. Many critics and media personalities such as Trevor Noah referred to Trump by using '45' as a way to express their resistance to associating his name with the presidency. I applaud this and resist using his name as much as is possible.

17. Judith Butler's book *The Force of Nonviolence* (2020) offers an interesting

take on how we ought to respond to violence as well as how the non-violent resistance to violence is often portrayed as itself the most violent by political institutions. Reading this as the BLM protests were unfolding in summer 2020 and as the American administration started to demonise non-violent protesters referring to them as Antifa and anarchists to be feared was an uncanny experience to say the least.

18. For a glimpse of this, see this article from the *Intelligencer* on the 2018 midterms in the US and young people's intention not to vote: <http://nymag.com/intelligencer/2018/10/12-young-people-on-why-they-probably-wont-vote.html?fbclid=IwAR2zwCfZxN-Ohh7SpnSkyod4g4ZVSeCaanQmvOoJXZHB-PAf1IWNwdavCMQQ> (last accessed 15 May 2022).

19. The unfolding social unrest in the USA and the heightened crisis following the murder of George Floyd and ensuing BLM protests are potent signs of the erosion of the social fabric in that country, as well as a reassuring indication that resistance can be revived. The BLM movement is not new but was suddenly and powerfully revived by this act of hatred as well as other killings of black people at about the same time. As mentioned earlier, this has been a long-standing problem in the USA, and the almost daily occurrence of such killings may have caused some short-term desensitisation. But the capacity, and duty, to be angry remained and has been revived (more on this duty in the conclusion). At the time of finalising this chapter, Justice Ruth Bader Ginsburg died, and many activists are feeling great despair at the loss of such a champion of the rights of women and minorities. At the same time, a movement of resistance is building as the same activists reshape their despair into a mode of anger that is aiming at continuing Justice Ginsburg's lifelong fight. Perhaps it is the case that the higher the degree of despair, the higher the anger and resistance must be.

References

Alaimo, S. (2010), *Bodily Natures: Science, Environment, and the Material Self*, Bloomington: Indiana University Press.

Alaimo, S. (2016), *Exposed. Environmental Politics and Pleasures in Posthuman Times*, Minneapolis: University of Minnesota Press.

Arendt, H. (1966), *The Origins of Totalitarianism*, new edn, New York: Harcourt, Brace and World.

Arendt, H. (2006), *Eichmann in Jerusalem: A Report on the Banality of Evil*, New York: Penguin.

Bargetz, B. (2018), 'Longing for Agency: New Materialisms' Wrestling with Despair', *European Journal of Women's Studies*, 26 (2): 181–94.

Bennett, J. (2010), *Vibrant Matter. A Political Ecology of Things*, Durham, NC: Duke University Press.

Bond, A., and M. Liboiron (2018), 'Science with Heart: Dealing with Pollution, Harm, and Suffering as a Scientist', 3 December, <https://civiclaboratory.nl/2018/12/03/science-with-heart-dealing-with-pollution-harm-and-suffering-as-a-scientist/> (last accessed 6 April 2019).

Braidotti, R. (2018), 'A Theoretical Framework for the Critical Posthumanities', *Theory, Culture & Society*, 36 (6): 31–61.

Butler, J. (2020), *The Force of Nonviolence: An Ethico-Political Bind*, London: Verso.

Chun, W. H. K. (2017), *Updating to Remain the Same: Habitual New Media*, Cambridge, MA: MIT Press.

Chun, W. H. K. (2018), 'Queerying Homophily', in C. Apprich, W. H. K. Chun,

F. Cramer and H. Steyerl, *Pattern Discrimination*, Minneapolis: University of Minnesota Press, pp. 59–97.

Daigle, C. (2017), 'Trans-subjectivity/Trans-objectivity', in H. Fielding and D. Olkowski (eds), *Feminist Phenomenology Futures*, Bloomington: Indiana University Press, pp. 183–99.

Eco, U. (1995), 'Ur-Fascism', *The New York Review of Books*, 42 (11).

Feinstein, A. (2017), 'Violent News: Psychological Trauma a New Risk in Digital Age', *The Conversation* (Canada edition), 9 July, <https://theconversation. com/violent-news-psychological-trauma-a-new-risk-in-digital-age-79161> (last accessed 6 April 2019).

Frost, S. (2016), *Biocultural Creatures: Toward a New Theory of the Human*, Durham, NC: Duke University Press.

Johnson, L. M. (2015), 'On Teaching our Incapacity to Unexperience', October, <http://www.readmorewritemorethinkmorebemore.com/2015/10/on-teaching-our-incapacity-to.html?q=unexperience> (last accessed 27 March 2019).

Marche, S. (2019), 'America's Next Civil War', *The Walrus*, 22 October (updated 12 March 2019), <https://thewalrus.ca/americas-next-civil-war/> (last accessed 5 April 2019).

Sadagopan, S. M. (2019), 'Feedback Loops and Echo Chambers: How Algorithms Amplify Viewpoints', *The Conversation* (Canada edition), 4 February, <https:// theconversation.com/feedback-loops-and-echo-chambers-how-algorithms-amplify-viewpoints-107935> (last accessed 6 April 2019).

Specht, D. (2018), 'Violent Videos Put Journalists at Increased Risk of Post-traumatic Stress', *The Conversation* (Canada edition), 12 October, <https://theconversa tion.com/violent-videos-put-journalists-at-increased-risk-of-post-traumatic-stress-103179> (last accessed 6 April 2019).

Vince, G. (2013), 'Cities: How Crowded Life is Changing Us', 17 May, <http:// www.bbc.com/future/story/20130516-how-city-life-is-changing-us> (last accessed 25 September 2020).

West, C. (2008), *Hope on a Tightrope*, Carlsbad, CA: Hay House Publishers.

Chapter 16

Reclaiming Vital Materialism's Affirmative, Anti-fascist Powers: A Deleuzo-Guattarian New Materialist Exploration of the Fascist Within

Delphi Carstens and Evelien Geerts

Introduction

In these times of pandemic uncertainty, socio-economic devastation and ecological catastrophe, extractivist capitalism continues to widen the gap between 'grievable' and 'ungrievable lives' (Butler 2020: n.p.). As neo-liberal exploitation, radical inequality, racism and xenophobic nationalism reproduce and strengthen one another in the globalised arena, the troubling spectre of fascism manifests itself yet again, necessitating a turn to several Deleuzo-Guattarian lines of critical-creative analysis and inquiry. As Gilles Deleuze writes, the broad aim of the schizoanalytical programme he developed alongside his philosophical companion Félix Guattari, is to bypass 'the strange detour of the other' (B, 356), whereby desire becomes entangled in a polarised politics of identity during times of crisis and *ressentiment*. If, as these philosophers argue, fascism – and various types of neo-fascism – can be conceived of in terms of desire, then ethical, political and philosophical projects must work towards mediating desire's pure flows of affective yearning and preventing these flows from violent stratification (fascism) or radical destratification (madness). In this respect, the concepts and strings of thought that have been developed in Deleuze and Guattari's individual writings, as well as in their collective oeuvre and various reinterpretations, are essential to contemporary critical theoretical projects that are concerned with the problematics of desire, alterity and (inter)subjectivity.

In this essay, we explore how several Deleuzo-Guattarian anti-fascist concepts, such as the Body without Organs (BwO), together with (mainly Deleuzo-Guattarian-influenced) new materialist approaches towards affirmation, nomadism and vitalism, may help us to 'keep an eye on all that is fascist, even [the fascist] inside us' (TP, 165). Such an analysis is needed to frame the rise of neo-fascist political and economic regimes operating under the guise of neoliberal capitalism today – regimes we are both well acquainted with due to our situated positionalities as inhabitants of an increasingly interconnected world and as citizens of respectively South Africa and Belgium, where race and ethnicity-based apartheid and separatist movements are triggering cyclical eruptions of fascism. Key to such a Deleuzo-Guattarian analysis of (anti-)fascism is an understanding of vitalism's genealogy as well as the ethico-political debates around desire conceived of as *élan vital* (vital force). We begin our investigation, therefore, by contouring and reclaiming a more affirmative, anti-fascist and thus potentially emancipatory vitalism from certain *Lebensphilosophien* that are currently being exploited to fuel fear-mongering neo-fascist ideologies as well as exploitative neoliberal economics.

From Philosophies of Life to Fascist Biopolitics: A Mapping of Vitalism and its Critical Variants

Although many contemporary thinkers (for example, Wolfe 2010; Braidotti 2013; Haraway 2016) have labelled today's zeitgeist as de-anthropocentric and posthumanist, spotlighting what could be regarded as the era of 'vital politics, of somatic ethics, and of biological responsibility' (Rose 2007: 40), the critical theoretical focus on matters of life (and death) is not new: *Lebensphilosophien* – the philosophies of life (*Leben*) and of living experience (*Erleben*) – played a major role in the nineteenth century. This collection of vitalism-emphasising philosophies[1] formed a cultural-philosophical resistance movement, eventually mutating into the pan-European idea that 'an aesthetic view had to be politicized in order to be realized' (Lebovic 2006: 35). Bio-aesthetical, and then biopolitical, *Lebensphilosophien* drew on German Romanticism, anti-Kantianism and anti-positivism, and were fuelled by the logocentrism-attacking philosophies of Kierkegaard, Schopenhauer and Nietzsche.

By the first decades of the twentieth century, the ranks of this movement had swelled to include Ludwig Klages, Henri Bergson, Jacob van Uexküll, Georg Simmel, Hans Driesch and Wilhelm Dilthey. While *Lebensphilosophie* and its German antecedents form one strand of vitalist philosophy, another strand grew around British Romanticism and American Transcendentalism. Branching from this strand is what we term Continental philosophy's critical vitalist tradition, which draws its origins from the likes of Spinoza and Bergson, leading to modern-day Deleuzo-Guattarian as well as new materialist, often

Deleuzo-Guattarian-inspired, praxes. Despite their entanglements, it is nevertheless possible to detect a clear break in the vitalist tradition. This rupture occurred when the German branch of *Lebensphilosophie* took a turn into the direction of fascism and Nazi bio-/necropolitics;[2] a vicious turn led by philosopher Ludwig Klages that subconsciously continues to haunt the entire vitalist tradition and hence needs to be examined.

In the 1920s the aesthetic conceptualisation of *Lebensphilosophie* became heavily politicised, constellating around the troubling pairing of so-called blood and soil politics and driving the supposedly heroic realism of the Spanish, Italian and German fascist and National Socialist states, along with even more racialised spin-offs such as South African apartheid. What had started out as a critical take on modernity's techno-logical advances and hyper-individualism – a valid critique later repeated in *Dialectic of Enlightenment* (1944), written by Frankfurt School-founding critical theorists Max Horkheimer and Theodor W. Adorno – morphed into a politically recuperated bio-/necropolitical philosophy of selective/selected life. Unmoored from its Spinozist/Bergsonian as well as more Romanticist/Transcendentalist variants, *Lebensphilosophie*, instead of celebrating life in all its different manifestations, became a destructive *Vitalpolitik* – a politics of vitalism – that fuelled sketchy Nazi undertakings such as phrenology, characterology and biocentrism. This bio-/necropolitical variant encompassed other mutations that connected the individual's supposed life rhythms to that of the collective and of nature (such as *Lebenskunde*, the science of life, the racialised Nazi biology curriculum, as well as eugenics). Sketching out the full genealogy of this cancerous *Lebensphilosophie* mutation's ambiguous pulls might lead us too far astray,[3] but for the purposes of this chapter it is necessary to examine the anti-fascist counter-arguments of critical theorists Walter Benjamin, Giorgio Agamben, Roberto Esposito and Alexander Weheliye in order to gain a better understanding of how vitalism has informed contemporary understandings of bio-/necropolitics as well as critical Deleuzo-Guattarian and new materialist attempts to come to grips with neoliberal capitalism's dark vitalism.

Frankfurt School affiliate Benjamin diagnosed *Lebensphilosophie*'s emphasis on the notion of life as extremely contemporary. During the early 1920s Benjamin was drawn to the mystical core of *Lebensphilosophie* as articulated by Klages and anthropologist Johann Jakob Bachofen, and even conceptualised his own philosophy of *Rausch* (intoxication) to relate his ideas about *Jetztzeit* (now-time) to Klages' oeuvre (see Benjamin 1999; Lebovic 2006). What differentiated Benjamin from Klages, however, was his emphasis on political accountability[4] – and this is an aspect that, as we will see shortly, also makes an appearance in many Deleuzo-Guattarian and new materialist vitalist undertakings. For the more conservative adherents of *Lebensphilosophie* – and particularly Klages – political self-reflexivity and accountability vis-à-vis the political recuperation of the aesthetic were not things worth considering. In fact, many of *Lebensphilosophie*'s adherents all too easily lent themselves to Führer-led racialised reworkings of the philosophy of life.

Critical analyses of the ambiguous history of *Lebensphilosophie* by Agamben and Esposito are also revealing in this regard. While investigating the rise of biopolitical regimes, Agamben and Esposito in *Homo Sacer* (1995) and *Bíos* (2004) follow in the footsteps of Benjamin as well as poststructuralist Michel Foucault. Agamben rejects Foucault's thesis that biopower[5] is purely modern by claiming that biopower and sovereign power are completely entwined in the modern state. He furthermore highlights the importance of distinguishing between *zoē/bios* or 'bare life/political existence' (Agamben 1998: 8) – a distinction we will return to when discussing critical vitalism – as well as between *zoē* and the politicisation of both life and death. With this move, Agamben links the biopolitical to the politicisation of life in totalitarian states and the Nazi death camps. Esposito, who in *Bíos* uses his ideas about (auto-) immunity to demonstrate modern politics' evolution into biopolitics, argues the same: the Nazi biopolitical state not only negated the powers of philosophy but also placed politically racialised biology on a pedestal. The Nazi state for Esposito (but also Agamben) therefore forms the 'culmination of biopolitics' (Esposito 2008: 10), in which biopolitics stands for how life itself becomes 'encamped in the centre of every political procedure' (2008: 15). Esposito then examines the foundations of biopolitics, which he locates in an 'organistic, anthropological, and naturalistic approach' (2008: 16) as developed in the Germany of the 1920s as well as by the Swedish political scientist Rudolph Kjellén, whose *Lebensform* (life-form) eventually changed into the notorious *Lebensraum* (life-space) ideology. The body of the German nation-state became fully politicised under Nazism between 1932 and 1945. This was a state which took a very literal strange detour of the other when it accorded political privileges (including the right to live) to the so-called racially pure body (construed as *bios*) so as to protect it against the pollution of supposedly lesser, impure races (construed as dehumanised *zoē*).

Neither Esposito nor Agamben, however, explicitly draw links with European imperialism and colonialism when connecting the biopolitical to Nazi fascism – thereby mirroring Foucault's underestimation of the analytical role of race and colonialism in the bio-/necropolitical project (see Stoler 1995, for a similar critique of Foucault).[6] Weheliye's *Habeas Viscus* addresses this non-engagement through an extensive analysis of the impact of what he calls 'racializing assemblages' (2014: 1) or the Deleuzo-Guattarian-influenced idea that race should not be regarded as a fixed biological or cultural label, but as a 'set of sociopolitical processes that discipline humanity into full humans, not-quite-humans, and nonhumans' (2014: 4). Weheliye here demonstrates how race, gender and their intersections have contributed to the disciplining of a very specifically embodied type of the human subject, while accentuating how the modern-day extermination camp is rooted in various colonial precursors – therefore nuancing Agamben's and Esposito's claims.

Esposito and Agamben furthermore insufficiently deal with the ways in which globalised neoliberal capitalism – rooted in the colonial modernity project and thus characterised by a racial logic (Robinson 1983; Chakravartty and Ferreira Da Silva 2012), or to put it even more specifically, a 'colonial ontology of anti-black racism' (Winnubst 2020: 103) – has rendered the distinctions between *zoē* and *bios* moot while ramping up the dark vitalist project of fascism. Neoliberal capitalism transforms all of life into surplus life, always starting with those who were already dehumanised. In this regard, political scientist Melinda Cooper adds several important qualifications to the former biopolitical thinkers' writings: 'Neoliberalism and the biotech industry', she states, 'share a common ambition to overcome the ecological and economic limits to growth . . . by reinventing life [itself] beyond the limit' (2008: 11–12). Having gone beyond bare life's commodification under fascist bio-/necropolitical regimes, neoliberal extractivist capitalism eventually financialises all of life; privileged or not, deemed human or not. 'With its vested interest in biological catastrophism, neoliberalism is [moreover] intent on profiting from the "unregulated" distribution of life's chances' (2008: 12). Seen through the lenses of neoliberal governmentality and driven by a toxic combination of hyper-individual atomism, hyper-responsibilisation and self-disciplining subjectivity, every little piece of matter is commodified by neoliberal bio-/necropower. This more 'equal', or, better said, flattening commodification process driven by extractivist capitalism does not contradict the fact that various embodied subjects have always been made to matter less than others (Butler 1993; Wynter 2003; Jackson 2020).

While economisation's brutal claws appear inescapable, a counter-response to neoliberal capitalism's corruptions of vital life is made by nomadic philosopher Rosi Braidotti's formulation of *zoē*-centred egalitarianism (2006b; 2013) to demonstrate the connections between all manifestations of lively matter without forgetting the role of geo-politically laden power relations that play out between differently embodied subjects. As with Foucault, Agamben, Esposito, Weheliye and political theorist Hannah Arendt (1958),[7] but far closer in spirit to Deleuzo-Guattarian thought, Braidotti's reformulation of *zoē* expounds on risks to life (in all its actualisations) and its reduction to pure, brute matter rendered destroyable. In this new materialist formulation, the realities of global bio-/necropolitical regimes are acknowledged, while the shared material vitality of all beings – including the formerly and currently dehumanised, non-human and more-than-human – is emphasised. This stands in stark contrast to the racialised privileging of particular human subjects in non-critical vitalist philosophies, as demonstrated earlier, as well as to capitalism's reinvention of life beyond the limit.

Capitalism and Life: Staying with(in) the Trouble

Despite the brutality unleashed by state-sponsored experiments with *Vitalpolitik* during the first half of the twentieth century, by the 1960s vitalism had got over the duplicities of *Lebensphilosophie*. A distinctly Romantic/Transcendentalist philosophy of life was writ large over youth culture, 'the eruption' of which 'thrust reason to one side' in a counter-response that privileged music's affective intensities and the 'wonder world of the night' against the 'mundane reality' (Blanning 2011: 185) of corporatisation and its necrotic values. As youth culture and various counter-cultural protest movements continue to demonstrate, the vocabulary of life is no less of a burning issue today. On the other side of the divide, the vocabulary of life is showing its darker fascist roots too. While political fascism is no longer solely propelled by European-based racism, nationalism and white supremacy, the impulse behind (neo-) fascist, nationalist ideology remains the same today as it was in the early twentieth century; namely the need to escape the 'modern darkness' of mechanised reason by inventing a collective 'imagined community' (Anderson 1991: 11–12) that constellates around the strange detour of the other. Contemporary peddlers of imagined communities of race, ethnicity and religion outside the West have come to uncannily resemble their European antecedents. Connected to their rivals by 'an irresistible memetic desire', they are trapped, along with 'all the inhabitants of the modern world', by a 'logic of self-assertion' and 'ressentiment' (Mishra 2018: 159).

Just as during the Reich, and equally during the psychedelic 1960s, imagined communities have gestated around Romanticised cultures of feeling; reclaiming a vitality of allegedly über-healthy bodies, clear-cut identities and durations from the political disaffection and ideological crises engendered by capitalism's deterritorialisations of social, religious and other living arrangements. Clearly this disaffection can go in one of two ways politically – either towards a fascist *Lebensphilosophie* that privileges *bios* and centralises otherness, or towards a Romanticised vitalist materialism that deprivileges *bios*, centralises *zoē* and is less interested in the detour of otherness that has become so central to much of contemporary identity politics. Resistance to 'the deadening interplay between fatality, technology and capitalism' have, of late, been endowed on the left 'with a new vivacity and a new radical aura', as Anderson puts it (1991: 43) – thanks in no small part to the biopolitics of Foucault and Agamben, the schizoanalytical project of Deleuze and Guattari, as well as new materialist emphases on *zoē* and the vibrancy of matter. Such critical vitalist moves are arguably all the more pressing in the face of neoliberalism's cheerless utopia. In these hyper-individualising borderline times (see De Wachter 2012) of movement and psycho-social crisis, the search for something more desirable than the present has been financially proscribed. In the words of one of neoliberalism's principal proponents, political theorist Francis Fukuyama, from here on in, 'daring, courage, imagination, and idealism will be replaced by economic calculation [. . .] and the satisfaction of consumer demands' (cited in Kumar 1995: 207).

In a move intended to escape the deathly facticity of such neoliberal triumphalism and the fascist spectres it could unleash, deconstructivist Jacques Derrida asks that we conceive of the future as an 'abyssal desert' (1994: 28), devoid of figures and empty of all objects of desire. Yet in waiting for nothing in particular, we declare the impossibility of changing anything – a move that resigns the future to the vagaries of fate. Against this paralysing impulse, we need tangible ethico-political modes of critical-creative analysis, positions and proposals in our search for more self-accountable ways of being with others while avoiding the pitfalls and cancerous tumefactions of desire. The spawning of relativisms needs to be brought to a halt, and our collective fixations on the past and future need to be disrupted. Only the production and articulation of accountable knowledges and models that are invested in theorising from the material ground up can save us now. Or as posthumanist scholar Donna Haraway put it so poetically in *Staying with the Trouble*, we need to start 'learning to be truly present . . . as mortal critters entwined in myriad unfinished configurations of places, times, matters, meanings' (2016: 1). Because if we do not stay with(in) the trouble now, the future will be stillborn.

In our quests to become intrepid creative agents (who stay with the trouble for life created by neoliberal economising and stand with minoritarian builders of differently thought-out anti-fascist imagined communities of practice), we need to remain constantly vigilant. Because '[f]ascism', as Guattari warns us, 'seems to come from the outside, but it finds its energy right at the heart of everyone's desire' (CS, 171). Moreover, as Deleuze and Guattari are at pains to point out in *A Thousand Plateaus*, all aspects of life today are overcoded by capitalism. While this system relentlessly deterritorialises social, political, theoretical and other formations/codes from their original contexts, it simultaneously reterritorialises them elsewhere. Thus, while capitalism has deterritorialised *zoē* and *bios* distinctions from the perspective of economics, it has reterritorialised them elsewhere in the form of problematic political fascist revanches.

Microfascisms: The Hauntings of Neoliberal Capitalism

'We have been led to believe that fascism was just a bad moment we had to go through', writes Guattari (CM, 239). Foucault takes this up in his introduction to *Anti-Oedipus*, claiming that it is 'not only historical fascism' that should concern us, but 'the fascism . . . in our heads, and in our everyday behaviour, the fascism that causes us to love power, to desire the very thing that dominates and exploits us' (Foucault in AO, xiii). Fascism, in short, is desire basically turning against itself. As Deleuze and Guattari underline it in *A Thousand Plateaus*: '[I]t's too easy to be antifascist on the molar level, and not even see the fascist inside you, the fascist you yourself sustain and nourish and cherish with molecules both personal and collective' (TP, 215). While we might call out the molar fascism of totalitarian bio-/necropolitical regimes, with their oppressive legislation and tyrannical apparatuses, we hardly seem to notice the 'microfascisms' (TP, 214) – the tiny (inter)personal habits and rules of (dis)engagement – that are 'already shaping [our own] postures, attitudes, perceptions, expectations, semiotic systems, etc.' (TP, 215). In the Deleuzo-Guattarian sense, desire is not propelled by lack or excess, but is, on the contrary, regarded as a vital affirmative force, embedded in a social field. So-called fascism-within is thus shaped by the micro-forces and micro-machines of socially produced desires and yearnings, birthing a type of internalised, paranoid self-repression.

'Desire is never an undifferentiated instinctual energy'; instead it can be thought of as an economy of desire; 'a whole supple segmentarity that processes molecular energies and potentially gives desire a fascist determination' (TP, 215). What then is this fascism of the internalised *eco* (household) and the repressive *nomoi* (habits and rules) that govern it? And how does this relate to the double pull of vitalist philosophies and our previous sketch of neoliberal capitalism? And, moreover, how can desire 'desire its own repression' (TP, 215)?

Deleuze and Guattari in *A Thousand Plateaus* are at pains to explain that capitalism has set about unlocking the unfettered power of desire conceived of as a kind of dark *élan vital*. While capitalism is always deterritorialising and reterritorialising desire, it is feeding on the disruptive qualities of desire, creating unstable monetary economies and volatile political-psychic economies. In today's borderline times, extractivist capitalism and neoliberal governmentality entrench social instability and the ongoing atomisation of subjects, fuelling anxieties over climate crisis and worsening precarity. People are consequently afraid of what is yet to actualise itself. Fascism's pathological desire, which Deleuze and Guattari detect in *Anti-Oedipus*, constellates around the longing of people to escape the no-long-term/no-future situation of late capitalism by desiring the very thing that dominates and exploits them. As philosopher John Protevi also notes, for these two thinkers, 'the fascist state is the most fantastic re-territorialization of capitalism', and 'fascism is on the side of paranoia and reterritorialization, the counter pole to [capitalism's] schizophrenia and deterritorialization' (2000: 167). So, the problem today is not simply a revival of political fascism, but of liberalism's (whether classic, modern or neoliberal) gestation of microfascist tendencies. In an era of endless global war in which pre-emptive drone strikes, CCTV cameras, state of emergency laws as well as infinite detention, internment and torture camps have sprung up, along with militant nationalisms and fanaticisms, it is difficult not to detect the re-hauntings of the spectre of political fascism. Yet, as Arendt (1965) also pointed out, the brutalities of the Nazi state were sustained by ordinary people. The same banal evil that Arendt detects at work in Nazi Germany is operating at the back end of the society of the spectacle. Egged on by a fascist-mediated imperative to 'live more and desire better', consumers are catapulted into a war of all against all (and, most alarmingly, against the biosphere itself); a war committed 'in all our names and for all our sakes' (Evans and Reid 2013: 9). In this modality by which the vitality of biological-social systems is rendered surplus in the service of the dark vitalism of consumerism, financial formations and bio-/necropolitical power gaming, we are confronted with the Satanic majesty and dynamism of global capital, whose covert multinational crack troops and supply chains have taken on all 'the invisible, promiscuous forces of the occult' and 'whose equally intangible movements . . . have such devastating effects' on ecosystems, economies and individuals (Cooper 2008: 71). Bio-/necropolitical capitalism finds cancerous growth opportunities in pandemic panics, (neo-)fascist revanches, socio-economic collapses and ecological wreckage. Quite literally everyone and everything has now been transformed into (data)minable materials.

As such, we can already diagnose microfascisms congealing around innumerable conspiracy theories and allegations of so-called fake news that have sprung up in response to all this promiscuous occultism. This is a social media situation that Deleuze and Guattari would undoubtedly have diagnosed as symptomatic of a paranoid body-social – bodies, both personal and collective, that can no longer tolerate the pressures, precarities and surfeit of desire that capitalism peddles. Sociologist Jean Baudrillard mused that the contemporary human subject 'only has to be deprived of breakfast' (1996: 19) to take on the most belligerent of acts and attitudes; a truth uncomfortably borne out in the age of social media by high levels of anonymous racist and sexist trolling (Fuentes 2018) that bank on dubious moral positions rooted in politicised misinterpretations of biology (such as social Darwinism). This takes us back to the nineteenth century, when Herbert Spencer refurbished Darwin's ideas, giving the survival of the fittest a moral, meritocratic twist: those with higher positions had ended up there because of their capacity to fight themselves to the top, earning themselves a supposedly biological and moral right to claim a privileged position on the uppermost branches of the tree of life. Similarly, men had allegedly won their privileges over women and Caucasians had won their ascendancy over supposed lesser races, and so on. Historical fascism, along with contemporary resurgences of micro- and macropolitical fascisms (evident in online trolling and alt-right memes) have exploited such ideologically coloured interpretations of Darwinism.

Capitalism therefore joins fascism in its exploitation of the very desires that underwrite life, and that, together with neoliberal rationality's hyper-individualising powers, pit individuals against one another (and set humans in opposition to all other forms of life). Biotechnological capitalism's political economy 'multiplies and distributes "differences" for the sake of profit' while unhinging the 'dialectical bond' between 'otherness' and the 'processes of its discursive formation', as Braidotti aptly explains this process (2006a: 1). In hijacking the creative potentials of life, neoliberal capitalism seems to be 'stealing our very insides' (Culp 2016: 6), to hungrily devour them. How then might Deleuzo-Guattarian and new materialist philosophies of connectivity, affirmation and situatedness assist us when, as Andrew Culp writes, their vitalist attributes have become the very mantras of 'rhizomatic capitalism' (2016: 7)?

Vibrant Materialism(s): Towards Affirmative Relational Futures

In an age of disaster capitalism and ecological tragedy, capitalism has undertaken a wholesale reclamation of life, which includes vitalism. In this scenario 'the new political economy of life' – presented as 'self-organising biological complexity' – 'begins to sound suspiciously like the new political economy of neoliberalism' (Cooper 2008: 42). In terms of this bio-/necropolitical rationale, 'vitalism comes dangerously close to equating the evolution of life with that of capital' (2008: 42). Simultaneously, in the Anthropocene, *élan vital* is presumed in a Spencerian fashion to have endowed (the anthropocentric, exclusivist conceptualisation of) Man, or rather *homo oeconomicus*, a favoured position at the apex of all creation.

Deleuze and Guattari, along with an array of new materialist theorists such as Braidotti, Elizabeth Grosz and Jane Bennett, by contrast, have reclaimed vitalism from such unsavoury connections, using it to articulate a non-hierarchical type of process that does not favour humans specifically, but includes, as for example Bennett writes, 'a heterogenous series of actants with partial, overlapping and conflicting degrees of power and affectivity' (2010: 33). This non-anthropocentric attitude informs the new theories of affect in which, as per Deleuze, *élan vital* is conceived of as something that inheres in all forms of matter-energy. This life-force, argues Deleuze, is 'a virtuality in the process of being actualised, a simplicity in the process of differentiating' (B, 94). Anticipating the recuperations of neoliberal bio-/necropolitical capitalism, Deleuze, as cited in correspondence mentioned in *Essays Critical and Clinical*, moves vitalism away from the biological, claiming that it is all about 'a conception of life as a non-organic power' (CC, xiii). This is a position that Bennett, Grosz and Braidotti all develop further – not by deprivileging life as such, but by treating it as a non-autonomous relational force inhering to subjects, objects and concepts as well as assemblages of these.

Deleuze and Guattari describe their collaborative approach as an attempt to 'create concepts that are always new' (WP, 5) by finding relations of resonance and exchange not only between themselves, but between oppositional domains that are usually determined by their own variant systems of thought and classification. These domains include nature and culture, human and machine, literature and philosophy, as well as art and science. This is a transversal outlook that seeks to find openings or lines of flight that allow thought to escape from the constraints defining and enclosing creativity in the search for new meanings. Deleuze and Guattari use the term haecceity to denote a spatial sensation of time that is oriented around pre-personal affects. Haecceity, they write, denotes 'a climate, a wind, a fog ... an hour, a season, an atmosphere, an air, a life' (TP, 262). An aesthetic approach oriented around such a reconceptualisation enables us to theorise our own experiences in non-anthropocentric ways and open ourselves to different perceptions and possibilities of rhythm and movement that inhere in the non-human, the geological, the meteorological and so on. When we create, we should move away from identity and habit, orienting ourselves around the production of novel constellations of affects as well as projecting our creations forward towards the creation of new sensations for a people yet-to-come. An orientation towards the future is of critical importance. There are two ways in which we might approach affect – by nostalgically turning towards an imaginary past, or by turning in a Deleuzo-Guattarian sense towards the as-yet-to-be-actualised future. The first, a sentimental move, is potentially fascist and carcinogenic. While corporeal bodies (individual and collective) inhere in the present, both the future and the past are metaphysical surfaces that can be poisoned by desire. Nostalgia reveals a dangerous desire to relocate a desired past in the present; a nostalgic ennui that is nihilistic and affectively toxic, poisoning bodies and trapping us in a negative logic of representation. Deleuze and Guattari accentuate this critique by stating that a 'complete curettage' of the guilt-laden 'Oedipal death drive' needs to be performed; 'a whole scouring of the unconscious' (OL, 311) if we wish to remove the cancerous tumour of fascist nostalgia that wants to shape the future in the form of a supposed Edenic past that never really was, and which will always be problematically oedipal.

How to Build a Body without Organs

Deleuzo-Guattarian vitalist philosophy, in contrast, promotes a radical symbolic operation; namely, the building of Bodies without Organs (BwOs) and the fashioning, in this way, of lines of flight or escape (with the caveat that such an operation does not in and of itself guarantee success). Bodies (and even bodies such as capital, or hyper-objects such as the Earth-system) cannot be reductively analysed as collections of forms, organs or subjects: Instead bodies are subject to forces, movements, rests and the capacity to affect and be affected. Both human and non-human embodied subjects are kinetic, dynamic and intensive; considering them otherwise deprives them of these powers.

Taking their cue from Artaud, Spinoza and Nietzsche, Deleuze and Guattari write of an affective material body, pregnant with possibilities, transversed by flows of multiple energies (chemical, thermal, kinetic, electrical), and perpetual movements between these energy states. The body – whether textual or physical, actual or imagined – involved in the virtual's visceral theatre is what Deleuze and Guattari label as a BwO. This is an attempt to escape the regimes of bio-/necropower by describing the body outside of organic or biological terms. As philosopher Manuel DeLanda also explains, the BwO was formulated 'in an effort to conceive of the genesis of form (in geological, biological, and cultural structures) as related exclusively to immanent capabilities [inherent in] the flows of matter-energy information' (2000: 263). As such, the BwO is an attempt to get rid of all the organising mechanisms of the (necro-) biopolitical/fascist state:

> the three great strata that concern us ... the organism, signifiance, and subjectifi-cation ... You will be organized ... You will be signifier and signified, interpreter and interpreted ... You will be a subject, nailed down as one, a subject of the enunciation recoiled into a subject of the statement. (TP, 159)

'The [biological] organism', continue Deleuze and Guattari, 'is not at all the body, [the true body is] the BwO' (TP, 159). Resisting attempts at being concretised, the supposed true body is unfixed and immanent. The aesthetic foundation of such a non-biological yet vitalist conception of the body remains the Romantic sublime – a peculiar aesthetic encounter, as Deleuze (CC, 35) writes, of 'dissonant accords' that engages the senses in 'such a manner that they struggle against each other like wrestlers, pushing each other to new limits and new inspirations' (CC, 34). Whereas the vitalism of *Lebensphilosophie* concerned itself with biology, Deleuze and Guattari push *élan vital* in the direction of all forms of matter/energy and duration, locating it in assemblages of haecceities, virtual potentials, and organs and symbiotic partners.

The BwO is not, however, simply a metaphysical conception but also a unified, intensive and lived physicality. Linked to other bodies, objects and fields of intensity around it via connective flows, this affective body is the key to a kind of creative mutation. DeLanda (2000: 264) writes that because they represent 'intense, destratified matter-energy', BwOs are free to act as 'probe heads' or 'exploratory agents' that scan 'abstract spaces of possibility' to retrieve or discover new arrangements or processes of organisation that can be grafted on to existing bodies. Conceptually, the BwO denotes one way in which we might imaginatively dissolve our subjectivities, travel across the plane of consistency in search of a better destiny for humanity (and not only for humanity, but for all forms of life), transcending neoliberal microfascisms and other fascist manifestations. The BwO, haecceity, affect, vitality and becoming are folding concepts in the philosophy of Deleuze and Guattari; concepts that might enable us, if we use them carefully and with vigilance, to produce healthier alternatives to the dominant, divisive representationalist identity-based logics.

Deleuze and Guattari identify three different kinds of BwOs. The first are full or well-constructed experiments, which can sustain dynamic flows and energies without interruption (TP, 153). The second are empty or poorly constructed 'frozen' (TP, 153) experiments, full of blockages and prone to icy stratification. The last and most volatile type are cancerous; 'terrifying caricatures of the plane of consistency' (TP, 163) in which abhorrent tumours proliferate on the 'debris of strata destroyed by too violent a destratification' (TP, 163). Capitalism, which is prone to acts of destructive deterritorialisation, 'tends toward a threshold of decoding that will destroy the socius in order to make it a body of organs [the exact opposite of a BwO] and unleash the flows of desire upon this [splintered] body' (AO, 33). In other words, capitalism – especially extractivist capitalism and hyper-individualising neoliberalism (the anticipated subjects of A Thousand Plateaus) – are aberrant BwOs within which bits and pieces of microfascist longing/desire might easily mutate into cancerous BwOs. These could constellate under the right conditions to form collective assemblages along the axes of what could be called imagined communities of desire – as they did in the formation of various bio-/necropower political regimes during the twentieth century. At a certain point, when the conditions are right, a whole array of microfascist desires might assemble into a 'mass movement' that is less the inherent expression of a political or economic 'organism' or organisation than it is the expression of a mutant war machine engaged in fulfilling the oedipal death drive; 'a cancerous' (TP, 215) vortex that pulls the BwO of the body-social into a self-destructive organisation.

As Benjamin Noys explains, in *Anti-Oedipus* an argument was made to counter the formation of fascist cancers within capitalised bodies by radicalising 'capitalism's deterritorialising tendencies' (2010: 1) in the direction of schizophrenia. The point was to create unexpected possibilities for counterattacks against fascist formations, and to launch unforeseen initiatives for creating revolutionary, popular, minority, mutant desiring-machines or BwOs. In *A Thousand Plateaus*, Deleuze and Guattari are more circumspect about the building of such experimental probes. They warn frequently against violent deterritorialisations and issue pointers for building full rather than empty BwOs. The point, however, is to continuously search for new weapons to use against the proliferation of cancerous formations. Instead of fruitlessly searching for radical contradictions at the heart of social relations, they suggest that we should look for our weapons among variegated specialised theories, cultural practices and lived experiences so that we might schizoanalytically wield them in constructing new assemblages. From social forms, write Deleuze and Guattari, capitalism's line of flight 'tears away particles, among which there are now only relationships of speed and slowness, and from subjects it tears away affects' (OL, 81). It is along lines of flight or dynamic movement that individual and social collectives of resistance themselves must take shape. After all, 'history's greatest adventures' have taken shape around such 'lines of flight ... It's always along a line of flight that we create because there we are tracing the real and composing a plane of consistency, not simply imagining or dreaming' (OL, 92). Our argument here is that Deleuze and Guattari, together with earlier-named new materialist thinkers, offer effective ways of conceptualising and creatively rethinking not only how we might prevent the formation of cancerous fascist assemblages, but also how we might go about building better individual and collective assemblages.

Conclusion: Critical Vitalism(s): For all Forms of Life and Matter/Energy

Sociologist Saskia Sassen (2014: 217) writes that the 'subterranean effects' and affects of neoliberal capitalism are 'cutting across familiar conceptual and historical ways of analysing', rendering them incapable of effectively resisting the way this system operates. For Deleuze and Guattari, who already detected this problem in the early 1970s, knowledge-production systems have become bogged down by semiotics and linguistics, linear/hierarchical historical diagrams as well as deterministic theories. Instead, they reason, we should be opening ourselves up to the transversal, virtual and vibrant potentials of materiality. The problem, for them, as well as for various new materialists, is an ethico-political one. Put in Braidottian terms, for example, there is a pressing need to reclaim desire from the ethical vacuum of 'advanced capitalism', which, like (neo-)fascist interpretations of *Lebensphilosophie*, 'leaves untouched the qualitative issue of what constitutes the core of an ethical subject' (2012: 170); a gap into which have sprung not only a host of microfascist habits and tendencies, but also some worrying political revampings of the fascist project. Here, the Deleuzo-Guattarian and new materialist restaging of the Romantic and Bergsonian/Spinozist philosophies of life holds some promise. But only if we, as these philosophers insist, cultivate attentiveness, acceptance of situated positionalities and self-accountability. Because 'every politics is simultaneously a macropolitics and a micropolitics' (TP, 213), and because the macropolitical is continuously immersed in and carried by the micropolitical, political subjects have an ethical duty of care to remain vigilant at all times against the relentless upwelling of microfascist tendencies. Moreover, just as 'liberalism has to be comprehended, not as exceptional to, but coextensive with the very form of fascism it claims to have "conquered"', many contemporary left-wing 'discourses and practices that declare themselves to be avowedly "anti-fascist"' (Evans and Reid 2013: 4) show some alarming fascist tendencies.

New materialists, along with Deleuzo-Guattarian scholars, call upon us to enact new sensorial and affective domains of possibility in our individual capacities (as the producers and consumers of resources and knowledge practices) as well as in our social capacities (as members of macropolitical and macroeconomic formations). We cannot escape the fact that today, as Guattari writes, deepening social divides, growing economic precarities and worsening ecological crises are messily entangled with capitalism's 'systems of [negative] modelling in which we are entangled, and which are in the process of completely polluting us, head and heart' (CM, 132). In such a situation of relational entanglement, our ethical duty, as Grosz (2017: 257) additionally underlines, is to acknowledge that we are all 'living beings' with a responsibility to perform onto-ethical acts that seek to 'liberate and transform [the] material processes' in which we are entangled.

Primarily concerned with the problematic of change, a schizoanalytical approach, as Guattari explains, works with 'sad' passions and suicidal/destructive desires, recognising them as 'the potential bearers of new constellations of universes of values or reference' (CM, 18) as well as sensorial, affective domains of possibility. Such an onto-ethics asks that we embrace a kind of conceptual pragmatism and even optimism regarding the difficulties of creating and sustaining personal and collective change. As Joshua Ramey writes, paraphrasing Deleuze, we are asked to keep 'faith that the traumatic and fateful character of events and their effects upon our lives are not irreversible and may [yet] be subject to [affirmative] intervention' (2012: 151). There are, of course, many perils to avoid in undertaking such a project. Political philosopher Erin Manning, for example, warns of the dangers of the linguistic turn in the humanities and social sciences with its 'politics of recognition' discourses. Here tendencies 'toward fascism' build 'on dichotomies of inclusion/exclusion, perpetrator/victim, [which] reify the human in the name of race, identity [and] gender' in the name of a 'universalising' discourse of the human (2016: 113). 'Fascism . . . travels through the finest weaves', warns Guattari; 'it is in constant evolution . . . [appearing] to come from the outside . . . it [arises and] finds its energy in the heart of each of our desires' (cited in 2016: 113).

Deleuze and Guattari's schizoanalytical thinking, to conclude, thus favours a conjunctive approach, emphasising inclusiveness, relationality, mutability and multiplicity. Their onto-ethical methodology requires that we foster a critical awareness that 'reframes [the] systems of knowledge and representation' (Grosz 2017: 257) by which we conceive of the world and our relations to it. As a panacea to the cancerous growth of microfascisms within as well as to the spectre of fascism on the streets, they, in tandem with several new materialists, call upon us to cultivate new depths of engagement. Such a call is critical-vitalist; asking for attention to the 'generative power that flows across all species', and promoting the cultivation of pleasure grounded in 'life itself' (Braidotti 2013: 103). This vitalism, as we have argued, is radically different from the type of vitalism invoked in the service of (neo-)fascist ideologies and is, moreover, constructed around an immanent Bergsonian/Spinozist onto-ethics of embedded, affecting-affected bodies. There are, as we have argued, crucial and critical ethico-political differences between bare life (*das blossen Leben*) invoked in the name of *bios* (or privileged life) by (neo-)fascist *Lebensphilosophien* and the *zoē*-egalitarianism invoked in the name of all life by Deleuzo-Guattarian and new materialist vitalist philosophies. The foregoing are crucial differences to take into consideration if we are to remain vigilant against becoming, even in small ways, that which we feel in our hearts to be politically and ethically abhorrent.

Notes

1. Although life philosophy and vitalism differ from one another, *Lebensphilosophie* is often seen as combining both. See Reill 2005 for more information.
2. With the bio-/necropolitical, we, among others, refer to philosopher Achille Mbembé's 'Necropolitics' essay, in which Foucauldian biopolitics is elaborated upon by means of an analysis of the entanglements between the disciplinary, the biopolitical and the necropolitical – or the politics of death – in colonial, race-relations-structured regimes. Mbembé's essay can be read as following in poet Aimé Césaire's footsteps by accentuating how colonial bio-/necropolitical violence prefigured Nazi fascism. See Césaire 1972; Mbembé and Meintjes 2003.
3. For more information on the contextualisation of the evolution of *Lebensphilosophie*, see Lemke 2007; Jones 2012; Lebovic 2013.
4. Benjamin's essay analyses the relationship between violence and power – both expressed by the German *Gewalt* – law and justice. Benjamin argues that the relationship between law and violence is intimate, as violence has both a 'law-making' and a 'law-preserving function' (1978: 284). Without violence, there is no state. The problem for Benjamin is that the borders between these two functions are blurred when it comes to the state's police force committing police violence (1978: 286). Law then becomes violence itself, which is highly problematic, and for him furthermore counters the theological-political signification of justice.
5. Biopower relates to the productive powers of and control over subjects and entire populations rendered livable or killable via specific technologies, standing in contrast to the idea of one, easily top-down sovereign power deciding a subject's right over life or death. See Foucault 1981.
6. It is only in Foucault's *Society Must Be Defended* (1975–76) lectures that the category of race is touched upon. See Foucault 2003.
7. Although Arendt's philosophy is mostly understood as a political philosophy that counters totalitarian, fascist regimes by accentuating human plurality, Arendt can also be read as a bio-/necropolitical thinker. See Diprose and Ziarek 2018.

References

Adorno, T. W., and M. Horkheimer (1997), *Dialectic of Enlightenment*, trans. J. Cumming, London: Verso. Translation of *Dialektik der Aufklärung: Philosophische Fragmente*, Querido Verlag, 1947.

Agamben, G. (1998), *Homo Sacer: Sovereign Power and Bare Life*, trans. D. Heller-Roazen, Stanford: Stanford University Press. Translation of *Homo sacer: Il potere sovrano e la nuda vita*, Turin: Guilio Einaudi, 1995.

Anderson, B. (1991 [1983]), *Imagined Communities: Reflections on the Origin and Spread of Nationalism*, London: Verso.

Arendt, H. (1958), *The Human Condition*, Chicago: University of Chicago Press.

Arendt, H. (1965 [1963]), *Eichmann in Jerusalem: A Report on the Banality of Evil*, New York: Viking.

Baudrillard, J. (1996), *Cool Memories II: 1987–90*, trans. C. Turner, Cambridge: Polity. Translation of *Cool Memories II: 1987–90*, Paris: Éditions Galilée, 1990.

Benjamin, W. (1978 [1921]), 'Critique of Violence' in *Reflections: Essays, Aphorisms, Autobiographical Writings*, ed. P. Demetz, New York: Schocken Books, pp. 277–300.

Benjamin, W. (1999 [1930]), 'Theories of German Fascism', in *Selected Writings, vol. 2, part 1: 1927–1934*, ed. M. W. Jennings, H. Eiland and G. Smith, Cambridge, MA: Harvard University Press, pp. 312–321.

Bennett, J. (2010), *Vibrant Matter: A Political Ecology of Things*, Durham, NC: Duke University Press.

Blanning, T. (2011), *The Romantic Revolution*, London: Phoenix.

Braidotti, R. (2006a), 'Affirming the Affirmative: On Nomadic Affectivity', *Rhizomes*, 11/12 (1), <http://www.rhizomes.net/issue11/braidotti.html> (last accessed 21 April 2019).

Braidotti, R. (2006b), *Transpositions: On Nomadic Ethics*, Cambridge: Polity.

Braidotti, R. (2012), 'Nomadic Ethics', in D. W. Smith and H. Somers-Hall (eds), *The Cambridge Companion to Deleuze*, Cambridge: Cambridge University Press, pp. 170–97.

Braidotti, R. (2013), *The Posthuman*, Cambridge: Polity.

Butler, J. (1993), *Bodies That Matter: On the Discursive Limits of 'Sex'*, London: Routledge.

Butler, J. (2020), 'Capitalism Has its Limits', <https://www.versobooks.com/blogs/4603-capitalism-has-its-limits> (last accessed 10 May 2020).

Césaire, A. (1972), *Discourse on Colonialism*, trans. J. Pinkham, New York: Monthly Review Press. Translation of *Discours sur le colonialisme*, Paris: Editions Presence Africaine, 1955.

Chakravartty, P., and D. Ferreira Da Silva (2012), 'Accumulation, Dispossession, and Debt: The Racial Logic of Global Capitalism – An Introduction', *American Quarterly*, 64 (3): 361–85.

Cooper, M. (2008), *Life as Surplus: Biotechnology and Capitalism in the Neoliberal Era*, Seattle: University of Washington Press.

Culp, A. (2016), *Dark Deleuze*, Minneapolis: University of Minnesota Press.

DeLanda, M. (2000), *A Thousand Years of Nonlinear History*, New York: Swerve.

Derrida, J. (1994), *Specters of Marx: The State of the Debt, the Work of Mourning, and the New International*, trans. P. Kamuf, New York: Routledge. Translation of *Spectres de Marx*, Paris: Éditions Galilée, 1993.

De Wachter, D. (2012), *Borderline Times: Het Einde van de Normaliteit*, Leuven: LannooCampus.

Diprose, R., and E. P. Ziarek (2018), *Arendt, Natality and Biopolitics: Toward Democratic Plurality and Reproductive Justice*, Edinburgh: Edinburgh University Press.

Esposito, R. (2008), *Bíos: Biopolitics and Philosophy*, trans. T. Campbell, Minneapolis: University of Minnesota Press. Translation of *Bíos: Biopolitica a filosofia*, Turin: Guilio Einaudi, 2004.

Evans, B., and J. Reid (2013), 'Introduction: Fascism in all its Forms', in B. Evans and J. Reid (eds), *Deleuze & Fascism*, New York: Routledge, pp. 1–12.

Foucault, M. (1981), *History of Sexuality, Volume 1: An Introduction*, trans. R. Hurley, London: Penguin. Translation of *La Volenté de savoir*, Paris: Éditions Gallimard, 1976.

Foucault, M. (2003), *Society Must Be Defended: Lectures at the Collège de France, 1975–76*, trans. D. Macey, New York: St. Martin's. Translation of *Il Faut Défendre la Sociéte: Cours au Collège de France*, Paris: Gallimard/Seuil, 1997.

Fuentes, A. (2018), 'Are We as Awful as We Act Online?', *National Geographic*, 234, <https://www.nationalgeographic.co.uk/2018/07/are-we-really-as-awful-as-we-act-online> (last accessed 14 June 2022).

Grosz, E. (2017), *The Incorporeal: Ontology, Ethics and the Limits of Materialism*, New York: Columbia University Press.

Haraway, D. J. (2016), *Staying with the Trouble: Making Kin in the Chthulucene*, Durham, NC: Duke University Press.

Jackson, Z. I. (2020), *Becoming Human: Matter and Meaning in an Antiblack World*, New York: New York Press.

Jones, D. V. (2012 [2010]), *The Racial Discourses of Life Philosophy: Négritude, Vitalism, and Modernity*, New York: Columbia University Press.

Kumar, K. (1995), 'Apocalypse, Millennium and Utopia Today', in M. Bull (ed.), *Apocalypse Theory and the Ends of the World*, Oxford: Blackwell, pp. 200–24.

Lebovic, N. (2006), 'The Beauty and Terror of Lebensphilosophie: Ludwig Klages, Walter Benjamin, and Alfred Baeumler', *South Central Review*, 23 (1): 23–39.

Lebovic, N. (2013), *The Philosophy of Life and Death: Ludwig Klages and the Rise of a Nazi Biopolitics*, New York: Palgrave Macmillan.

Lemke, T. (2007), *Biopolitik zur Einführung*, Hamburg: Junius Verlag.

Manning, E. (2016), *The Minor Gesture*, Durham, NC: Duke University Press.

Mbembé, J.-A., and L. Meintjes (2003), 'Necropolitics', *Public Culture*, 15 (1): 11–40.

Mishra, P. (2018), *Age of Anger: A History of the Present*, London: Penguin.

Noys, B. (2010), 'Apocalypse, Tendency, Crisis', *Monthly Review*, 5 February, <http://mrzine.monthlyreview.org/2010/noys050210.html> (last accessed 21 April 2019).

Protevi, J. (2000), '"A Problem of Pure Matter": Deleuze and Guattari's Treatment of Fascist Nihilism in *A Thousand Plateaus*', in K. Ansell-Pearson and D. Morgan (eds), *Nihilism Now! 'Monsters of Energy'*, Basingstoke: Palgrave Macmillan, pp. 167–88.

Ramey, J. (2012), *The Hermetic Deleuze: Philosophy and Spiritual Ordeal*, Durham, NC: Duke University Press.

Reill, P. H. (2005), *Vitalizing Nature in the Enlightenment*, Berkeley: University of California Press.

Robinson, C. J. (1983), *Black Marxism: The Making of the Black Radical Tradition*, London: Zed Books.

Rose, N. (2007), *The Politics of Life Itself: Biomedicine, Power, and Subjectivity in the Twenty-First Century*, Princeton: Princeton University Press.

Sassen, S. (2014), *Expulsions: Brutality and Complexity in the Global Economy*, Cambridge, MA: The Belknap Press of Harvard University Press.

Stoler, A. L. (1995), *Race and the Education of Desire: Foucault's History of Sexuality and the Colonial Order of Things*, Durham, NC: Duke University Press.

Weheliye, A. G. (2014), *Habeas Viscus: Racializing Assemblages, Biopolitics, and Black Feminist Theories of the Human*, Durham, NC: Duke University Press.

Winnubst, S. (2020), 'The Many Lives of Fungibility: Anti-blackness in Neoliberal Times', *Journal of Gender Studies*, 29 (1): 102–12.

Wolfe, C. (2010), *What is Posthumanism?*, Minneapolis: University of Minnesota Press.

Wynter, S. (2003), 'Unsettling the Coloniality of Being/Power/Truth/Freedom: Towards the Human, after Man, its Overrepresentation – An Argument', *CR: The New Centennial Review*, 3 (3): 257–337.

Chapter 17

'Soy Boy', Ecology and the Fascist Imaginary

Ruth Clemens and Becket Flannery

The political landscape in the United States has shifted rapidly throughout the last decade, as a far-right social and ideological formation (represented most dramatically by the populist rise of Donald Trump) has overtaken a major political party and reshaped public discourse about politics. In 2020 the global spread of the Covid-19 virus fuelled xenophobic fears of migration, while, in the face of nationwide protests in the United States against police brutality, the president turned towards a rhetoric of 'law and order', inspiring far-right militias and white supremacist groups to mobilise against movements for racial justice.[1] One of the most prominent features of the rise of this right-wing formation has been a loose proto- or neo-fascist community or movement stemming from online message boards and social media accounts and known collectively as the alt-right. In this chapter we examine some of the ways in which internet-based memes have been conceptualised in order to understand how online communities act as a kind of breeding ground for affects, discourses and imagery, and how the alt-right uses memes to spread a new fascist imaginary. This task is of the utmost importance in an age in which memes are 'increasingly central to how large numbers of predominantly young citizens experience politics' (Dean 2018: 2). Furthermore, the necessity of the scholarly community to overcome what Dean terms 'squeamishness' relating to popular new media is all the more urgent if we are to account for the causes and effects of recent political events such as the Brexit and Trump votes, the 'post-truth' phenomenon and the global rise of a proto-fascist 'New Brutality' (Braidotti et al. 2017).

This New Brutality includes a new language of irony, scatology, casual racism and misogyny under the guise of 'edginess'. This language has emerged from the so-called 'digital natives' of the internet age. What began as a reactionary formation in the online culture wars of the 2010s has grown into a movement embracing white supremacy, antisemitism, misogyny and violent nationalism. The vehicle for this tendency has been online meme culture, which incubated and smuggled this far-right vision into the mainstream:

> what we call the alt-right today could never have had any connection to the mainstream and to a new generation of young people if it only came in the form of lengthy treatises on obscure blogs. It was the image- and humor-based culture of the irreverent meme factory of 4chan and later 8chan that gave the alt-right its youthful energy, with its transgression and hacker tactics. (Nagle 2017: 13)

We posit that this language is proto-fascist and signals growing forms of fascist desire. We use the term 'proto-fascist' here with a genuine emphasis on the current conditions of political crisis in Europe and the United States and the uneasy sensation of the possibilities of escalation. As Christopher Hutton reminds us, 'many of the ideas that are now picked out as fascist were common currency among educated Europeans during the first half of the Twentieth Century' (2012: 2). If talking about fascism is tricky, defining it is even trickier. As Stanley G. Payne acknowledges, '*Fascism* is probably the vaguest of contemporary political terms' (1980: 4). In his recent study, Roger Griffin highlights the necessary contingency of any working definition of fascism to the social, political and cultural contexts in which it proliferates (2018: 90–1). As such, we must delineate our own conception of this brutal proto-fascism as informed by *Capitalism and Schizophrenia*, while simultaneously asserting the efficacy of Deleuze and Guattari's political philosophy for comprehending contemporary forms of fascism.

In this chapter we examine a specific linguistic meme, 'soy boy', as an example of what Gregory Bateson called an 'ecology of bad ideas' (1987: 489). In short, soy boy is a textual meme: a figuration used in internet-based discourse on social media or forums such as Reddit to name an inferior, weak and feminised male subject. Within this narrative, a soy boy typically sympathises or identifies with left-wing and liberal causes and groups. He does so because of an overconsumption of soy-based products which, according to pseudo-scientific neo-supremacist logic popularised in right-wing forums, leads to high levels of so-called 'female' hormones in men. According to this logic, this makes soy boy less masculine and therefore more susceptible to liberal politics. In the soy boy meme, which we introduce in detail below, ecological and cultural 'contamination' are conflated in multiple ways, allowing the alt-right to condense anxieties over gender, cultural identity, industrial food production, the body–mind relationship and globalisation, among others.

Using the realities of soy production in advanced capitalism as a point of comparison, we analyse how flows of capital produce deterritorialisations that challenge stable ideological, gender and racial identities. Following Felix Guattari's *The Three Ecologies*, we see how subjective, social and environmental ecologies are linked. This makes it necessary to analyse the figure of soy at every level, and examine what relations prevail between capitalism, ecology and the norms that the alt-right espouses. We read these racial and gender norms – such as the violent proliferation of an idealised hypermasculine, patriarchal, white supremacist, hypernationalist subject – as 'neo-archaisms'. According to Deleuze and Guattari, these are forms of social identity that reintroduce fragments of code; archaic conceptions that nonetheless 'are archaisms having a perfectly current function' (AO, 280). The function of these norms is to impose them in the present rather than return to any particular form of the past, which is constructed in dialogic folkloric terms, becoming a figure within the norm more than a historical tradition from which it emerges. As such, they are archaic only in the realm of the present imaginary: they are *neo-archaic*. These exclusionary neo-archaisms help us to arrive at the question posed by Deleuze and Guattari in their political philosophy of fascism: 'Why does desire desire its own repression, how can it desire its own repression?' (AO, 215). To begin to answer this question, we must try to comprehend how fascist desire works on an intimate, personal and often mundane level: the level of microfascism. Thus, the desire for hypermasculine perfection along neo-archaic lines via the fearful rejection of the emasculating potential of soy consumption becomes a desire for destruction, a rejection of intimate, psychological, bodily, social and environmental flows. This microfascist desire is no small matter: for Deleuze and Guattari, 'microfascisms are what make fascism so dangerous' (AO, 215). From Deleuze and Guattari's analysis of the micropolitics of fascist desire, we situate the alt-right as a rigid reterritorialisation of codes that simultaneously deterritorialises social life along a fascist line of flight, thus creating in its wake a 'postfascism' of 'the peace of Terror or Survival' (TP, 421). We will elaborate more on the role of survivalism later in the chapter.

The rise of the movement or community known as the alt-right is tied to the proliferation of internet memes on online forums such as Reddit (in subreddits such as r/The_Donald), 4chan and 8chan (Nagle 2017). Always playful and sometimes political viral figurations which proliferate on social media, memes are multiple and varied and move across diverse social strata. However, their power has been self-consciously harnessed by a community of political extremists to spread conspiracy and fear, most famously in the lead-up to the 2016 presidential election in the US. In *Making Sense of the Alt-Right*, Richard Hawley mentions memes before he mentions the eponymous movement itself (2017: 1–4). In fact, his introduction to the alt-right is framed by a meme of particular significance known as Pepe the Frog: 'For reasons that are difficult to discern, Pepe became the mascot of the "Alt-Right", short for "alternative right." The Alt-Right is, like Pepe, vulgar, irreverent, ironic, and goofy' (Hawley 2017: 2–3). The alt-right persists and proliferates online by creating and sharing memes. The circulation of these memes links the movement to more mainstream political actors within the state apparatus, while also allowing it to articulate its values and its enemies. What is clear here is that the alt-right has succeeded in utilising some quality of meme-mediality in furthering its own political ends. Meme-mediality is successful because it is not fuelled by semantics. Rather, it is fuelled by desire in a very dynamic way: with the click of a 'share' button flows the desire to speak or to be heard, the desire to create, the desire to be 'in' on the joke (to belong to the 'in-group'). However, what is at stake here is an understanding of how memes work between the micro and macro scales: an ecology of memes which accounts for the multiple relations of these phenomena.

In order to begin to discern what we mean by an ecology of memes – how this ecology of memes works and how it persists – it is first necessary to map the history of the meme itself. We follow the contemporary definition of memes as 'digital objects that riff on a given visual, textual or auditory form and are then appropriated, re-coded, and slotted back into the internet infrastructures they came from' (Nooney and Portwood-Stacer 2014: 249). However, meme genealogy stretches deeper: discussion of memes often begins with Richard Dawkins's inclusion of memes in *The Selfish Gene* (1976), written well before the internet age, in which the meme relates to cultural phenomena in general rather than the familiar internet meme. Nonetheless, several of his criteria are still used to define a meme's viability: indeed, the discourse of 'survival' from Dawkins is still applied to memes as a mark of success (Literat and van den Berg 2019). However, Dawkins's genocentric error, which although widely criticised in the developmental systems theory of recent biology scholarship (Oyama 2000), has often been repeated in media analyses of memes (Knobel and Lankshear 2007; Brideau and Berret 2014), is to take the meme as unit-in-itself which passes from (cultural or human) body to body via imitation and flat replication in order to propagate itself. This ignores the very qualities of its multiple political relations for which it is imperative to account in the current age. As Tony Sampson points out, memes are 'all too often analogically reduced to the workings of an evolutionary code which problematically fixes all contagious phenomena to stringent biological laws' (Sampson 2012: 355).

Contrary to Dawkins's suggestion that the gene (or meme) is the unit of selection, we reference Gregory Bateson's approach to ecology, which suggests that individuals (gene, organism, species) are always the wrong unit:

> Formerly we thought of a hierarchy of taxa – individual, family line, subspecies, species, etc. – as units of survival. We now see a different hierarchy of units – gene-in-organism, organism-in-environment, ecosystem, etc. Ecology, in the widest sense, turns out to be the study of the interaction and survival of ideas and programs (i.e., differences, complexes of differences, etc.) in circuits. (Bateson 1987: 489)

Rather than reading a meme in a 'survivalist' way merely through its quantitative proliferation and flat imitative replication, we focus on the qualities of its multiple and different relations. In this way, we can see how it participates in various circuits (in Bateson's terminology) or assemblages (in Deleuze and Guattari's) to produce new political territorialities.

Thinking ecologically along the lines of Guattari's *The Three Ecologies*, we are better able to see how soy boy is a discursive formation at the interconnection of subjective, social and environmental ecologies. Guattari insisted on the production of subjectivity as a crucial approach to how larger social and environmental ecologies are shaped. Even the 'subject' of the mental ecology is not restricted to the individual consciousness, but instead 'organizes itself in systems or "minds", the boundaries of which no longer coincide with the participant individuals' (TE, 36). In his distinction from segregated approaches to the environment, politics and the individual, Guattari suggested a 'common ethico-aesthetic discipline' (TE, 47). Guattari's work emphasises that existential territories in each of the three ecologies can be directed towards 'deathly repetitions' or 'a praxis that enables it to be made "habitable" by a human project' (TE, 35). Ecosophy is a way to both understand the persistence of deathly repetitions and a call to new ethical, political and aesthetic praxes for collective survival. In soy boy we see at every level the same mechanisms at work in a negative feedback loop: an anxiety over the deterritorialisation of capital recoded into a fascist imaginary, breeding toxic forms of identification that reinforce social and environmental degradation.

The Multiple Becomings of Soy in the Capitalist Schizophrenic Machine

The question we turn to in the following section of this chapter is: why soy? It might seem odd that the alt-right and its followers have chosen to appropriate a humble bean into their derisive figuration of non-fascism. It is especially strange when one considers the multiple becomings of soy in the capitalist schizophrenic machine: through capital, soy dissolves and becomes heterogeneous. The success of the soy boy figuration rests upon a perceived correlation between the increase in the Western world of food products which display their soy content as a selling point – such as soy-based meat replacement products, 'health' foods, soy milk – with the increase of a popular liberalism concerned with issues of environmental sustainability, social equity and ethical consumption. However, this is just one way in which the difference engine of capitalism has appropriated the desire to live otherwise into a profitable and marketable difference. The intimate realities of soy paint a completely different picture of increasing meat consumption, environmental degradation and global agricultural monopolisation. It is thus necessary to demystify soy and trace its multiple becomings as flex crop, food and fuel.

Until recently, soy production was a global oligopoly held mostly by North American and European companies. In 1986–87 the US produced 77 per cent of the world's soybeans (USSEC 2011). In the early 1990s the US and the European Union accounted for over 50 per cent of soybean crushing, the process by which soy is rendered into oil and meal, which can then be processed into other materials such as animal feed, cooking oil and, increasingly, industrial uses (Oliveira and Schneider 2016). According to a 2014 report by the World Wide Fund for Nature (WWF), global soybean production has exploded by 1,000 per cent over the last fifty years, from 27 to 269 million tons (WWF 2014). At the same time, major agribusinesses began to integrate technology and research-driven approaches to soybean cultivation, such as genetically modified seeds and agrochemicals (Turzi 2011). Corporate concentration and the expansion of soy production has led to a situation where a positive feedback loop is established between capital, growing production and growing markets. The ability of capital to create new markets for soybeans depends on continually multiplying the flexible uses for soy at an accelerated rate.

The use of soy in many industries, its literal molecular flow, takes it far from the familiar bean. Oliveira and Schneider show how pervasive the flow of this plant is in global capitalism, arguing that 'in terms of production volume, land use and international trade, soy is among the most important crops in the world today' (2016: 167). Of the world's total soy production, only 6 per cent is consumed as a bean or as bean-based products such as tofu (WWF 2011) with the remainder used in various forms taken from crushed beans, which yield meal, oil and a husk. The meal is used predominantly for feeding livestock, while the oil is refined into edible oil, with a small proportion being used as biodiesel and in industrial manufacturing as a petroleum replacement. Soy has been hailed as the founding material of a new green technology, the equivalent of coal in the new bioindustrial revolution (Oliveira and Schneider 2016): a becoming-mineral of soy. There are thus many ways in which soy illustrates the relation of capitalism and schizophrenia as explored by Deleuze and Guattari. In this case, it is specifically capital that makes soy flow into a global agro-industrial complex of 'food–feed–fuel', with a small number of conglomerates producing, processing and distributing soy *en masse*. In its transformation into many forms according to its chemical potential and protein content, soy seems closer to carbon fuel than to a commodity harvested and sold as such: soy is decomposed and converted into other forms of matter, other commodities, crossing thresholds with animals, meat, petroleum, condiments, bodybuilders and so on. The corporate concentration of production and distribution, the vertical integration of all aspects of the soy industry and the role of biotechnology highlight the role of capital in the multiple becomings of soy.

Aside from the vertical integration that provides the organisational capacity for turning soy into a flex crop, companies also market this multiplicity through terms such as 'green fuel' and 'sustainability'. There are many reasons to be sceptical of these claims for soy's sustainability and environmental friendliness, including the carbon dioxide emissions from burning forests to clear land for cultivation, the effects of mono-agriculture and the use of soy in many environmentally destructive industries such as livestock farming (Rulli 2007). In fact, 75 per cent of the world's soy is processed into livestock feed (WWF 2014), meaning that far from being the sustainable answer to the instrumentalisation of non-human life and climate degradation caused by meat overconsumption (as the soy boy meme would have it), in reality soy is an integral part of the supply chain that upholds the deathly acceleration of the global meat and dairy industry. Nonetheless, these terms are coded in European and American political discourse with liberal eco-reformism, concealing their compatibility with the most exploitative forms of neo-liberal capitalism.

Soy Boy and the Fascist Imaginary

Because of these aforementioned liberal associations, soy has been adopted as a pejorative for liberals and leftists by members of the alt-right. Soy has become a fetishistic figure for the alt-right, but its emergence has much less to do with the supposed environmental politics of liberals, and instead reveals a neo-fascist paranoia: anxiety over the stability of gender, the body and modernity. Soy boy is used to reinforce categories and hierarchies, particularly between genders (as well as between 'naturally' masculine and 'unnaturally' feminine men), as we will see by tracing the meme's development and use. The efficiency of soy boy, however, is that it condenses several strands of right-wing discourse. Soy boy does this first by dovetailing patriarchal and racial supremacy, conflating soy-consuming Western liberals and neo-colonial stereotypes of perceived Asian weakness and effeminacy via the popularity of new diets consisting of traditional Asian food staples. Secondly, soy boy conflates agribusiness oligopoly with a feminist conspiracy via the proliferation of these new diets, which are marketed to (usually white middle-class) women via the health food and wellness industries. Finally, soy boy expresses anxiety over the possibility of multiple fluidities of gender away from the binaristic gender system with the dietary and chemical flows that produce the body in contemporary capitalist society. This reveals a further schizophrenic logic: the belief that the active mind and the passive body are separate and bounded entities is simultaneously strengthened and threatened through soy boy's implicit concession that, as human beings, our environment affects us. According to this alt-right discourse we are masters of our environment, yet 'we are what we eat'.

The early beginnings of soy boy are traceable as far back as 2005, when a contributor to far-right website WND, Jim Rutz, created a six-part series, the first part of which is titled 'Soy is Making Kids "Gay"' and the rest titled 'The Trouble with Soy', in which he alleges that soy is 'poison' and 'feminizing'. In 2009 an article by Jim Thornton in *Men's Health* – far from a niche or radical publication – repeated these claims in a less sensational way, asserting that 'There may be a hidden dark side to soy, one that has the power to undermine everything it means to be male.' The *Men's Health* article made the link that, because soy contains phytoestrogens (so named because they are structurally similar to oestrogen), their consumption in humans causes increased levels of oestrogen, which then causes so-called 'feminising' effects in male bodies such as breast growth, sexual impotence and genital shrinkage. To bolster their arguments, Rutz and Thornton cite a number of studies which they say prove that soy consumption leads to dysfunctional oestrogen levels in men. However, these studies were either carried out on rodents or on men who were already experiencing hormone-related problems, and subsequent meta-studies have shown that soy consumption does not affect levels of sex hormones in humans (Messina 2010). Not only does the article in *Men's Health* promote bad science, but it also repeats assumptions that gender, the body and certain hormones are aligned along a male–female binary, that a hormone can be 'female' and that 'femininity' can be located in a hormone.

Although there is little or no scientific evidence to support this claim, or indeed the claim that soy is 'feminising', the idea continued to spread among the alt-right. In April 2017 the disyllabic pejorative 'soy boy' first appeared on Reddit to describe and name an inferior and feminised male subject who has achieved this state through consuming supposedly emasculating ideologies and products. Constructed in distinction to the mentally and physically 'strong', soy boys are men who are held to be too feminine. The phrase caught on in alt-right communities, and in November 2017 Paul Joseph Watson of the highly monetised libertarian fake-news website PrisonPlanet published a YouTube video called 'The Truth about Soy Boys'. This video uses a series of pseudo-scientific claims, scientific research taken out of context and imaginative leaps to position soy as the causative factor in supposedly declining testosterone levels in men and the perceived increase in their 'feminised' behaviour. According to this discourse, this emasculation is a very real bodily experience: the overconsumption of soy causes muscular wasting and sexual impotence, producing a chemical 'castration' in men and thereby 'feminising' society (somewhat unsurprisingly, the effects of soy consumption on women in this model are never mentioned in the soy boy discourse). Despite the lack of scientific evidence for this claim, the discursive work it performs was perhaps too irresistible to ignore over merely factual concerns, and it rapidly proliferated and mutated across the internet and into different communities in the form of a meme. Figure 17.1 shows the speed at which the soy boy figuration became an established part of online discourse.

Soy boy serves to reinforce the alt-right's hierarchies and divisions, including gender and race, as justified by pseudo-science. In the West, soy is still associated with Asian diets through the marketing of soy-based foods as healthy sustainable meat alternatives originating in traditional Asian cuisine such as tofu, tempeh and edamame. Furthermore, as a replacement for dairy products it is also coded as antithetical to a trait the alt-right associates with whiteness: lactose tolerance. More

Google Trends: Soy Boy

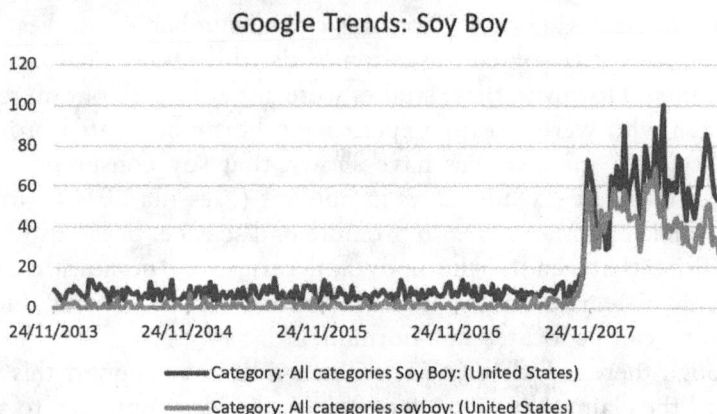

Figure 17.1 The number of Google searches for 'Soy Boy' in the US from 2013 to 2018. Source: Google Trends, <https://g.co/trends/bDa1v> (last accessed 4 October 2020).

recently, dairy milk has been used by alt-right protestors as a symbol of white supremacy. Exploiting a long line of cultural marketing in the style examined by Barthes' *Mythologies* (1972), white supremacists hold milk-chugging rallies and even use milk as a projectile to harass those it deems enemies, associating dairy with masculinity, nation and whiteness (Harmon 2018). Historically these same tropes of whiteness contrasted a diet of cow's milk and flesh with Orientalist notions of the inferior diets of racialised others, particularly in Asia, while ignoring the actual agro-political conditions of food and its frequent embeddedness with colonialism. The genocentric fixation on a genetic trait (lactose tolerance) exemplifies the pseudo-scientific discourse that undergirds alt-right racism. Distorting genetics into 'proof' of essential racial characteristics, contemporary white supremacy is couched in terms such as 'biodiversity', claiming that distinct racial groups exist and that cultural or social integration would result in the collapse of these (supposedly necessary and essential) differences. The alt-right appropriates the liberal discourse of diversity to justify racial separation: soy becomes the symbol of the inability to consume dairy on the part of some populations, and therefore of racial distinction *tout court*.

Soy's association with Western vegan and vegetarian diets (coded as politically 'liberal') allows the alt-right to contrast (liberal) soy boys with carnivorous (conservative) 'alpha males'. The link between meat, competition, predation and masculinity finds its apotheosis in soy boy's other, the 'crypto carnivore'. A trend among cryptocurrency enthusiasts, this all-meat diet relies on some of the same narrative tropes as crypto-currency in its libertarian mode: a 'return to nature', along with its sup-posedly natural gender roles and identities, and of course the completely natural free market. Journalist Jordan Pearson, in his 2017 investigation into these all-meat communities, writes how soy becomes the figure for 'artificial' food, while meat becomes properly 'authentic' nutrition.

Problematically for the alt-right, the vast majority of soy (as we have already mentioned) is used to feed livestock, flowing into the red meat and dairy milk prized as properly masculine sources of protein. Soy reveals the schizophrenic logic of a capitalist world in which a crop that is mainly used to fuel the meat industry on a global industrial scale becomes metonymic for the perceived liberal weakness of a meat-free diet. Soy flows under such simplistic political divisions as red meat conservatives and soy latté liberals. Soy protein is frequently used in protein powders and shakes, dietary supplements consumed to help build muscle mass and attain properly 'masculine' bodies – here the schizophrenic flows of soy as both feminising and masculinising come to the fore once more. Nonetheless, according to the soy boy discourse, the obsession with 'wellness' and sustainable consumption that prolif-erates soy-based products is actually a conspiracy by liberal feminists designed to emasculate men through the supposed oestrogen content of soy. The 'conspiracy' of feminists takes the place of the concentration of soy production by large agribusiness, combining anxiety over the content of food (such as the use of pesticides and genetically modified organisms) and the control of global corporations with anxiety over the constitution of gender. Agribusiness's assault on the environment becomes liberal feminism's attack on cisgender heterosexual men, and specifically white men.

The flow of soy into numerous products therefore causes it to become a figure for anxiety over the flow of gender. Even within the molar cat-egories of gender, there is still a 'multiplicity of molecular combinations bringing into play not only the man in the woman and the woman in the man, but the relation of each to the animal, the plant, etc.: a thousand tiny sexes' (TP, 235). The anxiety over masculinity expressed by the alt-right, its 'permanent molecular insecurity' (TP, 237) over its own recod-ing of gender categories, has fixed on soy as an emasculating symbol, referring to those who do not meet its standards of masculinity as soy boys. According to this discourse, gender categories are natural, essential and genetic givens undermined by cultural modernity. However, the fear of the power of soy encoded in soy boy implicitly supports an ecological mode which disregards the static, singular and bounded conception of

Vitruvian man who is master of nature in favour of a conception that accounts for the world via the power of its (non-human) relations. The anxiety of how to be 'properly' masculine or a 'real' man extends to anxiety over the chemical and material flows through the body, seeing the dangers of 'feminisation' as being dietary as well as ideological or cultural. It is the very prevalence of soy that feeds the paranoia over gender; contaminating the categories of 'male' and 'female', it seems to threaten the stability of these categories, not to mention a 'becoming-plant'. 'A thousand tiny sexes', indeed.

Contemporary masculinist and fascist discourses of ethnonational purity, rather than remaining totally ignorant of the structure of modern food production, use the deterritorialised nature of such a system to their paranoid advantage. This uncertainty is exploited not only to shift blame on to notions of a liberal feminist conspiracy, but also for profit. The popular conspiracy-laden radio show and website *Infowars* has gone so far as to provide its own line of dietary supplements. These supplements, for example Alex Jones's 'Brain Force' supplement, are specifically marketed as combating the various substances supposedly placed in the food and water supply to inhibit resistance to the larger scheme of subjugating white men and reducing their 'natural' propensity for freedom. Nonetheless, this supplement as well as others which aim to combat the 'feminising' effects of soy – as well as the protein powders of bodybuilders – of course contains soy. The schizophrenic allegiance between capitalism and fascism is always present.

What 'force' does the brain exert? What kind of 'potency' would it possess? Without taking too seriously the marketing claims of a dietary supplement sold by a conspiracy theorist, we might ask what concepts of mind and body are being proposed. The paranoid framework of *Infowars* portrays the mind and body as under constant assault from a conspiracy aimed at 'weakening' minds (and bodies) through a confluence of ideology and matter: leftism, feminism and oestrogen. The mind is seen as a purely rational capacity that must maintain mastery over the body in which it is housed, without falling prey to emasculating ideological or chemical influences. The premium placed on rationalism, on a pure reliance on the autonomous mind, becomes a paranoid hermeneutics in which diet (including media) becomes the curative measure. In short, it is the figurative 'red pill' of alt-right and misogynist internet discourse taken from the 2000 film *The Matrix*, which causes the scales of illusion to fall from the eyes of the ingesting party (*Infowars* also sells a supplement called 'The Real Red Pill'). The position of the body in this discourse, meanwhile, is only as a flow of chemicals and proteins, a conception of the self that (in a very different context) Guattari critiqued as scientism: 'it is as though a scientistic superego demands that psychic entities are reified and insists that they are only understood by means of extrinsic coordinates' (TE, 25). The subject, in this pseudo-scientific discourse, can only be the product of external, biochemical, linguistic or systemic factors.

The subject thus being proposed by soy boy is a body and *cogito* constantly under threat of deterritorialisation through the confluence of flows. Nonetheless, soy boy disavows the embodiedness of cognition and the heterogeneous 'vectors of subjectification' (TE, 25) by supposedly preserving the mind from contamination. Guattari reminds us that the fallacy of the mind–body split inaugurates two simultaneous tendencies: the entirely extrinsic construction of the subject by behavioural-empirical models, the body as purely chemical and mechanistic, as well as the independence of the mind and disavowal of the body by the *cogito*. Both of these modes are present in the soy boy discourse: the reduction of the body to biochemical inputs, but also the supremacy of the mind as a will to master its own embodiment. Rather than a truly ecological figure, this will take the embodiedness of the mind as its object, dictating to itself a diet of certain ideological and chemical inputs.

Memes and the Fascist Line of Flight

We have seen how the content of soy boy functions, and we turn now to our analysis of its form: its meme-mediality. Soy boy and other alt-right memes inscribe these schizophrenic notions of threatened supremacist masculinity into existential territories and produce subjectivities. The phrase 'soy boy' acts as a refrain, the repetition of which unifies disparate codes, from the misogynistic trope of persecuted masculinity to the scientific racism of the right's distortion of genetics. It also is able to form assemblages that link online communities and macropolitical actors, molecular desire with the state apparatus, and individuals in technological circuits. Memes not only organise a territory through their capacity to proliferate and mutate, but even use hashtags to track both the magnitude and reach of a refrain. Nonetheless, we should not automatically accept the neo-Darwinian framework for analysing memes, but instead see the ways that competition and selfishness are inscribed into the territorialities organised by memes.

Deleuze and Guattari's analysis of birdsong is instructive here. Rather than describing birdsong as a method to claim a territory for functions such as hunting and sexual reproduction, Deleuze and Guattari claim that 'these functions are organized or created only because they are *territorialized*, and not the other way around. The T factor, the territorializing factor, must be sought elsewhere: precisely in the becoming-expressive of rhythm or melody' (TP, 348). Defining the meme through aggression and 'selfishness' attempts to explain its territorialising quality through its self-replicating function. However, it is in fact the meme-relation which creates territories through which functions (such as replication, competition, etc.) are possible. The difference is not trivial: assuming genocentric 'selfishness' as the primary driver of a meme's proliferation naturalises competitive and aggressive behaviour, placing it prior to the territoriality by which behaviours are possible or legible.

The prosody of soy boy should not be quickly discounted as part of its territorialising function. As Deleuze and Guattari write: 'What is primary is the consistency of a refrain, a little tune, either in the form of a mnemic melody that has no need to be inscribed locally in a center, or in the form of a vague motif with no need to be pulsed or stimulated' (TP, 366). This is why soy boy territorialises even as the alt-right simultaneously disavows its actual content, claiming that the very absurdity of soy boy and its various interlocked narratives is only a joke. It is the repetition itself that draws the territory, and soy boy's lack of seriousness is crucial in this regard, allowing the meme to circulate through audiences that might otherwise find its content offensive. Hawley (2017) suggests that perhaps the irreverence of the meme makes it politically malleable, or maybe it is the meme's propensity for an 'ironic' ambivalence of intent. The meme has an aesthetics of propagation in which meaning adapts to a virtual flatness, allowing it to duplicate its own image at a dizzying speed in a multiplicity of different contexts and situations. Due to their molecular power, these viral representations are used by large assemblages such as macropolitical agents and corporations as tools of constraining power or *potestas*. The path of certain memes from the fringe right-wing to the Twitter feed of Donald Trump testifies to this pipeline, as a 2018 piece for the *New York Times* by journalists Keith Collins and Kevin Roose shows. The power of memes has less to do with their content (and therefore also the sincerity of that content) than the ability to build new assemblages, larger networked circuits, through which fascism (in this case) can operate.

The alt-right does not have a specific ideology; it values the transgression of norms rather than instantiating a particular norm (Nagle 2017: 28–39). This is precisely why it can treat its 'ideas' so lightly, how it can spread through its own self-disavowal and yet pursue the fascist path towards abolition: because fascism is also not an ideology but a line of flight. Deleuze and Guattari identify fascism first as a form of desire, following Wilhelm Reich in observing of the masses that 'at a certain point, under a certain set of conditions, they *wanted* fascism, and it is this perversion of the desire of the masses that needs to be accounted for' (AO, 31). Fascist desire does not merely wish to abolish a particular political enemy in favour of establishing something, but rather 'is constructed on an intense line of flight, which it transforms into a line of pure destruction and abolition' (TP, 230). Soy boy does not have to be serious to be deadly; indeed, what else would we expect of 'realized nihilism' (TP, 230) than that it would believe in nothing? What the alt-right has realised is that it does not need to believe in anything to trace its violent path, a path that runs through a deterritorialising fascism towards a state that Deleuze and Guattari call 'postfascism' (TP, 465).

The 'feminist conspiracy' behind soy production is a ridiculous fantasy, but as we saw above, the alt-right takes mental and physical 'weakness' very seriously, even if the figure of the soy boy is in jest. Basic assumptions about individualism and the primacy of aggression, even if expressed as a joke, proliferate and emerge in forms that are deadly serious. This is evident, for example, in the hyper-misogynistic violence of 'incels', which is often preceded by statements so bizarre that they are easily mistaken for absurdist riddles.[2] Even if it were possible to distinguish between earnest and ironic, the meme's ability to circulate and adapt in many different contexts makes it at best misleading to claim that a particular statement may or may not be serious – the question to ask is rather *for whom* is this meme serious, and what are the effects of this. The sites where these memes are (re-)produced, circulated and consumed have particular audiences with established ways of reading. In many communities, the ironic reading of a meme is understood as a logical step in its circulation which extends its life (Literat and van den Berg 2019). Multiple entanglements of meaning are present in memes, which does not suggest a denial of any meaning but rather a situated and contextual reading according to which one audience may see an offensive joke and another a call to arms. The relation of the meme should be the basic unit of reference, as some new media theorists such as Jenkins (2014) and Bratich (2014) suggest. Such entanglements of meaning both emerge from and actively produce these different sites of reception, as irony, absurdity and offence are used to delimit insider from outsider groups. One can call out an outsider for taking a meme too seriously, while simultaneously speaking to insiders who might take the same meme deadly seriously in a different manner. We can understand the 'irony' of the alt-right as part of its deterritorialising effect and still recognise the white supremacist and patriarchal reterritorialisations in its wake.

The meme helps circulate in an ecological feedback loop between epistemological fallacies, environmental and social degradation, and fascist desire. As Gregory Bateson wrote in his essay 'Pathologies of Epistemology', 'There is an ecology of bad ideas, just as there is an ecology of weeds, and it is characteristic of the system that basic error propagates itself' (1987: 491–2). For Bateson, bad ideas propagate, crowding out and undermining other ideas and subjectivities, altering the ecology in their favour. Guattari uses the example of algae to describe this process, comparing the proliferation of images on television with the invasion of mutant algae in Venice (TE, 28). From this overwhelming of the subjective ecology, Guattari then demonstrates how such pathogens spread through cities and social systems, where the resulting conditions reinforce in a negative feedback loop the spread of bad ideas in the mental ecology. Soy boy is one of many mutant algae in the alt-right ecology of bad ideas, which by its very spread alters the water for the further proliferation of toxic notions. For the rest of this section, we examine specifically how this neo-archaic construction of masculinity figures a 'postfascist' state of survival.

According to Guattari, capitalism's tendency towards dissolving subjectivities and disrupting existential territories results in a 'subjective conservatism' in which 'hierarchical structures [. . .] have become the object of an imaginary hypercathexis' (TE, 31). The hierarchies that soy boy manifests, the elevation of masculinity, individualism, aggression and competitiveness, are reinscribed precisely at the moment that masculinity is deterritorialised by capitalism. To support its neo-archaisms, the alt-right and its spokespeople such as Alex Jones circulate memes and narratives that advocate (when it comes to gender) a return to mythologised archaic norms, constructing an image of the ancient past that accords with its vision for the future. Jones and *Infowars* sell a line of (largely mundane, expensive and ineffective) dietary supplements, including products called 'Caveman', which was discontinued due to a ruling by the California Office of the Attorney General after it was found to contain excess levels of lead, and 'Ultimate Bone Broth', which use tales of ancient aggression and survival in their product description. From the description of 'Ultimate Bone Broth' on the *Infowars* website:

> In ancient times, man roamed the Earth in a constant state of hunting and being hunted. There was no room for weakness: every time an animal was caught, all of its parts were put to good use – from skin and guts, to fur

and bone. From the way we interact with one another to the way we eat, our modern society has completely discarded many of the ancient traditions and practices that our ancestors held dearly.

This opening statement identifies a state of survival with the state of nature, suggesting that the alt-right's own neo-Darwinian narratives and fetishisation of capitalist competition are a part of an essential human nature and a natural order. Central to this worldview are survival and predation (along with gender and 'man') as unchangeable givens neces-sary to produce 'healthy' subjects and societies, a state approaching Deleuze and Guattari's characterisation of 'postfascism':

> This worldwide war machine, which in a way 'reissues' from the States, displays two successive figures: first, that of fascism, which makes war an unlimited movement with no other aim than itself; but fascism is only a rough sketch, and the second, postfascist, figure is that of a war machine that takes peace as its object directly, as the peace of Terror or Survival. (TP, 465)

We view the discourse of soy boy thus as a contemporary manifestation of survivalist rhetoric, which 'can be understood as an especially extreme and violent manifestation of larger social forces that wed masculinity with militancy' (Belew 2018: 7).

The alt-right, in its ethos of competition, aggression and the individual versus their environment, echoes the political principles of survivalism, a paramilitary movement in the United States that emerged in the 1970s and early 1980s in the wake of demobilisation following the Vietnam War. Because Deleuze and Guattari understand the military itself to be a form of state appropriation of the nomadic war machine (TP, 464), the demobilisation after the Vietnam War thus functions as a nomadic war machine captured by the state apparatus, given war as its object, and then released from the state, even to the point of declaring war on the state itself (Belew 2018). The declaration of war on the state (and its own schizophrenic proliferation of industrial agriculture, food regulation and desire-based diets riding the waves of the free market) in this survivalist discourse is not insignificant. While fascism is often seen to culminate in the takeover of the state, it is thus necessary to separate the concept of fascism from the state. The fascist state was 'capitalism's most fantastic attempt at economic and political reterritorialization' (AO, 280), a cap-turing of the war machine by the state apparatus. Fascism itself, on the other hand, is a line of flight that, instead of crossing thresholds towards new becomings, falls into a line of abolition:

the line of flight crossing the wall, getting out of the black holes, but instead of connecting with other lines and each time augmenting its valence, *turning to destruction, abolition pure and simple, the passion of abolition.* Like Kleist's line of flight, and the strange war he wages; like suicide, double suicide, a way out that turns the line of flight into a line of death. (TP, 253)

This suicidal passion becomes evident in the way that environmental degradation is pursued unto death, the double suicide of both humanity and the circuit or environment that sustains it.

Following Guattari's *The Three Ecologies*, we can also see how this fascist line of flight is linked to mental and social ecologies, where soy boy celebrates exactly what propels us down this line of abolition. An epistemological error, the belief that the self is distinct from its environment, is reproduced as a domination of the mind over the body, and of the individual over society. The result is a society of survival, reinforcing the very same aggressive mindset that produced it, leaving individuals further isolated; finally, instrumentalising the planetary environment, the exploitation of which feeds subjective paranoias over the body, thus producing reactionary figures such as soy boy. Pulling ourselves away from this double suicide will not require merely an inversion of these identifications: as Bateson pointed out, the separation of the human mind from its environment is one of the basic errors that proliferates and despoils. To reverse the damage done to our environment, we need to think and act through an ecosophy that acknowledges the interlocked nature of the three ecologies. The will to dominate must be replaced by a full assumption of 'machinic ecology' (TE, 43), which neither continues the illusion of human supremacy nor refuses its responsibility.

Notes

1. For example, in the presidential debate of 29 September 2020, Trump urged the violent neo-fascist men's group Proud Boys to 'stand back and stand by' because 'somebody's got to do something about' [*sic*] anti-fascist activists (*Washington Post*).
2. Alek Minassian, who murdered ten and wounded fourteen in the Toronto van attack of 23 April 2018, preceded his massacre with a Facebook post that read: 'Private (Recruit) Minassian Infantry 00010, wishing to speak to Sgt 4chan please. C2324911. The Incel Rebellion has already begun! We will overthrow all the Chads and Stacys! All hail the Supreme Gentleman Elliot Rodger!' (BBC 2018).

References

Anonymous (2017), *Reddit.com*, 19 April, <https://archive.4plebs.org/tv/thread/817 90191/#q81791708> (last accessed 4 October 2020).

Barthes, R. (1972), *Mythologies*, trans. A. Lavers, New York: The Noonday Press. Translation of *Mythologies*, Paris: Editions du Seuil, 1957.

Bateson, G. (1987), 'Pathologies of Epistemology', in *Steps to an Ecology of Mind: Collected Essays in Anthropology, Psychiatry, Evolution, and Epistemology*, 2nd edn, Northvale, NJ: Jason Aronson, pp. 484–93.

BBC (2018), 'Alek Minassian Toronto Van Attack Suspect Praised "Incel" Killer', 25 April, <https://www.bbc.com/news/world-us-canada-43883052> (last accessed 4 October 2020).

Belew, K. (2018), *Bring the War Home*, Cambridge, MA: Harvard University Press.

Braidotti, R. T. Vermeulen, J. Aranda, B. K. Wood, S. Squibb and A. Vidokle (2017), 'Editorial – "The New Brutality"', *e-flux*, 83, June, <https://www.e-flux.com/journal/83/142721/editorial-the-new-brutality/> (last accessed 4 October 2020).

'Brain Force Plus', product description, *Inforwarsshop.com*, <https://www.infowarsstore.com/brain-force.html> (last accessed 4 October 2020).

Bratich, J. (2014), 'Occupy All the Dispositifs: Memes, Media Ecologies, and Emergent Bodies Politic', *Communication and Critical/Cultural Studies*, 11 (1): 64–73.

Brideau, K., and C. Berret (2014), 'A Brief Introduction to Impact: "The Meme Font"', *Journal of Visual Culture*, 13 (3): 307–13.

California Office of the Attorney General (COAG) (2017), '60 Day Notice 2017–02319', <https://oag.ca.gov/prop65/60-day-notice-2017-02319> (last accessed 4 October 2020).

Collins, K., and K. Roose (2018), 'Tracing a Meme From the Internet's Fringe to a Republican Slogan', *New York Times*, 4 November, <https://www.nytimes.com/interactive/2018/11/04/technology/jobs-not-mobs.html> (last accessed 4 October 2020).

Dawkins, R. (1976), *The Selfish Gene*, Oxford: Oxford University Press.

Dean, J. (2018), 'Sorted for Memes and Gifs: Visual Media and Everyday Digital Politics', *Political Studies Review* 17 (3): 1–12.

Dunn, M. (2017), 'The Internet's Newest Insult', *The Daily Mercury*, 28 December, 32.

Gleeson, J. J. (2018), 'An Anatomy of the Soy Boy', *New Socialist*. 3 February, <https://newsocialist.org.uk/an-anatomy-of-the-soy-boy/> (last accessed 4 October 2020).

Griffin, R. (2018), *Fascism: An Introduction to Comparative Fascist Studies*, Cambridge: Polity.

Harmon, A. (2018), 'Why White Supremacists are Chugging Milk (and Why Geneticists are Alarmed)', *New York Times*, 17 October, <https://www.nytimes.com/2018/10/17/us/white-supremacists-science-dna.html> (last accessed 4 October 2020).

Hawley, G. (2017), *Making Sense of the Alt-Right*, New York: Columbia University Press.

Hickey-Moody, A. (2019), *Deleuze and Masculinity*, Basingstoke: Palgrave Macmillan.

Hutton, C. (2012), *Linguistics and the Third Reich: Mother-Tongue Fascism, Race and the Science of Language*, Abingdon: Routledge.

Jenkins, E. S. (2014), 'The Modes of Visual Rhetoric: Circulating Memes as Expressions', *Quarterly Journal of Speech*, 100 (4): 442–66.

Knobel, M., and C. Lankshear (2007), 'Online Memes, Affinities, and Cultural

Production', in M. Knobel and C. Lankshear (eds), *A New Literacies Sampler*, New York: Peter Lang, pp. 199–228.

Literat, I., and S. van den Berg (2019), 'Buy Memes Low, Sell Memes High: Vernacular Criticism and Collective Negotiations of Value on Reddit's MemeEconomy', *Information, Communication & Society*, 22 (2): 232–49.

Messina, M. (2010), 'Soybean Isoflavone Exposure Does not Have Feminizing Effects on Men: A Critical Examination of the Clinical Evidence', *Fertility and Sterility*, 9 (7): 2095–104.

Nagle, A. (2017), *Kill All Normies*, Winchester, UK: Zero Books.

Nooney, L., and L. Portwood-Stacer (2014), 'One Does not Simply: An Introduction to the Special Issue on Internet Memes', *Journal of Visual Culture*, 13 (3): 248–52.

Oliveira, G. de L. T., and M. Schneider (2016), 'The Politics of Flexing Soybeans: China, Brazil and Global Agroindustrial Restructuring', *The Journal of Peasant Studies*, 43 (1): 167–94.

Oyama, S. (2000), *Evolution's Eye: A Systems View of the Biology-Culture Divide*, Durham, NC: Duke University Press.

Payne, S. G. (1980), *Fascism: Comparison and Definition*, Madison: University of Wisconsin Press.

Pearson, J. (2017), 'Meat and Greet: Inside the World of the "Bitcoin Carnivores"', *Motherboard*, 29 September, <https://motherboard.vice.com/en_us/article/ne74nw/inside-the-world-of-the-bitcoin-carnivores> (last accessed 4 October 2020).

Power, N. (2017), 'The Language of the New Brutality', *e-flux*, 83 (June), <https://www.e-flux.com/journal/83/141286/the-language-of-the-new-brutality/> (last accessed 30 May 2019).

'The Real Red Pill', product description, *Infowarsshop.com*, <https://www.infowarsstore.com/the-real-red-pill.html> (last accessed 4 October 2020).

Rulli, J. (2007), 'Introduction to the Soya Model', in J. Rulli (ed.), *United Soya Republics: The Truth about Soya Production in South America*, trans. M. Bell, Buenos Aires: GRR Grupo de Reflexión Rural, pp. 14–31.

Rutz, J. (2006), 'Soy is Making Kids "Gay"', *WND.com*, 12 December, <https://www.wnd.com/2006/12/39253/> (last accessed 4 October 2020).

Sampson, T. D. (2012), 'Tarde's Phantom Takes a Deadly Line of Flight – from Obama Girl to the Assassination of Bin Laden', *Distinktion: Scandinavian Journal of Social Theory*, 13 (3): 354–66.

Sommer, W. (2017), 'How "Soy Boy" Became the Far Right's Favorite New Insult', *Medium*, 26 October, <https://medium.com/@willsommer/how-soy-boy-became-the-far-rights-favorite-new-insult-e2e988d365c7> (last accessed 4 October 2020).

Thornton, J. (2009), 'Is This the Most Dangerous Food For Men?', *Men's Health*, 19 May, <https://www.menshealth.com/nutrition/a19539170/soys-negative-effects/> (last accessed 4 October 2020).

Turzi, M. (2011), 'The Soybean Republic', *Yale Journal of International Affairs*, 6 (2): 59–68.

'Ultimate Bone Broth', product description, *Infowarsshop.com*, <http://www.infowarsshop.com/Ultimate-Bone-Broth_p_2296.html> (last accessed 4 October 2020).

USSEC (US Soybean Export Council) (2011), 'How the Global Oilseed and Grain Trade Works', <https://unitedsoybean.org/wp-content/uploads/2013/07/RevisedJan12_GlobalOilSeedGrainTrade_2011.pdf> (last accessed 4 October 2020).

Watson, J. (2015), 'Multiple Mutating Masculinities', *Angelaki*, 20 (1): 107–121, <https://doi.org/10.1080/0969725X.2015.1017387>.

Watson, P. J. (2017), 'The Truth About Soy Boys', video file, YouTube.com, 16

November, <https://www.youtube.com/watch?v=FTSvLKY7HEk> (last accessed 4 October 2020).

WWF (World Wide Fund for Nature) (2014), *The Growth of Soy: Impacts and Solutions*, Gland, Switzerland: WWF International.

Chapter 18

Pussy Riot vs. Trump: Becoming Woman to Resist Becoming Fascist

Natalie Dyer, Hollie Mackenzie, Diana Teggi, Patricia de Vries

Introduction

This chapter explores how protest punk rock group Pussy Riot reclaim the *vagina* in their songs 'Straight Outta Vagina' and 'Make America Great Again' by activating a non-normative and *fluid* feminist desire against the phallic micropolitical fascism emanating from former US President Donald J. Trump. Our analysis of these two Pussy Riot songs aims to conceptualise a feminist micropolitics centered on the pussy, a *labial* language and the multiple molecular *becomings* that such pussy politics generate. We eschew the trap of constructing a counter-penis concept, as Simone de Beauvoir warned (Appignanesi 2005). Instead, we imagine and interpret pussy politics by way of engaging with Pussy Riot's songs in order to offer a politics of feminist resistance to the micro-fascist psychic economies at work in the Trump presidency. By relating to the Trump presidency through Deleuze and Guattari's concept of the Face Machine, this politics of feminist resistance activates the disruptive power of a fluid feminist subject. We argue that it reclaims the pussy's multiplicity, fluids and flows both as a source of becoming and as an antidote to the microfascism witnessed today. We situate the music videos of 'Straight Outta Vagina' and 'Make America Great Again' as sources which stage a multiple and fluid feminist desire that intervenes in the toxicity of Trump's Face Machine and allows for the possibility of *'an "other meaning"'* inspired by Irigaray's feminist ethics (Irigaray 1985b: 29).

Trump's Face Machine: Staging a Phallic Microfascist Desire

As a celebratory crowd chants 'U.S.A!' with an unsettling military repetition, Trump takes the stage. It is 9 November 2016. The *Air*

Force One film soundtrack plays in the background, ushering in the new president who declares the American Dream dead and promises to bring it back. A micropolitical desire is forging, signalled by the highly emotive military music – all hail the new Sandman. The camera closes in on Trump's face as he thanks his audience and solemnly pledges himself to the nation. Of the political election process, he comments: 'difficult business'. We are reminded that he is first and foremost a businessman whose time is money, and money is king. He proceeds to apologise for keeping his audience waiting. This is *showbiz*, lest we forget it.

This is Trump's America proclaimed only months after he was caught on camera boasting about making sexual advances to a particular woman, although he seems to be speaking of women generally, when he states: 'I don't even wait. And when you're a star, they let you do it. You can do anything. Grab them by the pussy. You can do anything' (*New York Times* 2016). It is highly unsettling that these words should be spoken at all, let alone by the same man who promises to make America great again in his inauguration speech: 'From this day forward, a new vision will govern . . . it's going to be only America first, America first.' Trump's vision for America is prefaced by his self-ordained right to grab any woman 'by the pussy', and a revamping of feral misogyny, a classic in the canon of historical fascism. Therefore, we argue that reclaiming the pussy or indeed the vagina is an act of radical political protest against this misogynist fascism.

As Pankaj Mishra notes, citing Mary Wollstonecraft, the project of nationalist politics is fundamentally misogynistic. Women are always supposed to know their place in a vision of lost greatness. And many white, bourgeois women seem to opt to reside in that place, considering the voting results (Philpot 2018). For many minority groups, nationalist politics has failed and continues to fail to provide a common ground to begin with.

Exposed to microfascist nationalist politics that does not shy away from sexism, racism, classism and ableism on a daily basis, feminists, postcolonial and gender theorists, poets, activists and artists alike are, and have been for decades, challenging the protagonist of the dogma of an American Dream, as well as its entitlement to its land. Some dissidents have worked to bring into view the power structures inherent in what constitutes 'America' (Crenshaw 1989; hooks 2015; Lugones 2007; Mohanty 2003). Others have sought to expose the ethnocentrism and androcentrism of what is considered 'Great' (Haslanger 2008). Together they have argued for the need for a radically inclusive and fluid politics of feminist and fluid desire, with the capacity to rupture 'the American dream'.

It seems irrefutable that we are living in *interesting* times. Following Trump's election, America has faced rising inequalities and unpredictable politics, in which nothing can be considered sacred or solid, including the judiciary and civil rights. We have witnessed the horrors of police brutality against Black Lives Matter protesters, herd immunity as a response to COVID-19 and the revocation of constitutional abortion rights. Even a group of ultra-rich American men feel uneasy, with their palpable fears and concerns intensifying around the growing risks of social inequality and the possibility of tensions turning violent. To the extent that they have joined a movement for Survivalists,[1] or 'Preppers' as some call themselves, this group of ultra-rich American men are preparing for the moment the proverbial shit hits the fan by reterritorialising *their* land of the free under the ground.

Larry Hall, a former computer scientist at the Florida Institute of Technology and a billionaire specialist in networks and datacentres, started the Survival Condo Project – 'a fifteen-story luxury apartment complex built in an underground Atlas missile silo' somewhere in the north of Kansas (Osnos 2017). In a former nuclear silo, Hall has built his molehill where the ultra-wealthy can grit their teeth and hole up for five-plus years, underground, in twelve luxury condos tailored to the owner's needs. The shared amenities include a pool, a rock-climbing wall, a pet park, an Apple-Mac-equipped study room, a gym, a movie theatre and a library. The 'medical wing' of the Survival Condo is decked out with a hospital bed, a procedure table and a dentist's chair. In case of societal collapse, or in case of a Pussy Riot, a 'SWAT-team-style truck picks up any Survival Condo owner' within 650 kilometres, Hall explains (Osnos 2017). He has sold all the units of his Survival Condo. In its entirety his bunker can house and support a total of seventy-five wealthy people and their pets. Going off the grid, indulging in apocalypse talk, or 'taking sides with the death drive', as McKenzie Wark (2017) once argued, 'is the ultimate in white-boy privilege'.

The Survivalists are a product of the phallic vector mobilised by Trump's politics, which we conceptualise as the Trump Face Machine. Following Deleuze and Guattari (*Anti-Oedipus*, *A Thousand Plateaus*), a micropolitical analysis of Trump reveals the molecularity of fascist desire and its channelling on to the molar axes of subjectification. Microfascism operates at the level of the production of desire. The difference between microfascism and microrevolution is not in the content of desire, but in its ethics. Desire never happens in a vacuum, it is never floating without support, never disconnected, except when a line of flight breaks free. Desire is always already in an assemblage. It is always already connecting with and running through material, social and symbolic landscapes. Deleuze and Guattari explain this as desire being already plugged into a desiring-machine, that is a heterogeneous assemblage of the subject and her outside – assuming the two can be separated.

What makes the desiring-machine work? What makes the entanglement of such different entities hold together is the same energy, the same agentive principle running through them: impersonal desire. The desiring-machine actualises and transforms desire by displacing it on to newly assembled material and socio-semiotic landscapes. The desiring-machine is thus productive of subjectivities as well as worlds. We contend that desiring-machines essentially perform a qualitative shift in the ethics of desire – which has nothing to do with a choice of object. Drawing on Rosi Braidotti's reading of Spinoza's ethics (2006), a desiring-machine should be judged by what it does, that is, by the sorts of *passions* it produces rather than what it is. Affirmative/joyful passions expand a body's capacity to affect and be affected, while negative/sad passions reduce it. An affirmative ethics of desire will thus seek to maximise the subjects' potential to express themselves, while a negative ethics of desire will seek to restrain, block or even destroy it. Microfascism endorses the second mode by systematically obstructing certain desiring flows to the advantage of others.

The Face Machine, or Faciality, is one such desiring-machine connecting desire to a highly codified and rigid landscape of power (*pouvoir*) whose meaning and subject do not depend on the singular facial traits co-opted by it. On the contrary, they depend on the image of power that is latent at an unconscious level, which more often than not is the dominant one. According to Braidotti, the dominant image of a subject holding power – which too often coincides, but does not necessarily have to coincide, with its concrete appearance – is 'white, able-bodied, heterosexual, speaking a standard language, owning the land, the property, the families, the children, the nation' (Braidotti 2015: 243). Therefore, as Deleuze and Guattari explain, to make a Face recognisable as such, the faciality function makes the perceived traits 'conform in advance' to a dominant psychic reality (TP, 168). As Deleuze and Guattari conceive it, the Face is not personal nor is it a universal constant of human embodiment (TP). Not every human face is necessarily a Face, since not everyone's head is entangled in the production of systems of power (*potestas*). Only a few people's faces are also Faces of power. The production of political leaders always requires the production of a Face and this is especially true in today's highly visualised and mediatised information society.

In Western culture, what this Face of power does is to absorb all concrete faces and reject the ones it cannot assimilate, ordering them by degrees of difference from the pure, ideal template of the face of Christ – which Western Christian theology and art standardised as white (Siker 2007) while it most probably was dark-skinned (Wilson 2004). As such, the Face is not neutral, nor is it a representation of the average white man, rather it is the White Man himself (TP, 176.). The Face of power always works and behaves as the face of the White Man, with all the political, symbolic and affective consequences that go along with it. This is because, as already mentioned, Faciality is unconscious before being the assemblage of any facial trait. And any unconscious is social, it is a multiplicity of desiring-machines always connected to an outside, an environment, a territory, a whole world, that is extensively being shaped and dominated by the White Man.

All Face Machines capture the molecular desires of the masses and reterritorialise them along the axes of the white, male, heterosexual, able-bodied subject speaking a standard language. Trump's Face Machine functions exactly in the same way – it deterritorialises white male anger for a loss of status away from the problems of exploitation and poverty, while reterritorialising it on to the empty promise to 'Make America Great Again'. Empty because it is not supported by any viable social and economic policy. Yet promising because it resonates with the black hole of resentment for the questioning of white male privilege. Crucially, Trump's Face Machine both attracts and emits flows of negative passions revolving around the loss and restoration of white male supremacy over and against all the others it cannot assimilate, thus catalysing a microfascist economy of desire.

The machinic and microfascist function of Trump's face is exemplified by his tweets, in which a disembodied and iconised version of the US president builds a wall on the Mexican border, bans Muslims from entering the country, bans trans* people from the army, threatens North Korea with nuclear war, and retweets white supremacist videos falsely blaming Black Lives Matter for random acts of violence, thus inciting racial hate (Riotta 2020). Another emblematic example of Trump's facialisation is a propaganda video about the minting of commemorative presidential medals bearing an idealised version of his face (Donald J. Trump for President Inc. 2017). Here, the minting of the medals is linked to the success of the apprentices' policy targeting unskilled workers introduced by his government. The video is replete with demonstrations of love, gratefulness and esteem for Donald expressed by the workers as much as pride for 'living the dream' of helping him 'make America great again'.

Case Study: Pussy Riot's 'Straight Outta Vagina'

So, how do we 'dismantle the face?' (TP, 186). What alternative ways of desiring can be mobilised against Trump's Face Machine? As Rosi Braidotti points out in her article 'Punk Women and Riot Grrls', in so-called advanced capitalism 'the new wave of feminist movements operates through diffuse resistance to despotic regimes, the occupation of public spaces and quest for alternative modes of becoming political subjects' (Braidotti 2015: 239–40). Luce Irigaray explores the defection from the 'ruling symbolic' in terms of a *diffusion* of the phallocentric that correlates with a 'mechanics of fluids', and which is attributable to '*an other*' order of meaning aligned with women's expression and beyond discourse.

> It is already getting around – at what rate? in what contexts? in spite of what resistances? – that women diffuse themselves according to modalities scarcely compatible with the framework of the ruling symbolics. Which doesn't happen without causing some turbulence, we might even say some whirlwinds, ought to be reconfined within solid walls of principle, to keep them from spreading to infinity. Otherwise they might even go so far as to disturb that third agency designated as the real – a transgression and confusion of boundaries that it is important to restore to their proper order. (Irigaray 1985b: 106)

Irigaray suggests that a woman's meaning potentially 'overflows' a category of subjection, specifically on account of their sexual difference. Of course, it is important to point out that this has also been the means by which women have historically been excluded from culture or absorbed back into phallic modes of production, which has been exceedingly damaging. And yet Irigaray importantly conceives of women's sexuality, imaginary process and access to language as pertaining to a divergent and productive framework of enunciation (Irigaray 1985b: 76). Indeed, in contemporary Western feminist theory the embodied nature of the subject remains a central issue, specifically with respect to the radically shifting topography of sexual difference (Braidotti 1994).

In opposition to the molar reterritorialisations of desire in terms of subjectification, such as the ones enacted by the Face Machine, Deleuze and Guattari speak of molecular becomings. Among these, *becoming-woman* 'possesses a special introductory power' (TP, 248) as woman is the closest other to men in Western culture, and designates a space of anomaly culturally aligned with sorcery and hysteria (Clément 1986). However, all becomings are necessarily minoritarian as they cut across the binary distributions of power organising the social field, hence renouncing any molar and stable category. Reterritorialisation provides a different territory to a desire that was already deterritorialised. A deterritorialised desire is a desire whose connections with a given ground, a landscape of meaning and power, had already been released, thus creating a line of flight. Becoming is one such line of flight before it folds on to itself. Becoming produces 'zones of indiscernibility' in between the majority and minority groups and the constellations of power it disrupts (TP, 293). Majorities and minorities are not defined quantitatively, but rather qualitatively, which is to say in terms of what positions they hold within material socio-semiotic systems of power. Majorities or molar machines are ordinating (hegemonic) while minorities or molecular machines are subordinated (different than). On this basis, there is no becoming majoritarian as the majority cannot engender real change: revolution starts at the margins, not at the centre of power (*potestas*). Reterritorialisations happen when a molecular deterritorialising flow – a becoming, a line of flight – gets stuck and falls back on to itself. This stops desire from creating a new, smooth and open territory of its own. The blocking of a becoming results in the redistribution of desire along the rigid axiomatics of a gridded closed space, that is a majoritarian/molar territory such as the one enacted by Trump's Face Machine.

As Deleuze and Guattari advise:

> It is of course indispensable for women to conduct a molar politics, with a view to winning back their own organism, their own history, their own subjectivity: 'we as women . . .' makes its appearance as a subject of enunciation. But it is dangerous to confine oneself to such a subject, which does not function without drying up a spring or stopping a flow. (TP, 276)

Although women's *flow* has historically been stoppered up, gagged and silenced, to articulate it only along the lines of an identitarian and essentialist (majoritarian) subjectivity and desire would preclude its revolutionary potential to continue opening new spaces of desire and subjectification alternative and resistant to power (*potestas*). Hence, women's flow needs to be expressed as *an other* mapping of becoming, bringing about an active reimagining of the *real*, because it expresses a different desire intervening on the scene of discourse.

At this level, which is that of a micropolitics of desire, Irigaray alerts us that what has been refuted in the 'patriarchal psychic economy [. . .] organized around the phallus' are the properties and capacities of the *fluids* (1985b: 110). Nonetheless, this refuted woman-thing 'speaks' and in the terms of her *fluids* rather than those of a phallocentric language subjecting her, even at the cost of being incomprehensible (1985b: 111).

Irigaray explains that the fluids escape the systemitisation of meaning and culture in a way akin to that of music (1985b: 111). As Deleuze and Guattari state, 'musical expression is inseparable from a becoming woman' (TP, 299), and so Pussy Riot deploy their political vaginal rebirth musically. In 'Straight Outta Vagina' we are reminded that the vagina is where we all come from and as such we ought to celebrate it as a site of political rebirth, a threshold via which we can continue to become re-radicalised to fight the abstract machine of Faciality. Hence the vagina can be honoured as a threshold passed through not just at birth, but molecularly as fully grown sapiens towards all manner of becomings minoritarian, as revered by Riordan (2011). At least for the time being, humans are of woman born (for a feminist perspective on the artificial womb, see de Vries 2020), but they do not need have a vagina to enter processes of becoming-woman and becoming-feminist. In these terms Pussy Riot explore through playful mimesis a 'mother–matter–nature' category associated with their sex and a corresponding musical fluidity of disruption (Irigaray 1985b: 77). When carried away by such musical, contagious and affective flows of molecular becoming, 'Anyone can be Pussy Riot'.

'Straight Outta Vagina' is a radical feminist action targeted against Trump's Face Machine and regime of power, and that is especially true in light of their subsequent song/film clip 'Make America Great Again'. Pussy Riot stage a direct protest against 'dominant social representations of subjectivity' based on a phallocentric state-run apparatus, most identifiably the Trump Face Machine, by mobilising their 'carnal, psychic and social' micropolitical embodiment to express a feminist desire for transformation(s) (Braidotti 2015: 240). Indeed, we might uphold Pussy Riot as celebrating the 'joyful acts of insurrection' of the counter-subject, which defaces Trump's microfascistic political economy through a parodic display of sexual difference (Braidotti 2015: 241). In the first place Pussy Riot perform a counter-representation of feminist desire that *de-faces* a landscape of power ascribed by Trump's Faciality when they don their beanie masks with eye-holes and mouth-holes cut out – as they do in their song and film clip 'Straight Outta Vagina'.

> The radical political stance today consists in becoming-minoritarian or nomadic, in a viral manner: you put on your mask, you become Pussy Riot, you take it off, and you no longer are Pussy Riot. The process of becoming-Pussy Riot is subversive in that it is works actively towards the transformation of the signs, the social practices and the embodied histories of white institutionalised femininity, of resisting citizenship, of human rights campaigning, feminist and gender politics and art practices. (Braidotti 2015: 247–8)

Perhaps to avoid becoming fascist in the political climate following the Trump presidency, the most affirmative choice is to become Pussy Riot, that is, to put on the beanie mask and stand against the majority by becoming-minoritarian. But also, secondly, to align with a subversive anti-discourse of the vagina or the pussy in a playful celebration of sexual difference, which disrupts a dominant white male mode of signification, such as that of the Trump Face Machine. Pussy Riot demonstrate that it is women's sexual difference and corresponding musical *flow* that needs to be expressed through a remapping of becoming woman by women.

At the beginning of 'Straight Outta Vagina' we hear bells toll ominously – it's the end of an era. A young girl takes Communion, a heart-shaped candy with a red slitlike vulva pictured on top of it – a defaced crucifix. She is a Pussy Riot initiate. Nadezhda Tolokonnikova, from here on referred to by her nickname Nadya Tolokno, presides over the ritual, wearing her guerrilla-style beanie with eyes and mouth-holes cut out. A clinical white male voiceover advises us to 'pay attention' since we're about to get an 'education'. Women stand in a bathroom preening, posing, mocking the trope of *femininity* as it correlates with consumer culture – that old duality no longer serves. The women prefer to piss standing up and shake off their vaginas. In another scene women thrust their vaginas forward playfully covered by their hands. They reveal pale blue faux merkins taped over their vaginas, perhaps a parody of the unrealistic colours adopted by sanitary towel commercials to represent menstrual blood. A strong woman holds up the young girl, a rite of passage is unfolding, this is micropolitics feminist-style – pop-punk mayhem.

Leikeli47's rap gets underway: 'My pussy, my pussy is sweet just like a cookie, it goes to work, it makes the beats, it's C.E.O., no rookie . . .' Pussy Riot playfully point to their sculptural vaginas, much like a Sheela-na-gig,[2] thrusting them forward and chanting: 'Don't be stupid, don't be dumb, vagina's where you're really from.' They rap about the radical materiality of women's sexual difference – about feminist flow, an unstoppable deluge of women talking, screaming, chanting their own political rebirth. Pussy Riot musically and playfully demonstrate a diffuse micropolitical protest. If '*certain* social formations need face, and also landscape', then Pussy Riot attempt to dismantle that American landscape of abstracted white heterosexual power by celebrating a mimetic vagina with anarchic political rebirth and posing an affirmative counter-subject (TP, 180). Indeed, Pussy Riot engender a Deleuzian notion of becoming-woman as a means of exploring an elsewhere of desire that brings about a rhizomorphic release from subjection and garners an intensity extending beyond phallocentric structures. In this sense too we can be carried away by affective, contagious and connective flows of molecular becoming when we put on a beanie mask and identify with the vagina as a site of multiple political rebirths – 'Anyone can be Pussy Riot.'

A Pussy Riot: Staging a Fluid Feminist Desire

Irigaray posits the *labial* as the source of women's creative flows of expression and ethical relation to desire. Exploring the labial as a means of establishing a feminist discourse does *not* entail 'producing a discourse of which woman would be the object or the subject' (Irigaray 1985b: 135). As previously mentioned, this would produce molar axes of subjectification in terms of the feminine subject seeking to confine herself to a stable majoritarian category defined by essentialist, monolithic representations. Rather, Irigaray argues that it is from *within* the labial lips that women can express themselves in a counter-discourse of plurality and difference, which has the potential to disrupt the phallocentric mode of discourse. In following Irigaray's argument, we suggest that it is from within the labial that we might find a desiring-machine capable of producing a qualitative shift in the ethics of desire.

According to Irigaray, the labial designates the 'two' labial lips, which are not to be understood as a complementary dyad, but rather as the embodiment of irreducible plurality and difference. In a ceaseless exchange with each other, the 'self-caressing' labial lips express '*an "other meaning"*' that makes her 'whimsical, incomprehensible, agitated, capricious ... leaving "him" unable to discern the coherence of any meaning' (Irigaray 1985b: 28–9). Through her body she enunciates involuntarily what she feels: 'She steps ever so slightly aside from herself with a murmur, an exclamation, a whisper, a sentence left unfinished ... When she returns, it is to set off again from elsewhere. From another point of pleasure, or of pain' (1985b: 29). Hence,

Irigaray explains that it is useless to ask a woman to repeat herself in order to make sense of what she is saying, as when she does she would be repeating herself from another place in her flow of discourse: 'They have returned within themselves . . . within the intimacy of that silent, multiple, diffuse touch. And if you ask them insistently what they are thinking about, they can only reply: Nothing. Everything' (1985b: 29). This labial language of difference cannot be understood by the phallic symbolic order, because it 'sets off in all directions' making her enunciate 'contradictory words' that cause her to appear 'somewhat mad from the standpoint of reason, inaudible for whoever listens to them with ready-made grids, with a fully elaborated code in hand' (1985b: 29). Yet according to Irigaray, woman's fluidity and her multiplicity are her point of resistance to the ruling phallic symbolic subordinating difference to sameness, because it disrupts the linear coherence of his language.

Case Study: Pussy Riot's 'Make America Great Again'

In their music video 'Make America Great Again', Pussy Riot further interrupt the toxic flows of Trump's Face Machine and reinvent them in *an "other meaning"'* (Irigaray 1985b: 29). Through their parody, they interrupt the fixed masculine idea associated with the Trump campaign slogan, 'Make America Great Again', and bring into play a different idea of a great America. We argue that the use of drag throughout this music video advocates a schizoanalytical artistic process, which is capable of resisting the reterritorialising microfascist desires of Trump's Face Machine through an ethics of affirmation (see Mackenzie 2019 for a description of artistic practice as a feminist schizo-revolutionary process).

The music video begins with a 'Trump News Network special report', with Tolokno sporting a Trump-style blonde wig while reporting that Trump has won the presidential election. Real-life clips continually interrupt the mock news show displaying how Trump's microfascist economy of desire has been played out with recordings of the violence perpetrated by police and Trump supporters, on which Tolokno reports 'no more Muslims . . . no more Mexicans'. This mix of scenes speeds to its end and we are faced with the reporter in a Pussy Riot balaclava screaming into the camera – embodying a minoritarian position against the dominant chaos of Trump's America.

The music begins. This is *showbiz*, lest we forget it. We encounter the first example of reterritorialised Trump Faces as police officers aggressively escort a Russian Tolokno into the immigration office. 'Fuck you', she shouts, to which the police officers tell her to 'speak American'. Irigaray's critique is made manifest: even when this 'woman-thing speaks', she is misunderstood. Their misunderstanding is based both on her Russian accent, because she is 'non-American', and because she is a woman. She is judged and branded, with a hot iron, an 'OUTSIDER', in a geographical, linguistic and biological sense. Dressed as a male Trump police officer, another Tolokno judges and brands her, clearly enjoying inflicting this pain and finding almost sexual pleasure in the subordination of the foreign female outsider. We witness the fetishisation of Western patriarchal power over foreign bodies. Captured by Trump's Face Machine, Trump's police officers reproduce its toxic flow of desire. In Foucault's famous words, this is 'the fascism in us all, in our heads and in our everyday behaviour, the fascism that causes us to love power, to desire the very thing that dominates and exploits us' (AO, xiii). The potential to love and enjoy fascism is in us all because malleability is in the nature of desire to the extent that we are prone to any sort of investments. Where does the difference lie then?

'Let other people in, Listen to your women, Stop killing black children, Make America Great Again': Trump Tolokno reinvents Trump's campaign slogan, while we are confronted with another Tolokno wearing a glamorous jewelled balaclava giving us the middle finger. A symbolic gesture that cannot be misunderstood: *Fuck you and your exclusive borders, your creeping disrespect for women's pussies and constitutional rights, and bone-chilling disregard for black lives*. By donning the Pussy Riot balaclava, Tolokno performs deterritorialisations that stop Trump's Face Machine from emitting flows of toxic affects. Opening it up, Pussy Riot create a space for *'an "other meaning"'* for a different America.

'How do you picture the perfect leader? Who do you want him to be?' We now encounter Tolokno queering the Trump drag in an image of a Trump clown playing with a globe in the Oval Office. Her questions demand that we challenge the consensus to vote for a president who toys with the whole world and holds the power to demolish it. The next image demands our intervention within this consensus by examining our own microfascist desires that condition us to want a 'strong male leader' and to desire our own oppression (Braidotti and Dolphijn 2017). Tolokno admiringly strokes a piñata figure of Trump, yet another enactment of Trump's Face Machine. However, Pussy Riot intervene by mocking Trump's Face and grabbing the Trump piñata by the balls, uncovering the fragility of power and inviting us to bring him down.

In encountering this second example of Tolokno's schizoanalytical process of drag, we are forced to acknowledge our malleability in the nature of desire and to proceed with resisting Trump's microfascist economy of desire with caution. That is to say, by embodying Trump, Tolokno signals the risk that resisting fascism can induce its own forceful instilling of negativity, a freezing paralysis that forms a dogmatic, fixed, standardised position or identity (that is being used to resist with), and thus can in turn lead to the emergence of microfascism in our engagements with difference(s). On the other hand, and as an affirmative response, we propose that the multiple characters Tolokno embodies as Trump present Pussy Riot's ethics of affirmation and transmit the need to be continuously unfixed, flexible, schizoanalytical and non-dogmatic. By performing queer versions of Trump, Tolokno escapes the microfascist desires that seek to reterritorialise her face. Therefore, we argue that by smashing the piñata's enactment of Trump's Face Machine, Pussy Riot are inviting us to perform a deterritorialisation that ruptures Trump's Face Machine and its flows of toxic affects in a joyful and playful celebration. We suggest that this deterritorialised piñata creates an opening for different possibilities for the idea of a great America based on an ethics of affirmation. This new meaning is not, and should not be, fixed, as we have already noted. Take it up and dress it in drag. Do a Pussy Riot: interrupt the toxic flows of Trump's Face Machine and create a different space, and have fun while you're at it.

Pussy Riot have found a way of protesting in a joyful affirmative performance:

> politics is all the more effective as it is joyful, affirmative; it puts wings on your feet even as its practitioners lie behind bars. Pussy Riot's creative acts of insurrection prove conclusively the point that Deleuze and Guattari make more ponderously when they stated that: 'You don't have to be sad in order to be militant, even though the thing you are fighting is abominable' ... Affirmation, not sadness, fuels feminist politics. (Braidotti 2015: 252)

According to Braidotti, Pussy Riot, in the face of terror and torture, ground their embodied resistance as a 'radically immanent materialist' practice that empowers their vaginas through creative interventions (Braidotti 2015: 241). As Donna Haraway argues in *Staying with the Trouble: Making Kin in the Chthulucene* (2016), there is a fine line between acknowledging the extent of the trouble we are in and succumbing to abstract futurisms or sublime despair and its concomitant politics of indifference. Her plea is for a politics of showing up. To show up for each other, Haraway contends, requires us to reject the cynics, the techno-fixers and the game-over attitude. Pussy Riot not only show up, but intervene, like a glitch, a missing pixel, a burst of lightning, a sudden scream, a fluke, or burning desire. 'Make America Great Again' illustrates what is 'fucked' about a worldview focused on the molar, the solid, the proprietary and the binary instead of on the molecular and fluid – the becoming-woman.

However, the ability to protest with joyful affirmation is difficult as we experience the abominable reterritorialising effects of misogynist fascism in the following scene. The convicted Russian Tolokno is thrown into a prison cell by the Trump police officers, reterritorialised again by Trump's Face Machine. One is undoing his trousers, as the other handcuffs her to the bars of the cell and undresses her. Two real-life clips interrupt the scenes with Trump saying 'Knock the crap out of her would ya' and 'I would like to punch them in the face I tell ya'. The Trump piñata is hit by Pussy Riot. Each beat symbolises the violent gestures of rape and murder. We are interrupted again by Trump telling us 'and I love the women'. With every movement of deterritorialisation, there are always movements of reterritorialisation that follow (TP, 226). In this case, the movements of deterritorialisation produced by Pussy Riot that rupture Trump's Face Machine in smashing the Trump piñata are followed by movements of reterritorialisation produced by Trump's Face Machine. These movements violently overcode any possibilities of difference to resubmit Pussy Riot to his systems of representation and establish a territory in which woman is subordinate once more.

We cannot ignore the violence that underlines Trump's use of language. Employing Irigaray's theoretical framework, Trump's discourse can be situated within a phallocentric mode. His enunciations about and of women symbolise man's isomorphic sexual imaginary by privileging a mechanics of solids based on the amplification of the masculine features of 'production, property (*propriété*), order, form, unity, visibility, erection' (Irigaray 1985b: 86). Trump's charged political rhetoric is not dissimilar to an ejaculatory flow enumerating a toxic white heterosexual normativity in the staging of the so-called American dream.

The following scene depicts this toxic white heterosexual normativity to the extent that the convicted Russian Tolokno is forced into a clinic called Trump Medical Aid, and strapped on to a hospital bed with stirrups, where her vagina is examined by a Trump doctor. 'Let other people in' Trump Tolokno sings; a phrase which is now heard as a dark phallic command. The Trump doctor shakes his head and confirms that there is nothing he can do for her, thus evoking the male phantom of the vagina as a dark cave triggering *'the horror of nothing to see'* (Irigaray

1985b: 86). By this time, Tolokno as Pussy Riot is giving her last punch to Trump's piñata face before pulling him down to rip multiple dollar notes from his head. A symbolic image to represent the business-minded billionaire that America desired, and the price they have paid for it with their civil rights. As it rains money in the Oval Office, the convicted Russian Tolokno is being branded with the hot iron again. The music stops and the brand reads 'SHE MADE AN ABORTION'. Her scream is then interrupted by a real-life clip from Trump, who begins to say 'Sadly . . .'. Seizing the opportunity presented by the interruption, Russian Tolokno kicks the Trump doctor to the floor. Trump continues to tell us on the television that 'the American dream is dead'. She is in pain and angry, at the evidence that her American dream of immigrating to the land of the free was deeply deceitful and impossible due to Trump's murderous migration policy. She pushes the Trump police officer and goes to flee. Trump appears again along with the music to tell us that he 'will bring it [the American dream] back'. Tolokno runs off, and while she is running for the door, the other Trump police officer shoots her in the back.

And yet, although shot down by the Trump police officer, Tolokno's feminist line of flight is not *really* dead. Pussy Riot's musical and visual intervention is an invitation to those-who-are-other to create further creative feminist lines of flight. By employing Trump's campaign slogan 'Make America Great Again', Pussy Riot borrow his rigid signifiers from the phallocentric symbolic order and in doing so liquefy them in a flow of 'contradictory words' in order to express *an "other meaning"* (Irigaray 1985b: 29). That is to say, according to Irigaray, women's mode of discourse is fluid and therefore different to the dogmatic rigidness of the phallocentric symbolic order, which privileges the one phallic signifier. Irigaray explains that women's expression flows in a style that symbolises a female sexual imaginary, which she associates with a mechanics of fluids. By approximating the properties of liquids, women's process of enunciating emphasises features that are 'continuous, compressible, dilatable, viscous, conductible, diffusible' (Irigaray 1985b: 111). As Irigaray remarks, a mechanics of fluids exerts 'pressure' through the solid mechanics privileged within the phallocentric mode of discourse.

Pussy Riot's feminist version of making America great again therefore stands as a reinvention of what Trump's presidency proposed. When they tell us to 'Make America Great Again', this slogan takes on an *other meaning* as Pussy Riot explain that it entails letting other people in, listening to your women, and ceasing to kill black children.

Although they employ Trump's signifiers, they cannot 'mark, or re-mark upon them' (Irigaray 1985a: 71). Rather, Pussy Riot speak from a space of morphological difference, and it is women's morphological dubiousness that makes them 'troublesome', as Braidotti describes (1994: 80). They have found a way of exposing their labial thinking that gives the exclamation prominence: a *pussycentric* language. We argue that this is how Pussy Riot are making trouble in the dominant phallocentric symbolic order. Pussy Riot's feminist lines of flight incited by their libidinal energy release a fluid feminist desire that Olkowski describes as 'the source of their creativity and ethical relation to the world' (Hiltmann 2007: 11). We propose that Pussy Riot *are* a line of flight that breaks through the molar masculine unconscious re-enacted by Trump's Face Machine.

In an interview, Pussy Riot band member Garadzha replies to Langston's (2012) question 'Why "Pussy Riot"?':

> A female sex organ, which is supposed to be receiving and shapeless, suddenly starts a radical rebellion against the cultural order, which tries to constantly define it and show its appropriate place. Sexists have certain ideas about how a woman should behave, and Putin, by the way, also has a couple thoughts on how Russians should live. Fighting against all that – that's Pussy Riot.

Pussy Riot unsettle, dislocate and disrupt. Their first famous insurrection in the Cathedral of Christ the Saviour in Moscow in 2012 answered Irigaray's call for an initial immediate response that, described by Braidotti, 'revealed the impotence of institutionalised power forever' (Braidotti 2015: 252). Ever since, Pussy Riot have continued to answer Irigaray's call by enduring a long and difficult process of struggle and transformation, which involved the incarceration of two group members. Among their many musical and visual interventions, 'Make America Great Again' and 'Straight Outta Vagina' show that Pussy Riot are not solely focused on attacking Russian despotic power, but also democratically elected Trump and his ultra-liberal capitalist America. That is not only institutional, but also micropolitical fascism. Through their musical lines of flight, Braidotti summarises that they become 'nomadic subjects' and 'global "net-izens"' who 'express a new trans-national political subjectivity that clashes with the unitary formations of church, nation and state' (2015: 251). We propose to continue the feminist discourse, or rather, a *pussycentric* language. Let's become Pussy Riot and stage fluid feminist desires as creative interventions that aim to disrupt the toxic flows of Trump's Face Machine and start a pussy riot.

Notes

1. Though not all preppers or survivalists are wealthy, and survivalism has a long history (see Kabel and Chmidling 2014; Marilyn 2014).
2. A Sheela-na-gig is a primitive Celtic figure of a woman with her labia spread open to expose her massive vagina. Perhaps the best-known example is at Kilpeck Church in Herefordshire, and there are estimated to be over a hundred at various religious sites in Ireland.

References

Appignanesi, L. (2005), *Simone De Beauvoir. Life & Times*, London: Haus.

Braidotti, R. (1994), *Nomadic Subjects: Embodiment and Sexual Difference in Contemporary Feminist Theory*, New York: Columbia University Press.

Braidotti, R. (2006), *Transpositions: On Nomadic Ethics*, Cambridge: Polity.

Braidotti, R. (2015), 'Punk Women and Riot Grrls', *Performance Philosophy*, 1 (1): 239–54, <https://www.performancephilosophy.org/journal/article/view/32/64> (last accessed 14 June 2022).

Braidotti, R., and R. Dolphijn (2017), Deleuze Seminar Series, 'Session 1: Introduction to the Non-Fascist Life', University of Utrecht.

Clément, C. (1986), 'The Guilty One', in H. Cixous and C. Clément (eds), *The Newly Born Woman*, trans. B. Wing, Minneapolis: University of Minnesota Press, 1–39. Translation of *La Jeune née*, Paris: Union générale d'éditions, 1975.

Crenshaw, K. (1989), 'Demarginalizing the Intersection of Race and Sex: A Black Feminist Critique of Antidiscrimination Doctrine, Feminist Theory and Antiracist Politics', *The University of Chicago Legal Forum*, 1989, Article 8, <https://chicagounbound.uchicago.edu/uclf/vol1989/iss1/8> (last accessed 15 May 2022).

de Vries, P. (2020), 'The Speculative Design of Immaculate Motherhood', *Digicult*, <http://digicult.it/design/the-speculative-design-of-immaculate-motherhood/> (last accessed 15 May 2022).

Donald J. Trump for President Inc. (2017), 'Donald J Trump Medallion – Medalcraft Mint 2017', <https://www.youtube.com/watch?v=NtQUJg6YjZo> (last accessed 15 May 2022).

Dyer, N. R. (2020), *The Menstrual Imaginary in Literature: Notes on a Wild Fluidity*, New York: Palgrave.

Haraway, D. J. (2016), *Staying with the Trouble: Making Kin in the Chthulucene*, Durham, NC: Duke University Press.

Haslanger, S. (2008), 'Changing the Ideology and Culture of Philosophy: Not by Reason (Alone)', *Hypatia*, 23 (2): 210–23.

Hiltmann, G. (2007), 'Introduction: Accounting for the Other: Towards an Ethics of Thinking', in H. Fielding, G. Hiltmann, D.Olkowski and A. Reichold (eds), *The Other: Feminist Reflections in Ethics*, New York: Palgrave Macmillan, pp. 1–20.

hooks, b. (2015 [1989]), *Talking Back: Thinking Feminist, Thinking Black*, London: Routledge.

Irigaray, L. (1985a), *Speculum of the Other Woman*, trans. G. C. Gill, Ithaca, NY: Cornell University Press. Translation of *Speculum de l'autre femme*, Paris: Les Éditions de Minuit, 1974.

Irigaray, L. (1985b), *This Sex Which Is Not One*, trans. C. Porter and C. Burke, Ithaca, NY: Cornell University Press. Translation of *Ce sexe qui n'est pas un*, Paris: Les Éditions de Minuit, 1977.

Irigaray, L. (1994), *Thinking the Difference: For a Peaceful Revolution*, trans. K. Montin, London: Athlone. Translation of *Le temps de la différence: pour une révolution pacifique*, Paris: Librairie générale française, 1989.

Kabel, A., and C. Chmidling (2014), 'Disaster Prepper: Health, Identity, and American Survivalist Culture', *Human Organization* [Online], 73 (3): 258–66, <https://doi.org/10.17730/humo.73.3.l34252tg03428527>.

Langston, H. (2012), 'Meeting Pussy Riot', *Vice*, 12 March, <https://www.vice.com/en_us/article/kwnzgy/A-Russian-Pussy-Riot> (last accessed 15 May 2022).

Lugones, M. (2007), 'Heterosexualism and the Colonial/Modern Gender System', *Hypatia*, 22 (1): 186–209.

Mackenzie, H. (2019), 'A Schizo-Revolutionary Labial Theory of Artistic Practice', in J. Sholtz and C. Carr (eds), *Deleuze and the Schizoanalysis of Feminism: Alliances and Allies*, London: Bloomsbury, pp. 260–75.

Marilyn, L. J. (2015), 'The Living Heritage of Prepping', PhD thesis, Arkansas State University, <https://www.proquest.com/openview/7b18de13936fffe5a424b85f9dd6912a/1?cbl=18750&parentSessionId=9ZX6K3ZksbZSZM4H8g8m2obWZvCZ5OPjIAtrsaHV2X8%3D&pq-origsite=gscholar&parentSessionId=wbs6A%2FV%2F6lML6uI5m%2BmIz%2BAtFVgQB%2Fl0N9Q%2FHx%2B%2Bg2c%3D> (last accessed 6 June 2022).

Mohanty, C. T. (2003), *Feminism Without Borders: Decolonizing Theory, Practicing Solidarity*, Durham, NC: Duke University Press.

The New York Times (2016), 'Transcript: Donald Trump's Taped Comments about Women', *The New York Times*, 8 October, <https://www.nytimes.com/2016/10/08/us/donald-trump-tape-transcript.html> (last accessed 15 May 2022).

Osnos, E. (2017), 'Survival of the Richest', *The New Yorker*, 23 January, <https://www.newyorker.com/magazine/2017/01/30/doomsday-prep-for-the-super-rich> (last accessed 15 May 2022).

Philpot, T. S. (2018), 'Race, Gender, and the 2016 Presidential Election', *PS: Political Science & Politics* [Online], 51(4): 755–61, <https://doi.org/10.1017/S1049096518000896> (last accessed 14 June 2022).

Riordan, G. (2011), 'Haemosexuality', in F. Beckman (ed.), *Deleuze and Sex*, Edinburgh: Edinburgh University Press, pp. 69–88.

Riotta, C. (2020), 'Trump Tweets Video Blaming Subway Attack on Black Lives Matter, Stirring Outrage', *The Independent*, 1 September, <https://www.independent.co.uk/news/world/americas/us-politics/trump-subway-attack-black-lives-matter-antifa-protests-nyc-a9697496.html> (last accessed 15 May 2022).

Siker, J. (2007), 'Historicizing a Racialized Jesus: Case Studies in the "Black Christ", the "Mestizo Christ", and White Critique', *Biblical Interpretation*, 15 (1): 26–53.

Wark, M. (2017), 'Facebook Post', Facebook, 1 May, <https://www.facebook.com/mckenziewark/posts/10100560870288587> (last accessed 15 May 2022).

Wilson, G. (2004), 'So What Colour Was Jesus?', BBC, 27 October, <http://news.bbc.co.uk/1/hi/magazine/3958241.stm> (last accessed 15 May 2022).

Notes on Contributors

Christian Alonso is Artistic Director of La Panera Art Centre (Lleida, Catalonia, Spain) and a lecturer in Art History at the University of Lleida. He holds a PhD in Art History, University of Barcelona (*cum laude*), 2020. His research links Félix Guattari's ecosophical perspective with a series of ethico-aesthetic practices in order to conceptualise the work of art as a technology for materialising contingent, multi-agential ecologies. He has worked on this subject as a curator (*Multispecies Imaginaries*, La Capella, 2022; *Soil Politics*, Centre d'Art Maristany, 2019; *Machinic Recompositions*, Can Felipa, 2017), as an author and editor of books and journals (*Transversal Ethico-Aesthetics*, REGAC, 2022; *Mutating Ecologies in Contemporary Art*, Universitat de Barcelona, 2019), as the coordinator of conferences, symposia, seminars and workshops on art and critical thought, and as director of applied artistic research projects (Transcorporal.org; Working Group on the Hybrid Ecologies of the Llobregat Delta). His website is at <http://caosmosis.net/>.

Lila Athanasiadou is a cultural worker, researcher and architect whose practice spans from visual and audio essays to teaching encounters and cultural activism. She has organised and moderated seminars, reading groups and lectures at TU Delft, ArtEZ, Stroom and Kunstinstituut Melly and has presented her work at academic conferences at KTH Royal Institute of Technology, RITCS School of Art, University of Lisbon, Goethe University, Utrecht University and the Estonian Academy of Arts. Her work explores feminist and queer pedagogical practices and intersections of digital data with human and territorial bodies. Between 2016 and 2018 she acted as the curator of the Corporeal Discourse programme for the Master of Interior Architecture at ArtEZ University of the Arts. She is currently teaching in Social Practices at Willem de Kooning Academy.

Angela Balzano is coordinator and professor of the science module of the Masters in Gender Studies and Policies at the RomaTre University; adjunct professor of the course in Diversity Management and tutor in Women and Law for the GEMMA Masters in Gender Studies at the University of Bologna; research fellow for the Department of Political Culture and Society of the University of Turin, for which she follows the H2020 Project MINDtheGEPs (Modifying Institutions by Developing Gender Equality Plans). She has translated for DeriveApprodi Rosi Braidotti's *The Posthuman* and Donna Haraway's *The Promises of Monsters*. In 2021 she published her first monograph with Meltemi, *Per farla finita con la famiglia. Dall'aborto alle parentele postumane.*

Simone Bignall is a political philosopher and Senior Researcher in the Jumbunna Institute Hub for Indigenous Nations and Collaborative Futures at the University of Technology Sydney, where she works with First Nations who are rebuilding their polities for sovereign self-determination. In addition to her widely published collaborative research in this area, she is the author of *Postcolonial Agency: Critique and Constructivism* (Edinburgh University Press, 2010) and the forthcoming *Exit Colonialism: Ethics after Enjoyment*. She has also co-edited *Deleuze and the Postcolonial* (with Paul Patton, Edinburgh University Press, 2010); *Agamben and Colonialism* (with Marcelo Svirsky, Edinburgh University Press, 2012); *Deleuze and Pragmatism* (with Sean Bowden and Paul Patton, Routledge, 2014); and *Posthuman Ecologies: Complexity and Process after Deleuze* (with Rosi Braidotti, Rowman and Littlefield, 2018).

Rosi Braidotti: BA Hons. ANU, Canberra 1978; PhD *cum laude*, Université de Paris, Panthéon-Sorbonne, 1981; Fellow Institute for Advanced Study, Princeton, 1994; Jean Monnet Fellow, European University Institute, 2000–01. Honorary degrees: University of Helsinki, 2007; University of Linkoping, 2013. Knight in the Order of the Netherlands Lion, 2005; Honorary Fellow of the Australian Academy of the Humanities, 2009; Member of the Academia Europaea, 2014. Distinguished University Professor and founding Director of the Centre for the Humanities at Utrecht University, 2007–16. Her books include *Patterns of Dissonance* (Polity, 1991); *Nomadic Subjects* (Columbia University Press, 1994; 2nd edn 2011); *Metamorphoses* (Polity, 2002); *Transpositions* (Polity, 2006); *Nomadic Theory* (Columbia University Press, 2011); *The Posthuman* (Polity, 2013) and *Posthuman Knowledge* (Polity, 2019). In 2016 she co-edited with Paul Gilroy, *Conflicting*

Humanities, (Bloomsbury Academic) and in 2018 with Maria Hlavajova, *The Posthuman Glossary.* Her personal website is at <www.rosibraid otti.com>.

Mónica Cano Abadía is a moral and political philosopher. She has been a postdoctoral fellow at the Center for Advanced Studies – South East Europe (University of Rijeka), and at the Section of Political Philosophy (University of Graz). She is currently a Senior Scientist and the Gender, Equality, and Diversity Specialist at the Research Infrastructure BBMRI-ERIC, as well as a lecturer at the Master's Programme in Interdisciplinary Women's and Gender Studies (University of Graz), teaching social movements and activism. Her current research foci include gender and ethics of Artificial Intelligence in biomedicine.

Delphi Carstens is a lecturer at the University of the Western Cape (UWC), South Africa. His research interests include applying feminist new materialist and Deleuzo-Guattarian methodologies to the formulation of processual, bewildering and ecosophic pedagogical movements. He holds a PhD in apocalyptic science fiction and theory-fiction from Stellenbosch University. Publications include chapters in the edited volumes *Higher Education Hauntologies* (Routledge, 2021), *Socially Just Pedagogies in Higher Education* (Bloomsbury, 2018) and *Ahuman Pedagogy* (Palgrave, 2022), as well as journal articles in *CriStal* (2020), *Somatechnics* (2020), *Alternation* (2019) and *Parallax* (2018).

Ruth Clemens is Lecturer in Literary Studies at Utrecht University. From 2017 to 2018 she was a visiting research fellow at the Utrecht Institute for Cultural Inquiry and in 2020 she completed her PhD in Comparative Literature at the University of Leeds. She is recipient of the UCL Tagore Scholarship and the ALCS Essay Prize. Formerly, she was committee member of the British Association for Modernist Studies and founding editor of *The Modernist Review.* Her work has appeared in *BSJ, Feminist Modernist Studies, Modernist Cultures* and *Comparative Critical Studies.* Her research interests include translation, multilingualism, experimental literature, book history and materiality, and the posthuman. She is currently working on a collaborative and interdisciplinary project about biomineralisation, teeth and poetics.

Christine Daigle is a Professor of Philosophy and Director of the Posthumanism Research Institute at Brock University. She is the author of *Le nihilisme est-il un humanisme? Étude sur Nietzsche et Sartre*

(Presses universitaires de Lyon, 2005), *Routledge Critical Thinkers: Jean-Paul Sartre* (Routledge, 2009) and *Nietzsche as Phenomenologist: Becoming What One Is* (Edinburgh University Press, 2021). She is the editor of *Existentialist Thinkers and Ethics* (McGill/Queen's University Press, 2006), to which she contributed a chapter on Simone de Beauvoir's ethics. She has also co-edited *Beauvoir and Sartre: The Riddle of Influence* (Indiana University Press, 2009), with Jacob Golomb, *Nietzsche and Phenomenology: Life, Power, Subjectivity* (Indiana University Press, 2013), with Élodie Boublil, and *From Deleuze and Guattari to Posthumanism. Philosophies of Immanence* (Bloomsbury, 2022), with Terrance H. McDonald. She is the author of a number of articles on Nietzsche, Sartre, de Beauvoir and most recently on posthumanism. She is currently completing a monograph on the ethical potential of posthumanist vulnerability.

Rick Dolphijn is an associate professor in Media and Culture Studies, Utrecht University, an honorary professor at the University of Hong Kong (2017–23) and a visiting professor at the Unversity of Barcelona (2019/2020). His books include *Foodscapes* (Eburon/University of Chicago Press, 2004), *New Materialism: Interviews and Cartographies* (Open Humanities Press, 2012, with Iris van der Tuin) and *The Philosophy of Matter: A Meditation* (Bloomsbury, 2021). His academic work has appeared in journals such as *Continental Philosophy Review*, *Angelaki*, *Rhizomes*, *Collapse* and *Deleuze Studies*. He edited (with Rosi Braidotti) *This Deleuzian Century: Art, Activism, Life* (Brill/Rodopi, 2014/15) and *Philosophy after Nature* (2017), and most recently *Michel Serres and the Crises of the Contemporary* (Bloomsbury, 2019/20). He is a PI in two international research projects: Food2Gather (HERA funded 2019–22) and IMAGINE (Norwegian Research Council 2021–24).

Natalie Rose Dyer completed a PhD in Creative Writing at the University of Melbourne (2017) where she also earned an MFA (2010) with an Australian Postgraduate Award. She was Researcher-in-Residence at the University of Amsterdam in 2018. She is the recent recipient of the Peter Steele Poetry Award 2021. She currently teaches poetry and supervises higher degree students at the University of Melbourne. Her poetry and essays are widely published in esteemed international literary journals including *Meanjin Quarterly*, *Australian Poetry*, *Cordite Poetry Review*, *Chiron Review*, *Wisconsin Review* and many more. Her book *Notes on a Wild Fluidity*, which takes a fresh look at the feminist politics of corporeality, was published with Palgrave in 2020. She is currently working on a book of essays on feminist activism, wandering and ecology. Her experimental blog project *Boundary Speak Diaries (2013–2021)* is at <https://natalierosedyer.com/blog/boundary-speak-diaries>.

Becket Flannery is an Amsterdam-based writer and artist. He received his MFA from the University of Southern California in 2014, and was a resident at the Rijksakademie van beeldende kunsten in 2016–17. He has recently exhibited his work as Becket MWN at the Grazer Kunstverein (Graz, AT), Kunsthalle Fribourg (Fribourg, CH) and SculptureCenter (New York, US), among others. His writing has been commissioned by Shimmer (Rotterdam, NL), S.M.A.K. (Ghent, BE), If I Can't Dance, I Don't Want to Be Part of Your Revolution (Amsterdam, NL), and *Revue Initiales* (Lyon, FR) among others. He is currently teaching at the Gerrit Rietveld Academie in Amsterdam, the Netherlands.

Zeynep Gambetti is an independent scholar, who taught as Associate Professor of Political Theory at Bogazici University from 2000 to 2019. Her research interests include nineteenth- and twentieth-century Continental thought, critical theory, theories of collective agency, ethics and public space. She has published extensively on social movements, with particular emphasis on space as a vector of relationality. Inspired primarily by Arendt, Marx, Deleuze and Foucault, her theoretical work focuses on contemporary forms of violence and resistance. Among her publications are *Rhetorics of Insecurity: Belonging and Violence in the Neoliberal Era* (SSRC/New York University Press, 2013), co-edited with Marcial Godoy-Anativia, and *Vulnerability in Resistance: Politics, Feminism, Theory* (Duke University Press, 2016), co-edited with Judith Butler and Leticia Sabsay. She is currently working on a theory of fascism that situates its rebirth within neoliberal societal dynamics. She also co-chairs the International Board at the UC Berkeley-based International Consortium for Critical Theory Programs.

Evelien Geerts is a multidisciplinary philosopher and Research Fellow at the University of Birmingham, UK. She holds a PhD in Feminist Studies and History of Consciousness from the University of California, Santa Cruz, and (research) MA degrees in Philosophy and Gender and Ethnicity Studies. Her research interests include new materialisms and Deleuzo-Guattarian philosophy, queer theory, and political philosophical questions of identity, difference and violence. She has previously published in *Philosophy Today*, *Women's Studies International Forum* and *Rhizomes: Cultural Studies in Emerging Knowledge* – publications that can be found at <www.eveliengeerts.com> – and is a Posthumanities Hub affiliated researcher.

Arash Ghajarjazi received his PhD from the Department of Philosophy and Religious Studies at Utrecht University. The particular focus of his research is on the relations between Iranian media, Islam and sciences from the nineteenth century onwards. More broadly, trained both as a cultural analyst as well as a historian, he explores the ways in which Islamic traditions have evolved in and as media. He approaches histories of Muslim material cultures as well as of Islamic thought together, understanding them as inseparable events. His research seeks balance between thick historical contextualisation and radical philosophical conceptualisation. He completed his master's degree in Media and Performance Studies, during which he engaged closely with the philosophy of Deleuze and Guattari. Positioned mainly in the field of Iranian and Islamic Studies, he tends to push history of Islam to its under-examined limits, to make history make concepts that can reshape the understandings of the Islamic past and present.

Woosung Kang is Professor in the Department of English and Comparative Literature at Seoul National University, Korea. He was a visiting scholar at the University of Pennsylvania (2012–13) and National Taiwan University (2019–20). His research area includes American literature and culture, politics of aesthetics, critical theories, psychoanalysis, film theory and Asian cinemas. He is the author of *Freud Seminar* (2019), *Painting as the Gaze of Philosophy* (2014), *Poe Translated* (2014) and *The Birth of a Style: Emerson and the Writing of the Moment in the American Renaissance* (2003). He has published articles on American literature, Japanese films, deconstruction, Deleuze, and other theorists. He translated Slavoj Žižek's *Pandemic!* (2020) and Avital Ronell's *Stupidity* (2015) into Korean, and is now working on *The Geographies of East Asian Cinema: The Taiwan Convergence* and *Political Derrida*.

Goda Klumbytė is an interdisciplinary scholar working between informatics and humanities and social sciences. Her research engages feminist new materialism, posthumanism, human–computer interaction and algorithmic systems design. In her doctoral research conducted at the Gender/Diversity in Informatics Systems group at the University of Kassel, Germany, she investigates epistemic premises of machine learning as a knowledge production tool and proposes innovative ways to work with intersectional feminist and new materialist epistemologies towards more contextualised and accountable machine learning systems design. She co-edited *More Posthuman Glossary* with R. Braidotti and E. Jones (Bloomsbury, 2022), and has published work in *Posthuman Glossary* (ed. Rosi Braidotti and Maria Hlavajova, Bloomsbury, 2018), *Everyday Feminist Research Praxis* (ed. Koen Leurs and Domitilla Olivieri, Cambridge Scholars, 2015), the journals *Online Information Review*, *Digital Creativity* and *ASAP*, as well as presented at informatics conferences such as ACM's CHI, nordiCHI and FAccT. She is one of the editors of the critical computing blog <https://enginesofdifference.org>.

Stavros Kousoulas is Assistant Professor of Architecture Theory in the Faculty of Architecture of TU Delft. He studied architecture at the National Technical University of Athens and at TU Delft. He received his doctoral title *cum laude* from IUAV Venice participating in the Villard d'Honnecourt International Research Doctorate. He has published and lectured in Europe and abroad. He has been a member of the editorial board of *Footprint Delft Architecture Theory Journal* since 2014.

Patricia MacCormack is Professor of Continental Philosophy at Anglia Ruskin University Cambridge. She has published extensively on philosophy, feminism, queer and monster theory, animal abolitionist activism, ethics, art and horror cinema. She is the author of *Cinesexuality* (Routledge, 2008) and *Posthuman Ethics* (Routledge, 2012) and the editor of *The Animal Catalyst* (Bloomsbury, 2014), *Deleuze and the Animal* (Edinburgh University Press, 2017), *Deleuze and the Schizoanalysis of Cinema* (Continuum, 2008) and *Ecosophical Aesthetics* (Bloomsbury, 2018). Her new book is *The Ahuman Manifesto: Activisms for the End of the Anthropocene*.

Hollie Mackenzie is a doctor in Political and Social Thought, an artist, and an escape game designer. Her publications explore a feminist philosophy of labial art-politics and critical pedagogy. She has been awarded multiple art awards and research grants, including a University of Kent 50th Anniversary Scholarship to pursue doctoral research and a teaching prize for her creative and experimental pedagogy. Her sculptures have also featured in *The Caitlin Guide*, *The State of Art: Sculpture and 3D* volumes and *The Sunday Times* magazine. She was the Lead Artist for the MA in Politics, Art and Resistance (University of Kent) in the Fairground at Tate Exchange, Tate Modern (2014–17). Currently, she is developing and implementing an artistic experiential pedagogical approach to designing and constructing innovative escape rooms that aim to engage, puzzle and challenge participants while simultaneously encouraging learning through collaboration and creativity. More about her can be found at <www.mackenzieartist.co.uk>.

Siddique Motala is an academic development senior lecturer in the Department of Civil Engineering at the University of Cape Town, South Africa. He is a trained land surveyor and holds a PhD in Education. His research interests are posthumanism, the scholarship of teaching and learning, spatio-temporal mapping, storytelling and innovative practices in engineering education. He co-edited *Higher Education Hauntologies: Living with Ghosts for a Justice-to-Come* (Routledge, 2021), with V. Bozalek, M. Zembylas and D. Hölscher. He was a recipient of the 2017 HELTASA/CHE National Excellence in Teaching and Learning Award. His current work is focused on augmented reality and mapping the stories of District Six, the historic site of apartheid forced removals in Cape Town.

John Protevi is Phyllis M. Taylor Professor of French Studies, and Professor of Philosophy, at Louisiana State University. He received his PhD in Philosophy from Loyola University Chicago in 1990. After early publications on figures such as Kant, Hegel, Heidegger and Derrida, his philosophical touchstone is now Deleuze, whom he tries to connect to research in the earth, life, social and cognitive sciences. His most recent books are with University of Minnesota Press: *Political Affect* (2009), *Life, War, Earth* (2013) and *Edges of the State* (2019). His website, with research papers and course materials, is at <www.protevi.com/john>.

Diana Teggi is a sociologist and lecturer in the Department of Social and Policy Sciences at the University of Bath, where she has recently completed her doctorate. Her thesis focuses on the experience of dying in English care homes and the care thereof. In the first substantial study of the topic in nearly twenty years, she sheds light on the management of residents' dying by care home staff. Her thesis concludes that dying in care homes is not a natural process, but a highly managed one. Her other research interests focus on sexual and intimate relationships in late old age. She gave the 2022 University of Bath Beatrice Godwin Memorial Lecture and her research features in *Social Science and Medicine*.

Patricia de Vries works as research professor at the Gerrit Rietveld Academy. She has published in *Big Data & Society*, *Rhizomes*, *nY*, *De Reactor*, *Press & Fold*, *Amsterdam Book Review*, and has written on art and philosophy for the art gallery MU in Eindhoven, Centraal Museum in Utrecht, Maxxi Museum in Rome, and the digital art center Chronus in Shanghai.

Shiva Zarabadi holds a PhD in Education, Gender, Feminist New Materialism and Posthumanism from UCL Institute of Education, and an MSc degree in Sociology from London School of Economics and Political Science. She is currently teaching an MA module Understanding Education Research at UCL Institute of Education. Her research interests include feminist new materialism, posthumanism and intra-actions of matter, time, affect, space, humans and more-than-humans. She uses walking and photo-diary methodologies to map relational materialities in ordinary practices. She is the co-editor of *Feminist Posthumanisms/New Materialisms and Education* (Routledge, 2019) and the author of 'Post-Threat Pedagogies: A Micro-Materialist Phantomatic Feeling within Classrooms in Post-Terrorist Times', in *Mapping the Affective Turn in Education Theory, Research, and Pedagogies* (2020).

Index